Springer Proceedings in Business and Economics

Springer Proceedings in Business and Economics brings the most current research presented at conferences and workshops to a global readership. The series features volumes (in electronic and print formats) of selected contributions from conferences in all areas of economics, business, management, and finance. In addition to an overall evaluation by the publisher of the topical interest, scientific quality, and timeliness of each volume, each contribution is refereed to standards comparable to those of leading journals, resulting in authoritative contributions to the respective fields. Springer's production and distribution infrastructure ensures rapid publication and wide circulation of the latest developments in the most compelling and promising areas of research today.

The editorial development of volumes may be managed using Springer Nature's innovative Meteor platform, which is a proven online submission, management and review system. This system is designed to ensure an efficient timeline for your publication, making Springer Proceedings in Business and Economics the premier series to publish your workshop or conference volume.

This book series is indexed in SCOPUS.

Nessrine Omrani
Francesco Schiavone
Francesco Paolo Appio • Marta Ballatore
Yosr Ben Tahar
Editors

Human-Machine Synergy and the Digital Future - Exploring Collaboration and Competition Volume 1

Proceedings from the 3rd DTS International Conference, Paris, France, May 22-23, 2025

Springer

Editors
Nessrine Omrani
Management Department
Paris School of Business
Paris, Paris, France

Francesco Paolo Appio
Management Department
Paris School of Business
Paris, France

Yosr Ben Tahar
Management Department
Paris School of Business
Paris, France

Francesco Schiavone
Management and Quantitative Studies
Department
Parthenope University of Naples
Naples, Napoli, Italy

Marta Ballatore
Management Department
Paris School of Business
Paris, France

ISSN 2198-7246 ISSN 2198-7254 (electronic)
Springer Proceedings in Business and Economics
ISBN 978-3-032-21346-4 ISBN 978-3-032-21347-1 (eBook)
https://doi.org/10.1007/978-3-032-21347-1

This Springer imprint is published by the registered company Springer Nature Switzerland AG
The registered company address is: Gewerbestrasse 11, 6330 Cham, Switzerland

Preface: Volume 1

This book, *Human-Machine Synergy and the Digital Future: Exploring Collaboration and Competition* (Volume 1), explores how AI and digital technologies reshape decision rights, routines, and value creation across sectors and societies. By human–machine synergy, we mean the designed interplay of human judgment and machine computation, where collaboration and competition jointly drive performance, accountability, and inclusion.

Originating from the Digital Transformation Society (DTS) conference 2025, this reviewed proceedings volume brings together empirical studies, conceptual advances, and practice-oriented cases. To capture the complexity and nuance of this transformation, the book is organized into 11 thematic parts, each addressing a distinct dimension of human–machine synergy.

Part I, *Digital Transformation and AI in Society,* examines the broader socio-technological changes brought about by digitalization, highlighting the ethical, cultural, and institutional implications of AI integration. Chapters span education road maps, SDG-aligned agriculture, organizational effectiveness in leading firms, and ethical restraint lessons from genome editing for advanced AI.

Part II, *AI and Open Innovation,* explores how AI enables new forms of collaborative innovation and knowledge creation beyond traditional organizational boundaries. Contributions include digital finance for SMEs/startups and the impact of collaborative strategies on patent value and technological significance.

Part III, *Digitizing Workforce Practices,* delves into the restructuring of work environments, talent management, and organizational behavior in a world where digital tools and AI are becoming integral to everyday professional routines. Topics cover workforce digitalization opportunities/risks, AI in human capital management, telework in public organizations, cobots adoption in Industry 5.0, technostress and productivity, and AI in the PhD journey.

Part IV, *AI in the Service Sector,* focuses on how service industries are reimagining customer engagement, service delivery, and operational efficiency through the adoption of intelligent technologies. Evidence ranges from FinTech in microfinance to AI-enabled platform models in communication agencies and graph-based sentiment analysis in retail.

Part V, *AI for Sustainability*, discusses the emerging role of AI in addressing environmental challenges, enabling sustainable practices, and supporting the transition toward greener business models. Chapters address circular business models, automated ESG reporting, sustainable BMI frameworks, green-finance mapping, RAG-enabled contingency planning, meta-reviews of AI-sustainability, and public procurement.

Part VI, *Predicting with AI,* investigates the growing reliance on predictive analytics and machine learning to inform strategic decisions in dynamic and uncertain environments. Applications include AutoML for air quality, explainable AI for SME governance, and financial behavior of failed firms during COVID-19.

Across methods, from case studies, surveys, and experiments to systematic and bibliometric reviews, network analysis, AutoML, graph-based natural-language processing, and retrieval-augmented generation, these chapters make mechanisms observable, comparable, and, where appropriate, replicable. For scholars, they sharpen constructs, boundary conditions, and measures that link AI capabilities to outcomes, enabling cumulative testing across contexts. For policymakers and regulators, they translate evidence into governance choices grounded in ethics, explainability, bias management, and sector-specific rules. For executives and practitioners, they offer design principles for augmenting human work, allocating decision rights, and assessing value beyond narrow efficiency metrics.

We are grateful to the authors and reviewers for their rigor and craft. Taken together, the contributions show that human–machine synergy is not a single recipe but a portfolio of designs, incentives, and norms tuned to purpose and context. Our aim is to provide a coherent and plural account of collaboration and competition between human and artificial intelligence—one that equips readers to build systems that are innovative, trustworthy, and inclusive.

Paris, France — Nessrine Omrani
Naples, Italy — Francesco Schiavone
Paris, France — Francesco Paolo Appio
Paris, France — Marta Ballatore
Paris, France — Yosr Ben Tahar

Acknowledgments

The successful completion of this book has been a collaborative effort, and we are deeply grateful to all those who have contributed to its development.

We extend our heartful gratitude to the authors for their participation in the DTS 2025 Conference. The event brought together 160 international participants from 83 institutions around the world, with 106 papers presented. We are especially thankful to the chapter authors whose research, insights, and commitment made this volume possible. Their diverse perspectives and scholarly rigor have enriched the book, offering a nuanced understanding of the evolving relationship between humans and intelligent machines.

Our sincere thanks go to the editorial and production team at Springer, whose professionalism, responsiveness, and guidance were instrumental in shaping the final product. Their support ensured a smooth publication process and helped bring this project to fruition.

Special thanks also go to the keynote speaker Pattie Maes and to the editors of prestigious journals Wim Vanhaverbeke, Luca Mora, Monica Masucci, Dominik K. Kanbach, and Rian Beise-Zee. We are equally grateful to the roundtable experts Mariagrazia Squicciarini, Elmar Lutter, Vincent Maret, and Emanuele de Rinaldis for their valuable insights.

We are also indebted to the reviewers and academic colleagues who provided thoughtful feedback throughout the editorial process. Their critical reflections helped refine the contributions and elevate the overall quality of the volume.

We would like to express our gratitude to the Paris School of Business and the DISAQ University of Naples Parthenope. Our sincere thanks also go to all the project partners: Know MedTech, UNESCO, Sanofi, Bouygues, Qatar Airways, Technovation, Technological Forecasting and Social Change, IEEE Transactions on Engineering Management, European Journal of Innovation Management, and Journal of Engineering and Technology Management.

Finally, we thank our families, friends, and colleagues for their patience and encouragement throughout the editing process. Their support sustained us during long hours of coordination, review, and revision.

We hope this book contributes meaningfully to ongoing conversations about human–machine synergy and inspires further inquiry and innovation across academic, professional, and policy domains.

We are also pleased to announce that the Digital Transformation Society Conference will take place next year at the University of Naples Parthenope on May 21–22, 2026!

Contents

Digital Transformation and AI in Society

Digital Transformation in Education: A Roadmap for Future Research . . . 3
Filomena Izzo, Ida Camminatiello, and Nessrine Omrani

Digital Transformation in Agriculture: Mapping Technological Adoption Through SDG Alignment 19
Maria Virginia Sirolli, Francesca Igini, and Andrea Rocchi

Digital Transformation and Organizational Effectiveness: An Analysis of the Mauritian Top 100 Companies 35
Saubah Poolee Cootee and Nessrine Omrani

Does the Ethical Restraint of Frontier Hereditary Human Genome Manipulation Provide a Model for the Ethical Restraint of Frontier "Super General Intelligence" Development 55
Robin Dickinson and Zubin Sethna

AI and Open Innovation

Digital Finance for SMEs and Startups: Literature Review and Research Proposals 63
Tindara Abbate, Fabrizio Cesaroni, Alessandra Costa, Antonio Crupi, and Elvira Tiziana La Rocca

AI and Open Innovation: Exploring the Impact of Collaborative Strategies on Patent Value and Technological Significance 69
Andrea Amanti, Alessandra Costa, Antonio Crupi, and Francesco Paolo Appio

Digitizing Workforce Practices

Eclecticism and Wishful Thinking in the Digitalization of Workforce Practices: Opportunities and Risks 77
Massimo Bianchi

Applicability of Artificial Intelligence in Human Capital Management 91
María del Valle Fernández Moreno, David Ballesteros Ruiz, and Marta Tolentino

Telework Satisfaction in Public Organizations: Examining the Roles of Hygiene and Motivators Factors 115
Costanza Baldrighi, Francesca Sanguineti, and Pietro Previtali

Navigating Cobot Adoption in Industry 5.0: Exploration of Key Success Factors for the Adoption of Cobots in Manufacturing 137
Nisar Ahmed Channa, Gian Luca Casali, Claudio Del Regno, Greg Hearn, and Mirko Perano

Artificial Intelligence, Technostress, and Organizational Support in Business Context? What Impact on Productivity Through a Typology Model 153
Raffaele Silvestre and Mauro Romanelli

Artificial Intelligence in the PhD Journey: Transforming Research, Mentorship, and Learning 171
Giuseppe Ceci, Mauro Gatti, and Michela Iannotta

AI in the Service Sector

Exploring the Spectrum of FinTech Innovations Implemented in Microfinance Companies: A Comprehensive Review 185
Uwakmfon Promise Offiong and Katarzyna Szopik-Depczyńska

AI and Platform Models in Communication Agencies Transforming Business Architecture Through Organizational and Revenue Model Innovation 199
Stefan Kemp

Graph-Based Sentiment Analysis: An AI-Driven Approach to Mapping Customer Feedback in Retail 213
Jérôme Baray

AI for Sustainability

Artificial Intelligence and Circular Business Model Innovation: A Dynamic Capabilities Perspective 243
Mauro Sciarelli, Lorenzo Turriziani, and Anna Prisco

Leveraging AI for Automation in ESG Reporting 269
Arnesh Telukdarie, Musawenkosi H. L. Nyathi, and Maddubailu Suresh Sai Vinod

Sustainable AI-Driven Business Model Innovation: A Theoretical Framework 287
Rosario Faraci and Rosaria Ferlito

Exploring the Role of AI and ML in the Evolution of Green Finance: A Systematic Bibliometric Review 309
Hossein Habibinejad, Paul Reaidy, and Morteza Alaeddini

Enhancing Real-Time Contingency Scenario Planning with Retrieval-Augmented Generation Models 321
Christophe Bisson and Thierry Warin

Mapping AI-Driven Sustainability Research: A Meta-Review Using Topic Modeling 335
Iandolo Francesca, La Sala Antonio, Maielli Giuliano, and Vito Pietro

Digital Innovation for Sustainable Public Procurement: Overcoming Barriers and Unlocking Opportunities with AI 353
Alessia Sciarrone, Mario Calabrese, and Kamel Ben Youssef

Predicting with AI

Addressing Air Quality Estimation Exploiting AutoML 363
Alessio Carachino, Davide Storelli, Enza Giangreco, and Marco Pinnella

Managing Risk with Meaning: Explainable AI and Cognitive Turn in SME Governance 377
Davide Liberato lo Conte, Giuseppe Sancetta, and Nicola Cucari

Characterizing the Financial Behavior of Failed Companies During the COVID Crisis 383
Manuel Ruiz Marín, M. Luz Maté Sánchez-Val, José Noguera Venero, and F. Javier Sánchez-Vidal

Conclusion 401

Digital Transformation and AI in Society

Digital Transformation in Education: A Roadmap for Future Research

Filomena Izzo, Ida Camminatiello, and Nessrine Omrani

Abstract The integration of digital technology has profoundly reshaped the educational landscape, influencing pedagogical practices, administrative strategies, and institutional governance. Despite the growing body of research on digital transformation in education, the field remains fragmented, lacking a comprehensive framework that bridges management studies and educational research. This study addresses this gap by conducting a bibliometric analysis of scholarly literature on digital technology in education, using the Web of Science database.

Employing the Bibliometrix package in the R environment, this research identifies key thematic areas and emerging research trends. The results highlight the increasing academic interest in the digitalization of education, with a particular focus on technological innovation, digital governance, and the acceptance of digital tools among educators and students. The analysis also reveals critical challenges, including systemic barriers to adoption, disparities in access to digital resources, and the need for interdisciplinary approaches.

By providing a structured overview of the existing literature, this study offers a roadmap for future research, emphasizing the importance of strategic investments, targeted teacher training, and policy frameworks that ensure an inclusive and effective digital transformation in education. The findings contribute to both educational and management research, offering insights for policymakers, educators, and scholars seeking to navigate the evolving landscape of digital education.

Keywords Digital technology · Digital transformation · Education · Bibliometric analysis

F. Izzo · I. Camminatiello (✉)
Economics Department, University of Campania Luigi Vanvitelli, Capua (CE), Italy
e-mail: filomena.izzo@unicampania.it; ida.camminatiello@unicampania.it

N. Omrani
Management Department, Paris School of Business, Paris, France
e-mail: n.omrani@psbedu.paris

N. Omrani et al. (eds.), *Human-Machine Synergy and the Digital Future - Exploring Collaboration and Competition Volume 1*, Springer Proceedings in Business and Economics, https://doi.org/10.1007/978-3-032-21347-1_1

1 Introduction

The development of digital technology has profoundly reshaped the educational landscape, leading to a widespread interest among researchers, educators, and policymakers. Digital tools and platforms are increasingly integrated into teaching and learning processes, creating new opportunities for innovation while posing challenges related to accessibility, implementation, and effectiveness. This ongoing transformation aligns with broader discussions within management literature on organizational adaptation, change management, and the strategic use of technology. Bharadwaj et al. [1] and Vial [2] highlight the pivotal role of digital transformation in enhancing performance, streamlining processes, and fostering collaboration across diverse contexts. Meanwhile, educational institutions face increasing challenges to modernize pedagogical practices, personalize learning, and optimize administrative functions. The implementation of digital solutions in education requires careful alignment with institutional goals and stakeholder expectations [3], raising questions about governance, resource allocation, and digital literacy.

Numerous studies have explored the relationship between education and digital technology, particularly in terms of e-learning, digital pedagogy, and technology-enhanced learning [4–6]. However, these contributions are often framed within pedagogical or psychological perspectives and lack a structured focus on strategic governance, leadership, and institutional transformation. Recent bibliometric reviews have begun to address these issues in specific contexts, such as SMEs or higher education institutions [7–9], but an overarching analysis that integrates the managerial dimension of digital transformation in education remains limited.

Despite the growing research on digital technology in education, the field remains fragmented, with research encompassing diverse subfields such as online learning, educational data analytics, and hybrid classrooms. While prior bibliometric analyses have addressed general trends in educational research [10, 11], few have systematically examined the intersection of digital transformation and education from a management perspective. Our study addresses this gap by conducting a bibliometric analysis using a dataset explicitly drawn from the "Management" category of the Web of Science database. This approach allows us to investigate how managerial concepts—such as performance optimization, innovation diffusion, digital governance, and institutional change—are reflected in the scholarly discourse on education and technology.

This study aims to provide a roadmap for future research on digital technology and education. Drawing on bibliometric insights, this article also identifies strategic opportunities for improving the implementation and governance of digital initiatives in educational settings. By bridging educational research with management studies, it offers an interdisciplinary framework that contributes to both theoretical understanding and practical policymaking. It contributes to both educational research and management studies by offering a structured overview of existing knowledge and highlighting avenues for interdisciplinary exploration.

2 Methodology

This study adopts a **quantitative bibliometric approach** to systematically review the scientific literature on digital transformation in education. Bibliometric analysis allows for the exploration of research trends, author and institutional collaborations, citation networks, and the conceptual structure of a research field [10–12]. The analysis was conducted using the **Bibliometrix** package within the **R environment**, which provides a replicable and transparent workflow for data processing, descriptive statistics, and science mapping [13, 14].

2.1 Data Source Selection

The bibliographic data were retrieved from the **Web of Science (WoS)** Core Collection. This database was selected over alternatives such as **Scopus** and **Google Scholar** for several reasons:

1. **Quality Control**: WoS includes only peer-reviewed and high-impact journals, ensuring greater data reliability compared to Google Scholar, which indexes a broader but less curated set of sources, including gray literature [15, 16].
2. **Field Categorization**: WoS enables advanced filtering by **subject categories**, which was crucial for this study's focus on the *Management* domain. Scopus lacks this same degree of categorical precision.
3. **Comparative Robustness**: Studies comparing WoS, Scopus, and Google Scholar consistently highlight WoS's advantages in terms of citation metadata consistency and analytical precision [12, 17].

2.2 Data Collection and Search Strategy

The literature search was conducted on **January 13, 2025**, using the following query:

- In the **Title** field of WoS: "Education AND Technology";
- Language: English;
- Subject Area: Management.
- Timeframe: unrestricted.

This search yielded **124 records**. After a **data-cleaning process**, including duplicate removal and manual abstract screening for thematic relevance, **56 articles** were retained for analysis.

2.3 Bibliometric Analysis Procedures

The final dataset was exported in **plaintext format** and processed in **RStudio** using **Bibliometrix** [13]. Two main types of analysis were conducted: **descriptive analysis and thematic mapping.**

The descriptive analysis included metrics such as the number of publications over time, the intra-country (SCP) and inter-country (MCP) collaboration indices, and document type distribution.

The SCP index is calculated by dividing the number of articles with multiple authors by the total number of articles; the MCP index is the ratio between the number of inter-country co-authored articles and the total number of articles.

These indicators allow an initial mapping of research productivity and geographic reach [11]. The thematic mapping and trend analysis is a co-word analysis performed to generate thematic maps based on keyword co-occurrence. Topics were plotted according to Callon centrality (importance within the research field) and Callon density (internal development), using the [18] framework adopted by Bibliometrix [10].

The Callon centrality can be expressed by:

$$CC_k = 10 \times \sum_{j \epsilon k, h \epsilon k'} AS_{jh} \tag{1}$$

where AS_{jh} is the association strength between two words j and h, belonging to two distinct topics, k and k'.

The Callon density can be calculated by:

$$CD_k = 10 \times \sum_{j, j' \epsilon k} \frac{AS_{jj'}}{n_k} \tag{2}$$

where $AS_{jj'}$ is the association strength between a couple of words j and j' belonging to a given topic k, and nk is the total number of words belonging to k.

These measures express the role of a topic in organizing the domain's conceptual structure. Callon centrality measures the relevance of the topic in the entire research domain, while Callon density is a measure of the topic's development [19].

The thematic map allows for the identification of:

(a) *Motor themes* (high density and centrality).
(b) *Niche themes* (high density, low centrality).

(c) *Emerging or declining themes* (low density and centrality).
(d) *Basic themes* (low density, high centrality).

2.4 Software and Reproducibility

All analyses were conducted using **R version 4.3.1** and **Bibliometrix version 4.2.1**. The full R script and cleaned dataset can be shared to ensure methodological transparency and **replicability**, in line with recent best practices in bibliometric research [11, 14].

3 Results

Table 1 summarizes the scientific production in the field of Education and Technology, providing information on the research timespan (1995–2025), the total number of analyzed documents (56) and the types of publications, categorized into articles, book chapters, and early access publications.

The analysis covers a 30-year period, suggesting a continuous evolution of academic interest in the integration of technology into education. The growth of scientific production aligns with the increasing spread of digital technologies in education, particularly in recent years, as illustrated in the following chart (Fig. 1).

The presence of early access publications ("article; early access") indicates that studies are currently in the publication process, reflecting a growing interest and dynamism in recent research.

The relatively low number of book chapters suggests that there may be opportunities for greater theoretical systematization of the topic through monographs and dedicated volumes.

Figure 2 illustrates the annual scientific production in the field of Education and Technology from 1995 to 2025, showing the number of articles published each year. The x-axis represents the years, while the y-axis indicates the number of published articles.

Scientific production on "Education and Technology" was relatively low and irregular in the early years (1995–2010). There were periods with no publications or

Table 1 Main information about data

Timespan:	1995:2025
Documents	56
Document types	
Article:	47
Article; book chapter:	5
Article; early access	4

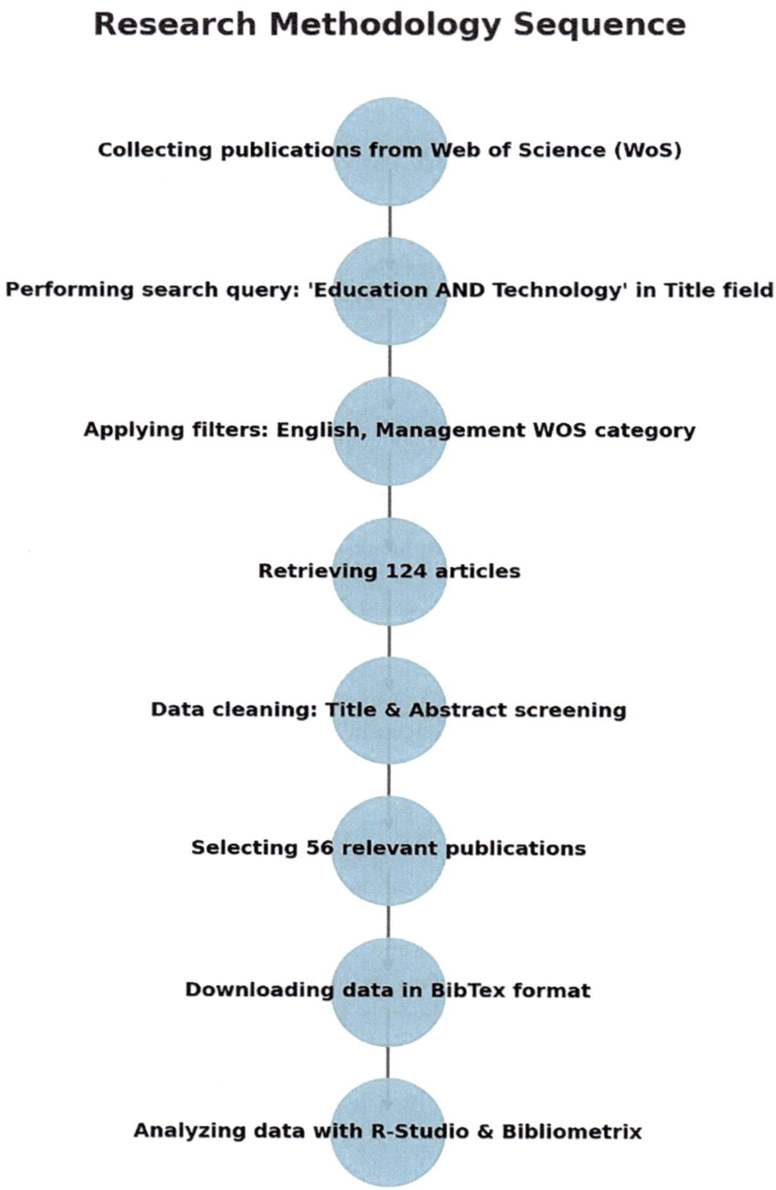

Fig. 1 Research methodology steps

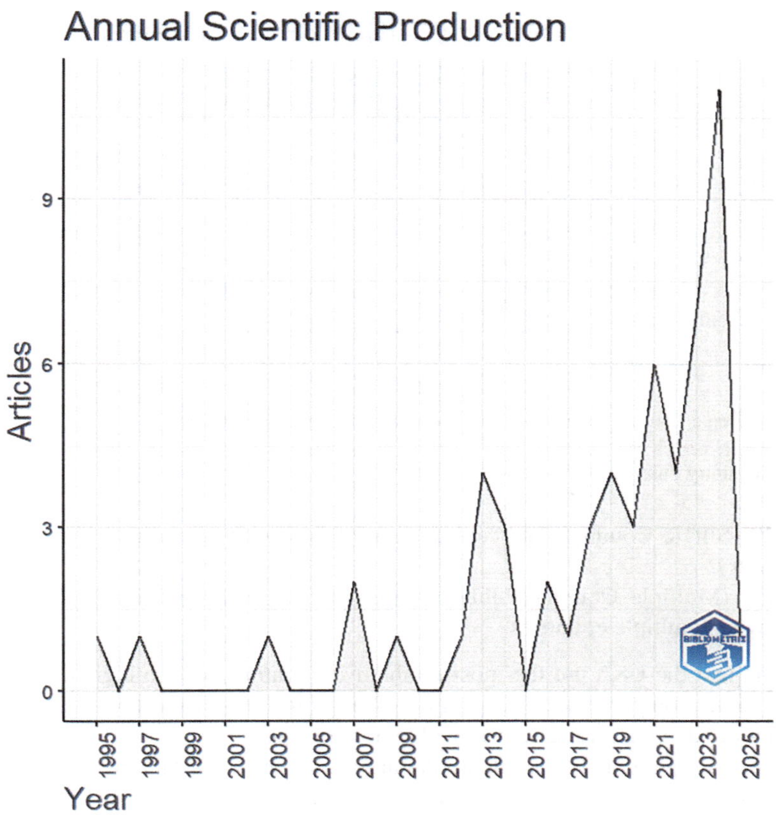

Fig. 2 Annual scientific production

very few articles published each year. This suggests that, before 2010, research in this field was not yet well-established or did not receive significant attention.

From 2011 onward, a gradual increase can be observed, which may be linked to the growing digitalization of education, the expansion of e-learning, and the large-scale adoption of early educational technologies.

From 2020 onward, there is an exponential increase in scientific production. This is likely due to the COVID-19 pandemic, which accelerated the adoption of digital learning and led to a significant rise in research on distance learning, digital tools, and educational innovation.

The decline in 2025 may not indicate a real decrease but rather an incomplete projection based on available data. In fact, it should be noted that the WOS research was conducted in early February 2025.

Figure 3 illustrates the countries with the highest number of scientific publications in the field of Education and Technology, distinguishing between:

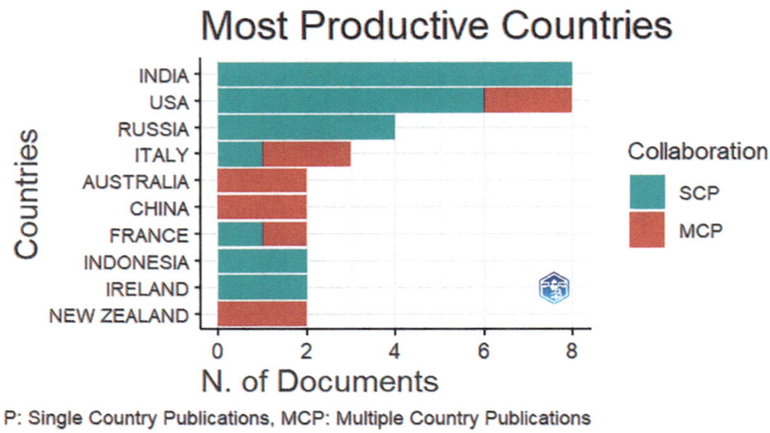

Fig. 3 Country publications

- SCP (Single Country Publications): Articles written by authors from a single country.
- MCP (Multiple Country Publications): Articles resulting from collaborations between multiple countries.

India and the USA are the most productive countries, with a higher number of publications compared to other nations. Russia and Italy follow with a moderate production, demonstrating active involvement in research.

Figure 3 highlights two publication patterns: countries with a higher proportion of SCP (domestic research) and countries with a greater presence of MCP (collaborative research).

Countries with a higher proportion of SCP (domestic research) include India, the USA, Russia, Indonesia, and Ireland. These countries primarily produce national research, with few articles resulting from international collaborations. This suggests that research in these nations might be more focused on local or institutional initiatives without a strong international network.

Countries with a greater presence of MCP (collaborative research) include Italy, Australia, China, France, and New Zealand. This indicates that these countries actively participate in international research networks, fostering knowledge exchange and resource sharing.

Given the increasing global interest in educational technology, a rise in international collaborations can be expected in the near future.

Figure 4 presents research topics positioned in a two-dimensional graph based on:

- Horizontal axis (Relevance degree–Centrality): Measures the relevance of the topic within the field of study;
- Vertical axis (Development degree–Density): Indicates the internal development level of the topic.

The map is divided into four quadrants, each with a distinct meaning.

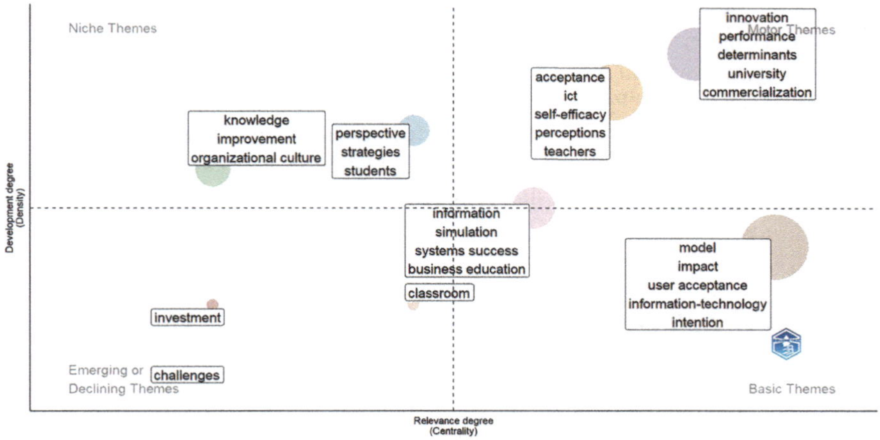

Fig. 4 Positioning map

3.1 *Upper Right Quadrant: Motor Themes (High Centrality—High Density)*

The topics in this quadrant are: Innovation, Performance, Determinants, University, Commercialization; Acceptance, ICT, Self-efficacy, Perceptions, Teachers.

These themes represent well-developed and highly relevant areas of research in "Education and Technology."

The first group of keywords ("Innovation," "Performance," "University," "Commercialization") suggests that technological innovation in Higher Education is a central aspect. The integration of technology into academic processes and its commercialization are key topics.

The second group ("Acceptance," "ICT," "Self-efficacy," "Perceptions," "Teachers") highlights research on teachers' perception and acceptance of technology, which is crucial for the success of digital initiatives in the educational sector.

3.2 *Upper Left Quadrant: Niche Themes (Low Centrality—High Density)*

The topics in this quadrant are: Knowledge, Improvement, Organizational Culture, Perspective, Strategies, Students.

These themes are highly developed but less connected to the rest of the field, indicating more specialized research areas.

The first group ("Knowledge," "Improvement," "Organizational Culture") suggests studies on knowledge management and the improvement of educational practices at an organizational level.

The second group ("Perspective," "Strategies," "Students") may refer to educational strategies aimed at students and their perspectives on technology use.

Although well-defined, these themes could benefit from greater integration with other research areas to increase their impact.

3.3 Lower Left Quadrant: Emerging or Declining Themes (Low Centrality—Low Density)

The topics in this quadrant are: Investment, Challenges.

This quadrant includes underdeveloped topics with low overall relevance in the current research field.

"Investment" and "Challenges" suggest that funding and difficulties in implementing technology in education are discussed topics but have not yet been fully explored in academic literature.

If these themes are emerging, they could become more central in the future. If declining, they may have lost relevance compared to more recent research topics.

3.4 Lower Right Quadrant: Basic Themes (High Centrality—Low Density)

The topics in this quadrant are: Information-Technology Intention, Information, Simulation, Systems Success, Business Education, Classroom.

These themes are crucial for research in "Education and Technology" but require further development and exploration.

The first group ("Model," "Impact," "User Acceptance," "Information-Technology Intention") indicates that IT acceptance in education is a fundamental topic but needs more specialization.

The second group ("Information," "Simulation," "Systems Success," "Business Education," "Classroom") highlights that simulation and the success of technological systems in business education and classrooms are discussed but require further investigation.

Since these topics are central but underdeveloped, future studies could explore specific aspects such as the impact of technologies on learning and improvements in technology adoption models.

3.5 Summary of the Positioning Map Analysis

Innovation and technological acceptance are dominant themes. Innovation and the commercialization of technology in Higher Education, along with teachers' perception and acceptance of technologies, are at the center of academic debate.

Educational strategies and knowledge management are specialized areas. Although well-developed, these topics remain relatively isolated and could benefit from stronger connections with more central themes.

Investment and challenges in technology adoption in education require more attention. This issue could become a key research area in the future.

Technology adoption models and their impact on students are fundamental for research. However, they require further investigation and more structured studies.

4 Discussion and Implication

The results of the bibliometric analysis underscore a dynamic and sustained growth in research focused on digital technology in education. This upward trend reflects increasing scholarly engagement with the complex intersection of pedagogy, institutional governance, and technological innovation. The quantitative rise in publications post-2010—and especially after 2020—signals a paradigm shift in how educational transformation is conceptualized, moving from isolated technological adoption to integrated institutional change [10, 11].

This shift has been further accelerated by external events, most notably the COVID-19 pandemic. During this period, schools and universities across the globe were compelled to rapidly implement online and hybrid learning solutions. This emergency-driven digital migration catalyzed the widespread adoption of educational technologies and triggered a substantial increase in academic publications related to e-learning, remote teaching, and virtual platforms [11, 20]. The temporal concentration of publications in 2020–2021 found in our dataset aligns with this external disruption, suggesting a strong link between crisis response and scholarly output.

Thematic mapping reveals several strategic research clusters. 'Motor themes' such as Innovation, ICT, and Teacher Acceptance are both central and well-developed, indicating a mature and relevant discourse. These findings resonate with literature emphasizing the pivotal role of educators in technological integration [6]. The presence of "Investment" and "Challenges" in the emerging themes quadrant points to a relatively underexplored yet critical area of research. This includes barriers to technology adoption such as lack of funding, infrastructure, and institutional readiness [5]. Additionally, 'Basic themes' like Information-Technology Intention and User Acceptance suggest that foundational adoption models are still evolving and require further contextualization within educational settings [4].

The findings carry important implications for education leaders and policymakers. Institutions should not only invest in digital infrastructure but also ensure that such investments are aligned with pedagogical goals and organizational culture [21, 22]. Training programs for teachers, strategic digital governance, and inclusive access models are essential to transform short-term solutions into long-term value. Furthermore, the analysis of international collaborations (SCP vs. MCP) indicates opportunities for greater global exchange of knowledge and practices, which can enhance institutional capacity building and policy learning across regions.

This study also highlights several research gaps. The limited attention to investment and governance challenges suggests a need for more research on the structural and systemic dimensions of educational digitalization. In addition, future studies should expand on co-citation and cluster analysis to deepen the understanding of intellectual trends and author networks. Methodologically, the use of mixed approaches combining bibliometric data with qualitative case studies could enhance contextual understanding of digital transformation processes in diverse educational systems.

Overall, this discussion integrates empirical findings with theoretical insights and offers a roadmap for both future academic research and practical interventions. By bridging bibliometric analysis with managerial and policy perspectives, the study contributes a comprehensive framework for understanding and guiding the digital transformation of education.

5 Conclusion

This study examined the evolution of digital transformation in the educational sector through a bibliometric analysis, highlighting the growing academic interest in the topic and the main emerging research trends.

The findings confirm that the digitalization of education is not merely a transient trend but rather a structural shift that is redefining both teaching practices and the organizational strategies of educational institutions.

One of the most significant contributions of this research lies in the identification of the most developed thematic areas. Among these, technological innovation and the digitalization of educational processes emerge as the most extensively studied topics, often analyzed in relation to the acceptance and adoption of technology by students and teachers.

In this context, the role of teachers proves to be crucial for the effectiveness of technological integration: their training, digital competencies, and attitude toward innovation significantly influence the level of adoption of new technologies in school and university settings.

Furthermore, the study highlights some research areas that remain relatively unexplored but are gaining increasing relevance. In particular, systemic challenges emerge concerning investments, digital infrastructure, and organizational barriers that hinder the effective dissemination of technologies in education.

The difficulties in implementation are not solely due to resistance to change or a lack of digital skills but also to structural issues such as insufficient funding, the lack of standardization across digital platforms, and governance challenges.

From an applied perspective, the findings of this research suggest that the integration of technology in education should be approached strategically and systematically. Simply introducing digital tools into curricula is not enough; it is essential to develop digital governance policies that ensure the effective and sustainable use of new technologies. This requires targeted investments in infrastructure, continuous professional development programs for teaching staff, and careful regulation of data usage and digital platforms in education.

Only through coordinated collaboration among educational institutions, policymakers, and technology companies will it be possible to promote an inclusive and effective digital transformation.

Finally, this research provides a reference framework for future studies, emphasizing the need to further explore the long-term impact of digitalization on learning outcomes, educational inclusion, and the administrative efficiency of institutions. A more in-depth analysis of these aspects will be essential to understanding how technology can genuinely contribute to improving the quality of education and reducing the digital divide among different segments of the student population.

6 Study Limitations and Directions for Future Research

While this study provides a bibliometric analysis of the literature on digital transformation in education, it presents certain methodological limitations that could be overcome by adopting a more articulated and in-depth approach.

Currently, the bibliometric analysis primarily focuses on descriptive aspects and thematic mapping of existing research, without fully leveraging the advanced techniques available in Bibliometrix software. The descriptive analysis provides basic information, such as the number of publications and their temporal distribution; however, it could be enhanced by incorporating more detailed metrics, such as the number of citations per author and publication, the productivity index of authors, the identification of the most influential sources, and the analysis of the distribution of the most commonly used keywords in studies.

Another limitation of this study is the absence of cluster analysis, which would allow for the identification of groups of studies with similar characteristics, thereby facilitating a more structured understanding of research trends. For instance, clusters could be identified in areas such as the adoption of digital technologies by teachers, barriers and challenges to digitalization in education, and the role of educational policies in digital transformation.

Moreover, a co-citation analysis is missing, which would be particularly useful for identifying connections among the most cited studies and outlining the intellectual structure of the discipline. This approach would highlight key authors and theories shaping the debate on digitalization in education.

Another aspect that has not been considered is the identification of international collaborations. An analysis of collaboration networks among authors and institutions would have made it possible to identify major research hubs and understand the dynamics of global scientific cooperation in the field of digital transformation in education.

To address these limitations and enhance the effectiveness of the study, the following improvements should be considered:

- a more detailed analysis of bibliometric metrics, with a focus on citations and author productivity;
- a cluster analysis to identify macro-themes and emerging research groups;
- a co-citation and keyword co-occurrence analysis, to highlight connections among the most relevant studies and map the theoretical landscape of the discipline;
- an analysis of collaborations between authors and institutions, to gain deeper insight into the global academic network on digital transformation in education.

Integrating these advanced methodologies would provide a more comprehensive and structured overview of the existing literature, improving the understanding of research trends and identifying new study opportunities.

Finally, the primary aim of this study was to explore and map scientific dynamics through well-established bibliometric methodologies. Future developments could involve a more in-depth thematic analysis, such as topic modeling using LDA (Latent Dirichlet Allocation), to enrich and validate the findings obtained through bibliometric analysis.

References

1. Bharadwaj, A., El Sawy, O.A., Pavlou, P.A., Venkatraman, N.: Digital business strategy: toward a next generation of insights. MIS Q. **37**(2), 471–482 (2013)
2. Vial, G.: Understanding digital transformation: a review and a research agenda. J. Strateg. Inf. Syst. **28**(2), 118–144 (2019)
3. Selwyn, N.: Education and Technology: Key Issues and Debates. Bloomsbury Publishing, London (2016)
4. Davis, F.D.: Perceived usefulness, perceived ease of use, and user acceptance of information technology. MIS Q. **13**(3), 319–340 (1989)
5. Ertmer, P.A.: Addressing first- and second-order barriers to change: strategies for technology integration. Educ. Technol. Res. Dev. **47**(4), 47–61 (1999)
6. Hew, K.F., Brush, T.: Integrating technology into K-12 teaching and learning: current knowledge gaps and recommendations for future research. Educ. Technol. Res. Dev. **55**(3), 223–252 (2007)
7. Ganga-Contreras, F., Suarez-Amaya, W., Alarcón-Henríquez, N.: Scientific production of the relationship between leadership, higher education and digital transformation: a bibliometric analysis. Interciencia. **49**(1) (2023)
8. Marino-Romero, J.A., Palos-Sánchez, P.R., Velicia-Martín, F.: Evolution of digital transformation in SMEs management through a bibliometric analysis. Technol. Forecast. Soc. Chang. **199**, 123014 (2024). https://doi.org/10.1016/j.techfore.2023.123014

9. Salazar-Sepúlveda, G., Toledo-Aceituno, P., Villarroel-Molina, A.: Digital transformation in higher education institutions: bibliometric analysis (2023) [Preprint]. https://www.researchgate.net/publication/372388413_Digital_Transformation_in_Higher_Education_Institutions_Bibliometric_Analysis
10. Cobo, M.J., López-Herrera, A.G., Herrera-Viedma, E., Herrera, F.: Science mapping software tools: review, analysis, and cooperative study among tools. J. Am. Soc. Inf. Sci. Technol. **62**(7), 1382–1402 (2011)
11. Donthu, N., Kumar, S., Mukherjee, D., Pandey, N., Lim, W.M.: How to conduct a bibliometric analysis: an overview and guidelines. J. Bus. Res. **133**, 285–296 (2021). https://doi.org/10.1016/j.jbusres.2021.04.070
12. Zhu, J., Liu, W.: A tale of two databases: the use of Web of Science and Scopus in academic papers. Scientometrics. **123**(1), 321–335 (2020)
13. Aria, M., Cuccurullo, C.: Bibliometrix: an R-tool for comprehensive science mapping analysis. J. Informet. **11**(4), 959–975 (2017)
14. Aria, M., Misuraca, M., Spano, M.: Mapping the evolution of social research and data science on 30 years of Social Indicators Research. Soc. Indic. Res. **149**(3), 803–831 (2020)
15. Mongeon, P., Paul-Hus, A.: The journal coverage of Web of Science and Scopus: a comparative analysis. Scientometrics. **106**(1), 213–228 (2016)
16. Singh, V.K., Singh, P., Karmakar, M., Leta, J., Mayr, P.: The journal coverage of Web of Science, Scopus and Dimensions: a comparative analysis. Scientometrics. **126**(6), 5113–5142 (2021)
17. Visser, M., van Eck, N.J., Waltman, L.: Large-scale comparison of bibliographic data sources: Scopus, Web of Science, Dimensions, Crossref, and Microsoft Academic. Quant. Sci. Stud. **2**(1), 20–41 (2021)
18. Callon, M., Courtial, J.P. & Laville, F. Co-word analysis as a tool for describing the network of interactions between basic and technological research: The case of polymer chemsitry. Scientometrics 22, 155–205 (1991). https://doi.org/10.1007/BF02019280
19. Aria, M., Cuccurullo, C., D'Aniello, L., Misuraca, M., Spano, M.: Thematic analysis as a new culturomic tool: the social media coverage on COVID-19 pandemic in Italy. Sustainability. **14**(6), 36–43 (2022). https://doi.org/10.3390/su14063643
20. Williamson, B., Bayne, S., Shay, S.: The datafication of teaching in higher education: critical issues and perspectives. Teach. High. Educ. **25**(4), 351–365 (2020)
21. Brynjolfsson, E., Hitt, L.M.: Paradox lost? Firm-level evidence on the returns to information systems spending. Manag. Sci. **42**(4), 541–558 (1996)
22. Zhu, K., Kraemer, K.L.: Post-adoption variations in usage and value of e-business by organizations: cross-country evidence from the retail industry. Inf. Syst. Res. **16**(1), 61–84 (2005)

Digital Transformation in Agriculture: Mapping Technological Adoption Through SDG Alignment

Maria Virginia Sirolli, Francesca Igini, and Andrea Rocchi

Abstract Digitalization is transforming agriculture, improving productivity and resource efficiency. However, the extent to which digital technologies contribute to broader sustainability objectives remains uneven. This study examines the intersection of digitalization and sustainability in agriculture through the lens of the Sustainable Development Goals (SDGs), using empirical data from the FAO AgriTech Observatory. The findings reveal a strong concentration of digital initiatives aligned to economic and productivity-oriented SDGs (SDG 9 and 12), while environmental (SDG 14 and 15) and social goals (SDG 5) remain significantly underrepresented. This pattern suggests that digital transformation in agriculture primarily follows market-driven priorities, favoring efficiency and competitiveness over a more holistic approach to sustainability. Web-based platforms, mobile applications, and AI are widely adopted, whereas technologies with potential for governance and environmental monitoring—such as GIS, remote sensing, and blockchain—are less integrated. Gender-responsive solutions remain scarce, raising concerns about digitalization reinforcing existing inequalities rather than addressing them. While digital tools can support sustainability, their impact depends on enabling policies, infrastructure, and targeted investments. Bridging these gaps requires a strategic shift in AgriTech development, ensuring innovation extends beyond productivity gains to support climate resilience, social inclusion, and governance. Aligning digitalization with sustainability-driven priorities will be key to fostering a more equitable and resilient agrifood system.

M. V. Sirolli (✉) · F. Igini
Department of Management, Sapienza University of Rome, Rome, Italy
e-mail: mariavirginia.sirolli@uniroma1.it; francesca.igini@uniroma1.it

A. Rocchi
Department of Communication and Social Research, Sapienza University of Rome, Rome, Italy
e-mail: andrea.rocchi@uniroma1.it

N. Omrani et al. (eds.), *Human-Machine Synergy and the Digital Future - Exploring Collaboration and Competition Volume 1*, Springer Proceedings in Business and Economics, https://doi.org/10.1007/978-3-032-21347-1_2

Keywords Agriculture · Agritech · Digital transformation · Sustainability · Sustainable development goals

1 Introduction

Agriculture is at the core of global development, providing food, employment and raw materials while shaping ecosystems. However, the sector faces mounting challenges as the global population, projected to reach nearly ten billion by 2050 [1], intensifies pressure on food production while demanding reduced environmental impact. A core paradox of agricultural sustainability is that, while essential for human survival, farming has historically contributed to environmental degradation. Intensive agriculture drives deforestation, excessive water use, soil depletion and high greenhouse gas emissions—especially methane (CH_4) from livestock and nitrous oxide (N_2O) from fertilizers, both with greater warming potential than CO_2 [2, 3]. Land-use changes further erode biodiversity and release stored carbon [4]. Overuse of irrigation depletes water reserves, while runoff from fertilizers and agrochemicals pollutes ecosystems [5]. Additionally, food waste and long-distance transport worsen emissions, compounding agriculture's environmental footprint [6–8]. Thus, the sector risks undermining its own long-term viability.

This complexity makes agriculture distinct from other industries, given its deep interdependencies with ecological, climatic, and socio-economic systems. Unlike most sectors, agriculture operates within a dynamic natural environment where technological interventions must balance productivity with sustainability. Digitalization exemplifies this duality: while enhancing efficiency, it has also reinforced unsustainable production models. Understanding this dynamic is crucial for shaping agrifood systems, as the sector navigates multiple, interconnected drivers. Climate change increases extreme weather events, threatening yields, yet innovations like precision agriculture and drought-resistant crops mitigate these risks. Improved value chains, such as better storage and logistics, reduce food waste and strengthen resilience [9]. Meanwhile, demographic shifts—including population growth and urbanization—alter food consumption patterns, driving increased demand for processed and protein-rich foods. This shift raises concerns about sustainability, food security, and nutrition-related diseases [10]. Geopolitical instability disrupts food markets globally, driving price volatility and trade restrictions, while policies, subsidies, and trade agreements further shape food accessibility [11]. Moreover, environmental degradation and resource scarcity threaten productivity, underscoring the need for sustainable land and water management, which remains highly dependent on regional infrastructure disparities. Shifting consumer expectations add complexity: growing awareness of sustainability, health, and ethical sourcing is driving R&D in alternative proteins, climate-friendly farming, and biodegradable packaging, though regulatory constraints often slow adoption [12]. The COVID-19 pandemic also exposed vulnerabilities in food systems, underscoring the need for resilient infrastructure and knowledge-sharing to help farmers adapt to future shocks [13].

Addressing these challenges requires a holistic approach that balances technology, policy, market adaptation, and environmental sustainability. The resilience and inclusivity of future agrifood systems depend on effectively integrating these elements. In this context, digitalization is a key driver of sustainable transformation. Despite its growing role in agricultural policy and sustainability, there is limited assessment of its alignment with SDG targets. This study examines the intersection of digitalization and agricultural sustainability through the lens of the UN 2030 Agenda, which frames global development around poverty reduction, environmental protection, and equitable resource access. Using empirical data from the FAO AgriTech Observatory [14], this paper examines how digital technologies contribute to sustainability objectives, providing insights into their applications, challenges, and opportunities, highlighting digitalization as a key enabler of agricultural sustainability in the face of growing environmental and demographic pressures.

2 Literature Review

Digital transformation refers to the integration of digital technologies into core agricultural activities, aiming to enhance productivity, decision-making, and sustainability [15]. In this context, the Sustainable Development Goals (SDGs) provide a comprehensive framework for evaluating the broader impact of such technologies, encompassing economic, environmental, and social dimensions. Mapping digital initiatives across the 17 SDGs offers a structured lens to assess where digital agriculture is making tangible progress—and where critical gaps remain (cf. Table 1).

The evolution of digitalization in agriculture has transformed the sector from traditional manual labor to highly sophisticated, data-driven systems. For millennia, agriculture relied on human and animal labor, rudimentary tools, and an extreme dependence on environmental conditions. Despite occasional advancements—such as sophisticated irrigation techniques in Mesopotamia [16]—farming remained largely unchanged until the industrial era [17]. Mechanization, chemical input, and the Green Revolution dramatically increased productivity, shifting agriculture toward large-scale, capital-intensive models. However, this shift also introduced challenges related to environmental sustainability, soil depletion, and inefficient resource use [18]. Precision farming emerged in the 1980s as a response to these challenges, leveraging GPS-based technologies, remote sensing, and variable-rate applications to optimize input use. Unlike traditional uniform management, precision agriculture enabled farmers to monitor soil conditions, crop health, and environmental factors in real time, applying fertilizers, pesticides, and water more efficiently to reduce waste while maintaining yields. However, adoption has been uneven, favoring large, mechanized farms with greater access to capital and infrastructure [19, 20]. Building on precision farming, Agriculture 4.0 applies the Industry 4.0 model to agriculture, integrating smart technologies, automation, and

Table 1 Summary of drivers for agrifood sector transformation

Category	Driver	Explanation
A. Systemic (overarching) drivers	1. Population dynamics and urbanization	Urbanization is increasing rapidly, with an estimated 70% of the global population living in urban areas by 2050, impacting agrifood systems
	2. Economic growth, structural transformation and macroeconomic outlook	Macroeconomic trends influence inclusive economic transformation, with risks of declining labor shares and weakened household spending
	3. Cross-country interdependencies	Global interdependencies of food systems create both opportunities and risks, as food security is vulnerable to economic downturns
	4. Big data generation, control, use and ownership	Big data enhances real-time decision-making in agriculture but raises concerns over market dominance and data control by a few entities
	5. Geopolitical instability and increasing conflicts	Conflicts, including those over resources and energy, contribute to food insecurity, affecting millions in conflict-prone regions
	6. Uncertainties (e.g., COVID-19 pandemic)	Uncertainties like the COVID-19 pandemic impact food production and distribution, highlighting vulnerabilities in agrifood systems
	7. Rural and urban poverty	High levels of poverty in rural and urban areas affect food security, as healthy diets remain unaffordable for many people
B. Drivers affecting food access and livelihoods	8. Inequalities	Economic and social inequalities limit access to resources, job opportunities and essential services, disproportionately affecting women
	9. Food prices	Food price fluctuations, despite long-term trends, fail to capture full social and environmental costs, affecting affordability
	10. Innovation and science	Advancements in biotechnology, genetics and agroecology offer solutions but also present challenges in agrifood transformation
C. Drivers affecting food and agricultural production and distribution	11. Public investment in agrifood systems	Public investments in agrifood systems have declined significantly in recent years, affecting agricultural productivity and sustainability
	12. Capital and information intensity of production	Mechanization, automation and digitalization increase capital requirements while reducing labor demand in agriculture and manufacturing
	13. Input and output market concentration	Market concentration in input and output sectors creates barriers to competition and resilience in agrifood systems
	14. Consumption and nutrition patterns	Consumer preferences shape food demand, requiring governance mechanisms like carbon labeling to promote sustainability
	15. Scarcity and degradation of natural resources	Unsustainable farming leads to soil degradation, biodiversity loss and increased vulnerability to crop failures

Table 1 (continued)

Category	Driver	Explanation
D. Drivers regarding environmental systems	16. Epidemics and degradation of ecosystems	Agricultural expansion into forests and antimicrobial resistance heightens risks of zoonotic diseases and ecosystem degradation
	17. Climate change	Agriculture contributes significantly to greenhouse gas emissions, necessitating climate adaptation and mitigation strategies
	18. Sustainable ocean economies	Expanding sustainable ocean economies is a key to balancing environmental, social and economic sustainability in fisheries and aquaculture

Source: authors' own elaboration based on "The future of food and agriculture. Drivers and triggers for transformation" [22]

real-time data processing across the agrifood system [21]. Often referred to as "Smart Agriculture" or "Digital Farming," it creates a fully networked ecosystem where digital platforms connect farmers, suppliers, and consumers, facilitating data-driven decision-making across the value chain [22]. This transition is driven by key enabling technologies such as IoT-connected sensors, cloud computing, and artificial intelligence (AI). These tools enhance farm management, predict risks, and improve supply chain efficiency. Smart farming introduces a networked ecosystem, where digital platforms connect farmers, suppliers, and consumers, facilitating transparency and efficiency throughout the food system: AI-powered models forecast crop diseases before outbreaks occur; autonomous machinery performs precision tasks with minimal human intervention; and decision support systems (DSS) optimize farm operations [15, 23, 24].

Digitalization in agriculture is closely tied to sustainability, promoting resource efficiency and circular economy principles. Precision technologies minimize water and chemical inputs, while AI applications enhance crop planning and reduce food waste [25, 26]. However, this digital shift also introduces risks, including increased energy consumption from data centers and automation, digital inequalities that exclude small-scale farmers from technological benefits, and ethical concerns over data ownership and corporate control of agricultural platforms [27]. This paradox underscores the dual role of digitalization: while a powerful enabler of sustainable agriculture, it also presents challenges that require policy interventions, infrastructure investments, and inclusive innovation strategies. The Food and Agriculture Organization (FAO) has identified 18 drivers of change shaping agrifood systems, emphasizing their interconnected nature (Table 1), which will shape the future of agrifood systems, emphasizing that these factors do not operate in isolation but rather interact in complex and dynamic ways. Climate change, for example, intensifies extreme weather events, threatening crop yields, yet technological innovations such as precision irrigation and drought-resistant crops help mitigate these risks. Similarly, shifting demographics and urbanization alter food consumption patterns, while resource availability, policy frameworks, and market dynamics influence agricultural production and food security [1, 28–30]. These complex interactions highlight the need for resilient supply chains, efficient resource management, and adaptive strategies to navigate an increasingly uncertain global landscape.

3 Methods

This study adopts a mixed-method approach, combining exploratory analysis with empirical data drawn from FAO's AgriTech Observatory to assess how digitalization supports progress across the Sustainable Development Goals (SDGs). While FAO explicitly associates SDGs 1, 2, 5, 6, 10, 12, 14, and 15 with agriculture, our analysis extends to all 17 SDGs, reflecting agriculture's systemic relevance to economic resilience, environmental protection, and social equity.

The analysis is based on the AgriTech Observatory developed by the FAO Regional Office for Europe and Central Asia. The Observatory is a structured and validated repository of global digital agriculture initiatives linked to SDGs. The dataset includes 400 initiatives launched between 2015 and 2023, and is continuously updated by FAO staff and partners through institutional monitoring and standardized reporting procedures.

The dataset covers initiatives from 219 countries and territories, ensuring wide geographic and contextual diversity. Each initiative is classified by:

- Technology type (e.g., mobile apps, AI, drones, blockchain);
- Geographic region (country and subregion);
- SDG alignment, based on FAO's internal tagging system;
- Initiative type, grouped into six categories: Digital/Smart Village, Good Practice, Policy, Project, Resource, and Solution.

For this study, only operational categories were considered (i.e., Project, Solution, Good Practice, Digital/Smart Village, and Resource), while Policy initiatives were excluded, as they function primarily as enablers rather than direct implementations. After filtering, the final sample included 377 digital initiatives directly linked to the implementation of SDG-relevant actions.

The dataset was manually curated and quality-checked to ensure consistency with FAO classifications. This process preserved the original SDG mappings while excluding duplicates, incomplete entries, and initiatives unrelated to digitalization.

To understand how digital solutions are distributed across the SDGs, a two-step process was applied. First, an exploratory count assessed the frequency of each SDG among the 377 initiatives. Second, a quantitative matrix was constructed to evaluate the presence of each technology across SDGs. Technologies were placed in rows, SDGs in columns, and values represented the frequency of each technology within initiatives aligned with a given SDG.

To enable proportional comparisons, a normalization procedure was applied using the formula:

$$C_{ij}^{norm} = \frac{C_{ij}}{T}$$

where:

C_{ij}^{norm} = the normalized presence of technology (i) in initiatives in aligned with SDG (j);
C_{ij} = the raw contribution value;
T = is the total number of initiatives analyzed (377).

Normalized values range from 0 to 1, where 1 indicates the highest relative presence. A heatmap was generated to visualize these patterns, with:

- technologies on the Y-axis;
- SDGs on the X-axis;
- a color gradient from dark blue (low presence) to dark red (high presence), representing normalized frequency.

This matrix structure supports comparative assessments across SDGs, identifying key enablers (e.g., mobile/web platforms, big data, AI) and areas with limited digital integration. It also facilitates identification of patterns that may relate to the maturity, scalability, or contextual fit of different technologies.

The Observatory covers initiatives from both high-income and low- and middle-income countries. Preliminary exploration of geographic distribution reveals higher densities in EU and Eastern European countries, with relatively fewer initiatives documented in Central Asian and Western Balkan countries. These differences may reflect disparities in infrastructure, investment capacity, digital literacy, and institutional reporting practices. As the dataset is based in part on voluntary reporting and institutional contributions, it may under-represent regions with limited digital engagement or reduced participation in global development platforms. Additionally, the SDG classifications reflect institutional tagging and may not fully capture the intensity or quality of impact. Despite these limitations, the Observatory offers a consistent and validated foundation for identifying macro-patterns in the relationship between digitalization and sustainable development.

4 Findings

The first analysis reveals a strong concentration of digital initiatives in SDG 9 (Industry, Innovation, and Infrastructure, 218 initiatives) and SDG 12 (Responsible Consumption and Production, 209). This confirms the central role of digitalization in infrastructure enhancement and the promotion of sustainable production models. SDG 8 (Decent Work and Economic Growth, 174) and SDG 2 (Zero Hunger, 129) also show high engagement, reflecting increasing demand for technology to boost productivity and food security.

SDG 17 (Partnerships, 119) and SDG 11 (Sustainable Cities, 99) emphasize collaboration and innovation in urban systems. Conversely, SDG 5 (Gender Equality, 20) and SDG 14 (Life Below Water, 6) are markedly underrepresented, suggesting uneven digital integration across thematic areas. These patterns may reflect the varying levels of digital readiness, investment incentives and enabling infrastructure across sectors.

Figure 1 identifies the most widely adopted technologies: desktop/web platforms (69%) and mobile applications (48%), which benefit from high accessibility and usability. Cloud computing (32%), IoT (29%), GPS (29%), and big data (27%) also feature prominently, supporting scalable and connected services. AI (22%) and machine learning (18%) show growing traction, though still less pervasive than foundational technologies.

Emerging or resource-intensive technologies—such as robotics (11%), blockchain (10%) and AR/VR (6%)—exhibit limited uptake, likely due to cost, complexity, or narrow applicability. Social media (14%) and online communities (10%) tend to complement rather than drive innovation. The low incidence of "other technologies" (1%) reinforces the reliance on mature digital solutions.

The analysis also explores the relationship between technologies and their usage within initiatives addressing the 17 SDGs through a heatmap visualization (Fig. 2). The results reveal notable disparities in technology adoption across different SDGs:

Big Data (26.5%) and AI (22%) are most frequently used in initiatives linked to SDG 9 (Industry, Innovation, and Infrastructure) and SDG 8 (Decent Work and Economic Growth), highlighting their role in sustainable production and infrastructure development.

Both technologies are also key enablers in SDG 2 (Zero Hunger), supporting advancements in agriculture and food security.

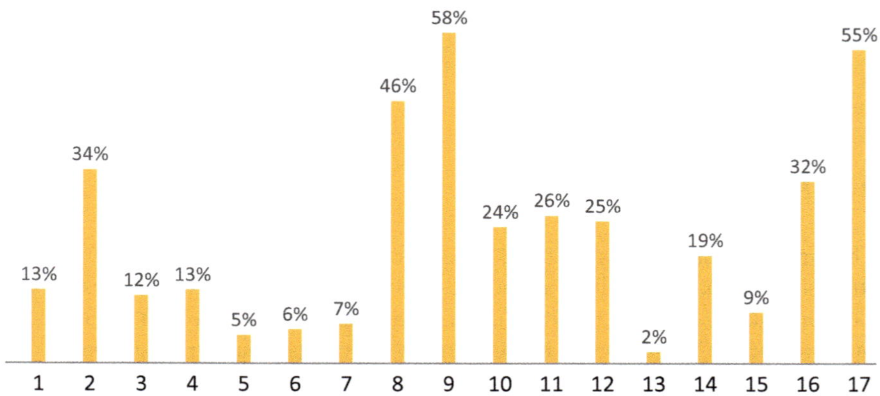

Fig. 1 Percentages of related SDGs out of total initiatives. (Source: authors' own elaboration based on "The future of food and agriculture. Drivers and triggers for transformation" [22])

Fig. 2 Percentage of use of technology in the total number of initiatives. (Source: elaboration by the authors based on Agritech Database (FAO) [14])

Bluetooth and AR/VR technologies are minimally used, particularly in SDG 14 (Life Below Water) and SDG 6 (Clean Water and Sanitation). AR/VR is moderately represented in SDG 9 (0.056) and SDG 8 (0.037) but remains marginal elsewhere.

Economic and industrial SDGs, including SDG 9, SDG 8, and SDG 12 (Responsible consumption and production), show higher technology adoption, particularly in Big Data (0.138) and AI (0.109) applications for sustainable production and resource efficiency. In contrast, environmental SDGs such as SDG 14 (Life below water) and SDG 15 (Life on land) show lower technology integration, suggesting a limited focus on digitalization in environmental sustainability efforts. Mobile applications, web-based platforms, and AI-driven solutions play a key role in initiatives that are aligned with:

- SDG 1 (No poverty), supporting economic vulnerability mapping and resource allocation;
- SDG 2 (Zero hunger), enhancing agricultural efficiency and food security;
- SDG 3 (Good health and well-being), generating digital solutions for hospital nutrition management, food safety audits, and consumer protection platforms;
- SDG 4 (Quality education), endorsing a digital education ecosystem for agribusiness, including e-learning platforms, electronic libraries, and ICT training applications;
- SDG 5 (Gender equality), empowering women farmers by strengthening agrifood market linkages.

Despite the strong role of digital platforms in sustainable development, certain SDGs remain underrepresented in terms of technology adoption. SDG 14 (Life Below Water) exhibits minimal digital innovation for ocean sustainability, while SDG 16 (Peace, Justice, and Strong Institutions) shows limited integration of AI-driven governance solutions. In contrast, technologies such as GIS, GPS, drones, and sensor-based systems demonstrate high uptake in economic and industrial SDGs.

For instance, SDG 9 (Industry, Innovation, and Infrastructure) makes extensive use of GIS (0.2626), GPS (0.2944), drones (0.1088), remote sensing (0.2997) and sensor technologies (0.3740) for infrastructure planning and automation. Similarly, SDG 12 (Responsible Consumption and Production) leverages these tools to monitor resource use and support circular economy practices.

These findings suggest that economic and production-oriented goals attract greater technological investment, whereas social and environmental SDGs remain comparatively under-integrated. Such disparities may stem from broader structural differences, including unequal access to infrastructure, gaps in digital literacy, and fragmented policy frameworks—highlighting opportunities for more inclusive and balanced digital development (Fig. 3).

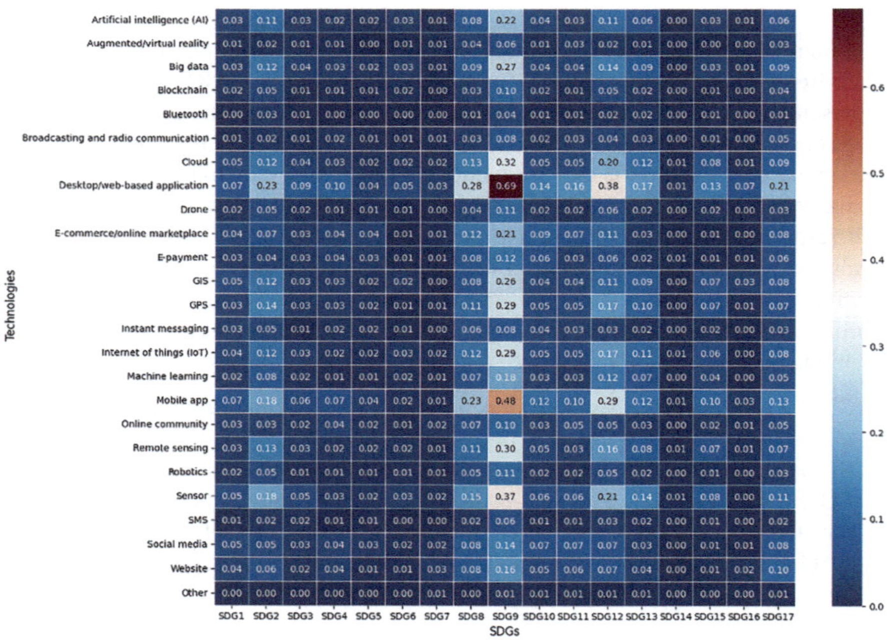

Fig. 3 Heatmap of the relationship between technologies and their use in total initiatives related to the 17 Sustainable Development Goals. (Source: authors' own elaboration)

5 Discussion and Implications

The findings reveal that digitalization in agriculture remains uneven across SDGs, with a clear emphasis on economic growth and productivity (SDGs 9 and 12), while environmental (SDGs 14 and 15) and social dimensions (e.g., SDG 5) are comparatively underrepresented. This distribution suggests that digital transformation in agriculture is still predominantly market-driven, shaped by efficiency gains and return on investment rather than holistic sustainability goals.

This imbalance is particularly critical considering the ecological footprint of agriculture. The limited presence of SDG 14 (*Life Below Water*) and SDG 15 (*Life on Land*) points to missed opportunities for using technologies such as remote sensing and AI to support biodiversity and ecosystem management. A key barrier here is the misalignment between existing AgriTech solutions—largely designed for terrestrial crop systems—and the technological or regulatory needs of marine and conservation-focused domains. Similarly, the underrepresentation of SDG 5 (*Gender Equality*) reflects structural inequities: despite women representing a significant portion of the agricultural workforce, they face barriers to land ownership, financing, and participation in digital innovation ecosystems [1]. Without targeted efforts, digitalization risks reinforcing pre-existing inequalities.

Moreover, the minimal engagement with SDG 16 (*Peace, Justice, and Strong Institutions*) highlights a broader limitation: digital tools in agriculture are predominantly operational, with limited application in governance, transparency, or institutional capacity-building. While some goals—such as SDGs 5, 14 and 16—may appear less "technologically addressable," their integration remains essential for sustainable food systems.

Underlying these trends are structural enablers and barriers. On the enabling side, the widespread use of web and mobile platforms is facilitated by their accessibility and low deployment costs. Cloud computing, GPS, and IoT have been successfully integrated into high-input systems due to their compatibility with automation and precision agriculture. However, persistent barriers include infrastructure gaps in rural areas, digital literacy deficits among smallholders, limited interoperability of data systems, and inconsistent regulatory frameworks. These challenges are particularly acute in low- and middle-income countries and in traditional, subsistence-based agricultural systems, where return on investment in digital technologies is perceived as uncertain or low.

Technological adoption also varies by level of maturity. While big data, AI and IoT are increasingly mainstream, emerging tools such as blockchain, AR/VR and robotics remain marginal. This may reflect high entry costs, lack of contextual adaptation, or uncertainty regarding their real value in field conditions. These barriers are further compounded by limited experimentation, training infrastructure, and cross-sectoral collaboration.

From a policy perspective, governments and international organizations should adopt a more proactive role in steering digital transformation toward inclusive and sustainability-oriented outcomes. This includes supporting public infrastructure, incentivizing environmental and social innovation through targeted subsidies or procurement and embedding digital equity into agricultural policy design.

For academia, future research should explore the underlying mechanisms behind technology uptake, considering factors such as system type (e.g., smallholder vs. commercial farming), regional disparities, and socio-political context. Cross-disciplinary approaches are needed to examine the intersections between technology, equity, and sustainability in agriculture. In particular, the underexplored potential of emerging technologies (e.g., AR/VR for farmer training or blockchain for supply-chain transparency) warrants greater investigation.

For the private sector, there is a growing opportunity to diversify innovation beyond productivity. AgriTech firms should co-develop solutions with local actors to ensure relevance and usability across diverse agricultural systems. Market expansion into underrepresented SDGs—particularly through low-cost, inclusive and environmentally responsive technologies—can generate both social impact and competitive advantage.

In sum, addressing current asymmetries requires rethinking the direction of digital innovation in agriculture. Strengthening the contribution of digitalization to all SDGs—not just those tied to productivity—demands a systemic shift in how technologies are designed, deployed and supported across agricultural contexts.

6 Conclusion and Limitations

This study highlights how digitalization in agriculture is not neutral but reflects the sector's long-standing priorities and structural biases. The findings indicate a strong concentration of digital initiatives on economic and productivity-oriented SDGs (SDG 9 and 12), while environmental (SDG 14 and 15) and social goals (SDG 5) remain underrepresented. This clear inclination toward efficiency-driven innovations suggests that digital transformation has primarily been leveraged to optimize agricultural output, rather than address broader sustainability challenges. Without targeted interventions, this imbalance risks reinforcing existing disparities rather than mitigating them.

Despite the increasing availability of AgriTech solutions over the past decade, adoption at scale remains limited, particularly in emerging economies [1]. Technologies such as GIS, remote sensing and AI-driven analytics have the potential to support governance by improving land tenure security, monitoring illegal deforestation, and enhancing policy enforcement. Yet, these aspects remain largely unexplored, indicating that strengthening digital governance mechanisms could contribute to more resilient and equitable agricultural systems. Similarly, gender-responsive AgriTech solutions have the potential to bridge critical gaps in access and decision-making, yet they are scarcely represented in the dataset, suggesting a need for more targeted investment.

Moreover, structural barriers—including unequal access to technology, climate variability, and socio-economic disparities—continue to hinder progress in achieving sustainability objectives [29]. While digitalization can be a powerful enabler, it cannot operate in isolation. Ensuring its benefits are equitably distributed requires complementary policy frameworks, infrastructure investments, and capacity-building initiatives. Technology alone cannot address climate-related challenges without supportive governance structures, nor can it ensure food security without improvements in logistics, equitable market access, and adaptive supply chains.

These findings suggest that digital agriculture, like many technological transitions, mirrors existing sectoral biases. The relative lack of focus on the fisheries sector, for example, may stem from the dominance of terrestrial farming in AgriTech innovations, while limited investment in governance-related applications reflects the sector's historical emphasis on operational efficiency over policy oversight. Recognizing these biases is crucial for ensuring that digital transformation does not deepen existing inequalities but rather serves as a tool for a more sustainable and inclusive agrifood system.

To make digitalization a true driver of sustainability in agriculture, future efforts should focus on three key areas: (1) incentivizing the use of technology for environmental objectives, such as biodiversity conservation and water resource management; (2) promoting more inclusive initiatives to support women and underrepresented groups in agriculture; and (3) ensuring that digital innovation is accessible to regions with limited technological infrastructure. Dedicated funding mechanisms—such as sustainability-linked subsidies and policy-driven AgriTech investment programs—could play a critical role in steering digital transformation toward these priorities.

While this study provides valuable insights into the distribution of digitalization initiatives across SDGs, it also has certain limitations. The analysis is constrained by the scope of the FAO AgriTech Observatory dataset, which may not fully capture the breadth of digital agricultural innovations occurring outside its reporting framework. Additionally, while the study identifies trends in digital adoption, it does not assess the actual impact of these technologies on sustainability outcomes. Future research should aim to address these gaps by incorporating additional datasets, conducting field-level impact assessments, and exploring the socio-economic implications of digital transformation in agriculture.

Further research could also focus on the underrepresented SDGs, investigating why digital initiatives struggle to integrate governance, gender equality and environmental conservation. Additionally, given the early-stage adoption of technologies such as AR/VR and blockchain in agriculture, future studies could explore their potential applications and barriers to scalability. Understanding how digitalization can be harnessed not just for economic efficiency but also for social and environmental resilience remains a crucial area of inquiry.

Ultimately, ensuring that digital transformation serves as a catalyst for sustainable agriculture will require a concerted effort from policymakers, researchers, and industry stakeholders. The long-term impact of AgriTech will depend on its ability to drive meaningful change—enhancing sustainability, improving inclusivity, and strengthening resilience—while ensuring that innovation remains accessible, ethically governed, and aligned with broader sustainability goals.

Acknowledgement This research was partially financed by the European Union—Next Generation EU, Mission 4 Component 1 CUP B53C23001650006.

References

1. World Economic Forum: Agritech: shaping agriculture in emerging economies, today and tomorrow. https://www.weforum.org/publications/agritech-shaping-agriculture-in-emerging-economies-today-and-tomorrow/ (2024)
2. Eyhorn, F., Muller, A., Reganold, J.P., Frison, E., Herren, H.R., Luttikholt, L., Smith, P.: Sustainability in global agriculture driven by organic farming. Nat. Sustain. **2**(4), 253–255 (2019). https://doi.org/10.1038/s41893-019-0266-6
3. Wang, G., Wang, Y., Li, S., Yi, Y., Li, C., Shin, C.: Sustainability in global agri-food supply chains: insights from a comprehensive literature review and the ABCDE framework. Foods. **13**(18), 2914 (2024). https://doi.org/10.3390/foods13182914
4. Gao, L., Bryan, B.A.: Finding pathways to national-scale land-sector sustainability. Nature. **544**(7649), 217–222 (2017). https://doi.org/10.1038/nature21694
5. Pânzaru, R.L., Firoiu, D., Ionescu, G.H., Ciobanu, A., Medelete, D.M., Pîrvu, R.: Organic agriculture in the context of 2030 agenda implementation in European Union countries. Sustainability. **15**(13), 10582 (2023). https://doi.org/10.3390/su151310582
6. Širá, E., Kravčáková Vozárová, I., Kotulič, R., Dubravská, M.: EU27 countries' sustainable agricultural development toward the 2030 agenda: the circular economy and waste management. Agronomy. **12**(10), 2270 (2022). https://doi.org/10.3390/agronomy12102270
7. Borrelli, P., Lugato, E., Montanarella, L., Panagos, P.: A new assessment of soil loss due to wind erosion in European agricultural soils using a quantitative spatially distributed modelling approach. Land Degrad. Dev. **28**(1), 335–344 (2017). https://doi.org/10.1002/ldr.2588
8. Borsellino, V., Schimmenti, E., El Bilali, H.: Agri-food markets towards sustainable patterns. Sustainability. **12**(6), 2193 (2020). https://doi.org/10.3390/su12062193
9. Parfitt, J., Barthel, M., Macnaughton, S.: Food waste within food supply chains: quantification and potential for change to 2050. Philos. Trans. R. Soc. B Biol. Sci. **365**(1554), 3065–3081 (2010). https://doi.org/10.1098/rstb.2010.0126
10. United Nations: Report of the UN Economist Network for the UN 75th Anniversary: shaping the trends of our time. United Nations, New York (2020) https://digitallibrary.un.org/record/3884187?v=pdf
11. Food and Agriculture Organization of the United Nations (FAO): Digitalization: it is time to bridge the gap between urban and rural areas. FAO Newsroom. https://www.fao.org/newsroom/detail/digitalization%2D%2Dit-is-time-to-bridge-the-gap-between-urban-and-rural-areas/en (2022a)
12. Food and Agriculture Organization of the United Nations (FAO): The state of agricultural commodity markets 2018: agricultural trade, climate change and food security. FAO. https://openknowledge.fao.org/handle/20.500.14283/i9542en (2018)
13. Food and Agriculture Organization of the United Nations (FAO): Tracking progress on food and agriculture-related SDG indicators 2021: a report on the indicators under FAO custodianship. FAO. https://openknowledge.fao.org/server/api/core/bitstreams/aa111548-8458-4ea2-9b04-e10297dd0369/content (2021)

14. Food and Agriculture Organization of the United Nations: AgriTech Observatory. FAO. https://agritechobservatory.fao.org/analytics (2024)
15. Wolfert, S., Ge, L., Verdouw, C., Bogaardt, M.J.: Big data in smart farming: a review. Agric. Syst. **153**, 69–80 (2017). https://doi.org/10.1016/j.agsy.2017.01.023
16. Gruber, J.W.: Irrigation and land use in ancient Mesopotamia. Agric. Hist. **22**(2), 69–77 (1948)
17. De Herrera, G.A.: Ancient Agriculture: Roots and Application of Sustainable Farming. Gibbs Smith, Utah (2006)
18. Pingali, P.L.: The green revolution and crop biodiversity. In: Routledge Handbook of Agricultural Biodiversity, pp. 213–223. Routledge, London (2017)
19. Evenson, R.E., Gollin, D.: Assessing the impact of the green revolution, 1960 to 2000. Science. **300**(5620), 758–762 (2003). https://doi.org/10.1126/science.1078710
20. Finger, R., Swinton, S.M., El Benni, N., Walter, A.: Precision farming at the nexus of agricultural production and the environment. Annu. Rev. Resour. Econ. **11**(1), 313–335 (2019). https://doi.org/10.1146/annurev-resource-100518-093929
21. Araújo, S.O., Peres, R.S., Barata, J., Lidon, F., Ramalho, J.C.: Characterising the agriculture 4.0 landscape—emerging trends, challenges and opportunities. Agronomy. **11**(4), 667 (2021). https://doi.org/10.3390/agronomy11040667
22. CEMA—European Agricultural Machinery: Digital farming: what does it really mean? https://www.cema-agri.org/images/publications/position-papers/CEMA_Digital_Farming_-_Agriculture_4.0__13_02_2017_0.pdf (2017)
23. Zhai, Z., Martínez, J.F., Beltran, V., Martínez, N.L.: Decision support systems for agriculture 4.0: survey and challenges. Comput. Electron. Agric. **170**, 105256 (2020). https://doi.org/10.1016/j.compag.2020.105256
24. Mohamed, E.S., Belal, A.A., Abd-Elmabod, S.K., El-Shirbeny, M.A., Gad, A., Zahran, M.B.: Smart farming for improving agricultural management. Egypt. J. Remote Sens. Space Sci. **24**(3), 971–981 (2021)
25. Ozdogan, B., Gacar, A., Aktas, H.: Digital agriculture practices in the context of agriculture 4.0. J. Econ. Finan. Account. **4**(2), 186–193 (2017)
26. Liu, S.Y.: Artificial intelligence (AI) in agriculture. IT Profess. **22**(3), 14–15 (2020). https://doi.org/10.1109/MITP.2020.2986121
27. Elijah, O., Rahman, T.A., Orikumhi, I., Leow, C.Y., Hindia, M.N.: An overview of Internet of Things (IoT) and data analytics in agriculture: benefits and challenges. IEEE Internet Things J. **5**(5), 3758–3773 (2018)
28. Food and Agriculture Organization of the United Nations (FAO): The future of food and agriculture—drivers and triggers for transformation. FAO. https://doi.org/10.4060/cc0959en (2022b)
29. Food and Agriculture Organization of the United Nations (FAO): Tracking progress on food and agriculture-related SDG indicators 2023: a report on the indicators under FAO custodianship. FAO. https://doi.org/10.4060/cc7088en (2023)
30. FAO, IFAD, UNICEF, WFP, WHO: The state of food security and nutrition in the world 2024—financing to end hunger, food insecurity and malnutrition in all its forms. FAO. https://doi.org/10.4060/cd1254en (2024)

Digital Transformation and Organizational Effectiveness: An Analysis of the Mauritian Top 100 Companies

Saubah Poolee Cootee and Nessrine Omrani

Abstract Digital transformation drives the future of establishments and countries socially, technologically, and competitively stimulating thousands of researchers in this field. Surprisingly, few past studies have been conclusive on the role of digital transformation on organizational effectiveness in all sectors of the economy. This gap is the motivation for this research work. A conceptual framework is introduced and a survey of the top 100 companies in Mauritius substantiates that increased digitalization boosts organizational effectiveness. In this study, 89% of respondents have started their digital journey, and around half (50%) are in the initial phase of digitalization. Multiple regression was conducted, establishing that Customer Experience and Strategy significantly impacted the Digital Maturity Level. Moreover, the result of Culture and Expertise was significant, so it deserved to be considered a determinant of Digital Maturity Level. This study's contribution to the literature is manifold with the conception of a framework that enables measuring digital maturity level and its relationship to organizational effectiveness by level.

Keywords Digital transformation · Digital maturity · Organizational effectiveness · Organizational strategy

1 Introduction

Digital, digitalization, and digital transformation are globally referred to by governments and companies as the drivers of success for companies, countries, and the world [1]. Improvement of the internet, mobile devices, and interactive tools is the primary enabler of the digital transformation experienced in all industries [2]. The economy is moving toward digital transformation; thus, chief executive officers

S. Poolee Cootee · N. Omrani (✉)
Paris School of Business, Paris, France
e-mail: n.omrani@psbedu.paris

N. Omrani et al. (eds.), *Human-Machine Synergy and the Digital Future - Exploring Collaboration and Competition Volume 1*, Springer Proceedings in Business and Economics, https://doi.org/10.1007/978-3-032-21347-1_3

have an interest in understanding how digitalization impacts their company [3]. The evolution of products and services with digital transformation is diverse. Porter and Heppelmann [4] took the example of the music industry, which moved from a product to a service industry: from CDs to streaming and media services providers such as Spotify, Pandora, iTunes, Deezer, YouTube Music, and Tidal. In this industry, studios have been replaced by artists.

The question of whether digital transformation leads to better effectiveness has been researched by scholars and proved that digital transformation leads to organizational effectiveness [5–7]. However, research on the relationship between digital maturity stages and organizational effectiveness has not been made for organizations across economic sectors. Furthermore, there is limited research on digital maturity across industries and organizations. This gap in the literature review offers the opportunity to analyze the relationship between digital maturity stages and organizational effectiveness and to research the digital maturity status of organizations across sectors.

The first question is to determine whether there is a correlation between digital maturity and organizational effectiveness; the second question is on the relationship between digital maturity stages and organizational effectiveness; the third question focuses on the stages of digital maturity of organizations across sectors. As digital transformation is becoming increasingly critical for organizations to sustain in this competitive world, these questions are of prime importance for organizations in all sectors and Top 100 companies of Mauritius. To conduct this analysis, a theoretical research model was designed based on the relationship between the levels of the Digital Maturity Model and the Balanced Scorecard (Fig. 1).

This framework theorizes the link between digital transformation, digital maturity, and organizational effectiveness. It describes the possible links between the digital maturity dimensions, the stages of digital maturity, and organizational effectiveness with the four perspectives of the Balanced Scorecard. The digital

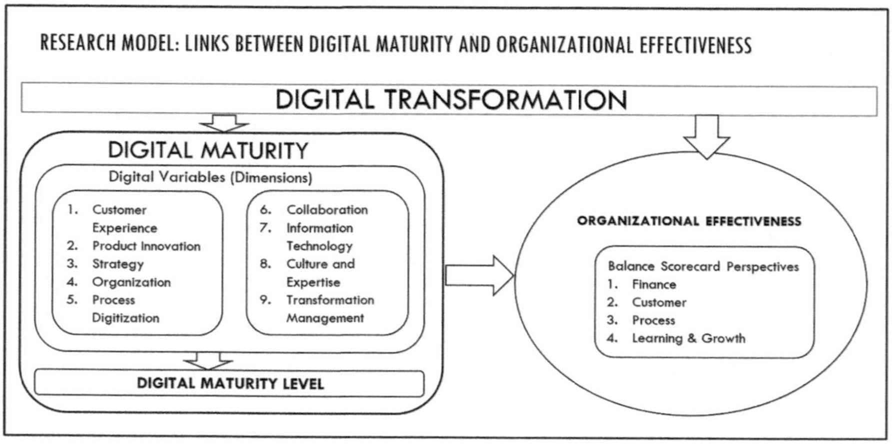

Fig. 1 Theoretical framework

development related to the nine digital variables enables digital maturity; these are the basis for improved organizational effectiveness in all or any of the four variables: Finance, Customer, Process, and Learning and Growth. According to this model, the effective development of digital transformation leads not only to digital maturity but also to increased organizational effectiveness.

2 Literature Review

2.1 Digital Transformation and Digital Maturity

There is a plethora of research from scholars on digital, digitization, digitalization, and digital transformation [8–16]. Scholars such as [9, 17, 18] even discussed and debated the understanding and application of the terms digitization, digitalization, and digital transformation as well as how these are deployed. The importance of measuring Digital Maturity is "the status of a company's digital transformation toward full growth" [9, 19]. It is important [13] for awareness of the level reached and provides the opportunity to identify the gaps to full maturity level. Digital Maturity is measured by the digital maturity model (DMM).

Digitization is the replacement of analog products with digital products with the same features [17] and the conversion of products to digital format [20]. According to Legner et al. [18], digitization is changing analog signals into digital ones. The use of digital technologies and innovation by people, enterprises, and society is usually referred to as digitalization [18], leading to related changes in the networking of people, businesses, and products [21], customer products, and journeys [22].

Schallmo et al. [23] define digital transformation as a continuous transformation with new or improved corporate models and operations made possible by digitization that adds value to enterprises' performance and profitability. It is about process improvement reached when organizations use technology to reorganize economies and streamline institutions and society [20].

Truant et al. [24] endeavored to simplify the understanding of digital transformation that should be viewed as a "two-dimensional construct" (1) "technology-enabled digital services" that is including digital elements in products [24] (2) about digital abilities that are included in organizations' processes such as radio-frequency identification, big data, cloud 4 computing, machine-to-machine, touch interface, 3D printing, smartphone apps, augmented reality, blockchain [25]. Digital transformation of business processes is mainly used for data creation and analysis for performance improvement [3], which provides customer information that enables the conception of improved products and services [26]. Digital transformation is viewed by Mergel [27] as a "holistic approach."

Digital Frameworks were developed by researchers to understand, deploy, or analyze digital transformation in organizations. Wade [28] proposed a Digitization Piano (Digital Business Transformation Framework) with an enterprise approach to analyzing digital endeavors [29]. Kavadia et al. [30] framework links technologies and markets. Berman and co-authors [31, 32] propose an "experience-first" approach. Nylén and Holmström [33] proposed a "Digital Innovation Strategy Framework" with a systematic approach to improve digital products and services' customer journey. The Digital Transformation Framework of [34] focuses on customer experience perspectives to understand the customer and digitalize to improve processes technically. These theoretical frameworks analyze technology but do not necessarily provide insight into different industry segments [29].

Digital Maturity Models have been developed as a tool to analyze "the status of a company's digital transformation toward full growth" [9, 19]. Several DMMs exist and some are for specific sectors. Literature on the analysis of maturity models was researched. Remane et al. [35] analyzed archetypes in 20 DMMs and Minonne et al. [36] evaluated 15 DMMs with 85 digitization factors and tested these with Archimate 3.0. They identified 147 variables/dimensions and found they were not the same for all models; important variables like customer or innovation are not in all models. They concluded that all maturity models are not suitable to evaluate a company's digital maturity. Teichert [13] analyzed 22 DMMs and 125 dimensions and found that 41 variables were the same across all models while 84 variables were unique denominations and 55% used defined stages for describing maturity and concluded comparability is impossible. Berghaus and Back [17] made an analysis of 17 DMMs and ascertained that only 3 defined the term Digital Maturity, different dimensions were used, nine DMMs were without theoretical basis, and only six models were peer-reviewed and published in academic outlets. In these research studies, the DMM of 5 [17] suited the most cross-sectorial analysis and their work analyzed 70 publications and 16 existing maturity assessments to develop their model. The model had 9 Dimensions and 5 Digital Maturity Stages that were tested (2015–2017) in a survey of 417 companies in Germany and Switzerland.

With internet access and mobile phones available everywhere, all sectors of the economy and companies of all sizes can aim to digitalize. In Tourism, the tendency is Digital tourism era [37] with no need for travel agencies [37] as customers get the possibility to make all the bookings online. The Finance Sector digitalization is expanding as financial technology is innovative, has great efficiency, low cost, optimized process, and innovation [38–41]. The Agricultural Sector involves precision-agriculture equipment, robotics, and apps (weed identification apps, weather apps) as well as farm management platforms [42]. In Manufacturing, there is a huge trend toward digitalization [43] enabling enhanced products [44, 45] and improved long-term profitability [26]. The Retail Sector has new business models and multi-sided digital platforms, such as Alibaba and Amazon [46], improving business efficiency. Retail literature enriched new concepts such as multi-channel and omnichannel retailing [47]. The Construction Sector is more slow in its implementation as the main challenge is re-skilling staff [48]. However, it is viewed that these advancements are more effective: less staff costs and time and the use of automated workflows, and robotics: less loss of materials with tracking systems [49].

2.2 *Digital Transformation and Organizational Effectiveness*

Organizational Effectiveness is the degree to which an organization realizes its goals, objectives [50–52]. Some of the theories are Goal Approach which defines effectiveness by the attainment of goals; resource-based that focuses on how best rare resources are used by organizations 6 [53]; the Internal Process Approach and the Balanced Scorecard [51].

Amit and Zott [54] in their study warned that theories of effectiveness have limitations when applied in the highly interconnected market while Marchand et al. [55] proposed the use of multi-dimensional effectiveness measures. [56, 57] proved that firms with superior digital capability sustain better firm performance. Chen and Zhang [38] in their study on digitalized SMEs found a strong positive relationship between portal functions and organizational performance and that training impacts the digitalization of SMEs' performance. They used the perspectives of the Balanced Scorecard to measure the effectiveness of these organizations. Eremina et al. [58] who studied the relationship between digital maturity and corporate financial results and performance were not very conclusive on the growth in process automation and online business. Lecerf and Omrani [59] proved that technologies enable a decrease in transaction costs as fewer data errors, thus fewer labor costs and the ability to tap into a customer base worldwide [59]. The study of Truant et al. [24] listed companies in Italy and found a positive relationship between digitalization and financial performance. The study of Chen and Zhang [38] was found to be more appropriate for this study as it used several perspectives on the organizational effectiveness of the Balanced Scorecard. They researched the Taiwanese textile industry's web portal and used a digital maturity model and the Four Drivers of Balance Scorecard dimensions [51].

Hypothesis: Digital Maturity stages positively impact organizational effectiveness.

3 Methods

This research is based on a quantitative deductive approach [60]. It is to be noted that this study did not reject other approaches of analysis, which can be used in future related research studies. The positivist approach is more appropriate than other approaches in this case as it structures its assumptions on the singularity and objectiveness of reality. Quantitative data was collected by using a self-administered questionnaire based on tools found in literature: seven digital maturity is analyzed based on the questionnaire used for the digital maturity model of [61] and the organizational effectiveness based on the studies of [38] using perspectives of the balanced scorecard. A survey method was favored as it provides the respondents the independence to choose and to respond to the questionnaire at the time that is best for them.

The Top 100 Companies in Mauritius in terms of profitability have been chosen as samples for this study. Management cadre of the Top 100 firms of Mauritius who are well versed in the digitalization of their companies participated in the survey. This study used a self-administered questionnaire as it is less costly and more accurate [62–64]. About 33 members of management of these companies agreed to take the survey, which makes around 21% and received a link to the questionnaire. Around 29 responses were received online. Two responses were not valid. Even if 27 companies responded, they were from 9 companies and 18 groups of companies which accounted for 252 companies in various sectors of the Mauritian economy (Figs. 2 and 3).

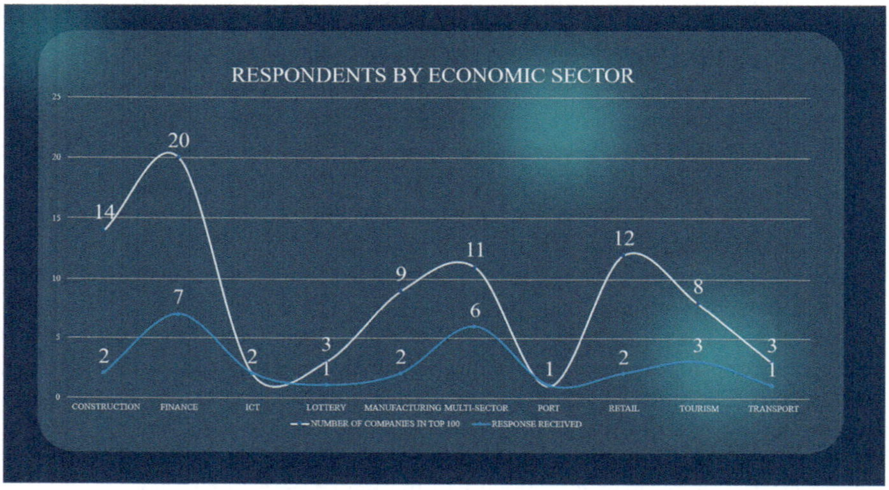

Fig. 2 Respondents by economic sector

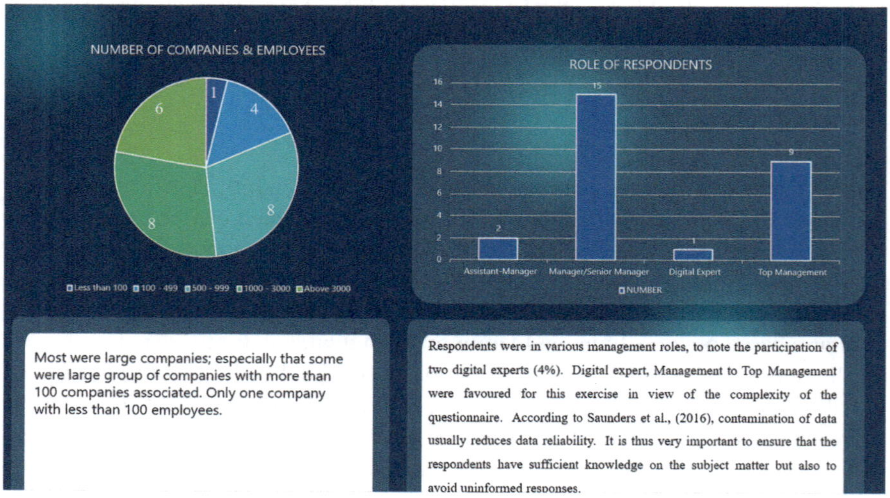

Fig. 3 Respondent companies and respondents' profile

4 Findings

A Test of Reliability and Construct Validity was conducted to verify whether statements representing the main research construct showed uni-dimensionality [65]. Reliability tests of the responses concurred. An alpha coefficient lying between 0.6 and 0.95 is an acceptable proof of an instrument's reliability [66, 67]. Construct validity was tested in SPSS by means of factor validity and each p-value for Bartlett's test of sphericity was less than 0.001: the questionnaire also passed construct validity tests [68]. Kaiser-Meyer-Olkin (KMO) statistics obtained for the sets of statements were at least 0.5, so the sample was considered adequate for inferential analysis [68].

4.1 Descriptive Statistics

The Rasch algorithm was used to analyze the survey data to derive a metric for each item that represents its level [69, 70]. Results show that 24 (89%) had started digitalization out of 26: 11% not digitalized. Correlation Analysis of the Digital Variables and Digital Maturity Level was performed to ascertain whether the testing of a multiple regression model was justified [71]. All nine variables positively correlated with Digital Maturity Level at the 1% level. It was also noted that correlation does not necessarily imply causality [72]. Both assumptions 9 and 10 were satisfied. Multiple regression analysis was conducted to test the validity of the model, as well as the significance of the impact of each predictor on Digital Maturity Level (DML). Nine hypotheses were implicitly tested in SPSS (Tables 1 and 2).

Table 1 Results of data-assumption checking (multiple regression analysis—DML)

Assumption	Observations	Satisfied
Outliers	None. All standardized residuals were between −1.287 and 2.130	✓
Multicollinearity	All VIF values $\leq$9.202	✓
Independence of residuals	Durbin-Watson statistic = 2.565	✓
Normality of residuals	Mean = 1.85×10^{-15}, standard deviation = 0.8	✓
Homoscedasticity	Scatterplot shows just a slight departure from homogeneity of variance	✓
Linearity	Residuals may be fitted by the x-axis	✓
Non-zero variances of predictors	*Customer experience* (0.766) *Product innovation* (0.648) *Strategy* (0.599) *Organization* (0.621) *Process Digitilization* (0.665) *Co-operation* (0.807) *Information technology* (0.675) *Culture and expertise* (0.461) *Transformation management* (0.718)	✓

ANOVAb DML: p-value less than 0.05 = the regression model was significant at the 5% level. Coefficient of determination R2 = 0.945: nine predictors = 94.5% variability in Digital Maturity Level. The model fits for the data (Table 3).

Coefficients—DML: Customer Experience (β = 0.317, t = 3.238, p = 0.005), Strategy (β = 0.346, t = 3.795, p = 0.002) significantly on Digital Maturity Level at the 1% level. Culture and Expertise (β = 0.232, t = 2.037, p = 0.059) were significant at the 6% level. From the data of the DML of the respondents, the Digital Maturity Model was classified for ease of understanding in which stage of the digital maturity of each sector. Using descriptive statistics of table and mean, the five Digital Maturity levels are calculated and listed in Table 4. The model comprises five levels of digital maturity namely: (1) Initial, (2) Active, (3) Engaged, (4) Competitive, and (5) Mature:

Table 2 Model summary[a]

Model	R	R square	Adjusted R square	Std. error of the estimate	Change statistics: R square change	F change	Sig. F change	Durbin-Watson
1	0.972[b]	**0.945**	0.914	0.33745	0.945	30.489	**0.000**	**2.565**

[a] Dependent variable: digital maturity level
[b] Predictors: (constant), customer experience, product innovation, strategy, organization, process digitalization, co-operation, information technology, culture and expertise, transformation management

Table 3 Coefficients[a]

Model	Unstandardized coefficients: B	Std. error	Standardized coefficients: Beta	Collinearity statistics: Tolerance	VIF
(Constant)	−7.872	0.668			
Customer experience	0.519	0.16	0.317	0.36	**2.78**
Product innovation	0.081	0.27	0.042	0.172	**5.801**
Strategy	0.783	0.206	0.346	0.414	**2.418**
Organization	−0.223	0.317	−0.116	0.125	**7.991**
Process digitalization	0.253	0.232	0.136	0.221	**4.534**
Co-operation	−0.12	0.188	−0.076	0.243	**4.123**
Information technology	0.013	0.259	0.007	0.188	**5.314**
Culture and expertise	0.53	0.26	0.232	0.264	**3.782**
Transformation management	0.504	0.315	0.285	0.109	**9.202**

[a] Dependent variable: digital maturity level

A cross-sectional analysis was carried out to check whether there were marked differences between the DML of sampled companies. This was made possible by computing a mean score for the DML of companies based on their operating sectors. H0: The mean DML scores for all the sectors are equal. H1: At least two of the mean DML scores are different. SPSS generated the following table (Table 5):

The p-value of 0.750 was higher than 0.05, the default significance testing level used in SPSS, there was not enough evidence to reject the null hypothesis at the 5% level. Therefore, the DML of all the sectors was practically equal. Even though the differences may have seemed quite big from descriptive analysis, the fact that there was only one company from the retail, port, and engineering sectors may have caused the p-value to be large. Companies are not digitally mature, but most sectors (except retail) that responded are in the process of digitalization. Most are in Digital Maturity Level 1.

Hypotheses: Digital maturity stages positively impact organizational effectiveness (OE) in organizations.

4.2 Results

To analyze this hypothesis, it was important to use the same methodology to measure Organizational Effectiveness. The Rasch algorithm was used and as per survey results, 22 (85%) organizations were effective out of 26, and 4 (15%) were not digitalized. Correlation analysis was carried out first to know if a multiple regression model should be conducted, with the dependent variable Organizational Effectiveness (OE) and its prospective predictors, namely Finance (FIN), Customer-oriented (CUST), Process (PROC) and Learning and Growth (GROW). Using Pearson's correlations, the following results were obtained: $**p < 0.01$. All positively correlated with Organizational Effectiveness Level at the 1% level. Finance is the main

Table 4 Digital maturity levels

DML	NAME OF DML
1	Initial
2	Active
3	Engaged
4	Competitive
5	Mature

Table 5 Digital maturity level by sector

	Sum of squares	df	Mean square	F	Sig.
Between groups	7.472	8	0.934	0.620	**0.750**
Within groups	25.598	17	1.506		
Total	33.070	25			

Table 6 Organizational effectiveness levels

OEL	Level name
1	Preliminary
2	Intervening and taking action
3	Evaluating and feedback
4	Operational
5	Effective

organizational effectiveness variable supported in other research whereby it has been proved that organizations that have deployed digitalization successfully have about 26% more profits than those organizations that are not digitalized.

ANOVAb OEL p-value that is very close to zero (less than 0.05): multiple regression model significant at the 5% level. Coefficient of determination R2: 0.986; the four predictors = 98.6% of the shared variance with Organizational Effectiveness. The model was an excellent fit for the data. Coefficientsa—OEL: Finance ($\beta = 0.432$) had the greatest significant impact on Organizational Effectiveness; Learning and Growth ($\beta = 0.320$), Customer-oriented ($\beta = 0.223$), and Process ($\beta = 0.137$). Based on the responses, an Organizational Effectiveness Model was developed and mapped to the following Organizational Effectiveness Level (OEL) (Table 6):

From the above SPSS output, a p-value of 0.072 was obtained: no significant differences in mean OE scores at the 5% level. The result was significant at the 8% level ($0.072 < 0.08$), which is non-negligible in terms of implication. However, the results for ANOVA post hoc tests were not 13 available to identify and confirm these significant differences in SPSS, given that some sectors had only one company representing them. This discrepancy did not allow the multiple comparisons table to be generated. One may deduce that there are possibly significant differences, mainly between transport and/or manufacturing and the three low-rated sectors (construction, ICT, and tourism).

4.2.1 The Impact of Digital Maturity Level on Organizational Effectiveness Level

Correlation analysis of DML and OEL results: DML and Organizational Effectiveness were significantly and positively correlated at the 1% level, with a correlation coefficient of 0.567 and a p-value of 0.003 (Tables 7 and 8).

The regression model was found to be significant at the 1% level ($F = 5.804$, $p = 0.009$). 15 It may be observed that the control variable Company Sector ($p = 0.493$) did not have any significant bearing on Organizational Effectiveness. DML positively impacts the dependent variable at the 1% level ($\beta = 0.579$, $t = 3.351$, $p = 0.003$). Null hypothesis rejected and DML is a significant determinant of Organizational Effectiveness, even when controlled by the Company Sector. Result: An increase in Digital Maturity Level would increase the company's Organizational Effectiveness (Table 9).

Table 7 Correlations

		Digital maturity level	Organizational effectiveness
Digital maturity level	Pearson correlation	1	**0.567**[a]
	Sig. (2-tailed)		**0.003**
	N	26	26
Organizational effectiveness	Pearson correlation	0.567[a]	1
	Sig. (2-tailed)	0.003	
	N	26	26

[a] Correlation is significant at the 0.01 level (2-tailed)

Table 8 ANOVA[a, b]

Model	Sum of squares	df	Mean square	F	Sig.
Regression	26.668	2	13.334	5.804	0.009
Residual	52.835	23	2.297		
Total	79.503	25			

[a] Dependent variable: organizational effectiveness
[b] Predictors: (constant), company sector, digital maturity level

Table 9 Coefficients[a]

	Unstandardized coefficients		Standardized coefficients		
Model	B	Std. error	Beta	t	Sig.
(Constant)	1.060	0.765		1.387	0.179
Company sector	−0.073	0.105	−0.118	−0.697	0.493
Digital maturity level	0.884	0.264	0.570	3.351	0.003

[a] Dependent variable: organizational effectiveness

The overall mean of means of DML and OEL was computed as a development indicator while keeping the same ratings to find the impact of digitalization on organizational effectiveness by sector. As per survey results, Transport is first-ranked, but it should be noted that only one company participated, as not all are in the Top 100 companies. Thus, this result may not reflect the real level of this sector. Manufacturing and Finance are at Level 4, but when clustered, it was found that there are two groups in Finance: some at Level 4 and some at another. Multi-sectorial companies are at Level 3, and Retail at Level 2. Tourism, ICT, Construction, and Other are still in their early stage of development in terms of digital maturity and organizational effectiveness.

Cluster by Economic Sectors according to Digital Maturity Level and Organizational Effectiveness. Nine clusters were identified among the 26 companies; 6 of the 9 clusters (one each in Finance and Multi-Sectorial, and the Manufacturing, Tourism, ICT and Other clusters), were still in their early stages merely Initial in terms of DML and preliminary level in Organizational Effectiveness.

However, the second Finance cluster was level 4 of DML 16 (competitive) and level 3 of Organizational Effectiveness (intervening and taking action); while the second multi-sectorial cluster was at level 2 of Digital Maturity Level (active) but reached level 4 of Organizational Effectiveness Level (evaluating and feedback). This cluster mapping confirms that the more organizations are digitalized the more effective they are. As for the two remaining, the Transport company was at the Engaged level for Digital Maturity and Organizational Effectiveness at Effective level 5, while the Retail company was still at the initial phase but at level 3 of Organizational Effectiveness.

4.2.2 Relationship Between Digital Maturity and Organizational Effectiveness Levels at the Company Level

DML and OEL are positively correlated. Organizational effectiveness does depend on digital maturity (Fig. 4).

Correlation is not perfect. Organizations with the same DM level do not necessarily have the same OE level. A larger sample is needed. Previous Research: Scholarly research found that digitalization investment amount does not ensure better effectiveness [59] 17. In view of the period of the survey, a question was on the impact of COVID-19. Above 70% of respondents agreed that COVID-19 impacted the digitalization pace of the organization positively.

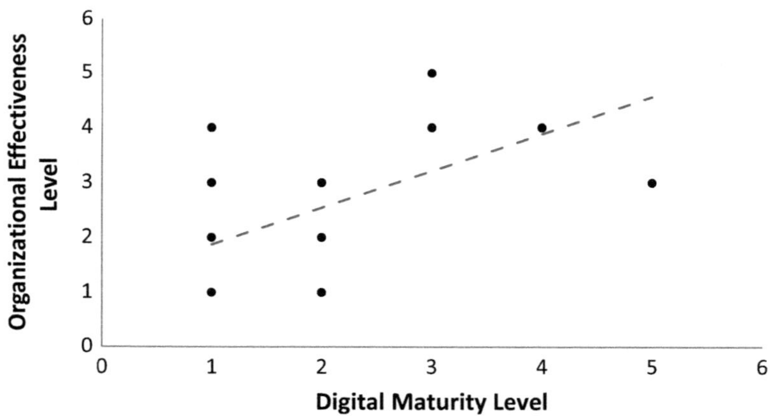

Fig. 4 OE level against DM level (individual companies)

5 Discussion and Implication

This study reveals that 53% of the Top 100 Companies in Mauritius are in their initial phase of digitalization. In this study, 23% were in Level 2 and 15% in Level 3. Only two companies had not started their digitalization; this result was not as per [73] whose study revealed that a few companies are digitalizing but it was not in the same period. The result is positive to the advice of [74] and concurs with [24] in that most are in the initial phase of digitalization, while most companies were on Levels 2 and 3 in the studies of [8].

Economic sectors exhibit diverse levels of Digital Maturity: studies by Berghaus and Back [8], as well as those by Truant et al. [24], adopt a cross-sectoral approach. Berghaus and Back [17]: retail/wholesale ranked second with (2.98) while in this study, retail is the only sector with the least DML (M = −0.06) third in their studies is transportation/logistics (2.94), almost the same mean as in Mauritius. The lowest mean maturity was in the banking sector (2.42), the machine sector (2.38), and the consumer goods sector (2.23). They were surprised by the banks' results and confirmed that the banks that participated were small banks, which impacted the results. Banks rank very well in this study with two clusters.

The Variables (Dimensions) of Customer Experience and Strategy impact Digital Maturity with the support of Culture and Expertise. This concurs with the study of [8]: "customer experience" (37%) had the lowest mean, followed by "process digitization" (41%). Their study also found that "strategy" (mean 51%) positively impacted digital maturity. Culture and expertise differ for [75], where it was found that organizations face resistance from employees.

Digitalization leads to better organizational effectiveness in organizations even when controlled by the company sector. Most researchers concurred that digitalization is positively related to organizational effectiveness [6, 24, 38, 74, 76, 77], even if not guaranteed [59], contrary to [75] who claimed it is only a marketing fad.

5.1 *Managerial Contribution*

The aim of this study was to analyze whether organizational effectiveness is improved with digitalization in companies. The findings of this study are of value to the management of organizations in that it proves that well-planned digitalization reaps better effectiveness. Three variables of digital maturity, notably customer experience, strategy, and culture and expertise, are found to be the most developed in Top 100 organizations in Mauritius, and these enabled better effectiveness more so in the finance variable. While the objective of organizations is definitely to use digitalization to improve effectiveness and to sustain in this competitive world, there was no evidence of the same. Thus, with new evidence, organizations can use these findings to ultimately develop and link their digital strategy to their overall strategy for better effectiveness in other variables too, such as product innovation, which is linked to customer experience as well as process digitization. Organizations cannot invest in full digitalization of the organization at one go; this is very risky in terms of the profitability of the organization. The findings of this study confirm that the strategy to have a step-by-step approach to digitalization in organizations is reaping its fruits toward better organizational effectiveness.

This study also provides organizations without digitalization or with limited digitalization with proof of the positive impact of digitalization in organizations. It is essential that Mauritian organizations start their digital journey by preparing the necessary infrastructure, policies, intellect, and procedures in place. It provides a guide on which variables to focus on initially, especially on the importance of integrating digitalization in the strategy as a roadmap to improve the effectiveness of their organizations. The main contribution of this study to managers is the importance of digitalizing the customer experience while including the same in the strategy and 19 ensuring that the culture and expertise of staff are aligned with these objectives. It is worth noting that this study shows the importance for employees to have the required skills to enable organizational effectiveness while digitalizing.

5.2 Theoretical Contribution

To formulate the Conceptual Framework of this study, literature was reviewed taking into consideration all related characteristics related to digitalization in companies and also their impact on organizational effectiveness. The digitalization variables and organizational effectiveness perspectives that best correspond to the research objectives were analyzed with reviews in literature on related concepts. This comprehensive review enabled the identification of theories, concepts, approaches, and research on digital maturity in organizations and organizations' effectiveness. To analyze digital maturity, the variables identified by Berghaus and Back [17] in their study were found to be the most appropriate as these variables derived from studies carried out in Switzerland and Germany in more than 400 companies and have been peer-reviewed and recommended by scholars as the variables identified include most dimensions required by an organization. To understand whether digitalization enables improved organizational effectiveness, the Balanced Scorecard perspective was taken into consideration as it encompasses all aspects of effectiveness. It was found more appropriate not to use the full KPI analytics analysis of the Balanced Scorecard for simplification and ease for respondents to the survey.

The main gap identified in this Literature Review is that while a tremendous amount of research focuses on digitalization in society, business, and specific sectors of the economy, most studies analyze the level of digitalization, the variables of digitalization in organizations, and the digital maturity level. However, very few focus on whether digitalization leads to better effectiveness and, more importantly, a study that encompasses all economic sectors.

As developed in previous chapters, this research provides new findings in the literature in that the model developed took into consideration the use of several digital maturity and organizational effectiveness variables used in two studies to ensure that this study embraces the most perspectives of these two broad research topics. This research contributes to the literature in the field of digitalization and its impact on organizational effectiveness. With this methodology, a positive relationship between digitalization and organizational effectiveness could be established, while other researchers could not establish organizational effectiveness from all perspectives except for [24].

This study takes into consideration the importance of each variable in the successful implementation of digitalization as not implementing may have other impacts that have not been studied in this research. As this study used several variables of digital maturity and organizational effectiveness, it is also clearer what prerogatives are taken into consideration by these companies that achieve better organizational effectiveness while digitalizing.

Consequently, the main theoretical contribution of this research work is the development of a new theoretical framework that includes all empirically tested variables of digital maturity and organizational effectiveness.

While most research focused on one sector of the economy, this research endeavored to analyze all sectors of the economy in the Top 100 companies. Also, most previous studies could not fully establish the link between digitalization and organizational effectiveness. Taking into consideration the consequent investment required for digital technological deployment in organizations, this research focused on Top 100 companies as these companies are the most profitable in the country and thus more apt to have the required funds. Truant et al. [24] had the same argument when they chose listed companies in Italy. Thus, both this study and that of [24], although employing different methodologies, were able to establish a positive relationship between digitalization and organizational effectiveness in financially stable and viable companies. However, these results by no means underpin the other research findings and their importance in the literature.

Thus, a second theoretical contribution of this study is that it confirms that most profitable organizations' digital transformation is positively linked to their organizational effectiveness. 21 This is by no means a coincidence; it clearly denotes that these organizations' digital strategy and/or overall strategy are aligned to reach objectives and progress with effectiveness improvement as the goal. Digital strategy is a variable that has been selected as a determinant of digitalization.

6 Conclusion and Limitations

The data analysis does not support all initial assumptions: (1) Companies per sector in Mauritius are digitally mature: the results show that not all sectors of the economy in Mauritius are digitally mature. (2) Top 100 Companies in Mauritius in all sectors are digitally mature: findings are that not all organizations are digitally mature in Mauritius. None have reached maturity level; that is, Level 5 of digital maturity. Around 13 organizations out of the 26 tested are still in their initial phase of digitalization, while 3 companies in the Finance sector were at the competitive level (Level 4). Limitations are in the sample size, in that the response rate is usually not very high for this type of survey. It is also noted that with quantitative data, it is difficult to establish causality; thus, a mixed method may have given better results and longitudinal data may also provide more reliable data. The period of the survey that was post-confinement created issues for companies to respond. Most were focusing on sustaining their business, and some of these were most profitable in 2019/2020 and were having financial difficulties in this post-pandemic period. It was also noted that the complexity of the questionnaire did not allow employees at all levels to participate, thus only experts and managers could be surveyed. The questionnaire did not have a section to analyze the deployment of technologies used in these companies. For future research, it would be beneficial to have more companies per sector. The use of a simplified questionnaire with the participation of more employees per company may provide other insights into the digitalization path of organizations. Longitudinal data will definitely help to analyze whether the actual results are corroborated. The period also should be without the constraint of pre or post-pandemic. It is also viewed that more government-owned companies should participate as they are part of the Top 100 companies and their digitalization level is of major importance for the country.

References

1. Ministry of Technology Communication and Innovation: Digital Mauritius 2030 Strategic Plan. http://mtci.govmu.org/English/Documents/2018/Launching Digital Transformation Strategy 191218/DM 2030 17 December 2018 at 12.30hrs.pdf. Last accessed 20 Jul 2021
2. Bholanauth. J.: Digital Maturity of Marketing Agencies in Mauritius (2018)
3. Björkdahl, J.: Strategies for digitalization in manufacturing firms. Calif. Manag. Rev. **62**(4), 17–36 (2020)
4. Porter, M.E., Heppelmann, J.E.: How smart, connected products are transforming companies. Harv. Bus. Rev. **93**, 97–114 (2015)
5. Bleicher, J., Stanley, H.: Digitization as a catalyst for business model innovation a three-step approach to facilitating economic success. J. Bus. Manag. **4**(12), 62–71 (2016)
6. Ismail, M.H., Khater, M., Zaki, M.: Digital business transformation and strategy: what do we know so far? Manufacturer Article, 36 (2017)
7. Kagermann, Wahlster, W., Helbig, J.: Recommendations for implementing the strategic initiative INDUSTRIE 4.0. Final report of the Industrie 4.0 WG (2013)
8. Berghaus, S., Back, A.: Stages in Digital Business Transformation; Mediterranean Conference on Information Systems (2016b)
9. Chanias, S., Hess, T.: How digital are we? Maturity models for the assessment of a company's status in the digital transformation. Manag. Rep. **2**(16), 1–14 (2016)
10. Kane, G.C., Palmer, D., Phillips, A.N., Kiron, D., Buckley, N.: Aligning the organization for its digital future. MIT Sloan Manag. Rev. **58180**, 1–29 (2016)
11. Mueller, M., Baer, T., Weber, C.: The digital maturity map—motivation for an EDM-based digital validation method. In: 9th International Design Conference, pp. 1359–1366 (2006)

12. Scott, J.E.: Mobility, business process management, software sourcing, and maturity model trends: propositions for the IS organization of the future. Inf. Syst. Manag. **24**(2), 139–145 (2007)
13. Teichert, R.: Digital transformation maturity: a systematic review of literature. Acta Univ. Agric. Silvic. Mendel. Brun. **67**(6), 1673–1687 (2019)
14. Valdez-de-Leon, O.: A digital maturity model for telecommunications service providers. Technol. Innov. Manag. Rev. **6**(8), 19–32 (2016)
15. Westerman, G., Bonnet, D., Mcafee, A.: The nine elements of digital transformation opinion & analysis, l. http://www.capgemini.com/resources/digital- (2014)
16. Westerman, G., Tannou, M., Bonnet, D., Ferraris, P., McAfee, A.: The digital advantage: how digital leaders outperform their peers in every industry. MIT Sloan Manag. Rev., 1–24 (2012)
17. Berghaus, S., Back, A.: Disentangling the fuzzy front end of digital transformation: activities and approaches. In: ICIS 2017: Transforming Society with Digital Innovation, 0–17 (2018)
18. Legner, C., Eymann, T., Hess, T., Matt, C., Böhmann, T., Drews, P., Mädche, A., Urbach, N., Ahlemann, F.: Digitalization: opportunity and challenge for the business and information systems engineering community. Bus. Inf. Syst. Eng. **59**(4), 301–308 (2017)
19. De Carolis, A., Macchi, M., Kulvatunyou, B., Brundage, M.P., Terzi, S.: Maturity models and tools for enabling smart manufacturing systems: comparison and reflections for future developments. IFIP Adv. Inf. Commun. Technol. **517**, 23–35 (2017)
20. Unruh, G., Kiron, D.: Digital transformation on purpose. MIT Sloan Manag. Rev. (2017)
21. Gartner: "IT Glossary". http://www.gartner.com/it-glossary/digitalization (2016). Accessed 2 Mar 2021
22. Reis, J., Amorim, M., Melao, N., Matos, P.: Digital transformation: a literature review and guidelines for future digital transformation research. In: 10th European Conference on Information Systems Management. Academic Conferences and Publishing Limited, vol. 1, pp. 20–28 (2016)
23. Schallmo, D., Williams, C., Boardman, L.: Digital transformation of business models—best practice, enablers, and roadmap. Int. J. Innov. Manag. **21**, 1740014 (2018)
24. Truant, E., Broccardo, L., Dana, L.P.: Digitalisation boosts company performance: an overview of Italian listed companies. Technol. Forecast. Soc. Chang. **173**, 121173 (2021)
25. Conner, B.P., Manogharan, G.P., Martof, A.N., Rodomsky, L.M., Rodomsky, C.M., Jordan, D.C., Limperos, J.W.: Making sense of 3-D printing: creating a map of additive manufacturing products and services. Addit. Manuf. **1**, 64–76 (2014)
26. Lenka, S., Parida, V., Wincent, J.: Digitalization capabilities as enablers of value co-creation in servitizing firms. Psychol. Mark. **34**(1), 92–100 (2017)
27. Mergel, I.: Agile innovation management in government: a research agenda. Gov. Inf. Q. **33**(3), 516–523 (2016)
28. Wade, M.: Digital Business Transformation: a Conceptual Framework. International Institute for Management Development, Lausanne (2015)
29. Nwaiwu, F.: Review and comparison of conceptual frameworks on digital business transformation. J. Compet. **10**(3), 86–100 (2018)
30. Kavadia, S., Ladas, K., Loch, C.: The transformative business model. Harv. Bus. Rev. **94**, 91–98 (2016)
31. Berman, S.J., Korsten, P.J., Marshall, A.: A four-step blueprint for digital reinvention. Strateg. Leadersh. **44**(4), 18–25 (2016)
32. Berman, S.J., Bell, R.: Digital Transformation, vol. 35(4), pp. 16–21. IBM Global Business Services (2011)
33. Nylén, D., Holmström, J.: Digital innovation strategy: a framework for diagnosing and improving digital product and service innovation. Bus. Horiz. **58**(1), 57–67 (2015)
34. Corver, Q., Elkhuizen, G.: A Framework for Digital Business Transformation, pp. 1–10. Cognizant (2014)

35. Remane, G., Hanelt, A., Wiesboeck, F., Kolbe, L.: Digital maturity in traditional industries—an exploratory analysis. In: 25th European Conference on Information Systems, May, pp. 1–16 (2017)
36. Minonne, C., Wyss, R., Schwer, K., Wirz, D., Hitz, C.: Digital maturity variables and their impact on the enterprise architecture layers. Probl. Perspect. Manag. **16**(4), 141–154 (2018)
37. Happ, É., Ivancsó-Horváth, Z.: Digital tourism is the challenge of future—a new approach to tourism. Knowl. Horizons Econ. **10**(2), 9–16 (2018)
38. Chen, S., Zhang, H.: Does digital finance promote manufacturing servitization: micro evidence from China. Int. Rev. Econ. Financ. **76**, 856–869 (2021)
39. Dapp, T.F.: Fintech: the digital transformation in the financial sector. In: Sustainability in a Digital World, pp. 189–199. Springer, Berlin (2014)
40. Muthaura, M.K., Kinyua, G.M.: Analysis of the role of technological alignment on organization performance: a perspective of commercial banks in Nyeri County, Kenya. Int. J. Innov. Res. **8**(6), 38–57 (2021)
41. Rahmonolawale, S., Rabilionaolapo, O.: Financial technology and business operations of selected financial technology firms in Lagos. Glob. J. Appl. Manag. Soc. Sci. **20**(1), 53–62 (2020)
42. Prause, L., Hackfort, S., Lindgren, M.: Digitalization and the third food regime. Agric. Hum. Values. **38**(3), 641–655 (2021)
43. Schiavone, F., Sprenger, S.: Operations management and digital technologies. Prod. Plan. Control. **28**(16), 1281–1283 (2017)
44. Davies, A.: Moving base into high-value integrated solutions: a value stream approach. Ind. Corp. Chang. **13**(5), 727–756 (2004)
45. Zhou, Y., Liu, G., Chang, X., Wang, L.: The impact of HRM digitalization on firm performance: investigating three-way interactions. Asia Pac. J. Hum. Resour. **59**(1), 20–43 (2021)
46. Hänninen, M., Smedlund, A., Mitronen, L.: Digitalization in retailing: multi-sided platforms as drivers of industry transformation. Balt. J. Manag. **13**(2), 152–168 (2018)
47. Verhoef, P.C., Broekhuizen, T., Bart, Y., Bhattacharya, A., Qi Dong, J., Fabian, N., Haenlein, M.: Digital transformation: a multidisciplinary reflection and research agenda. J. Bus. Res. **122**, 889–901 (2021)
48. Moshood, T.D., Adeleke, A.Q., Nawanir, G., Ajibike, W., Shittu, R.A.: Emerging challenges and sustainability of industry 4.0 era in the Malaysian construction industry. Int. J. Rec. Technol. Eng. **9**(1), 1627–1634 (2020)
49. Oesterreich, T.D., Teuteberg, F.: Understanding the implications of digitisation and automation in the context of industry 4.0: a triangulation approach and elements of a research agenda for the construction industry. Comput. Ind. **83**, 121–139 (2016)
50. Georgopoulos, S.B.: The Study of Organizational Effectiveness—Price (1972)
51. Kaplan, R.S., Norton, D.P.: The balanced scorecard—measures that drive performance. Harv. Bus. Rev. **70**, 71–79 (1992)
52. Price, J.L.: The study of organizational effectiveness. Sociol. Q. **13**(1), 3–15 (1972)
53. Seashore, S.E., Fichman, M., Fakhouri, J., Ford, L., Rousseau, D., Sutton, R.I., Johnson, E.M.: Empirical studies of organizational effectiveness (1983)
54. Amit, R., Zott, C.: Value creation in E-business. Strateg. Manag. J. **22**(6–7), 493–520 (2001)
55. Marchand, D., Kettinger, W., Rollins, J.: Information Orientation: the Link to Business Performance. Oxford University Press, New York (2002)
56. Bharadwaj, A.S.: A resource-based perspective on information technology capability and firm performance: an empirical investigation. MIS Q. Manag. Inf. Syst. **24**(1), 169–193 (2000)
57. Santhanam, R., Hartono, E.: Issues in linking information technology capability to firm performance. MIS Q. **27**, 125–153 (2003)
58. Eremina, Y., Lace, N., Bistrova, J.: Digital maturity and corporate performance: the case of the Baltic states. J. Open Innov. Technol. Mark. Complex. **5**(3), 54 (2019)
59. Lecerf, M., Omrani, N.: SME internationalization: the impact of information technology and innovation. J. Knowl. Econ. **11**(2), 805–824 (2020)

60. Sekaran, U.: Research Methods for Business: A Skill-Building Approach, 4th edn. John Wiley & Sons, New York (2003)
61. Berghaus, S., Back, A.: The fuzzy front end of digital transformation. Dissertation, St. Gallen School of Management, 4704, 0–17 (2017)
62. Aaker, D.A., Kumar, V., Day, G.S., Leone, R.: Marketing Research, 10th edn. John Wiley & Sons, Hoboken (2010)
63. Collis, J., Hussey, R.: Business Research: a Practical Guide for Undergraduate and Postgraduate Students. Palgrave Macmillan, Basingstoke (2014)
64. Saunders, M.N.K., Lewis, P., Thornhill, A.: Research Methods for Business Students, 7th edn. Pearson Education Limited, London (2015)
65. Ahmad, N.S., Sabri, A.: Assessing the uni-dimensionality, reliability, validity and fitness of influential factors of 8th-grades students' mathematics achievement in Malaysia. Int. J. Adv. Res. **1**(2), 1–7 (2013)
66. Karandashev, V., Evans, N.D.: Test of Implicit Associations in Relationship Attitudes (TIARA): Manual for a New Method. Springer, Berlin (2017)
67. Malhotra, N.K.: Marketing Research: an Applied Orientation, 7th edn. Pearson/Prentice Hall, Upper Saddle River, NJ (2019)
68. Field, A.: Discovering Statistics Using IBM SPSS Statistics: and Sex and Drugs and Rock "N" Roll, 4th edn. Sage, London (2013)
69. Friedel, D., Back, A.: Determination of enterprise 2.0 development levels with a maturity model. In: Proceedings of the IADIS International Conference, ISPCM 3–9 (2012)
70. Lahrmann, G., Marx, F., Mettler, T., Winter, R., Wortmann, F.: Inductive design of maturity models: applying the Rasch algorithm for design science research. Lecture Notes in Computer Science 6629 LNCS, pp. 176–191 (2011)
71. O'Brien, D., Scott, P.S.: In: Chen, H. (ed.) Correlation and Regression, in Approaches to Quantitative Research—A Guide for Dissertation Students. Oak Tree Press, Cork (2012)
72. Singh, S.: Why correlation does not imply causation? https://towardsdatascience.com/why-correlation-does-not-imply-causation-5b99790df07e. Last accessed 20 Oct 2021
73. Kane, B.G.C., Palmer, D., Phillips, A.N., Kiron, D., Buckley, N.: Digital maturity. MIT Sloan Manag. Rev., Summer (2017)
74. Barclay, C., Duggan, E.W.: Rethinking the digital divide: towards a path of digital effectiveness. In: Proceedings of the Annual Hawaii International Conference on System Sciences (2008)
75. Abraham, C., Junglas, I.: From cacophony to harmony: a case study about the IS implementation process as an opportunity for organizational transformation at Sentara Healthcare. J. Strateg. Inf. Syst. **20**(2), 177–197 (2011)
76. Kagermann, H.: Change through digitization, value creation in the age of industry 4.0. In: Management of Permanent Change, pp. 1–240. Springer, Berlin (2015)
77. Loebbecke, C., Picot, A.: Reflections on societal and business model transformation arising from digitization and big data analytics: a research agenda. J. Strateg. Inf. Syst. **24**(3), 149–157 (2015)

Does the Ethical Restraint of Frontier Hereditary Human Genome Manipulation Provide a Model for the Ethical Restraint of Frontier "Super General Intelligence" Development

Robin Dickinson and Zubin Sethna

Abstract Super General Intelligence, a form of Artificial Super Intelligence, is a Frontier Technology that has yet to be derived from General Artificial Intelligence. If developed, it could present an existential threat to human development. This conceptual paper proposes a model for Ethical Restraint as utilized in Hereditary Human Genome Manipulation, a Frontier Technology, along with a study to determine the model's applicability to the development of Super General intelligence.

Keywords Super general intelligence · Hereditary human genome manipulation · Ethical restraint · Frontier technology development

1 Introduction

Buchanan in a book entitled "Better than Human: The promise and perils of enhancing ourselves" examined the ethical dilemmas of human enhancement including Super General Intelligence [SGI]. Artificial Intelligence [AI] can be described as a Frontier Technology [FT]. The development pathway for AI has broadly been divided into three Frontiers: Narrow AI [NAI], General AI [GAI], and Artificial Super Intelligence [ASI] [1–3]. ASI could be developed from GAI and if so could be categorized as SGI. SGI could present an existential threat to human development [4–8]. There are many potential dimensions to this threat, including: the agency of the digital global human political economy to transcend the digital and manifest the physical, not least through the deployment of the internet of things [9]; through the non-human SGI physiology and psychology arising from SGI undergoing self-development [7]; AI-driven enhancement of human cognition [10] and the

R. Dickinson (✉) · Z. Sethna
Regent's University London, London, UK
e-mail: robin.dickinson@regents.ac.uk; zubin.sethna@regents.ac.uk

N. Omrani et al. (eds.), *Human-Machine Synergy and the Digital Future - Exploring Collaboration and Competition Volume 1*, Springer Proceedings in Business and Economics, https://doi.org/10.1007/978-3-032-21347-1_4

development of socialization between SGI entities [11]. Much of this work was built on some early cautions by [12] who argued for restraints in AI and biotechnology and warned of irreversible consequences. Therefore, SGI development needs significant ethical restraint [13, 14].

It is important to note the impact of digital technology which is currently pervasive across the global human political economy [9, 15–17]. One component of digital technology, NAI, is being deployed globally [18, 19]. The ethical restraint of organizations engaged in the development of the third frontier of AI, SGI is currently insignificant [19–22].

Genome Manipulation has been on a FT development pathway for many decades [23, 24] and from various perspectives including military applications of genetic enhancements [25]; eugenics and moral dilemmas in genome editing [26]; One strand of Frontier Genomics is Hereditary Human Genome development which presents an existential threat to human physiology and human socialization [27, 28]. Hereditary Human Genome Development is possible through a widely accessible technology [29] but its development has been significantly ethically restrained at multiple levels within and without of the organizations engaged in its development [30, 31]. Add to this Moore's exploration of how the long-neglected human right of Freedom of Thought might protect the integrity of the mind, and all of a sudden we experience a whole new dimension in frontier technology [32].

2 Hypothesis

Building on the premise that SGI development needs rapidly deployable, significant mechanisms of ethical restraint, this paper develops two hypotheses (Fig. 1):

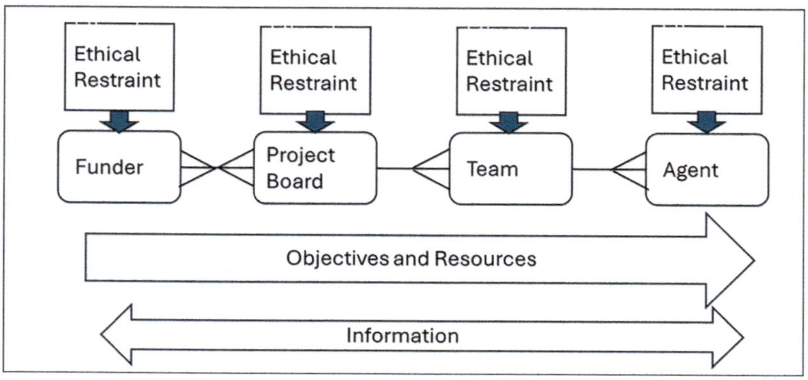

Fig. 1 Hypothecated Model 1 for the human delivery and ethical restraint of frontier developments [Author]

Hypothesis 1: Digital AI development organizations and Genome development organizations organize their delivery and ethical restraint of Frontier technology using a similar model.

Hypothesis 2: The mechanisms of ethical restraint operated within organizations that develop Hereditary Human Genome technology could be deployed within organizations that develop SGI [33].

3 Objectives

1. Validate the hypothecated Model 1 for the human delivery of frontier hereditary Human Genome manipulation.
2. Validate the hypothecated Model 1 for the ethical restraint of frontier hereditary Human Genome manipulation.
3. Validate the hypothecated Model 1 for the human delivery of "SGI" system developments.
4. Validate Hypothesis 2

4 Methods

A standard Mixed Methods approach will be utilized, with a Convergent Parallel Design for qualitative and quantitative data gathering focused on assembling a statistically valid sample of institutions engaged in frontier Human Genome manipulation and then case studies of institutions engaged in frontier Artificial General Intelligence. Leveraging a multi-stage approach using Grounded Theory for metrics definitions, data collection, result coding and analysis proceeding hypothesis development and validation. If a need to converge findings arises, a Mixed Methods Matrix iteration will be deployed.

Human Genome manipulation has been practiced for many decades by an increasing number of institutions, so it is not anticipated that access to an adequate number of institutions will be a problem. There are a smaller number of institutions engaged in frontier Artificial General Intelligence, and while generally access is restricted, the scope of the hypothecated model is not seen as contentious nor sensitive.

5 Implications

SGI has existential implications for all humanity and is appearing on developmental roadmaps [13] but has yet to be created. The contemporary output of AI development ethical governance bodies is weighted toward transformation challenges arising from the use of NAI [34, 35]. This paper could contribute to the rapid deployment of enhanced ethical restraint mechanisms for third frontier AI, SGI development.

References

1. Alvarez-Teleña, S., Díez-Fernández, M.: Advances in Artificial Super Intelligence: Calm is All You Need. https://doi.org/10.2139/ssrn.4924496 (2024)
2. Bory, P., Natale, S., Katzenbach, C.: Strong and weak AI narratives: an analytical framework. AI Soc. **40**, 2107–2117 (2025). https://doi.org/10.1007/s00146-024-02087-8
3. Hua, C., Cao, X., Liao, B., Li, S.: Advances on intelligent algorithms for scientific computing: an overview. Front. Neurorobot. **17**, 1190977 (2023)
4. Aithal, P.S.: Super-intelligent machines—analysis of developmental challenges and predicted negative consequences. Int. J. Appl. Eng. Manag. Lett. **7**(3), 109–141 (2023)
5. Barrett, A.M., Baum, S.D.: A model of pathways to artificial superintelligence catastrophe for risk and decision analysis. J. Exp. Theor. Artif. Intell. **29**(2), 397–414 (2017)
6. Johnson, L.S.M.: Existing ethical tensions in xenotransplantation. Camb. Q. Healthc. Ethics. **31**(3), 355–367 (2022)
7. Mostufa, S., Chakrabarti, K.: A genre of cognitive evolutions through artificial superintelligence and robotics technology. In: Bandyopadhyay, A., Ray, K. (eds.) Brain-Like Super Intelligence from Bio-Electromagnetism. Studies in Rhythm Engineering. Springer, Singapore (2024)
8. Song, B.: Intelligence and Wisdom: Artificial Intelligence Meets Chinese Philosophers. Springer, Singapore (2021)
9. Rose, K., Eldridge, S., Chapin, L.: The Internet of Things: An Overview, vol. 80(15), pp. 1–53. The Internet Society (ISOC), Reston (2015)
10. Cheshko, V.: An evolutionary metaphysics of human enhancement technologies. https://philarchive.org/archive/CHEAEM-5 (2019). Last accessed 19 Feb 2025
11. Lean, S., Read, G.J.M., Thompson, J., Baber, C., Stanton, N.A., Salmon, P.M.: The risks associated with artificial general intelligence: a systematic review. J. Exp. Theor. Artif. Intell. **35**(5), 649–663 (2021)
12. McKibben, B.: Enough: Staying Human in an Engineered Age. Times Books, New York (2003)
13. Goyal, R., Sharma, N., Kaur, A.: Artificial super intelligence: barriers and limitations. In: AIP Conference Proceedings, vol. 3209(1). AIP Publishing, Melville (2024)
14. Thomas, A.: The Politics and Ethics of Transhumanism: Techno-Human Evolution and Advanced Capitalism. Bristol University Press, Bristol (2024)
15. Brass, I., Hornsby, D.J.: Digital technological innovation and the international political economy. In: Shaw, T.M., Mahrenbach, L.C., Modi, R., Yi-chong, X. (eds.) The Palgrave Handbook of Contemporary International Political Economy. Palgrave Macmillan, London (2019)
16. Demichelis, L.: The internet of things and the internet of human beings. In: Marx, Alienation and Techno-Capitalism. Marx, Engels, and Marxisms. Palgrave Macmillan, Cham. (2022)
17. Furr, N., Ozcan, P., Eisenhardt, K.M.: What is digital transformation? Core tensions facing established companies on the global stage. Glob. Strateg. J. **12**(4), 595–618 (2022). https://doi.org/10.1002/gsj.1442

18. Heuveline, V., Stiefel, V.: Artificial intelligence and algorithms: true progress or just digital alchemy? In: Holm-Hadulla, R.M., Funke, J., Wink, M. (eds.) Intelligence—Theories and Applications. Springer, Cham (2022)
19. Tai, M.C.-T.: The impact of artificial intelligence on human society and bioethics. Tzu Chi Med. J. **32**(4), 339–343 (2020)
20. Hagendorff, T.: The ethics of AI ethics: an evaluation of guidelines. Minds Mach. **30**, 99–120 (2020). https://doi.org/10.1007/s11023-020-09517-8
21. Mittelstadt, B.: Principles alone cannot guarantee ethical AI. Nat. Mach. Intell. **1**, 501–507 (2019)
22. Sigfrids, A., Nieminen, M., Leikas, J., Pikkuaho, P.: How should public administrations foster the ethical development and use of artificial intelligence? A review of proposals for developing governance of AI. Front. Hum. Dyn. **4**, 858108 (2022)
23. Hasanzad, M., Sarhangi, N., Naghavi, A.: Genomic medicine on the frontier of precision medicine. J. Diabetes Metab. Disord. **21**, 853–861 (2022). https://doi.org/10.1007/s40200-021-00880-6
24. Wilkins, M.: Proteome Research: New Frontiers in Functional Genomics. Springer Science & Business Media, Berlin (1997)
25. Monsen, I.H.L., Glenna, S., Rjaanas, M.: Genome editing for soldier enhancement—trends and implications. Front FFI-Note. **20**, 02378 (2020)
26. Sarkar, S.: A Brave New Eugenics? CRISPR and the Human Future. https://sahotra-sarkar.org/wp-content/uploads/2020/07/sarkar-eugenics.pdf (2020)
27. Andorno, R., Baylis, F., Darnovsky, M., Dickenson, D., Haker, H., Hasson, K., Lowthorp, L., Annas, G.J., Bourgain, C., Drabiak, K., Graumann, S., Grüber, K., Kaiser, M., King, D., Kollek, R., MacKellar, C., Nie, J.B., Obasogie, O.K., Tyebally Fang, M., Werner-Felmayer, G., Zuscinova, J.: Geneva statement on heritable human genome editing: the need for course correction. Trends Biotechnol. **38**(4), 351–354 (2020)
28. Lanphier, E., Urnov, F., Haecker, S.E., Werner, M., Smolenski, J.: Don't edit the human germ line. Nature. **519**(7544), 410–411 (2015)
29. Gautam, N., Na, R., O'Leary, D., Saks, H., Srinivas, N., Yim, S.: Germline gene therapy: is it ethical to edit an embryo? J. Ethics Sci. Technol. Innov. **1**, 7–12 (2023)
30. Evans, J.H.: Setting ethical limits on human gene editing after the fall of the somatic/germline barrier. Proc. Natl. Acad. Sci. U. S. A. **118**(22), e2004837117 (2021)
31. National Human Genome Research Institute: Ethical Concerns. https://www.genome.gov/about-genomics/policy-issues/Genome-Editing/ethical-concerns (2017). Last accessed 20 Feb 2025
32. Moore, M.: Freedom of thought at the ethical frontier of law & science. Ethics Behav. **32**(6), 510–531 (2021)
33. Mökander, J., Sheth, M., Gersbro-Sundler, M., Blomgren, P., Floridi, L.: Challenges and best practices in corporate AI governance: lessons from the biopharmaceutical industry. Comput. Sci. **4**, 1068361 (2022)
34. Viljanen, M., Parviainen, H.: AI applications and regulation: mapping the regulatory strata. Front. Comput. Sci. **3**, 779957 (2022)
35. Verdier, H.: Global governance of AI. In: Artificial Intelligence Action Summit, Paris. https://www.elysee.fr/admin/upload/default/0001/17/085eb85e11b563e0f0ee1c23cb9552a9cc8f1e83.pdf (2025)

AI and Open Innovation

Digital Finance for SMEs and Startups: Literature Review and Research Proposals

Tindara Abbate, Fabrizio Cesaroni, Alessandra Costa, Antonio Crupi, and Elvira Tiziana La Rocca

Abstract Digital finance is reshaping the entrepreneurial context by reshaping how businesses access and manage financial resources. In particular, tools such as crowdfunding and peer-to-peer (P2P) lending are contributing to reducing information asymmetries, broadening access to credit, and shifting trust toward algorithmic and reputational mechanisms. In this context, this study aims to develop a conceptual framework that clarifies the relationship between digital finance and entrepreneurial activity, while also assessing the current state of knowledge on the risks associated with digital financial instruments and the evolving role of credit rating systems. To address these goals, a systematic literature review based on 172 peer-reviewed articles was conducted in accordance with PRISMA guidelines. The results identify key thematic clusters and reveal the interdisciplinary nature of research in this area, reflecting the convergence of finance, entrepreneurship, and digital innovation. It offers a structured synthesis of existing literature and provides theoretical and practical insights for scholars, policymakers, and practitioners interested in the role of digital tools in entrepreneurial finance.

Keywords Digital finance · FinTech · Crowdfunding

1 Introduction

The literature on crowdfunding and FinTech solutions highlights their increasing relevance as complements or alternatives to traditional financing sources—such as venture capital, business angels, and bank loans—particularly for SMEs and startups. These instruments help reduce information asymmetries through mechanisms such as platform reputation, investor feedback, lead investors, and social

T. Abbate · F. Cesaroni (✉) · A. Costa · A. Crupi · E. T. La Rocca
University of Messina, Messina, Italy
e-mail: tindara.abbate@unime.it; fabrizio.cesaroni@unime.it; alessandra.costa@unime.it; crupi.antonio@unime.it; elviratiziana.larocca@unime.it

N. Omrani et al. (eds.), *Human-Machine Synergy and the Digital Future - Exploring Collaboration and Competition Volume 1*, Springer Proceedings in Business and Economics, https://doi.org/10.1007/978-3-032-21347-1_5

connections. Crowdfunding platforms act as digital intermediaries, offering screening, regulatory compliance, and fraud risk mitigation. Artificial Intelligence (AI) and Big Data improve transparency and risk assessment, while shifting the foundation of trust from personal relationships to algorithms and interfaces.

Global regulations, such as the JOBS Act in the USA and European and Chinese regulations, significantly influence the spread of crowdfunding, with the regulatory approach (more permissive in the UK, more restrictive in China) affecting growth trajectories.

Beyond the entrepreneurial domain, Crowdfunding also serves social and sustainable projects, attracting impact-driven investors. Campaign success depends on content quality (pitch, images, videos), network building, and active engagement, which trigger herding behavior and build reputation.

Financial digitalization is not merely a tool but a systemic transformation across the business lifecycle, underlining the centrality of transparency, trust, innovation, and sustainability. Digital tools such as P2P lending expand credit access and lower entry barriers for startups and SMEs, supporting the rise of business models oriented toward social and environmental value creation.

Significantly, digital platforms not only facilitate financing but also foster collaboration between entrepreneurs and investors, nurturing ecosystems based on resource sharing and collective development. Technological infrastructures—especially blockchain and big data—play a key role in reducing information gaps, improving risk perception, and reinforcing stakeholder confidence. Transparency and digital reputational cues (e.g., credit ratings, user reviews) are central to attracting investment and ensuring efficient capital allocation.

Digital financialization thus emerges not merely as a technical advancement, but as a systemic shift shaping the entire business lifecycle. It enables more inclusive access to credit, lowers entry barriers, and supports the rise of business models oriented toward innovation, sustainability, and shared value creation.

Building on this context, the present study aims to provide a conceptual and empirical foundation for understanding the role of digital finance in entrepreneurial ecosystems. Specifically, it addresses two research questions:

RQ1—What is the state of the art describing the logical connections between digital finance and entrepreneurial activities?

RQ2—What is the current state of the art regarding the risks of digital finance and credit rating for businesses?

Our findings provide practical insights and conceptual tools for entrepreneurs, policymakers, and researchers interested in leveraging digital finance to support inclusive and sustainable economic development.

2 Methodology and Data Analysis

To answer these research questions, a systematic literature review (SLR) was carried out, following the PRISMA guidelines (Preferred Reporting Items for Systematic Reviews and Meta-Analyses) [1, 2]. This methodological choice ensures transparency, replicability, and comprehensiveness in the identification, selection, and analysis of academic contributions relevant to the field. After identifying a comprehensive set of keywords reflecting the core themes of interest—such as crowdfunding, crowdlending, digital platforms, peer-to-peer lending, and online financial intermediation—the resulting search screen was employed in Web of Science (WoS), using Boolean operators and proximity functions to capture variations in terminology. To ensure the validity of the analysis, a multilevel filtering process was applied through inclusion and exclusion criteria. Specifically, inclusion criteria restricted the corpus to articles written in English, published within relevant WoS categories (Business, Management, Finance), with a further filter based on journal quality (e.g., indexed in ABS rankings). Importantly, the review focused exclusively on original research articles, excluding literature reviews. As a result, a final sample of 172 peer-reviewed articles was retained for analysis.

The collected data have been analyzed using bibliometric techniques [3, 4] through the Bibliometrix package. Specifically, co-citation analysis was used to uncover the underlying intellectual structure of the field, while bibliographic coupling allowed for capturing thematic similarities among recent contributions to detect emerging themes and interdisciplinary linkages.

3 Discussion of Results

The results of the bibliometric analysis reveal a structured and multidimensional research landscape in the field of digital finance, particularly in relation to crowdfunding and P2P lending. The co-citation analysis identified four main thematic clusters.

The first, labeled New Perspectives on Crowdfunding, P2P Lending, illustrates how crowdfunding platforms function not merely as intermediaries but as institutional entrepreneurs capable of shaping market norms and influencing the behavior of participants [5].

The second cluster, Recent Prospectives on Crowdfunding and Entrepreneurial Finance, includes studies on crowdfunding and alternative finance [6], emphasizing that project communication, reward structures, and the use of social networks significantly influence the success of funding campaigns.

The third cluster, titled Perspectives on Lending, Informational Asymmetries, and Financial Innovation, brings attention to the relevance of "soft" information in credit evaluation processes and the potential for discriminatory practices in peer-to-peer markets [7, 8]. It also explores how appropriate market mechanisms can reduce adverse selection, thereby positioning digital lending as a complement or alternative to traditional banking [9, 10].

Finally, the fourth cluster, Fintech and Innovation, draws on seminal literature on imperfect information in credit markets [11, 12], discussing how information asymmetries lead to credit rationing [13, 14], and how these can be mitigated through signaling theory [15] and the development of long-term lending relationships [16].

In parallel, the bibliographic coupling analysis revealed three principal thematic domains. The first cluster, New Frontiers in Alternative Finance, focuses on the disclosure practices and decision-making dynamics in unregulated markets such as Initial Coin Offerings (ICOs), emphasizing how the quality and quantity of available information affect investor behavior [17].

The second, P2P Platforms and Crowdfunding: Key Success Factors and Challenges for the Digital Financial Ecosystem, underlines how users' financial knowledge and risk tolerance shape their use of P2P platforms, and also documents the persistence of such biases, like "home bias," whereby lenders are more inclined to fund geographically and culturally proximate borrowers [18, 19].

Finally, the third cluster, Digitalization and the Creation of a Credit Ecosystem, shows that peer-to-peer (P2P) lending can operate both as a complement and an alternative to traditional banking credit, particularly for medium-risk borrowers or those located in financially underserved areas [10].

4 Conclusions

The findings of this study provide an integrated view of the evolving literature on crowdfunding and peer-to-peer (P2P) platforms. The results demonstrate a growing convergence of research across disciplines such as finance, entrepreneurship, sociology, and psychology [20–22], reflecting the inherently multidimensional nature of digital finance. One of the most salient outcomes of this transformation is the democratization of credit and the promotion of financial inclusion, enabled by the reduction of geographical and socio-economic barriers through digital infrastructures.

Parallelly, the integration of various emerging technologies has amplified the capacity of platforms to assess and manage risk, reinforcing their role as credible and efficient financial intermediaries. Furthermore, at the same time, the study highlights the importance of reputational mechanisms, social capital, and digital engagement in influencing campaign outcomes and investor behavior.

These findings provide several implications for both theory and practice. From a theoretical perspective, the study contributes to the conceptualization of digital finance as an institutional and technological shift in entrepreneurial funding, providing a structured framework that integrates risk, trust, information asymmetry reduction, and digital innovation. From a practical standpoint, the results inform entrepreneurs, platform designers, and policymakers about the mechanisms that enhance the effectiveness of digital financial tools, with a specific focus on investor engagement and reputational signals.

Acknowledgments This study was funded by the European Union—NextGenerationEU—Mission 4, Component 2, in the framework of the GRINS—Growing Resilient, INclusive and Sustainable project (GRINSPE00000018—CUP J43C24000200007). The views and opinions expressed are solely those of the authors and do not necessarily reflect those of the European Union, nor can the European Union be held responsible for them.

References

1. Moher, D., Liberati, A., Tetzlaff, J., Altman, D.G., PRISMA Group: Preferred reporting items for systematic reviews and meta-analyses: the PRISMA statement. Ann. Intern. Med. **151**(4), 264–269 (2009)
2. Page, M.J., McKenzie, J.E., Bossuyt, P.M., Boutron, I., Hoffmann, T.C., Mulrow, C.D., et al.: The PRISMA 2020 statement: an updated guideline for reporting systematic reviews. Int. J. Surg. **88**, 105906 (2021)
3. Liu, X., Bollen, J., Nelson, M.L., Van de Sompel, H.: Co-authorship networks in the digital library research community. Inf. Process. Manag. **41**(6), 1462–1480 (2005)
4. Kraus, S., Brem, A., Muench, S., Gast, J., Gleich, R.: Mapping the field of entrepreneurship and sustainability: past, present and future. Bus. Strateg. Environ. **29**(8), 3409–3429 (2020)
5. Mollick, E., Nanda, R.: Wisdom or madness? Comparing crowds with expert evaluation in funding the arts. Manag. Sci. **62**(6), 1533–1553 (2016)
6. Mollick, E.: The dynamics of crowdfunding: an exploratory study. J. Bus. Ventur. **29**(1), 1–16 (2014)
7. Iyer, R., Khwaja, A.I., Luttmer, E.F.P., Shue, K.: Screening peers softly: inferring the quality of small borrowers. Manag. Sci. **62**(6), 1554–1577 (2016)
8. Pope, D.G., Sydnor, J.R.: What's in a picture? Evidence of discrimination from prosper.com. J. Hum. Resour. **46**(1), 53–92 (2011)
9. Wei, Z., Lin, M.: Market mechanisms in online peer-to-peer lending. Manag. Sci. **63**(12), 4236–4257 (2017)
10. Tang, H.: Peer-to-peer lenders versus banks: substitutes or complements? Rev. Financ. Stud. **32**(5), 1900–1938 (2019)
11. Akerlof, G.A.: The market for "lemons": quality uncertainty and the market mechanism. Q. J. Econ. **84**(3), 488–500 (1970)
12. Diamond, D.W.: Financial intermediation and delegated monitoring. Rev. Econ. Stud. **51**(3), 393–414 (1984)
13. Stiglitz, J.E., Weiss, A.: Credit rationing and collateral. In: Edwards, J., Franks, J., Mayer, C., Schaefer, S. (eds.) Recent developments in corporate finance, pp. 101–135. Cambridge University Press, New York (1986)
14. Stiglitz, J.E., Weiss, A.: Credit rationing in markets with imperfect information. Am. Econ. Rev. **71**(3), 393–410 (1981)
15. Spence, M.: Job market signaling. Q. J. Econ. **87**(3), 355–374 (1973)
16. Petersen, M.A., Rajan, R.G.: The benefits of lending relationships: evidence from small business data. J. Financ. **49**(1), 3–37 (1994)
17. Bourveau, T., De George, E.T., Ellahie, A., Macciocchi, D.: The role of disclosure and information intermediaries in an unregulated capital market: evidence from initial coin offerings. J. Account. Res. **60**(1), 129–167 (2022)
18. Han, L., Xiao, J.J., Su, Z.: Financing knowledge, risk attitude and P2P borrowing in China. Int. J. Consum. Stud. **43**(2), 166–177 (2019)

19. Burtch, G., Ghose, A., Wattal, S.: Cultural differences and geography as determinants of online prosocial lending. MIS Q. **38**(3), 773–794 (2014)
20. Cumming, D.J., Leboeuf, G., Schwienbacher, A.: Crowdfunding cleantech. Financ. Manag. **49**(2), 331–365 (2020)
21. Cumming, D., Hornuf, L.: Marketplace lending of small- and medium-sized enterprises. Strateg. Entrep. J. **16**(1), 32–66 (2022)
22. Vismara, S.: Equity retention and social network theory in equity crowdfunding. Small Bus. Econ. **46**(4), 579–590 (2016)

AI and Open Innovation: Exploring the Impact of Collaborative Strategies on Patent Value and Technological Significance

Andrea Amanti, Alessandra Costa, Antonio Crupi, and Francesco Paolo Appio

Abstract The strategic adoption of collaborative approaches has become a critical factor in shaping innovation trajectories within the field of Artificial Intelligence (AI). As firms engage in open innovation, the nature of their partnerships, ranging from alliances with research institutions to joint ventures with technology firms, plays a fundamental role in determining the effectiveness of their AI-driven initiatives. Understanding the structure, dynamics, and outcomes of these collaborations is essential for assessing their impact on firms' innovation performance, technological progress, and market competitiveness. This study investigates how the diverse typologies of firms' collaborative strategies in AI influence their performance outcomes. Specifically, we explore how different modes of cooperation, cross-industry partnerships, and university-industry collaborations in AI-related innovations impact on firms' performance. By adopting a mixed-method quantitative approach, integrating continuous and discrete regression models, our findings suggest that firms engaging in OI strategies tend to exhibit higher performances

Keywords Artificial intelligence · AI patents · Open innovation · Innovation dynamics

A. Amanti (✉) · A. Costa · A. Crupi
University of Messina, Messina, Italy
e-mail: andamanti@unime.it; alessandra.costa@unime.it; crupi.antonio@unime.it

F. P. Appio
Paris School of Business, Paris, France
e-mail: f.appio@psbedu.paris

N. Omrani et al. (eds.), *Human-Machine Synergy and the Digital Future - Exploring Collaboration and Competition Volume 1*, Springer Proceedings in Business and Economics, https://doi.org/10.1007/978-3-032-21347-1_6

1 Introduction

AI development is profoundly influenced by access to diverse knowledge sources, fostering new forms of recombined knowledge [1]. In this context, companies that embrace Open Innovation (OI) strategies demonstrate greater effectiveness in transforming external knowledge into patentable innovations, resulting in more advanced and higher value AI patents. By leveraging Open Innovation, firms can access a broad spectrum of expertise and technological resources, accelerating the creation of innovative solutions [2, 3]. AI patents serve as a key indicator of entrepreneurial activity within the artificial intelligence sector, reflecting both the pace of innovation and the ability of firms to translate widely distributed knowledge into distinct technological assets [4]. The diffusion of AI patents highlights how firms engaged in OI gain a competitive advantage in identifying unique innovation patterns and transferring knowledge across industries [5]. This process is particularly relevant for companies operating in high-uncertainty, technology-intensive sectors, where patent protection plays a crucial role in balancing innovation risks and returns [6]. By granting temporary monopolies, patents incentivize investments in high-risk areas requiring substantial financial resources and advanced technical expertise [7]. However, the OI model helps mitigate these barriers by facilitating knowledge-sharing and access to diverse capabilities, essential for developing stronger and more versatile AI patents [8]. Moreover, integrating OI and AI accelerate patent development by expanding the available knowledge [2]. Firms adopting OI strategies can tap into expert networks, collaborate with universities and startups, and leverage shared data to enhance the quality of their AI patents. In this sense, OI is not merely a mechanism for generating new ideas but also a fundamental driver for strengthening patenting capability and fostering long-term sustainable technological competitiveness [3, 9].

Within this framework, the intersections between AI and OI, as well as the mutually reinforcement mechanisms, require further investigation to understand how they reshape firms' organizational and innovation strategies in an increasingly open and technologically-integrated environment. Our research focuses on examining the nature of firms' collaborative strategies in AI-related innovation and their relative impact on performance outcomes. Therefore, the research goal is twofold: first, to assess the interplay between OI and AI-related patented innovations; second, to assess the casual effects between the heterogeneous set of OI strategies and firms' performances. Therefore, our study contributes to the advancement of innovation management literature, while also shedding light on the underlying mechanisms of innovation commercialization and providing actionable insights for managers and policymakers navigating the complex landscape of OI strategies for AI.

2 Methodology and Data Analysis

To investigate the nature of firms' collaborative strategies in AI and their relative impact on performance outcomes, this study adopts a quantitative methodological approach, directly applied to AI patents. Specifically, we analyze how Open Innovation (OI) collaborative strategies influence firm's performance. line with the OECD methodology of Baruffaldi et al. [10], we employed a systematic approach combining technological classification codes, like International Patent Classification (IPC) codes, and a keyword-based search. This approach ensures a comprehensive identification of AI-related patents, leveraging both the standardized classification system and a targeted keyword search. More specifically, following the above-mentioned research strategy, we identified a patent as AI-related if its English abstract or claims matched at least one AI-related keyword and was assigned at least one of the IPC AI-related codes. Using these dual criteria is crucial and has been found to be and effective research strategy, because complementing IPC classification codes with a keyword search allow to better identify patents that incorporate AI solutions, even if not explicitly classified under AI-related IPC codes, thus increasing the likelihood of better capturing the underlined linkages between OI strategies and AI-related patenting activities. We applied this AI patent search strategy to Questel-Orbit patent database, covering more than 60 patent authorities, including the European Patent Office (EPO). Additionally, to avoid double counting, we focused on patent families rather that individual patents. After selecting and screening the AI-related patents, our analysis involves a subsequent combination of AI-related patent database with ORBIS Intellectual Property Bureau van Dijk (BvD) database (to retrieve additional patent information, like number and types of owners and applicants, count of both forward and backward citations, patent value, etc.). We applied a mixed quantitative methodological approach to examine the causal relationship between Open Innovation strategies and firms' performance. Since performance was assessed in terms of both innovation output and market competitiveness, the distinct nature of these dependent variables required different regression models. Specifically, we employed a multivariate regression model for innovation output, given its continuous nature, while market competitiveness, being a discrete variable, was best analyzed using a negative binomial regression. To ensure the robustness of our estimates, we addressed potential biases such as multicollinearity, heteroskedasticity, endogeneity, and overdispersion by applying robust standard errors and different parameter specifications.

3 Discussion of Results

Our preliminary findings yielded several findings regarding the linkages between Open Innovation collaborative strategies and AI patent performance. First, we found a positive and significant relationship between firms' engagement in OI collaborative strategies in AI-related innovation and firms' performances. Further, we found that tapping into diverse knowledge and innovation sources through OI strategies enhances firms' overall performance, fostering greater innovation output and market competitiveness. Moreover, deepening the analysis by considering the types of partnerships, we observed a mixed effect on firms' innovation efficiency suggesting that companies navigating the complex landscape of OI must identify the optimal level of external knowledge and innovation inflows to maximize their strategic and operational benefits. Second, the regression models employed demonstrated a clear causal effect. Firms that actively establish and strengthen OI strategies are more likely to experience significant improvements in innovation performance and competitive positioning, thus supporting the existence of synergistic positive effects arising from the integration of external and diversified knowledge sources. Third, by considering different combination of external knowledge sources and the resultant heterogeneity of partnerships, by means of both Herfindhal–Hirschman indices and multiple categorical variables, our results help evaluate which alternatives collaborations are most effective in spurring firms' innovation performances, also unveiling the importance of strategic decision-making in selecting appropriate OI partners when developing and commercializing AI-related patents. Fourth, our descriptive results still show the prominent role of firms as collaborative partners, rather than other institutions. This suggests not only the greater ability of firms in accessing more technological advanced resources but also their more flexible organizational structures that allow to easily recombine knowledge from different sources to develop new value. Moreover, comparing the coefficients of both estimation approaches, our results suggest that technological impact of AI innovations and patent values follow the same dynamic patterns of evolutions.

4 Conclusions

This study provides an integrated perspective on the emerging intersection between Artificial Intelligence (AI) and Open Innovation (OI), with a specific focus on how collaborative R&D strategies can enhance the performance of AI-related patents. By analyzing a validated dataset of AI patents and classifying OI strategies according to their breadth and type, we offer robust empirical evidence that supports and extends existing innovation management literature. Our findings suggest that engaging in OI strategies—by leveraging external knowledge sources and digital capabilities—can significantly improve AI patent performance, both in terms of value and technological impact.

From a theoretical standpoint, this research contributes to the understanding of digital innovation by shedding light on the mechanisms through which different forms of OI collaboration influence innovation outcomes. The study emphasizes the importance of selecting OI strategies aligned with firms' strategic goals, particularly when navigating complex ecosystems shaped by AI technologies. Moreover, the inclusion of multivariate continuous and discrete regression models allows us to detail causal effects, offering additional insights into how OI can be effectively implemented across different industries and regions.

At the same time, we recognize the limitations of our approach. Our AI patent search strategy may not fully capture non-patented innovations—especially those involving software, algorithms, or informal collaborations—and some industrial sectors may be underrepresented in our database. These aspects highlight avenues for future research, particularly in extending the analysis to other indicators of AI innovation and considering multiple outcome variables beyond patents.

From a managerial perspective, our study provides actionable insights for decision-makers aiming to remain competitive in global markets. It underscores the importance of carefully selecting diverse and complementary OI partnerships to optimize value creation. Firms are encouraged to build structured, open, and technology-driven collaborations that integrate risk management, digital capability enhancement, and alignment with strategic objectives. Ultimately, our findings help illuminate the pathways through which OI strategies can be harnessed to maximize the potential of AI innovation across a wide range of organizational and technological contexts.

References

1. Messeni Petruzzelli, A., Murgia, G., Parmentola, A.: Opening the black box of artificial intelligence technologies: unveiling the influence exerted by type of organisations and collaborative dynamics. Ind. Innov. **30**(9), 1213–1243 (2023)
2. Büttner, B., Firat, M., Raiteri, E.: Patents and knowledge diffusion: the impact of machine translation. Res. Policy. **51**(10), 104584 (2022)
3. Pantanowitz, L., Bui, M.M., Chauhan, C., Elgabry, E., Hassell, L., Li, Z., et al.: Rules of engagement: promoting academic-industry partnership in the era of digital pathology and artificial intelligence. Acad. Pathol. **9**(1), 100026 (2022)
4. Appio, F.P., Martini, A., Fantoni, G.: The light and shade of knowledge recombination: insights from a general-purpose technology. Technol. Forecast. Soc. Chang. **125**, 154–165 (2017)
5. Liu, J., Chang, H., Forrest, J.Y.L., Yang, B.: Influence of artificial intelligence on technological innovation: evidence from the panel data of china's manufacturing sectors. Technol. Forecast. Soc. Chang. **158**, 120142 (2020)
6. Kemp, A.: Competitive advantages through artificial intelligence: toward a theory of situated AI. Acad. Manag. Rev. **49**(3) (2023)
7. Liu, N., Shapira, P., Yue, X., Guan, J.: "Mapping technological innovation dynamics in artificial intelligence domains: Evidence from a global patent analysis.", Plos One, vol. 16, n. 12, pp.e0262050 (2021)
8. Zan, F., et al.: Knowledge sharing and innovation performance: the mediating role of open innovation. Glob. Bus. Organ. Excell. **43**(3), 32–45 (2024)
9. Gulati, R.: Managing Network Resources: Alliances, Affiliations, and Other Relational Assets. OUP, Oxford (2007)
10. Baruffaldi, S., Van Beuzekom, B., Dernis, H., Harhoff, D., Rao, N., Rosenfeld, D., & Squicciarni, M.: Identifying and measuring developments in artificial intelligence: Making the impossible possible., OECD (2020)

Digitizing Workforce Practices

Eclecticism and Wishful Thinking in the Digitalization of Workforce Practices: Opportunities and Risks

Massimo Bianchi

Abstract In the evolution of management control systems, the digitalization of Workforce Practices (WP) directly affects the competences of human resources and it includes numerous opportunities and risks.

On the one hand, digitalization promises to automate repetitive tasks and improve the employee experience. On the other hand, it implies some questionable topics regarding a new fashion of Scientific Management with the intrusion into the personal sphere of the workforce.

The current evolution of management control systems is not only technical but also involves some basic concepts related to the eclecticism that characterizes information and data to various sciences and applied knowledge included in digital platforms of WP coming, to this regard, from the diffusion in management Audit of ISO standards and from the promotion of business technologies like IoT and CoSo Framework.

Numerous corporate standards and business technologies produce complexity and questions about the adequacy of workforce competence, which can be evidenced by traditional analytical tools such as the Graiciunas span of control, the Peter's principle of incompetence, and the Jaques' control span.

The purpose of this paper is to analyze the opportunities and risks, connected to the increasing standardization of auditing processes and advances in the digitalization of management control systems expressed particularly by the IoT and Coso Framework.

Keywords Workforce practices · Digitalization · Eclecticism · Wishful thinking · Management control systems

---

M. Bianchi (✉)
University of Bologna, Bologna, Italy
e-mail: massimo.bianchi@unibo.it

N. Omrani et al. (eds.), *Human-Machine Synergy and the Digital Future - Exploring Collaboration and Competition Volume 1*, Springer Proceedings in Business and Economics, https://doi.org/10.1007/978-3-032-21347-1_7

1 Introduction

The digitalization of Workforce Practices (WP) plays a characteristic relevance in the evolution of management control systems, firstly because it impacts directly on the needs of Human Resources, secondly because it includes numerous issues and risks linked to the complexity of proposed tools.

The digitalization promises, among other things, to automate repetitive tasks, including onboarding and outboarding activities, to save time and improve the employee experience to enable a rational and advanced approach to decisions on human resources.

On the other, it implies some questionable topics regarding a new fashion of Scientific Management and an intrusion into the personal sphere. All these perplexities increase when we apply digital sensors to the control of attendance in the workplace or performance algorithms to performance evaluation, interventions that give rise to questions that are difficult to argue.

The confluence of accounting data, materials, relating to the work environment and personal profiles is characterized by multidisciplinarity. Even combining this multidisciplinarily with the poly, trans, cross approaches, the result is still complex in nature.

From this point of view, the issue of the complexity of these systems is also debatable, as it may distance the proposed digital tools from the requirement of immediacy, both in terms of usability and adequate control.

The current evolution is not only technical but involves some basic concepts regarding the eclecticism that characterizes Management Control Systems and deriving from the introduction in Business Management of ISO Standards and as well as Business Technologies like IoT and CoSo network with unrealistic proposals coming, in this regard, from the marketing of digital devices.

The proliferation of concepts in management has been welcomed as facilitating the understanding of organizations, such as, in entrepreneurship, the entrepreneurial mindset, orientation, hustle, intention, and leadership [1], but it produces complexity.

In addition to this trend, there is also a multidisciplinary approach to Human Resources that aspires to be embedded in a holistic perspective understood as a framework of different knowledge and quantifications [2].

In practice, complexity opens the door to the Graiciunas's span of control [3], of Peter's principle of incompetence [4], and of Eliot Jacques time span [5] as classical and analytical tools to evaluate the limits of the current evolution of management and risks, arising from WP Digitalization. These problems should be solved in order to ensure an adequate and correct application, to workforce practices, of Management Control Systems digitalization (Table 1).

The aim of this paper is to analyze, whether the latest approaches to Control Systems, whose diffusion has been facilitated by the increasing standardization of audit processes and by the progresses of digitalization linked to the IoT and to the Coso Framework, would produce opportunities and risks in their appliance to WP.

Table 1 Synopsis of principles to evidence risks in digitalization of management control systems

Name	Author	Definition	Performance index	Year
Span of control	Vjtautas Andrius Graiciunas	The number of subordinates that a chief can coordinate effectively	Effectiveness	1933
Level of incompetence	Laurence J. Peter	The most incompetence a person can achieve based on the complexity of the decisions they have to make	Adequacy	1969
Time span	Eliot Jaques	The period between two successive checks that the hierarchical superior carries out efficiently on the significant activity of a subordinate	Efficiency	1975

This analysis is set in a more general context, assessing whether, in the eclectic evolution of management [6] and despite the high expectations induced by digitalization (strongly supported by the marketing of companies operating with connected platforms) in can be considered wishful thinking [7].

2 The Evolution of Management Control Systems

Recently, criticism has emerged in management studies, preceded by the stream of critical studies [8] on the adequacy of theories and practices, which has become a widespread condition with respect to meeting expectations of entrepreneurs, managers and professionals [9].

This criticism emerged in parallel with the increasing efforts to differentiate and to enrich the methods and contents of management with a diffused eclecticism in the acquisition of knowledge and methodologies of other sciences and techniques.

An analysis, derived from previous works in Political Economy by Antonio Gramsci [10] and Federico Caffè [11], proposes a model in which the evolution of Managerial Thinking would be interpreted by linking eclecticism to wishful thinking.

In this regard, the term "Managerial Thinking" has been taken as the set of theories and practices developed in the field of management, traditionally characterized by multidisciplinarity and practical orientation [12].

The increase in the complexity of "Managerial Thinking" has been clearly expressed by the rise of Technological assets linked to information technology and digitalization, to the establishment of increasingly detailed and binding rules for organizational activities and to the differentiation in contributions coming to Management from other systems of knowledge such as engineering, neuroscience, psychology, sociology, and so on.

In recent times, this has resulted in an increasing differentiation regarding the objects of management and related decision-making processes. At the same time, it has induced an eclecticism of managerial response.

This orientation toward Eclecticism has been interpreted as a positive aspect both from the point of view of creativity and adaptability to different contexts, as opposed to specialization, since it has been observed that:

- excessive specialization may not be useful if problems are particularly complex;
- eclecticism is more motivating than a multidisciplinary approach as it allows the examination of perspectives other than the usual ones;
- specialization may limit the exchange of ideas and experiences.

On the other hand, eclecticism produces complexity and opens the door to risks in workforce management, as defined by the Graiciunas Span of Control, by the Peter's principle of incompetence, and by the Jaques Control Span, all of which are classic and analytical tools representing different kind of risk for WP.

Graiciunas, supported by his mentor Urwick, limited the number of subordinates to be controlled and defined as span of control, independently from accounting and managerial tools and linking the effectiveness to face to face relationships [13].

Peter's principle teaches us that as a person's level of competence increases, so does his level of incompetence which implies that, within a discrete number of career advancements, he becomes unable of adequately mastering all the information and problems he faces [14].

Peter's principle has been attributed mainly to distortions in recruitment and promotion and not, as we try to show, to the increasing multidisciplinary approach to management that managers are forced to apply in an attempt to deal with the complexity of the environment and increasingly complex tools.

Jacques introduces the concept of time into efficiency through the concept of control span, which is defined as the period between two successive checks on the significant activity on a subordinate, after which his hierarchical superior is certain that he is operating beyond his level of competence.

Based on these three traditional principles, we can also argue that the increasing eclecticism of the knowledge that the workforce must acquire within an organization leads to unrealistic and inappropriate choice. The combination of the phenomena of eclecticism and wishful thinking allows us to hypothesize an interpretative paradigm of concrete management development.

In the case of eclecticism, the wide range of terms, paradigms, theoretical and practical implications, strongly increased by the interdependencies linked to the connections of the systems, represents a real risk for the effectiveness, adequacy and efficiency of the managerial tools as it produces incompetence in their use and consequently increases the risk of wishful thinking in managerial decisions, negatively influencing the organizations.

The evolution of Management toward complexity is linked to increasing differentiation and contribution from other sciences and technical knowledge that produce a widespread eclecticism.

The main reason for this comes from the changing context with the repositioning of economic areas and the crisis in the manufacturing sector, particularly in Western countries, and the attempt of management to react to this trend and find new solutions.

A significant part of this reaction comes from professional auditors and their associations, who are concerned about the increased responsibilities and expanded role of auditors in corporate certification and the new takeover of ISO standards applied to Auditing and Managerial Control Systems.

3 The Role of ISO Standards

As a component of complexity, mention should be made of the establishment of many ISOs, which directly influence the Governance and Management of Organizations along with their control systems [15].

In particular, ISO Standards aim to:

- more efficient use of resources and improved financial performance,
- improve risk management and the protection of people and the environment,
- increase the ability to provide consistent and improved services and products, thereby increasing value for customers and all other stakeholders.

ISO standards applied to management system refer to performance improvement by specifying analytically repeatable steps that the organization must implement to achieve its objectives. In this process, employee awareness and management leadership are involved and the commitment must be supported by a corporate culture.

Although this explicit purpose, shared by most of the international Professional Community and Organizations such as the International Standard Organization, the nature of ISO prescriptions is a list of repetitive and, in some cases, redundant instructions and recommendations, such as those summarized for Internal Auditors according to UNI EN ISO 19011_2003 (Table 2).

At the same time, the demand for certification and assurance of compliance with its increasingly strict rules has increased.

Table 2 Recommendations from UNI EN ISO 19011_2003

• Being able to maintain control of the conversation • Be a good observer and able to listen (note answers, participate, visit) • Have no prejudices and personal opinions • Keep calm in nervous situations (calm, reassuring, balanced) • Have good judgment, analysis and synthesis (evaluate aptitudes, impulses, attitudes) • Have ease of communication (give trust and cooperation • Have the ability to communicate with the personnel involved in order to best achieve the purpose of the audit • Have sensitivity to the local conventions of the place • Do not fear being unpleasant or try to be pleasant • Do not have polemical or ironic attitudes • Be diplomatic but non-compliant, i.e., remaining adherent to the objective of the audit, without being diverted by distractions or delaying tactics • Having the ability to remain faithful to one's beliefs when subjected to pressure not based on adherence

Meanwhile, with globalization, standardization has led to a division of the market into two macro areas: the regulated and the unregulated one. In the unregulated area, not only criminal businesses operate, but a kind of opaque and hidden underworld of trade in which more tolerant or unwritten rules prevail.

All these dynamics increase the diversification and complexity of organizations' response to survive in an increasing challenging environment.

In this digitalization scenario, two main categories of tools have been conceived, each with its own main characteristics: IoT Internet of Things and CoSo Framework, both of which are involved in the workforces' practices.

The IoT is based on the sensing and subsequent processing of material data produced by sensors applied to organizational structures and processes. The CoSo Framework is an architecture of processes and operations that enables an integrated control system.

The aim of Iot and CoSo, almost in the intentions of their creators, is to improve the Adequacy of controls and, consequently, of the organizations in which they are applied.

4 Simplex and Complex: IoT and CoSo

"The "Internet of Things" refers to the coding and networking of everyday objects and things to render them individually machine-readable and traceable on the Internet" [16].

From a macro-structural point of view, IoT and Coso respond to two different logics within management control systems (Fig. 1). IoT responds to a hierarchical logic in which material data collected directly from biases and sensors are conveyed and processed. The CoSo framework, as a systematic protocol for verifying the adequacy of management, emphasizes the interaction between its levels and components in order to verify the multiple possibilities of risk that may occur.

Is evident that, despite the number of detection bias and points, the purpose of the IoT is to organize a manageable set of converging developments on

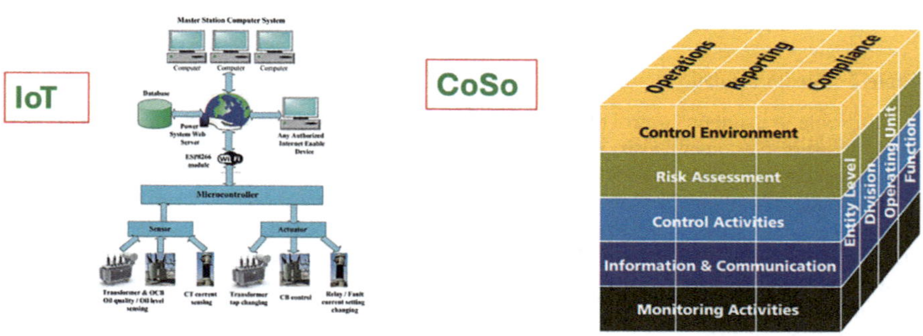

Fig. 1 IoT and Coso basic macrostructure [17, 18]

infrastructure, services, applications, and governance tools [19]. At the same time, the consideration of the third dimension, from Entity to Function Level, does not prevent the expression of risk combinations from reaching a considerable number of possibilities, as in the CoSo framework.

In a few words, the IoT focuses on technical devices accounting based on direct materials recording with the aim of simplifying and speeding up managerial control.

The IoT involves the use of detectors and biases for continuous data collection and analysis, which provide information on performances, workload allocations, and functional backups [20].

The CoSo Framework is a protocol to coordinate different processes and items in the Managerial Control System with the aim of ensuring their adequacy. In the CoSo, 17 principles and 5 components must be applied to ensure the adequacy of the control system and its ability to detect risks, without any gray areas [21].

Moreover CoSo is attributed to overcome "obstacles to continuous value delivery, but rip-and-replace efforts are costly, risky and time-consuming" while CoSo allows "using continuous modernization to minimize the cost, risk and impact of optimizing legacy applications" [22].

CoSo makes it possible to control recruitment, develop and retain competent people to achieve objectives. It saves human resources documentation related to recruitment, development, and retention. Meanwhile, it maintains the focus on individuals competence development [23].

Within these expectations, there is a gap with the actual benefits mentioned by the promoters [24].

This introduces the topic of the Adequacy, Efficiency and Effectiveness of WP digitalization as an interdependent system of performance indexes.

5 The Adequacy of WP Digitalization: Efficiency vs. Effectiveness

The stated key steps to introduce WP Digitalization are listed, from an IoT Promotional Material in Table 3.[1]

Also from the promotional material, in the manufacturing sector, "the digital application to workforce practices is promoted "to govern" end-to-end integrated product data, digital worker enablement and data-driven optimization of overall equipment effectiveness" (www.deel.com). Also, as it concerns the operational side most advantages are connected to the reduction of "Automate repetitive tasks such as onboarding and offboarding to save time and improve the employee experience" (www.deel.com).

To this end, always promotional materials, it is considered that IoT "helps new hires reach productivity faster, improves employee retention, and is particularly

[1] Freely derived from NOKIA Industry 4.0 www.nokia.com.

Table 3 Key steps of WP digitalization (www.deel.com)

STAGE 1: Digital connectivity and sensors
This stage is concerning the operation area and implies opportunities to improve productivity, quality and efficiency and better manage risk
STAGE 2: Digital engineering
Mainly focused on the growth through Industry 4.0 technologies to enhance product design and supply chains, develop smart products with intelligent automation
STAGE 3: Digital operations
The focus is on the increasing differentiation involving bioinformatics, nanotechnology and quantum technologies

important for remote employees or interns" (www.lumos.com/use-case). Furthermore, "it easily integrate with existing systems to support comprehensive, multichannel forecasting, aligning workforce deployment with actual demand" (www.ccmath.com).

Other expectations are cultivated in connection with Industry 4.0: Mass customization comes in here as well as a low-hanging opportunity. With the deployment of Industry 4.0 technologies, manufacturers can gain advantages by introducing degrees of product differentiation with high productivity and consistent quality.

For instance, is declared "Closed control loops enabled by sensor-based inline quality inspection and the flexible management of routing, scheduling, load balancing, and performance as well as the extension of automation to final assembly, contribute to this. High-volume production is a third area that deserves attention in its own right: fully automated production and maximization of overall equipment effectiveness with the flexibility to adapt to a given product mix" [25].

They criticize the detection of presence in the workplace as sensors to detect the departure from the workplace, the work timing, and the attention paid by the workforce to performance indicators. Other limitations concern the automatic transfer of this data to incentives or production bonuses.

Trade Unions may object to the violation of privacy and complain about the intrusion into the personal sphere of the employee. In any case the digitization conditions applied to the workforce should be regulated and shared at company level. The corporate code of ethics should also refer to these issues to avoid abuse or discrimination.

From another perspective, that of networking, the opportunities of CoSo Network's opportunities in workforce practices are extolled as a useful tool to "Sync Employee Profiles from HR to IT Role Based Access Control" [26] and "Easily search and filter your workforce by team, status, country, title, and more; see your organization in a snapshot and improve understanding between teams; manage compensation, titles, documents, with a change log for everything" [27].

All these expectations have to be compared with the recommendations provided to Managers and Auditors if not Employers, regarding the evaluation of the entrepreneurial decisions and the risk reduction. Moreover, the ISO rules declared their purposes to taking risks into control, preparing adequate prevention structures and prevention operations [28, 29].

In addition to these topics, there is a real concern about the preparation for the application of the IoT and the Coso Framework. To this regard, it is recommended an ad hoc education [30].

The application of the Graiciunas's Span of Control to the process structure also confirms that managers are unable to control a lot of data and its related indexes [31]. Moreover, the proliferation of indexes to measure the performance of subordinates would exceed the capability to evaluate it synthetically.

Peter, with his principle of incompetence, shows us that there is a limit in the adequacy of competencies, a limit that become prevalent as the number of problems to be addressed and the complexity of solutions [32].

Jaques derived from the empirical observation on management control systems, the definition of Time Span as the maximum time expired between two successive controls operated by the direct hierarchical superior, on the significant activity of the position [33]. According to this concept, the IoT would produce a flatting of the control span in small dimensions, while it implies, according to CoSo protocol, an excessive number of possible combinations, enabling any real control of risks.

Although the use of IoT and CoSo is not mandatory, meanwhile a professional training of auditors is requested to evaluate management control systems operating within these business technologies. The CoSo is particularly influential because it provides a framework against which risk management and internal control systems can be evaluated and its disapplication would increase the responsibilities of Auditors.

6 The Magic Ring

In both cases, the issue related to the Adequacy of the tools and their ability to fulfill the purposes they were designed and the due assessment, by Auditors, of the Adequate Organizational Structures to prevent risks in Management and to ensure that risks are identified and adequately controlled.

In this regard Adequacy, as a performance index, involves the concepts of Effectiveness and Efficiency which, as performance indexes (Fig. 2), are closely related to control time. It means that IoT and CoSo operate in real time, or, in any case, within a very tight span of control with the production of massive data.

The novelty lies in the fact that these concepts must operate not in an interaction of processes, no longer in competition, but as embedded, with feedback connected in a loop that Mella called Magic Ring [34].

This implies a dynamic process, involving almost all of these three performance indexes and related paradigms, concepts, and connections with Managerial Control Systems (Fig. 3) that produce in the Magic Ring, a process that is constantly evolving and with developments that are not completely predicted. The Magic Ring could also be considered the extreme product of eclecticism and a limit to the realism of Management Decisions [35].

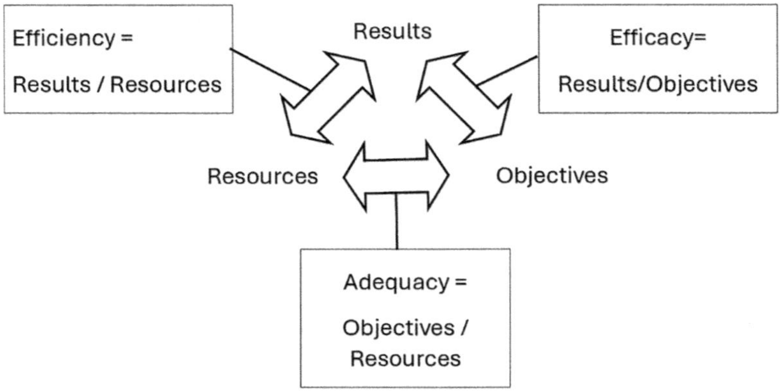

Fig. 2 The performance indexes system

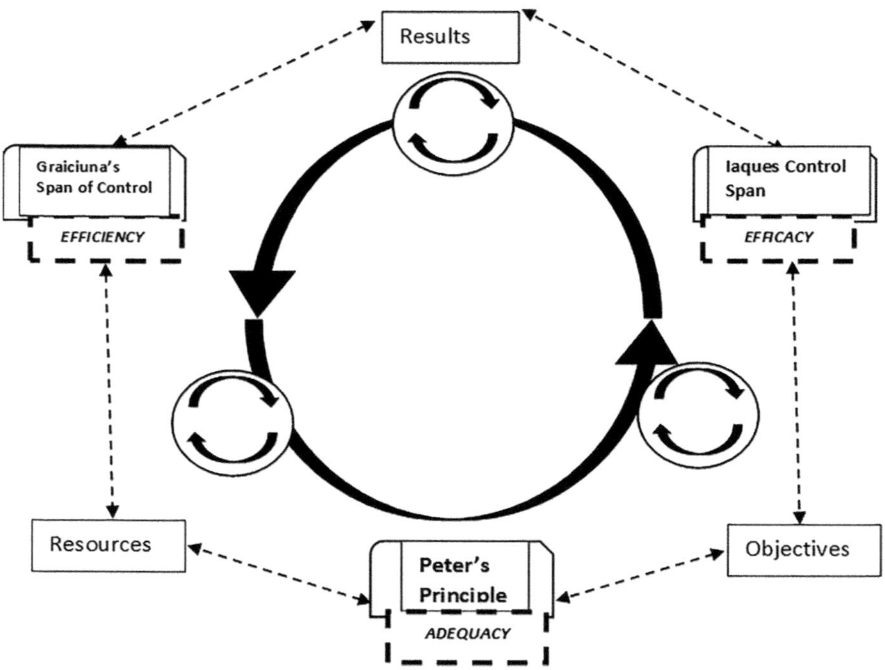

Fig. 3 The loop of risks control system with parameters (resources, objectives, results), performance indexes (effectiveness, efficiency, adequacy), and the guiding principles (Graiciunas, Jaques, Peter)

In particular, it is reasonable to think that a faster feedback period reduces the Effectiveness of consequential decisions, which are not fully supported by uncontrolled operators and numerous data.

From an empirical point of view, would it be possible that an early application of AI could have prevented the manufacturing crisis of recent times and, in more distant times, the financial crisis of 2007–2008? On the contrary, in the latter regard, the digitization of the stock exchange suffered the Flash Crash, a crisis caused by High Frequency Trading [36] resulting from the automatic feedback to market data [37], not controlled (by human operators), of stock transactions, which aggravated the situation [38].

Now, the dynamics highlighted by the Magic Ring could make the digitized market and business management even more unstable with the risk of wishful thinking in decision-making. In the latter regard, when these dynamics are referred to the workforce, all these assumptions become more relevant.

The manager who has to make decisions regarding the workforce, i.e., the human resources of the company, on the basis of the results of digitization and its synthesis, must avoid considering too many elements, exercising competence over too much knowledge, and deciding on a too narrow time span.

Another issue concerns the detection of the performance actuated instantly by IoT, which, in order to be meaningful, must be referred to a minimum time span and the choice of this time span, between two next periods on the significant activity of the position, is based on subjective elements and must be controlled to avoid frauds or inappropriate favoritism.

An adequate identification of the decision-making process raises significant questions regarding Adequacy and Ethics as:

- Privacy: Users may not be aware that the processing of their data also involves human beings, and this creates privacy issues, because sensitive information is not only handled by an algorithm.
- Accountability: Who is responsible for errors? Decisions resulting from errors are made by humans' beings or automatically. What are the limits of accountability?
- Compliance: A stricter regulation of AI has been established. Digitalization has led enterprises to face complex legal issues. Moreover, there is no evidence of compliance with established standards.

The application of AI to Workforce Management in its expressions such as IoT and CoSo presents high levels of complexity resulting from the evolution from eclecticism to the risk of making unrealistic decisions and due to the speed interaction of feedback from different elements of Management Control according to different perspectives of performances and related interactions.

7 Conclusions: The Dark Side of Overly Complex and Uneditable Records

Overly complex information and connected decision alternatives, when combined with the spread of blockchain in workforce management, reduce the opportunity for interaction between individuals and collaborative creativity.

This leads to the dark side of B2B relationships [39], extendable to interpersonal relationships when applied to workforce management and including negative effects of conflict, uncertainty, tension, and opportunism.

On the other hand, blockchain technology has not solved the problem, and the transparent recording of transactions weakens the use of trust-based relationship building [40].

Once again, eclecticism and wishful thinking are coupled in producing risks for the digitalization of workforce practices, confirming their connection in the evolution of Management thinking [41].

References

1. Read, D.: Philosophies of Organizational Change. Edward Elgar, Cheltenham (2020). https://doi.org/10.4337/9781788971966.00010
2. Russ, M.: Introduction and a holistic framework for human capital. In: Russ, M. (ed.) Quantitative Multidisciplinary Approaches in Human Capital and Asset Management, Business Science Reference. IGI Global, Hershey (2016)
3. Graiciunas, V.A.: Relationship in organization. In: Gulick, L., Urwick, L. (eds.) Papers on the Science Administration. Institute of Public Administration, New York (1937)
4. Farias, B., Rapôso, O., Penna, T.J.P., Girardi, D.: The Peter principle and learning: a safer way to promote workers. Phys. A Stat. Mech. Appl. **576**(C), 126023 (2021)
5. Jaques, E.: Time-Span Handbook. Cason Hall & Co. Publishers, Gloucester (1964)
6. Bianchi, M.: Network analysis and control system in mega projects. The case of PICASP erasmus project. In: Frenkel, D.A. (ed.) Comprehensive Anthology of Law—Ethics—Business, pp. 19–37. Athens Institute for Education and Research (2024)
7. Bianchi, M.: Deindustrialization and management sciences in italy. The shadow of velleitarism. In: 2024 Conference for the 11th Annual International Conference on Business, Law & Economics. Athens J. Law. 10(3). https://doi.org/10.30958/ajl_v10i30
8. Alvesson, M., Willmott, H.: Critical Management Studies. SAGE Publications, Thousand Oaks, CA (2011)
9. Mintzberg, H., Laasch, O.: Mintzberg on (ir)responsible management. In: The Research Handbook of Responsible Management. Edward Elgar, Cheltenham (2019). https://doi.org/10.4337/9781788971966.00010
10. D'Anna, G.: La 'scoperta' di Antonio Gramsci Le Lettere e i Quaderni del carcere nel dibattito italiano 1944–1952. Italia Contemporanea. **211**, 2 (1998)
11. Poettinger, M.: Velleitarismo: il giudizio storico di Federico Caffè sul secondo dopoguerra, RiSES Ricerche di Storia Economica e Sociale. J. Econ. Soc. Hist, Roma anno II, 2016 - fasc. 1-2 gennaio/dicembre, pp. 157–181 (2021)
12. March, J.C., Simon, H.A.: Organizations, p. 262. John Wiley & Sons, New York (1958)
13. Van Fleet, D.D., Bedeian, A.G.: A history of the span of management. Acad. Manag. Rev. **2**(3), 356 (1977)

14. Lazear, E.: The Peter Principle: a theory of decline. J. Polit. Econ. 112(S1), (2004). Papers in Honor of Sherwin Rosen: a supplement to volume 112, pp. S141–S163 (2004)
15. ISO/IEC 38500:2024: Information technology—governance of IT for the organization (2024)
16. Madakam, S., Ramaswamy, R., Tripathi, S.: Internet of things (IoT): a literature review. J. Comput. Commun. **3**(3), 164–173. Scientific Research, ISSN Print: 2327-5219 (2024)
17. www.IoT Free Images (2022)
18. Pastorino, S.: Il sistema di controllo interno. L'applicazione dei princìpi del CoSO2013-Introduzione al CoSO Report 2013, SCI, PWP (2023)
19. Van Kranenburg, R., Bassi, A.: IoT challenges. mUX J. Mob. User Exp. **1**, 9 (2012). https://doi.org/10.1186/2192-1121-1-9
20. Kumar, M.S., Prasanna, P.L., Lalitha, M., Joy, M., Jha, S.S., Pandey, B.K.: Utilizing the internet of everything and artificial intelligence for real-time workforce management. In: Role of Internet of Everything (IOE), VLSI Architecture and AI Real-Time Systems. IGI Global, Hershey (2025). https://doi.org/10.4018/979-8-3693-7367-5.ch011
21. McNally, S.J.: The 2013 COSO framework & SOX compliance. Strat. Financ. 5 (2013)
22. Van Der Zijden, S., Wan, D.D.K., Dodd, H.: The Gartner Report: Use Continuous Modernization to Optimize Legacy Applications. OutSystems, London (2024)
23. Riyadi, A., Yennisa, I., Sagita, L.: COSO's conceptual framework to internal control management risk in higher education management, ICED-QA 2019, September 11, Padang, Indonesia EAI. https://doi.org/10.4108/eai.11-9-2019.2298436 (2021)
24. Fotoh, L.E., Lorentzon, J.I.: Audit digitalization and its consequences on the audit expectation gap: a critical perspective. Account. Horizons. **37**, 43–69 (2023). https://doi.org/10.2308/HORIZONS-2021-027
25. NOKIA Industry 4.0: www.nokia.com (2025)
26. www.robomq.io
27. www.dell.com
28. Flückiger, I., Carbone, M.: From Risk Transfer to Risk Prevention. The Geneva Association, Zurich (2021)
29. Choo, D., Gai, K., Chiaraviglio, L., Yang, Q.: A multidisciplinary approach to Internet of Things (IoT) cybersecurity and risk management. Comput. Secur. **102**, 102136 (2021)
30. Christie, H., Clinton, F.: Hybridized professional groups and institutional work: COSO and the rise of enterprise risk management. SSRN Electron. J. (2014). https://doi.org/10.2139/ssrn.2379548.ISO/IEC38500:2024
31. Bianchi, M.: Perspectives for the extension of Graiciunas' principle to the process of control in public networks. In: 3rd International Symposium on the Development of Public Administration in South East (SE) Europe (Ljubljana) Proceedings, pp. 14, par. 5644 ch. 36823. ISBN 978-961-262-018-9 CD (2009)
32. Peter, L.J.: The Peter Principle: Why Things Always Go Wrong. William Morrow, New York (1969)
33. Jaques, E.: A General Theory of Bureaucracy. Heinemann Educational Books, London (1976)
34. Mella, P.: The Magic Ring. Springer, New York., ISSN 1568-2846 (2014)
35. Bianchi, M.: Il contributo di Piero Mella all'eclettismo degli studi di Economia Aziendale. Economia Aziendale. 15(2), (2024). https://doi.org/10.13132/2038-5498/15.2.241-259
36. Akansu, A.N.: The flash crash: a review. J. Cap. Mark. Stud. **1**(1), 89–100 (2017). https://doi.org/10.1108/JCMS-10-2017-001
37. Gennai, A.: 2012 Algoritmi e risparmio: come i software condizionano i prezzi, Il Sole 24 Ore, p. 6 (2012)
38. French, K., Roll, R.: Stock return variances: the arrival of information and the reaction of traders. J. Financ. Econ. **17**(1), 5–26 (1986)
39. Anderson, E., Jap, S.: The dark side of close relationships. MIT Sloan Manag. Rev. **46**(3) (2005)

40. Risius, M., Spohrer, K.: A blockchain research framework. Bus. Inf. Syst. Eng. **59**(6), 385–409 (2017)
41. Kuratko, D.F., Covin, J.G.: Fifty years of entrepreneurship: recalling the past, examining the present, & foreshadowing the future. J. Bus. Res. **186**, 114980 (2025)

Applicability of Artificial Intelligence in Human Capital Management

María del Valle Fernández Moreno, David Ballesteros Ruiz, and Marta Tolentino

Abstract This study explores the transformative impact of Artificial Intelligence (AI) on Human Resources Management (HRM) within the context of digital transformation and the Fourth Industrial Revolution. It examines how AI is reshaping traditional HR functions—such as talent acquisition, performance evaluation, and employee development—while introducing new strategic opportunities and ethical challenges. Drawing on theoretical frameworks including role theory, task substitution, and the resource-based view, the paper highlights the evolving competencies required of HR professionals in an increasingly digitalized environment. It also addresses the risks associated with AI implementation, such as algorithmic bias, surveillance, and the erosion of human-centric values in the workplace. Through case studies of companies like IBM, Uber, Glovo, and Ferrovial, the research illustrates practical applications of AI in HR and underscores the importance of balancing technological innovation with the protection of labor rights and human dignity. The findings suggest that while AI can significantly enhance efficiency and employee experience, its deployment must be guided by ethical governance and human oversight to ensure equitable and sustainable outcomes.

Keywords First keyword · Second keyword · Third keyword

1 Introduction

Artificial Intelligence has profoundly impacted the global socioeconomic landscape, driving a deep transformation in the functioning and dynamics of societies and businesses alike [1]. Indeed, new technologies, alongside phenomena such as globalization, have ushered in a new era—the era of digitalization—where

M. del Valle Fernández Moreno · D. Ballesteros Ruiz · M. Tolentino (✉)
University of Castilla–La Mancha, Ciudad Real, Spain
e-mail: mariavalle.fdez@uclm.es; David.ballesteros@uclm.es; marta.tolentino@uclm.es

N. Omrani et al. (eds.), *Human-Machine Synergy and the Digital Future - Exploring Collaboration and Competition Volume 1*, Springer Proceedings in Business and Economics, https://doi.org/10.1007/978-3-032-21347-1_8

industries, labor market dynamics, productivity, decision-making processes, and the delivery of services to citizens have been fundamentally revolutionized.

The business organization, as an entity that concentrates part of the decision-making capacity held by individuals and serves as a determining factor within the social system [2], along with its strategies and future visions, appears to be central to understanding the growing prominence of Artificial Intelligence in discourses on modernity and societal evolution. For this reason, our study will focus on business dynamics and structures, while maintaining broader premises—namely, that companies act as agents of social change and as drivers of the transformations currently shaping our society.

In light of the above, explaining what has changed—and what may yet change—within organizations is essential to understanding this new digital era, or Industry 4.0 [3], a transformation characterized by its multifaceted nature. Accordingly, we will direct our attention to a specific domain where Artificial Intelligence can be applied: human relations within and around the company. We will intentionally distinguish between Human Resources (HR) and Labor Relations within the organization, without neglecting a strategic business perspective on the use of AI.

Remaining within the promise of Artificial Intelligence [4] in the management and development of Human Resources, we aim to demonstrate its applicability across a wide range of HR functions. Our analysis will address aspects related to the current need to attract and retain talent, and the opportunities AI offers to achieve this through enhanced motivational and communicative strategies that foster new HR management models focused on employee experience. Clearly, the promise of AI does not end there; we will also explore theoretical frameworks that provide guidance for what is—and is becoming—a new model of Human Resources supported by cognitive technologies and a certain degree of corporate ethics.

This analysis must necessarily be conducted within the new conditions of labor relations that have emerged following the advent of Artificial Intelligence, highlighting the threat posed by this technology to a legal framework that has been outpaced by modernity and is currently evolving, thereby influencing certain business strategies. In this regard, we will examine the potential risks—and realities—that digitalization may entail within the workplace, both for emerging jobs and for traditional roles that are now subject to new, and potentially harsher, forms of labor exploitation than those seen in previous Fordist models.

Finally, we will devote a significant portion of this work to a practical section that illustrates how Artificial Intelligence is being applied in the business world for various strategic purposes. We will begin by analyzing this new reality in general terms, focusing on specific cases that exemplify developments related to our theoretical study. Subsequently, we will concentrate on the strategic approach adopted by a technology company, IBM, demonstrating how it leverages AI to establish a competitive advantage in the field of Human Resources.

2 Background and Conceptual Framework

The Human Resources function has undergone a significant transition from a purely administrative and transactional activity to a strategic position within organizations, gaining influence through the implementation of talent management practices, organizational development, and corporate culture design [5]. The emergence of Artificial Intelligence (AI) on the global stage has not only substantially altered socioeconomic dynamics [1], but also compels HR professionals to redefine their roles, competencies, and capabilities. In recent years, driven by digitalization, automation, and AI, a revolution in the workplace has taken place, radically transforming business models and the configuration of workforces [6].

The shift toward flexible, remote, and digital work models has forced HR departments to adopt emerging technologies in order to remain relevant and deliver organizational value [7]. In this context, AI emerges as a highly significant tool for fostering innovation, managing human capital, and redefining its role as a key intangible asset in achieving competitive advantage [8]. From a strategic business perspective, AI is not only a process optimization tool but also enables the development of highly personalized and adaptive value propositions [9] that can be directly applied to organizational personnel. Once integrated, this technology directly influences decision-making, operational efficiency, and the design of business models in which knowledge and information play a central role in wealth generation [10].

Focusing on HR management strategy, two fundamental theories can be identified to understand the evolution of HR's role in relation to the disruption caused by artificial intelligence [11]: role theory and task substitution theory. Brummette and Zoch [12] posits that each job position entails a set of expectations, behaviors, norms, and competencies anticipated by other stakeholders. In the HR context, this allows for an analysis of how emerging technologies are reshaping expectations and demands placed on HR professionals. The latter, task substitution theory [13], suggests that AI can gradually replace human tasks, beginning with those requiring lower levels of intelligence—mechanical and analytical activities—and progressively advancing toward tasks involving intuitive and empathetic capabilities. From this perspective, it becomes urgent for HR professionals to strengthen their human-centric competencies to maintain relevance and leadership in highly technologized environments.

In line with the above, based on an exhaustive analysis, Fitong Ketchiwou et al. [11] propose a competency framework structured around four major dimensions that will be essential for the future of HR in the current context of continuous change and exponential technological advancement. These four core competencies are as follows:

- Intrapersonal and Interpersonal Competencies: These include skills such as critical thinking, emotional intelligence, leadership, resilience, creativity, communication, teamwork, and empathy in managing interpersonal relationships. These competencies will be crucial in the current context, where Artificial Intelligence is still unable to replicate them effectively. As such, they provide organizations

with an intangible value embedded in human capital—one that is difficult to imitate and upon which a significant portion of HR strategy can be built.
- Technological and information competencies: These encompass digital literacy, the ability to use and integrate technologies, data analytics, knowledge of algorithm design, and the management of legal and ethical risks in digital environments. These skills enable HR professionals to function as an interface between people and machines, thereby helping to mitigate the potential risks that artificial intelligence may still pose when performing certain tasks and managing workforce operations.
- Competencies for Developing Human Capabilities: These refer to skills related to strategic talent planning, unemployment management, organizational culture, workplace well-being, diversity and inclusion, and continuous learning. In this way, HR professionals are expected to act as facilitators of human development in automated environments, where motivation also becomes a strategic factor for retaining human capital.
- Business value competencies: These include skills such as business knowledge, financial literacy, the ability to lead change, driving innovation, and generating sustainable impact. At a global level, these competencies can be significantly enhanced by Artificial Intelligence, which serves as a powerful enabler. Within the HR domain, they are equally critical for aligning human capital strategies with the broader strategic objectives of the organization.

In addition to the above, two other relevant theories applied to Artificial Intelligence in Human Resources have been proposed by İyem and Erer [14] and Ullah et al. [15]: human capital theory and the resource-based approach. Regarding the former, these authors concur in viewing human talent as a strategic asset for organizations, wherein AI becomes a significant tool for enhancing that human capital through improved identification, evaluation, and development of talent. As for the resource-based approach, Ullah et al. [15] argue that AI can help build distinctive capabilities that enable the acquisition of valuable, rare, inimitable, and non-substitutable resources, thereby providing firms with a sustainable competitive advantage.

Within the new digital environment in which the human resources function must operate, there already exists a broad body of studies offering an integrative and qualitative perspective that reveals a series of dynamics, the most prominent of which is the impact of AI on human resources. Authors Sakka et al. [16] and Schultz [17] agree that digital transformation has altered the nature of work and driven the adoption of technological tools across all HR functions—from automated recruitment to employee experience management through algorithmic platforms. Moreover, this transformation is not limited to task automation via AI; as noted by Huang and Rust [13], it also entails a qualitative shift in how data is analyzed, decisions are made, and people are managed. However, to navigate this shift effectively, it is essential to understand the capabilities and limitations of AI, as well as its legal, ethical, and cultural implications.

It is evident that, in light of the aforementioned context, human resources must pay close attention to competency management. On one hand, it is essential to promote new competencies, as emphasized by Conceição et al. [18] and Shet and Nair [19], who highlight the importance of digital literacy, data handling, applied artificial intelligence, basic programming, and the ability to strategically integrate technologies. Indeed, beyond their practical relevance, these competencies—alongside predictive analytics and the use of HR Tech—are becoming indispensable for HR teams. Accordingly, it is necessary to anticipate the emergence of new competency models, within which, following the contributions of [5], five key roles are defined for future HR professionals: business accelerators, human capability enablers, complexity simplifiers, information mobilizers, and collaboration facilitators. This model is widely referenced by Veldsman and Coetzee [20], who propose grouping competencies into four dimensions: intra- and interpersonal, digital, business-related, and human-value-oriented.

Nevertheless, it is also essential to acknowledge the importance of protecting and preserving irreplaceable human competencies, as these may prove to be a decisive factor in the success of an HR strategy. In this regard, Popo-Olaniyan et al. [21] and Minbaeva [22] emphasize that, in the face of the automation of repetitive tasks, human competencies—such as empathy, collaboration, emotional leadership, social intelligence, and creativity—assume a more strategic role.

Alongside competency management, the specialized literature also highlights the importance of change leadership and organizational culture. The transition toward digitalized work environments requires HR to act as the driving force of change within organizations, promoting adaptive, inclusive, and continuously learning organizational cultures [23, 24]. Consequently, fostering a culture that encourages collaboration between human beings and emerging technologies will be essential for sustaining talent engagement.

Artificial Intelligence, in relation to human resource management and human capital competencies, will also generate new dynamics in professional training and practice. In this regard, the literature identifies several lines of inquiry that underscore the urgent need to redesign HR vocational training curricula and incorporate complementary technological and human skills. These studies also highlight the key role of organizations in facilitating reskilling and upskilling processes to ensure a workforce prepared to navigate increasingly complex and dynamic environments. Accordingly, İyem and Erer [14] emphasize the importance of training and the active involvement of HR in technological integration, which becomes essential as the emergence of new technologies demands digital competencies that must often be cultivated within the enterprise, aligned with its own research and innovation strategies.

There are already studies that demonstrate specific applications of Artificial Intelligence in human resources. In particular, Ullah et al. [15] identify intensive use of AI in processes such as recruitment, performance evaluation, and succession planning through predictive algorithms, chatbots, CV-screening systems, etc. Similarly, İyem and Erer [14] examine the applicability of this new technology not only in recruitment but also in analyzing organizational climate sentiment and developing adaptive learning platforms, while also highlighting existing barriers to change that HR professionals will need to overcome.

In any case, beyond the theoretical framework and literature review presented, it is essential to examine the impact that new technologies may have on labor relations in the context of AI implementation in HR. In this regard, Murillo [8] and Sagaya and Momin [24] address the need for algorithmic ethics in HR management, stressing the importance of reliability, transparency, and non-discrimination in AI systems. Terrazas [25] emphasizes the risk of algorithmic bias inherited from human data, while Ginés [26] warns of the dangers of workplace privacy intrusion through predictive technologies. In line with these concerns, İyem and Erer [14] and Ullah et al. [15] advocate ethics and governance of AI based on core principles such as equity, transparency, explainability, privacy, and human role overseeing automated decision-making.

3 The Emergence and Applicability of Artificial Intelligence in Human Resources

In view of the various global considerations surrounding the emergence of artificial intelligence within the new digital socioeconomic order, this section focuses on a specific organizational domain in which this new technology may become particularly salient: the management of human resources within the enterprise.

In this regard, the primary objective that any organization must pursue remains the attainment of the collective common good. However, given that human resources constitute a specific department, its leadership does not hold exclusive responsibility for achieving overall organizational success. Rather, it contributes to this objective by ensuring the success of its own domain with the highest possible levels of efficiency and productivity—especially considering that human capital is the element that generates the greatest value within an organization. Consequently, artificial intelligence presents HR executives with a significant opportunity—and, as will be discussed, in some cases, a duty—to advance the global common good within the organization, benefiting both the enterprise and its workforce. Can the organization and management of human resources be transformed through AI? This is the question we aim to explore in the following pages.

3.1 Shifts in Human Resources Management: The Need for a Modern Orientation Toward the Employee Experience

The application of artificial intelligence within organizations is most intensely manifested in the management and development of employees' work—namely, in business production—fostering new forms of work organization that some scholars have described as a form of "digital neo-Taylorism" [27]. Indeed, the opportunities offered by new technologies in terms of value creation and productivity enhancement enable services to be delivered more swiftly, cost-effectively, and efficiently in order to outperform competitors. This is achieved, among other factors, through the complementarity of AI with human labor, which facilitates greater efficiency. However, such developments may also produce adverse effects within the workforce itself, and consequently, on its performance. Sociologists Murillo [8] warn that the use of AI may lead to a growing disconnect between employees and management, resulting in a diminished sense of belonging to the organization.

This is particularly relevant given that the competitive model in the new digital economy cannot be sustained solely through cost reduction via continuous employment adjustment. On the contrary, the emergence of new job roles—or those yet to be created—demands a set of digital competencies that many individuals currently lack. As del Prado [28] noted, at least ten million working-age individuals in Spain alone would require upskilling to qualify for future employment opportunities. More recently, Rocha [29] highlighted a paradoxical imbalance in this area: there are both shortages in the supply and demand of digital skills. Companies need qualified personnel, while skilled individuals remain unemployed due to a low level of innovation within the Spanish business sector. Furthermore, considering the need to implement innovation policies and AI strategies tailored to the specific competitive environment of each company, it becomes increasingly difficult to find individuals in the labor market with the requisite skills. More commonly, companies encounter candidates with generic digital competencies acquired through formal education, who must then undergo additional training to meet the specific qualifications required.

It is therefore essential to retain the human capital best suited to the company's needs. This task is complicated by the fact that, as Sennett [30] warns, new technologies may hinder internal communication and knowledge transfer. This is due to the disintermediation effect of AI, which distances the various layers of the organizational hierarchy [8]. The threat is significant, as internal communication is, according to García [31], "a manageable resource for achieving corporate, cultural, organizational, functional, strategic, and behavioral objectives," and is "not an end in itself, but an indispensable tool for developing new competencies." Thus, communication not only supports the effective execution of current business activities but also constitutes a key asset in modern and innovative organizational management—particularly in a context that demands agile, flexible organizations over bureaucratic structures. What is of particular interest here is the notion that internal communication represents "the new psychological contract that today binds individuals to organizations" [31].

Accordingly, the goal should be to foster a sense of belonging among employees to retain talent—without neglecting the essential objective of enhancing productivity and performance. Achieving this requires not only an effective communication strategy but also the creation of a suitable work environment capable of motivating individuals and promoting their integration into the organization. From our perspective, the key lies in recognizing the interdependent relationship between motivation and a sense of belonging [32]—a relationship that may be disrupted by obstacles such as poor communication, which can lead to frustration, individualism, or feelings of isolation within the company. Motivation, therefore, becomes a driver not only of talent retention but also of increased productivity and profitability.

Taking these factors into account in personnel management during the era of artificial intelligence may prove to be a decisive element in shaping a company's competitiveness. Organizational internal factors exert a strong influence on strategic outcomes and help explain the disparity in competitive positioning among organizations operating within the same environment [33]. Thus, despite the cognitive capabilities of current technologies, we maintain that human capital remains the key intangible asset in competitive strategy and the primary contributor to the value a company delivers. For this reason, it is essential to consider the various motivational factors that can be leveraged within the organization to foster employee well-being, promote a sense of belonging, reduce turnover, and, where possible, enhance productivity and profitability.

It is worth highlighting a paradox regarding the use of artificial intelligence within the context we are addressing: while it may generate a disintermediation effect between management and employees, it simultaneously presents an opportunity to establish a new model of human resources management—one grounded in communication and motivation. Just as AI has been recognized for its potential to add value to products and services that enhance customer satisfaction, we may also inquire into the possibility of building an internal organizational structure centered on the employee experience.

The concept of customer experience demonstrates that individuals are drawn to and appreciate personalized products and services tailored to their specific needs. However, despite also dealing with people, as Adams [34] points out, "when we enter the workplace, that personalization ends. Employment contracts, induction programs, performance and talent management, leadership competency models, training programs, reward frameworks: standardized, universally applied, one-size-fits-all." In other words, the individual needs of each employee are often overlooked, even as organizations obsessively seek to understand the specific desires of external stakeholders.

Cuatrecasas & Instituto Legal de RRHH [35] emphasizes the value of creating a new corporate culture that attracts talent and retains highly engaged employees through a strategy that places the employee experience at the core of HR management. Indeed, the objective is to identify the motivational drivers of each employee with the support of artificial intelligence, thereby overcoming traditional barriers to achieving comprehensive workplace motivation. In this regard, tasks traditionally assigned to HR departments for implementing motivational plans may be replaced by algorithmic processes capable of continuously and precisely identifying employees' concerns. Moreover, the goal is not merely to motivate, but to leverage new technologies—such as digital assistants—to understand employees, segment them, and support their professional development within the organization. This long-term approach appears to yield greater benefits than a narrow focus on productivity and performance alone.

Nevertheless, it is essential for organizations to adopt a communication strategy that conveys a clear, transparent, and trustworthy human-centered narrative. Such a strategy is necessary to articulate the change and its constructive potential for the future. Admittedly, this may entail the need for certain employees to reskill or upskill, which underscores the importance of effective communication to reassure workers that the organization is committed to their well-being. Beyond this, communication will be key to initiating coordinated and collaborative strategies between the organization and employees—particularly as the use of AI by employees increasingly occurs independently of managerial oversight. According to Cunha et al. [36], employees often adopt AI tools outside the scope of corporate strategies, with 78% reportedly using technologies not provided by their organizations with significant risks to alignment and adaptability.

Despite these challenges, the promise of artificial intelligence in human resources lies not only in its potential to enhance the employee experience but also in its strategic applicability to improve efficiency and optimize HR practices.

3.2 A New Development in Human Resources: Efficiency, Speed, and Artificial Intelligence

Over time, the omnipresence of AI within the organizational landscape has become so pronounced that it is not an overstatement to claim that one of the most significant forces shaping human resources today is the growing phenomenon of AI—alongside other technologies driving the digitalization of the economy. It is important to emphasize the cognitive—or "thinking"—nature of AI, a capability that allows this technology not only to perform routine and repetitive tasks but also to undertake more complex, highly qualified functions. While AI can serve as a substitute for human labor, its greatest potential—and promise—lies in its complementarity: enhancing workers' performance by increasing efficiency and speed, ultimately benefiting both the organization and the employee. This mutual benefit creates a shared interest in integrating AI into the workplace.

In this regard, the application of AI in human resources development is particularly compelling, as the technology can encompass nearly all activities related to the employment relationship—recruitment, selection, hiring, onboarding, task distribution, compensation and promotion, training… [8]. AI can streamline routine processes and support decision-making that would otherwise be delayed due to the human limitations in processing and analyzing large volumes of relevant data.

According to Business Insider [37], the trend indicates that AI is "increasingly gaining ground in the human resources departments of more traditional companies," in a context where 40% of large international firms have already adopted AI tools to complement human labor. However, many companies have yet to implement AI, particularly in HR, due to several barriers that hinder the evolution of HR departments [35]. Historically, the primary barrier has been the investment of time and financial resources required for such a transformative shift—an investment that often clashes with the short-termism prevalent in many organizations. Additional obstacles include a lack of commitment from both executives and employees, driven by resistance to change, limited future vision, poor understanding of technological transformation, or a lack of leadership skills necessary to guide the organization into a new technological era. Another significant challenge is the shortage of professionals with the skills needed to manage and adapt to change—particularly among women. Political and legal environments may also restrict the free development of AI, especially given its potential implications for individual and collective labor rights. Finally, the imperative to adopt a tailored innovation strategy highlights the asymmetries between regions and sectors, making it difficult for some organizations to keep pace with competitors, especially when focusing on internal management.

Overcoming these barriers presents a major opportunity for companies to manage their human resources more efficiently, particularly through more objective, data-driven decision-making processes that reduce the risks associated with personal discretion. Specifically, scholars Murillo [8] argue that algorithmic management "will improve decision-making, process coordination, and the identification of patterns that enable organizational self-learning," as well as "provide direction for work, automate performance evaluation, and anonymize disciplinary and reward mechanisms." The monitoring and control capabilities of AI can also track productivity and, through people analytics, assess employees' emotional states to inform decisions aimed at enhancing motivation and satisfaction. Furthermore, AI can support compliance with certain legal obligations, such as occupational risk prevention practices, which must be carried out continuously and dynamically—both at the general workplace level and for individual roles—by analyzing and mitigating risks in a personalized manner.

That said, it is crucial to acknowledge the risks of using AI as an autonomous decision-making agent, particularly in operations that directly affect a person's employability. Despite technological advancements, AI is not infallible and may produce outcomes that deviate significantly from expected behavior—a phenomenon known as "hallucination." In such cases, AI may introduce irrationality into HR management, making decisions that are detrimental to the organization. Therefore, human oversight must always be present to supervise the information and actions generated by AI systems.

4 The Impact of Digitalization of the Development of Labor Relations

Beyond the specific theories of organizational and human resources management, it is necessary to consider the broader socio-political dimension of labor relations. Without generalizing about deviant corporate behavior, it would be naïve to assume a utopian adherence to ethical principles in the use of artificial intelligence by organizations. Ultimately, labor relations are legitimately constituted through asymmetrical power structures and divergent—often conflicting—interests, despite the shared goal of preserving both employment and business continuity. The collective good of a company is not merely to achieve positive outcomes, but to maximize those outcomes, which may, in turn, generate tensions and conflicts between the parties involved. In this context, AI may become a tool through which organizations pursue greater profitability, potentially at the expense of the workforce.

The collective objective of a company is not merely to achieve positive outcomes, but to maximize those outcomes to their fullest potential. This pursuit of optimal results may, however, lead to conflicting interests and, at times, to disputes between the parties involved. Consequently, within the framework of corporate governance, organizations may find in artificial intelligence a mechanism that, while enhancing profitability, does so through means that may be detrimental to the working class.

Numerous studies and debates have addressed the quantitative risks that digitalization poses to existing jobs. These discussions reveal a complex and uncertain landscape, often yielding contradictory conclusions, with one clear consensus: work and its organization have undergone a radical transformation due to technological implementation. Therefore, it is more insightful to examine the qualitative effects of AI on labor relations. While the employment relationship is traditionally characterized by a contractual bond between hierarchically subordinate positions, the legitimate power of the advantaged party is bounded by a set of rights and guarantees designed to balance labor relations without eliminating managerial authority. These boundaries, however, are increasingly blurred in the context of digital transformation.

This dichotomy gives rise to divergent perspectives on the appropriateness of AI use, as outlined by the Economic and Social Council [38]: "On one side, the overly enthusiastic group bases its hypotheses primarily on idealistic assumptions. Digitalization enjoys widespread acceptance because it offers universal benefits, enables a circular economy with reduced waste, better utilization of underused assets (...), unprecedented opportunities for improved information, communication, connectivity, and transparency (...), easier work-life balance, and a new world of exchange and collaboration (...). The more skeptical group predicts a future marked by massive job losses, 24/7 availability, deteriorating working conditions, blurred boundaries between private and professional life, increased surveillance and control, job polarization (...), greater wealth inequality, and a new era of machines competing with a global labor pool."

Given the mythology surrounding AI, its applicability in personnel management remains questionable. Although workers may accept the use of new technologies, the conditions and purposes of their implementation are often unclear. For this reason, technological complementarity with human labor may, rather than support the organization and its workforce, generate conflict—particularly when perceived as a tool that reinforces the employer's unilateral power. This unilateralism manifests in the ability of companies to reduce or eliminate certain labor rights and guarantees within a new context of legal and social uncertainty, where the boundaries of managerial authority appear increasingly flexible or expansive.

The overcoming of the traditional legal labor model is evident in the rise of freelance workers operating through digital platforms under a supposed autonomy. These emerging forms of employment provoke debate over the appropriate regulatory framework and the guarantees that should apply. In the absence of clear answers, the prevailing approach seems to be the classification of such workers as self-employed or service providers under conditions of goodwill and neighborliness [39]. Following the implementation of algorithmic management, core features of employment such as subordination—and even others like alienation—become obscured within a confusing context.

Moreover, the potential for labor precarization in the digital transition extends to conventional jobs now subject to algorithmic organization. In these cases, the automation of personnel decisions leads to a dehumanization of workers, as algorithms—lacking empathy and consideration for personal circumstances—operate solely based on mathematical design and programmed self-learning [40]. This partly explains the emergence of discriminatory practices, but the consequences extend further, exacerbating the negative effects of the Fordist model [8].

One of the most concerning consequences of Artificial Intelligence implementation lies in the increased control it affords employers over the employment relationship—an influence that manifests across various domains. The most futuristic, and arguably most intrusive, aspect is the enhanced surveillance capacity enabled by techniques such as people analytics, which render traditional tools like video surveillance—already problematic in terms of privacy rights—virtually obsolete. As Ginés [26] explains, AI has enabled organizations to access "information about individuals that was previously inaccessible; information concerning not only their professional activity but also their private lives, rendering them virtually transparent." This situation is further exacerbated by the predictive capabilities of AI models, which "create a veritable voyeuristic window for the employer by predicting even more personal information." Organizations are thus increasingly encroaching upon personal privacy, seeking not only to identify behavioral patterns but also to infer sensitive data such as political ideology, sexual or gender identity, emotional state, and health status.

Moreover, the intensification of control and surveillance extends to the domain of work performance, where productivity and output are closely monitored—often in connection with disciplinary mechanisms. This dynamic leads to a disproportionate increase in workload, heightening the risk of physical injuries, accidents, and psychosocial hazards. Meanwhile, organizations gain greater flexibility in aligning working time with business needs, often at the expense of employees' personal needs. As a result, the potential benefits of AI as a complementary tool to human labor are diminished, leaving only the employer to profit from increased productivity and relative performance.

Consequently, workers may find their labor rights and personal dignity compromised, as the consensual nature of AI implementation within the employment relationship is displaced by unilateral employer decisions. As Baylos [41] notes, the use of technology "is presented to workers as a plan stemming from the uncontested authority of the employer—a power imposed by an external will that subordinates their activity to the employer's objectives, and whose development translates into pure despotism, as the employer increasingly asserts their power as a private legislator of production planning, extending progressively into the market and the external social sphere." This dynamic is, in part, consistent with a reality in which the employer is responsible for driving innovation to remain competitive and is the legal owner of both the organization and its managerial capacity, factors that enable the imposition of technical tools within the employment contract.

Indeed, the employer is granted entrepreneurial freedom and managerial authority within the employment relationship, which in principle permits the use of AI in the workplace. However, the existence of labor relations characterized by subordination and alienation does not preclude the worker from asserting a set of guarantees that, due to conflicting interests, may limit or condition the employer's organizational and managerial powers. As Casas [42] affirms, "the provision of labor does not absorb the worker's personality or life—not even their private life, but their personal life; it is only a part of their freedom, which in no way may undermine their dignity or the development of their personality."

5 Strategic Analysis of the Application of Artificial Intelligence: A Practical Study in the Business Environment

Given the theoretical framework outlined thus far, it is now appropriate to shift the focus toward a practical dimension that illustrates how new technologies have impacted human resources management within organizations. To this end, the analysis will be structured in two distinct sections: the first will examine the digitalization of four specific human resources management practices; the second will explore, in greater depth, the business strategy of a technology company, with particular attention to its approach to human capital management.

5.1 Practical Overview of Business Strategy: Concretization of the Applicability of AI in the Area of HR in Companies

5.1.1 New Organizational Models: The Cases of Uber and Glovo

The phenomenon of uberization has become widely recognized as a term that encapsulates the organizational transformations associated with the rise of digital platforms. In this context, a brief analysis of Uber and Glovo is particularly illustrative, as both companies follow a similar model: they offer services through mobile applications, where work is coordinated and controlled via digital and algorithmic systems.

Uber operates as a passenger transport company that connects riders with drivers through a mobile app. Drivers fall into two categories: freelancers and salaried employees, the latter of whom are provided with vehicles and other necessary tools to perform their work. In either case, services are delivered flexibly and remotely, without direct orders from a supervisor. Instead, the worker interacts with the company's app, which is powered by Artificial Intelligence capable of managing supply and demand in real time, efficiently assigning drivers to passengers based on variables such as proximity.

A similar model is employed by Glovo, a food and goods delivery company that manages its couriers through a proprietary AI-driven app. In this case, however, the employment structure differs: workers must provide their own equipment and enjoy a degree of autonomy in choosing their working hours and the specific orders they wish to accept. Task assignment is not automatic; rather, the app offers delivery opportunities to selected couriers based on various factors such as proximity, availability, acceptance rate, and delivery volume.

These companies clearly exemplify a new model of workforce management enabled by AI. They are able to direct and coordinate service delivery remotely, with advantages that go beyond cost savings associated with physical infrastructure. These include greater control over working time and productivity, as well as enhanced operational flexibility.

In addition, both companies employ novel compensation models. In Uber's case, wages are variable and depend on the quantity and quality of services rendered, measured through factors such as speed and customer ratings. Glovo follows a similar approach, where earnings are tied to the number of deliveries completed—each associated with a specific commission. However, the amount offered for each delivery is determined by the AI system based on the worker's availability, rating, speed, and delivery history. In short, these companies use AI to implement performance-based compensation models that align remuneration with individual success and productivity [35].

5.1.2 New Approaches to Job Search and Recruitment: Digital Employment Platforms

The labor market presents a paradoxical situation in which a qualified job seeker may struggle to find employment, while an employer simultaneously fails to fill a vacancy requiring the same qualifications. Although such mismatches are often temporary, over time they may lead both parties to accept less desirable options out of necessity. In this context, as noted by Adams [34], "what interests us is how Artificial Intelligence intervenes in the disintermediation of the labor market and reshapes it with characteristics previously unknown." AI not only optimizes the flow of information in the labor market but also has the capacity to match candidates and vacancies with unprecedented precision, revolutionizing recruitment and job search processes. Two platforms that exemplify this transformation are LinkedIn and Indeed.

LinkedIn, one of the most prominent digital employment platforms in the professional sphere, acts as an intermediary between organizations seeking to recruit and individuals who can create a professional profile akin to a CV, including work experience, education, achievements, and more. Additionally, it functions as a social network where professionals can share insights, engage in discussions, and expand their networks through connections, groups, and messaging.

What is most noteworthy about LinkedIn is its use of Artificial Intelligence to generate tailored recommendations for both job seekers and employers. Organizations can also create detailed company profiles and specify job conditions [37]. This facilitates rapid and efficient access to a wide range of job opportunities and candidate profiles. The platform is widely used by numerous organizations, including its parent company, Microsoft.

Since acquiring LinkedIn in 2016, Microsoft has optimized its recruitment strategy by leveraging the platform's tools to attract and select top industry talent [43]. Microsoft regularly posts job openings using LinkedIn Recruiter, an advanced tool that filters candidates by skills, experience, education, location, and more. The company also encourages employee participation in recruitment by allowing them to recommend candidates through their own networks (ibid.). Throughout this process, AI plays a key role as a complementary tool that enhances the efficiency and agility of recruitment—an aspect highlighted in Microsoft and LinkedIn's most recent [44].

Beyond candidate acquisition, LinkedIn offers Microsoft additional tools to strengthen its employer brand and talent retention strategy. The company regularly publishes diverse content on the platform to showcase its corporate culture and values, as well as the benefits of working at Microsoft. This employer branding strategy helps attract candidates whose skills and values align with the organization [45]. Furthermore, Microsoft uses LinkedIn Learning—another AI-powered tool offered by the platform—to support skill development among potential hires and current employees, including training in AI-related competencies.

Indeed, one of the largest and most popular job search platforms, serves a similar purpose but operates differently. Unlike LinkedIn, it does not function as a social network or offer CV-style profiles. Instead, it acts as a job search engine, allowing users to filter vacancies using keywords and criteria such as location, salary, education, work schedule, contract type, and posting date. What makes LinkedIn particularly interesting is that job listings can be posted directly by employers or aggregated from various sources—including job boards and company websites—through AI-driven data collection [46].

Although Indeed may initially appear less versatile than LinkedIn, it is used strategically by major companies such as Walmart, the global retail giant. According to its corporate website [47], Walmart uses Indeed to optimize its recruitment process by attracting qualified candidates and managing applications efficiently through job postings, online application systems, candidate tracking, and employee reviews.

Both LinkedIn and Indeed also offer job alert services, notifying users of relevant opportunities via email or messaging—even when they are not actively using the platform.

5.1.3 New Approaches in the Selection Process: The Case of Amazon Versus Other Companies

One of the most critical stages in human resources management is the selection process—that is, the step following recruitment in which companies must decide which candidates to hire. Interviews, screenings, tests, and other evaluation techniques can now be conducted or supported by artificial intelligence in a far more effective manner. AI emerges as a tool capable of analyzing candidates without the influence of personal discretion, thereby reducing recruiter bias and revealing internal characteristics of the applicant that may not be perceptible to a human interviewer. These include physical and psychological capabilities, adaptability, cultural fit, and even the detection of inconsistencies or fallacies in interview responses. In this regard, corporations such as Amazon have employed AI to support their selection processes [48].

In 2014, Amazon developed a proprietary algorithm at its Edinburgh engineering center to automate CV screening and accelerate the selection process while improving alignment with company needs. The AI system was designed to identify over 50,000 terms across CVs, analyzing data from a 10-year period to generate a model that would determine the most suitable candidates.

Despite its initial promise, the program was discontinued in 2018 due to a recurring flaw: the algorithm exhibited gender bias. Based on the data used to train it, Amazon's AI concluded that women were less suitable for certain technical roles, leading to their systematic exclusion from the process.

The Amazon case has since become a paradigmatic example of the discriminatory risks associated with AI—not only in selection processes but also in areas such as compensation, promotion, and even termination. In contrast, a newer platform called MYA System [35] offers an alternative approach. It employs algorithms designed to automate selection and data analysis while eliminating bias. Its AI includes a chatbot that interacts with candidates without prejudice, evaluating them based on job requirements, education, work experience, and other relevant criteria.

Beyond the discriminatory implications of the Amazon case, other companies have adopted AI in their selection processes in ethical and non-discriminatory ways. One such example is TechBullish, an online platform that provides guides, reviews, and solutions for issues related to computers, smart TVs, etc. TechBullish uses AI as a supportive tool to enhance human judgment, making the selection process more efficient, fair, and data-driven. This technology is key to optimizing resources and improving hiring quality [49]. According to HogoNext [50], the company's AI-driven selection practices include automated CVs screening and filtering via chatbots, bias-free candidate evaluation, automated interviews, and predictive analytics.

5.1.4 New Approaches to Talent Development: The Case of Ferrovial

Once a candidate has been selected and integrated into an organization, the management of this new human capital should not be limited solely to training, compensation, or performance monitoring. For the benefit of both the company and the employee, human resources must implement talent development strategies aimed at improving retention, fostering innovation, increasing productivity, enhancing adaptability to change, and strengthening employee engagement [51]. As in previous cases, artificial intelligence—particularly in its virtual assistant form—can serve as a powerful ally in carrying out these tasks in a more personalized and effective manner, as demonstrated by the company Ferrovial through its chatbot Qo [52].

Ferrovial, a Spanish company specializing in infrastructure and services, has adopted a strategy focused on the employee experience. In 2017, it launched a virtual assistant named Qo, designed to support talent development within the organization. This chatbot promotes physical, mental, and emotional well-being by encouraging various activities, including work-life-balance initiatives. In this way, the application of AI extends beyond talent development to encompass health and personal-professional equilibrium.

Focusing specifically on talent development, the Qo AI system aims to foster professional growth through a range of initiatives, including training and upskilling, individualized development plans, mentoring and coaching programs, internal mobility opportunities, recognition and reward schemes, and mechanisms for feedback and performance evaluation.

5.2 The IBM Case: Digitalization Strategy in Human Resources Development and Management

PIBM—International Business Machines Corporation, founded in 1911—is one of the oldest and most respected technology companies in the world, with a trajectory that has evolved from hardware to software, consultancy, and emerging technologies [53]. Over time, the company has expanded its portfolio of services and products, currently offering hardware and software (e.g., AIX, LINUX), digital infrastructures, consultancy services, and emerging technologies such as quantum computing, blockchain, and artificial intelligence.

Operating in over 160 countries and employing more than 300 million people, IBM stands out for its mission to lead the development of cutting-edge technologies and its vision of becoming the most successful and influential technology company globally. Its competitive advantage lies in delivering innovative solutions through an open innovation policy that combines internal development, academic collaboration, and strategic acquisitions such as Red Hat [54]. At the same time, it upholds values centered on diversity, innovation, authenticity, and adaptability. IBM's current strategy focuses on sustainability, innovation, and the advancement of emerging technologies, with particular emphasis on Artificial Intelligence—transforming both its internal processes and those of its clients, especially in the field of human resources.

5.2.1 Application of Artificial Intelligence in HR: IBM Talent and Transformation

IBM, as reflected in several of its reports [55], demonstrates a consistent concern for the digitalization of organizational processes, particularly in the area of human resources. The company notes that most organizations have yet to incorporate new technologies to support HR functions. For IBM, the integration of tools such as artificial intelligence represents a powerful source of competitive advantage—evidenced by its own results: following the digitalization of its HR functions, IBM generated over 300 million dollars in profit [56].

Indeed, IBM combines an HR policy focused on inclusion and diversity, talent development, and performance-based compensation with strong innovation in HR through the use of advanced technologies and a culture of innovation and entrepreneurship among its employees. The use of AI tools has become widespread across all stages of HR management and development: recruitment and selection, talent development and retention, employee experience, performance management, diversity and inclusion policies, and more. This automation of HR processes integrates predictive analytics—anticipating talent needs and optimizing workforce planning—with personalization practices, offering tailored solutions for each employee, and scalability, enabling the export of technological solutions to other companies regardless of their size or sector.

One notable example is IBM's collaboration with the well-known company Burger King, through which it developed a virtual assistant named TOP—Technology Orienting People. This algorithm communicates with employees via WhatsApp to provide various HR services, such as payslip summaries, income reports, and holiday requests, among others. The company's objective is clear: to introduce AI and automation into HR teams to shift manual and repetitive tasks to technology, thereby freeing human capital to focus on more strategic responsibilities.

The experience gained through these innovative practices has enabled IBM to open new business lines focused on consultancy and the commercialization of artificial intelligence and related technologies, aimed at helping client companies transform their organizational structures and human resources departments. In this context, IBM launched the IBM Talent & Transformation Program in 2018 to "transform workforces into the workforce of the future", using AI as a catalyst "to evolve HR departments from a service function to a growth engine for the business", and to "attract and retain a diverse and highly skilled workforce that drives and evolves the future of the business" [56]. The company places its trust in the reliability of this consultancy project based on its own internal implementation of these programs, and promises the following benefits and capabilities [57]:

- Reinvent and modernize HR experiences: Enhancing employee engagement through intelligent and personalized experiences.
- Increase operational performance: IBM's AI solutions streamline operations, boost productivity, and simplify processes through automation and intelligent chatbots.
- Unlock HR spending: Clients are offered operational cost savings through simplification and automation, freeing up resources to invest in other workforce priorities.
- Enable a transformative HR strategy: AI facilitates the development of a robust and practical HR strategy that integrates data, analytics, and workforce planning to meet organizational needs—developing processes, people, and technological capabilities for success.
- Redesign the operating model: A shift grounded in the alignment of new business objectives with organizational structure, vision, and emerging functionalities enabled by digitalization and AI.
- Cloud-oriented organizational structure: IBM offers services to migrate HR systems to cloud and AI-driven design, enhancing flexibility and aligning HR technology investments with broader organizational goals.
- Design an experience centered on the employee: IBM's AI leverages dynamic workflows to deliver a personalized and enhanced experience for each employee at a reduced cost, efficiently addressing individual needs.
- Talent acquisition and skills development: A key element in Industry 4.0, supported by IBM through strategic transformation and talent acquisition processes that balance people, AI, and data.

In short, IBM offers a genuine digital transformation of HR through more flexible and agile organizational models that consider both business and individual employee needs. This AI is integrated throughout the employee lifecycle via a suite of algorithms, most notably Watson.

Watson is defined as a high-level cognitive algorithm with advanced natural language understanding and machine learning capabilities, enabling it to solve complex problems and support more informed and objective decision-making ([58] Redbooks 2023). Its versatility makes it scalable across various functional domains—health sciences, financial services, customer service, marketing, cybersecurity, education, etc.—but here we focus on its specific application in HR practices, where the following Watson modules stand out (ibid.):

- Watson Recruitment: This tool supports recruitment and selection by analyzing and comparing CVs against job descriptions, identifying the most suitable candidates based on skills, experience, and other criteria. Its ability to process large volumes of data in a short time enables predictive automation of candidate success, allowing recruiters to focus on the assessment of candidates demonstrating the highest potential.
- Watson Career Coach: A system designed to provide employees with personalized recommendations for professional development opportunities, training courses, and career paths based on their skills and motivations. This helps

employees plan their future within the organization, increasing motivation, job satisfaction, and talent retention—while also enabling analysis of individual turnover risk.

- Watson Assistant: A suite of chatbots that respond to employee queries regarding company policies, benefits, procedures, and other HR-related topics. In addition to delivering fast and accurate responses, it analyzes employee sentiment to detect early signs of dissatisfaction or issues in specific areas.
- Watson Talent Frameworks: A tool that provides detailed role and competency descriptions to help organizations align their talent strategies with business objectives. It supports more effective and precise job design, career planning, and vacancy descriptions.

In addition, Watson offers a range of personalized functionalities within the HR domain that enable the automation of processes such as performance management—analyzing employees to conduct more objective and accurate evaluations—and diversity and inclusion policies—assessing workforce composition and identifying areas for improvement in this regard.

Alongside this algorithm, IBM also provides other Artificial Intelligence systems and tools for lesser-known HR areas, such as IBM SkillsBuild, a training program designed to equip individuals with essential digital skills and enhance their employability, and the Employee Assistance Program, which offers confidential support to employees facing personal or work-related challenges that may affect their performance or overall well-being.

6 Conclusions

Artificial Intelligence (AI) emerges as a driver of global socioeconomic transformation—a catalyst for change that has propelled the evolution toward the Fourth Industrial Revolution. This new era is characterized by a fusion of technologies that blur the boundaries between the physical, digital, and biological spheres, enabling the development of tools and techniques that surpass human cognitive capabilities in terms of efficiency and speed. Innovation, which is essential for the effective application of AI, has been enhanced by these new technologies, alongside the products and services offered by companies. This has given rise to new competitive dynamics, in which AI is increasingly seen as a source of business models and competitive advantage. In this context, data has become the new oil, and technology and innovation the decisive factors for business survival in an environment of constant change.

Within the field of human resources, AI also presents itself as a powerful promise—a tool capable of maximizing benefits in terms of speed, efficiency, and responsiveness in decision-making. Employment has been significantly impacted by the automation of tasks through AI, which has raised concerns in the academic literature regarding potential job displacement. However, this fear is accompanied by a degree of uncertainty—common to all industrial revolutions—that renders such claims inconclusive. In contrast to this uncertain outlook, a more immediate and tangible reality emerges: AI not only replaces but also complements human labor, and even enables the creation of new jobs—whether through new tasks or new organizational models—that may ultimately outweigh the losses.

What is most significant about AI in the HR domain is the opportunity it offers as a complement to human labor. It can enhance employee satisfaction by relieving them of repetitive and tedious tasks, while also supporting the development and strategic direction of the HR function itself. Although challenges remain—particularly in terms of communication breakdowns between employees and management due to technological intermediation—AI can also serve as a tool for building more effective communication and motivation strategies. These strategies can help shape a meaningful employee experience within the corporate culture, thereby improving retention. Moreover, if companies are able to overcome key barriers, AI can complement—or even automate—virtually all HR activities, improving speed, effectiveness, and objectivity, with the potential to reduce arbitrariness and bias in decision-making. This threat is already being addressed by specialized technologies.

The potential for AI to complement and enhance a wide range of HR tasks is clearly demonstrated by IBM, which, through its internal innovation strategy and technological development, has created new business lines focused on consultancy. These services assist other companies through algorithms such as Watson in specific areas like human resources.

Nonetheless, despite the wide range of possibilities for applying AI in these domains, full automation of decision-making and task execution may have negative consequences—not only for employees but also for the organization itself. While AI is undoubtedly a cognitive tool, it is also a form of bounded rationality, constrained by algorithms based on mathematical and statistical operations. This may lead to the exclusion of factors that, while irrelevant to the algorithm, are highly significant for the business. For this reason, the adoption of digitalization must be accompanied by human oversight, ensuring that business decisions are made through a hybrid model that combines human and technological reasoning.

This opens up a new and potentially more beneficial field for HR management and development compared to previous models. However, it also presents challenges that require companies to pursue effective internal communication strategies as a key element for successful operations and talent retention. It also demands the development of new digital capabilities, necessitating continuous and targeted training within the organization. Furthermore, companies must adopt new ethical business models for the application of AI—models that take into account and seek to mitigate or eliminate inherent risks such as bias, data protection, fair labor transitions, and cybersecurity.

Ultimately, and despite the potential threats to business interests, the dual nature of AI—as both a promise and a threat—manifests itself within the employment relationship. Digitalization expands and blurs the boundaries of managerial power, which must, by legal and social justice imperatives, remain subject to the safeguarding of human dignity and the fundamental labor rights of workers.

References

1. Rivas, P.: La aplicación de la inteligencia artificial al trabajo y su impacto discriminatorio. Aranzadi (2020)
2. Guarnizo, J.V.: Organización y dirección de empresas. Bremen (2005)
3. Schwab, K.: La cuarta revolución industrial. Futuro Hoy. **1**, 6–10 (2020)
4. Almirall, E.: Hacia una política de innovación en IA. In: Algoritmos, inteligencia artificial y relación laboral, pp. 25–46. Aranzadi (2023)
5. Ulrich, P., Frank, V., Buettner, R.: Artificial intelligence in small and medium-sized family firms: an empirical study on the impact of family influence. Corp. Gov. Organ. Behav. Rev. **7**(1), 72–80 (2023)
6. Morandini, S., Fraboni, F., De Angelis, M., Puzzo, G., Giusino, D., Pietrantoni, L.: The impact of artificial intelligence on workers' skills: upskilling and reskilling in organisations. Inform. Sci. **26**, 39–68 (2023)
7. Goetze, T.S.: Mind the gap: autonomous systems, the responsibility gap, and moral entanglement. In: Proceedings of the 2022 ACM Conference on Fairness, Accountability, and Transparency, pp. 390–400 (2022)
8. Murillo, D.: Algoritmos, decisiones automatizadas y desafíos éticos: Un análisis sociológico. In: Algoritmos, inteligencia artificial y relación laboral, pp. 47–76. Aranzadi (2023)
9. Tarziján, J.: Fundamentos de la estrategia empresarial: 6ta Edición. Ediciones UC (2023)
10. Thurow, L.: Construir riqueza: Las nuevas reglas para individuos, empresas y naciones en una economía basada en el conocimiento. Javier Vergara Editor (2000)
11. Fitong Ketchiwou, G., Schultz, C.M., Lessing, K.F.: A framework for future human resource management individual competencies: an integrative review. Athens J. Bus. Econ. **12**, 1–36 (2025). https://doi.org/10.30958/ajbe.X-Y-Z
12. Brummette, J., Zoch, L.M.: How stakeholders' personal values influence their value expectations for legitimate organizations. Corp. Commun. Int. J. **21**(3), 309–321 (2016)
13. Huang, M.H., Rust, R.T.: Artificial intelligence in service. J. Serv. Res. **21**(2), 155–172 (2018)
14. İyem, C., Erer, B.: Artificial intelligence applications in human resource management. Uluslararası Yönetim Akademisi Dergisi. **8**(2), 335–343 (2025). https://doi.org/10.33712/mana.1702990
15. Ullah, M., Din, M.U., Khan, F., Mushtaq, S.: Artificial intelligence in human resource management: a case of information technology sector of Khyber Pakhtunkhwa. Pak. J. Polit. Stab. Arch. **3**(1), 1099–1117 (2025)
16. Sakka, F., El Maknouzi, M.E., Sadok, H.: Human resource management in the era of artificial intelligence: future HRM work practices, anticipated skill set, financial and legal implications. Acad. Strateg. Manag. J. **21**(S1), 1–14 (2022)
17. Schultz, C.M.: The future and the role of human resource management in South Africa during the Fourth Industrial Revolution. SA J. Hum. Resour. Manag./SA Tydskrif vir Menslikehulpbronbestuur. **19**, a1624 (2021)
18. Conceição, L.C., Pereira, L.F., Dias, Á.L.: The key competencies for the future of work: a bibliometric study. J. Chin. Hum. Resour. Manag. **14**(1), 3–37 (2023)
19. Shet, S., Nair, B.: Quality of hire: expanding the multi-level fit employee selection using machine learning. Int. J. Organ. Anal. **31**(6), 2103–2117 (2023)
20. Veldsman, D., Coetzee, M.: Professional personas and capabilities of the future people practitioner: a thematic review. SA J. Hum. Resour. Manag. (2022)

21. Popo-Olaniyan, O., James, O.O., Udeh, C.A., Daraojimba, R.E., Ogedengbe, D.E.: Future proofing human resources in the US with AI: a review of trends and implications. Int. J. Manag. Entrep. Res. **4**(12), 641–658 (2022)
22. Minbaeva, D.: Disrupted HRM? Hum. Resour. Manag. Rev. **31**, 100820 (2021)
23. Cunha, M.P., Pina e Cunha, E., Gomes, E., Mellahi, K., Miner, A.S., Rego, A.: Strategic agility through improvisational capabilities: implications for a paradox-sensitive HRM. Hum. Resour. Manag. Rev. **30**(1), 100695 (2020)
24. Sagaya, A., Momin, M.M.: Global reverberation and prediction for HRM amid and after COVID-19: a technological viewpoint. Mater. Today Proc. **46**, 1–13 (2020)
25. Terrazas, I.: Inteligencia artificial y sus sesgos en el análisis de datos: Los riesgos de la nueva discriminación. Ensayos Ciberfeministas, pp. 221–233. Dykinson (2023)
26. Ginés, A.: Prólogo. In: Algoritmos, inteligencia artificial y relación laboral, pp. 17–24. Aranzadi (2023)
27. Brown, P.: The global auction: the broken promises of education, jobs, and incomes. Oxford University Press, Oxford (2011)
28. del Prado, D.P.: The challenges of algorithm management: the Spanish perspective. Białostockie Studia Prawnicze. **2**(29), 131–144 (2024)
29. Rocha, F.: La dimensión laboral de la economía digital: Reflexiones para un debate en proceso. Colección de Informes Fundación 1° de Mayo, (146) (2020)
30. Sennett, R.: El artesano. Anagrama (2009)
31. García, J.: La comunicación interna. Díaz Santos (1998)
32. Macías, S., Aguilar, J.J., Ramírez, I.A., Escobar, H.E.: El sentido de pertenencia como eje rector de la motivación laboral. Revista de Universidad Autónoma de Nuevo León. **1**, 3306–3325 (2016)
33. Miles, J., González, A., Mandirola, N.: Gestión de alto desempeño y su impacto en los resultados de la empresa: El caso de Uruguay y Argentina. J. Technol. Manag. Innov. **13**, 57–68 (2018)
34. Adams, L.: The HR change toolkit: your complete guide to making it happen. Practical Inspiration Publishing, Northwich (2020)
35. Cuatrecasas & Instituto Legal de RRHH: Inteligencia artificial y su impacto en los recursos humanos y en el marco regulatorio de las relaciones laborales. La Ley (2018)
36. Cunha, M.P., Pina e Cunha, E., Gomes, E., Mellahi, K., Miner, A.S., Rego, A.: (2020)
37. Business Insider: LinkedIn integra la IA para facilitar la búsqueda de empleo. https://www.businessinsider.es/linkedin-integra-ia-facilitar-busqueda-empleo-1391117 (2024)
38. Consejo Económico y Social: Hacia un trabajo digital justo. Informe El Futuro del Trabajo. Consejo Económico y Social (2016)
39. Álvarez, H.: Sindicalismo en crisis. The Economic Journal. Recuperado de. https://www.theeconomyjournal.com/texto-diario/mostrar/591639/sindicatos-crisis (2014)
40. Rodríguez, M.L., Pérez del Prado, D.: El impacto de la economía 4.0 sobre las condiciones de trabajo y empleo: Estudio de caso en dos empresas de base tecnológica. Cuadernos de Relaciones Laborales. **36**(2), 355–373 (2018)
41. Baylos, A.: Desequilibrio en la empresa y entorno digital: La importancia de los derechos colectivos. Las nuevas fronteras del poder de dirección y control del empresario en la transición digital, pp. 17–40. Bomarzo (2024)
42. Casas, M.E.: La plena efectividad de los derechos fundamentales: Juicio de ponderación (¿o de proporcionalidad?) y principio de buena fe. Relaciones Laborales. **12**, 141–156 (2004)
43. LinkedIn Blog: How Microsoft uses this one type of data to get ahead of talent trends. https://www.linkedin.com/business/talent/blog/talent-strategy/key-piece-of-data-that-drives-microsofts-global-talent-acquisition (2018)
44. Microsoft & LinkedIn: AI at work is here. Now comes the hard part: employees want AI, leaders are looking for a path forward. Work trend index annual report (2024)
45. Link Humans: How Microsoft uses social for employer branding. https://linkhumans.com/microsoft-social-employer-branding/ (2024)
46. Indeed: Acerca de Indeed. Recuperado de https://es.indeed.com/about (2024)

47. Walmart Careers: I finished my application—now what? What to expect in each step of the application process for stores & clubs. Recuperado de https://careers.walmart.com/application-process-step-by-step (2024)
48. Silveira, G.: Artificial intelligence, gender, and human rights: the case of Amazon. Justiça do Direito. **3**, 218–245 (2021)
49. Wonderlic: How AI in recruitment is changing the hiring process. https://wonderlic.com/blog/employee-selection/hiring/how-ai-in-recruitment-is-changing-the-hiring-process/ (2024)
50. HogoNext. How to apply AI effectively for candidate selection. https://hogonext.com/how-to-apply-ai-effectively-for-candidate-selection/ (2024)
51. Batt, R.: Managing customer services: human resource practices, quit rates, and sales growth. Acad. Manag. J. **45**(3), 587–597 (2002)
52. Ferrovial: Qo, el chatbot de Ferrovial para ayudar a sus empleados a alcanzar su máximo potencial. https://newsroom.ferrovial.com/es/noticias/chatbot-robot-conversacional/ (2017)
53. Business Model Analyst: Modelo de negocio de IBM. https://businessmodelanalyst.com/es/modelo-de-negocio-ibm/ (2023)
54. CTA: ¿Hacia dónde camina el futuro de la innovación y la tecnología según IBM? https://blog.corporaciontecnologica.com/es/listado-completo/Hacia-donde-camina-el-futuro-de-la-innovacion-y-la-tecnologia-segun-IBM/ (2023)
55. IBM Think España: Un nuevo estudio revela cómo la IA está cambiando el trabajo y qué deben hacer los responsables de RRHH al respecto. https://www.ibm.com/blogs/think/es-es/2023/08/21/unnuevo-estudio-revela-como-la-ia-esta-cambiando-el-trabajo-y-que-deben-hacer-los-responsables-de-rrhh-al-respecto/ (2023)
56. IBM: IBM Talent Business utiliza AI para repensar la fuerza laboral moderna. https://www.multivu.com/players/English/8247551-ibm-talent-transformation-ai/ (2018)
57. IBM Consulting: Consultoría de transformación de recursos humanos y talento. https://www.ibm.com/mx-es/consulting/hr-talent-transformation (2024)
58. Redbook: La era de los Sistemas Cognitivos. Una mirada al interior de IBM Watson y ¿Cómo funciona?, en IBM. https://www.redbooks.ibm.com/redpapers/pdfs/redp4955_es.pdf (2023)

Telework Satisfaction in Public Organizations: Examining the Roles of Hygiene and Motivators Factors

Costanza Baldrighi, Francesca Sanguineti, and Pietro Previtali

Abstract In many public institutions, telework—once considered a temporary fix during the COVID-19 crisis—has become a strategic element of modern organizations. This study examines telework satisfaction among technical and administrative staff at one of the oldest Italian public universities through the lens of Herzberg's two-factor theory. Using survey data and Path Analysis, our results indicate that hygiene and motivator factors both significantly influence telework satisfaction. These findings underscore that while a well-structured work environment with solid, trust-based, interpersonal relationships are essential to prevent isolation and disengagement, fostering a sense of accomplishment is equally important for sustainable telework practices. Implications for public management and recommendations for enhancing flexible work arrangements are discussed.

Keywords Telework satisfaction · Two-factor theory · Public sector

1 Introduction

Teleworking (TW) first emerged as an organizational practice about half a century ago and has since evolved in both its definitions and methods [1]. Its adoption has progressively increased alongside advancements in communication technologies. A dramatic surge in telework came with the COVID-19 pandemic [2], which forced many public and private organizations to rapidly implement remote work solutions to mitigate health risks [3]. In this emergency context, the ability to work remotely, especially from home, allowed many public institutions to continue delivering their services [4]. Even now that the emergency has subsided, many entities have decided

C. Baldrighi · F. Sanguineti (✉) · P. Previtali
Department of Economics and Management, University of Pavia, Pavia, Italy
e-mail: costanza.baldrighi01@universitadipavia.it; francesca.sanguineti@unipv.it; pietro.previtali@unipv.it

N. Omrani et al. (eds.), *Human-Machine Synergy and the Digital Future - Exploring Collaboration and Competition Volume 1*, Springer Proceedings in Business and Economics, https://doi.org/10.1007/978-3-032-21347-1_9

to maintain telework options—at least occasionally—recognizing the benefits it offers for both the institutions and their employees.

However, introducing flexible work arrangements (FWA) requires far more than the simple adoption of new technologies. It necessitates a significant organizational transformation, impacting cultural dimensions like employee-manager relationships and socialization patterns, as well as practical considerations such as the deployment of effective ICT infrastructures and work tools [3]. In consequence, organizations face several challenges in implementing such work modalities, and the literature presents mixed results regarding the impact of teleworking on organizations and their employees. While the overall perception of these arrangements is generally positive [5], potential downsides—such as reduced and deteriorated social interaction [6] or decreased organizational commitment [1]—cannot be overlooked.

Beyond these observed outcomes, a deeper look into what drives telework satisfaction (TWS)—defined as employees' overall evaluation of the telework arrangement in terms of its effectiveness in meeting their professional responsibilities and personal well-being—seems essential. At first glance, one might assume that the benefits of telework are clearly evident. Reality, however, is more complex. What truly enables employees to feel supported, engaged, and satisfied when adopting telework? How do factors that simply prevent dissatisfaction interact with those that actively foster a sense of achievement and fulfillment? These questions are particularly important in public settings, where technical and administrative staff typically hold permanent contracts and extrinsic rewards are standardized, thereby limiting the impact of conventional incentive schemes [7, 8]. As a result, understanding and leveraging intrinsic motivators, such as recognition, opportunities for professional growth, and the inherent meaningfulness of work, becomes fundamental for countering potential disengagement and enhancing both job satisfaction and performance.

To explore this complexity, we draw on Herzberg's two-factor theory, a seminal work that distinguishes between hygiene factors—those necessary to prevent dissatisfaction—and motivator factors—those that contribute to intrinsic satisfaction [9, 10]. Although this theoretical distinction is well-established, its relevance is evident in its capacity to explain nuanced employee responses in modern work environments [11], including those in which telework is an option.

Our study is based on data collected from the technical and administrative staff of one of the oldest Italian public universities, the University of Pavia. While our findings are derived from a single institutional setting, they provide valuable insights into the dynamics of telework satisfaction in the public sector and lay the foundation for future research on how public employees perceive and integrate telework into their daily routines.

2 Literature Review

Terms such as smart working, telework, remote working, and telecommuting are often used interchangeably: as a result, the one term informally adopted within an organization may not accurately reflect the actual work arrangements in place. While all these terms refer to flexible work arrangements, there are significant differences between them. For instance, smart working emphasizes balancing individual needs and organizational expectations [6, 12] and typically entails a higher degree of flexibility in time, space, methods, and autonomy [13, 14]. In contrast, teleworking, especially in its work-from-home form, often requires employees to replicate office dynamics within a remote setting, working synchronously with their on-site colleagues [13].

Today, TW is widely recognized as one of several flexible work arrangements [1]. The most commonly adopted definition in the literature [1, 15–17] is provided by Baruch (2001) [18], who defines telework as the situation "when employees perform all or a substantial part of their work physically separated from the location of their employer, using IT for operation and communication" ([18], p. 114).

An extensive body of literature has examined the effects of TW on various organizational outcomes, particularly in public sector contexts. Studies have explored its impact on job satisfaction, autonomy, organizational performance, employee engagement, and retention [1, 3, 15–17, 19]. However, findings in this field are mixed. Some suggest that allowing employees to choose their work location, even partially, is linked to higher job satisfaction and performance [20, 21]; Bae and Kim (2016) [20] specifically found a positive relationship between TW and job satisfaction, while the opportunity to TW is often associated with improved work-life balance [22], even during COVID-19 [23, 24]. Additionally, recent research indicates that TW enhances autonomy and has a positive impact on employee engagement [25].

On the other hand, TW is not always associated with positive outcomes and some studies present opposite results. For example, Caillier (2013) [15] found that teleworkers were not significantly more motivated than non-teleworkers. Similarly, De Vries et al. (2019) [1] found that working from home did not affect work engagement. With regard to TW's impact on performance, the literature suggests that the relationship is not direct [22], and the factors undermining or increasing it are yet to be completely identified [4]. This suggests that the relationship may be positive only under certain conditions, such as when trust-building management practices and result-based evaluations are in place [26]. Other scholars have highlighted the potential downsides of TW: Palumbo et al. (2023) [6] argue that smart working—a work arrangement where employees have the flexibility to choose both their workplace and working hours [13]—may lead to greater engagement, but can also generate feelings of isolation, negatively impact employees' sense of belonging, and worsen the relations with colleagues and supervisors [6]. Other scholars have highlighted the blurring of boundaries between work and personal life [14] and the difficulties for employees to adapt their work to a TW modality [5]. In essence, while TW is generally associated with positive outcomes, the literature emphasizes that this relationship is not straightforward and that certain conditions must be met for TW to be perceived as both beneficial [24] and a satisfactory work arrangement.

Bonacci and Scarozza (2024) [14] introduced the concept of Smart Working Satisfaction (SWS) by examining the factors that influence employees' satisfaction with SW. Similarly, our study focuses on employees' satisfaction with telework (TWS), aiming to identify the key variables that shape employees' perceptions of this particular work arrangement. Specifically, we seek to determine whether TWS is more strongly influenced by hygiene factors or by motivators, as defined by Herzberg's two-factor theory (1959) [27]. In other words, does TWS depend more on factors that prevent discomfort (hygiene) or on those that promote growth and self-actualization (motivators)?

2.1 Herzberg's Two-Factor Theory in Modern Workplaces: An Old Theory That Still Holds?

Despite its origins in the 1960s, Herzberg's two-factor theory remains highly relevant to modern work environments. As shown by Mitsakis and Galanakis (2022) [11] in their extensive literature review, Herzberg's framework continues to provide a valuable lens for understanding the key drivers of employee satisfaction and motivation.

In the public sector, for example, a 2024 study applying this theory to organizational commitment among public employees in South Korea found that motivators have the greatest impact on such an aspect, suggesting that human resource management practices should prioritize them to further boost commitment [8]. However, in different organizational contexts, hygiene factors may play a more significant role, either positively or negatively, in shaping job satisfaction among public employees [28]. These mixed findings underscore the complexity of determining which type of factor has the greatest impact on employee well-being, performance, and overall experience. Adopting Herzberg's theory provides a structured framework for categorizing and understanding the key drivers of motivation and satisfaction, which in turn can help organizations tailor their policies and interventions more effectively.

Additionally, the relative importance of hygiene and motivator factors appears to be influenced by cultural differences, as employees from different backgrounds may have varying priorities and expectations [28]. Generational turnover is another important consideration. Recent studies highlight the role of flexible work arrangements in enhancing job retention, talent attraction, and work commitment, particularly among younger employees [29].

In this perspective, understanding the key factors that ensure TW—an increasingly significant component of modern employment—is both fulfilling and positively perceived is crucial for maintaining the attractiveness of organizations in the long term. Herzberg's theory, with its clear distinction between hygiene factors, which address "the need to avoid unpleasantness," and motivators, which fulfill "the need for growth or self-actualization" ([30], p. 12), offers a widely recognized and established practical framework for investigating these dynamics.

Building on these constructs, as established in the literature, we propose the following hypotheses (Fig. 1):

H1a: Hygiene factors have the most significant impact on telework satisfaction.
H1b: Hygiene factors have a limited impact on telework satisfaction.

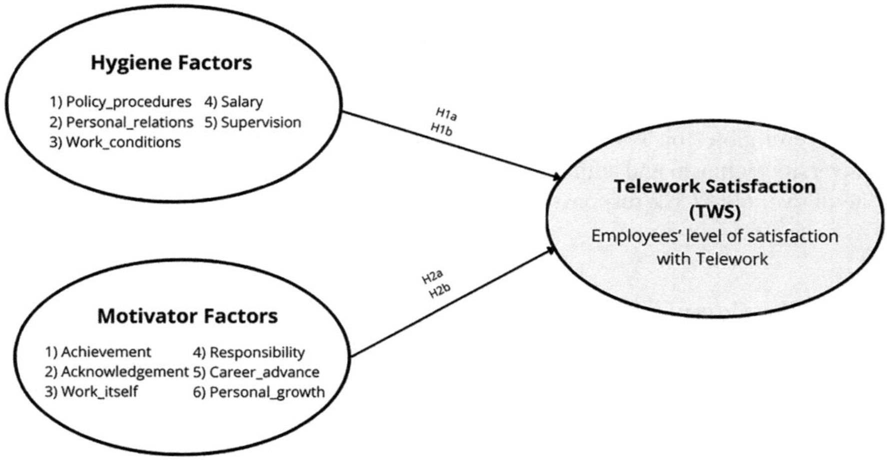

Fig. 1 Hypothesized model. (Source: authors' own elaboration)

And conversely:
H2a: Motivator factors have the most significant impact on telework satisfaction.
H2b: Motivator factors have a limited impact on telework satisfaction.

3 Methods

3.1 Data Collection

The data were collected through a survey designed as part of an internal inquiry initiated by the University of Pavia, in Italy. The main aim was to assess job satisfaction among the institution's technical and administrative staff, with a specific focus on telework, a practice that has been incorporated into the university's operational framework in recent years. This survey sought to evaluate telework's impact on key dimensions, including work-life balance, interpersonal relationships, work performance, and interactions with supervisors, thereby providing insights into both its advantages and potential drawbacks.

The survey underwent a two-step process. Initially, a pilot survey was drafted and distributed to a small group of selected employees to obtain feedback and refine the questionnaire. Subsequently, the final version was sent out to the whole university technical and administrative staff between December 14, 2024, and January 10, 2025, and was distributed online via Google Forms. Participation was voluntary, and responses were collected anonymously. For the purpose of this study, we adopted a convenience sampling technique, an approach already used in this field of research [31]. Thus, rather than selecting participants randomly, we targeted individuals who were accessible and willing to participate in the survey.

To ensure comprehensive data collection, the questionnaire was organized into three interconnected sections. The first section was addressed to all employees, regardless of whether their role allows for TW. The second section was specifically designed for those who regularly engage in TW, while the third was for employees who are eligible for TW but opt not to use it. The survey was distributed to all University technical and administrative staff (911 individuals), achieving a response rate of over 60% (572 responses).

3.2 The Sample

The age distribution of the employees in our sample aligns with national data [32, 33] with an average age of approximately 50 years and only 13.2% of respondents being under 35 years old. Over 70% of the sample are women, a figure that exceeds the national average of 58.8%.

Among the respondents, 63.8% have worked at the organization for at least 10 years, while newly hired employees (less than 3 years of service) account for 17.8%. Additionally, 57% of employees have at least one child, and 64.7% report regularly providing care for young children, elderly individuals, and/or people with disabilities.

In terms of work conditions, 93% of the respondents hold full-time employment contracts, while 87% do not live near their workplace (less than 5 km), with 37% commuting over 30 km to reach their office. The sample is composed of 65.6% administrative staff, 32% technical staff, and the remaining percentage holds other roles (e.g., directors, other types of collaborators).

For the purposes of this study, only the responses of employees who regularly engage in TW were considered, totaling 373 observations (65.2% of the total respondents). The data reveal a generally positive relationship between university employees and TW, with only 1.6% of those who have experienced remote work choosing to renounce this option. Currently, approximately two-thirds of the respondents who engage in TW perform their duties outside the office for 2 days per week. Table 1 provides a synthetic description of the survey's respondents' characteristics.

3.3 Variables

Independent Variables The independent variables were constructed based on Herzberg's theoretical model (1959) [27], which categorizes factors into hygiene and motivator factors. In total, 11 independent—latent—variables were identified, each representing an aspect potentially impacting telework satisfaction (TWS). Drawing on the literature [30], we identified five hygiene factors (Policy proce-

Table 1 Job characteristics of the sample ($N = 572$)

Role		Access to TW		Type of contract	
Administrative staff	65.6%	Yes, my current job allows for TW, and I use it	65.20%	Full-time	93%
Technical staff	32%	Yes, my current job allows for TW, but I choose not to use it	20.80%	Part-time	7%
Other roles	2.40%	No, my current job does not allow for TW	14%		

dures, Personal relations, Work conditions, Salary, Supervision) and six motivators (Achievement, Acknowledgment, Work itself, Responsibility, Career advancement, Personal growth). Each latent variable was measured through one or more survey items (manifest variables). These items, drawn from previous research, were adapted to suit the context of this study and ensure comparability.

Initially, items were grouped into variables solely based on their content. In a second step, to enhance robustness and internal consistency, the items for each variable were tested using Cronbach's alpha and Confirmatory Factor Analysis (CFA). Items with Cronbach's alpha values below 0.7 or factor loadings below 0.5 (rounded) were excluded. Finally, to address potential multicollinearity, the Variance Inflation Factor (VIF) was calculated for each item, and items with VIF values exceeding 3.3—the lowest threshold—were excluded [34]. All items were measured using a multi-item 5-point Likert scale [35], with responses ranging from "1 = strongly disagree" to "5 = strongly agree," or from "1 = not at all satisfied" to "5 = completely satisfied." The complete list of variables and items with their respective description is provided in Table 2.

Dependent Variable The dependent variable, *TW_Satisfaction*, represents the level of satisfaction with telework. It was calculated as the mean score of six different items measured on a 5-point Likert scale (e.g., "1 = strongly disagree" to "5 = strongly agree") included in the survey (Table 2). To ensure internal consistency, Cronbach's alpha, CFA, and VIF were assessed for these items, all of which were retained.

3.4 Model

We initially followed the approach of Metselaar and colleagues (2023) [22] and tested our hypotheses using a Structural Equation Model (SEM) after conducting a Confirmatory Factor Analysis (CFA). SEM was originally chosen because it allows for the investigation of relationships both among latent variables and between latent variables and their corresponding manifest items. We assessed model fit by examining internal consistency (via Cronbach's Alpha) and structural validity (through CFA), excluding weak items to ensure that the remaining ones accurately measured their respective latent variables.

Table 2 Variables and items

	Variable name	Variable definition	Item	Item definition	Adapted from
Hygiene factors	Policy procedures	Policy and procedures: Clear, fair, and consistently applied policies/ clear procedures	PP_item2	How satisfied are you with the training you received to carry out your current job?	Bae and Kim (2016)
			PP_item3	I know what's expected of me at work	Caillier (2012)
			PP_item4	I have enough information to do my job well	Caillier (2012)
			PP_item5	When changes are introduced, the reasons why they are introduced are explained to me	Giacomini and Palumbo (2023)
			PP_item6	I know how my job relates to organizational goals	Giacomini and Palumbo (2023)
			PP_item7	I know how my job relates to organizational priorities	Giacomini and Palumbo (2023)
			PP_item8	I get the information I need to do my job well	Giacomini and Palumbo (2023)
			PP_item9	I am aware of what happens in work areas/offices other than my own	Giacomini and Palumbo (2023)

	Personal_relations	Interpersonal relations: Positive relationships with colleagues and supervisors	PR_item3	With TW I felt more trust in myself from my colleagues	Bonacci et al. (2024)
			PR_item4	With TW I felt more confidence in myself from my parents from the management	Bonacci et al. (2024)
			PR_item5	TW allows me to have a better relationship with my colleagues	Bonacci et al. (2024)
			PR_item7	With TW, socialization with colleagues is improved (consider, for example, the time to talk about non-work topics, chat using instant messaging) compared to what happens when adopting the traditional working method	Bonacci et al. (2024) and Carbonara et al. (2022)
	Work_conditions	Work environment: A safe, comfortable, and well-equipped place to work. A general sense of stability and continuit	WE_item1	I would recommend my organization (UNIPV) as a good place to work	Kim and Lee (2020)
			WE_item6	Considering everything, how satisfied are you with the organization you work for (UNIPV)?	Kim and Lee (2020) and Ki and Lee (2024)
			JS_item2	I feel a deep sense of belonging to my organization (UNIPV)	Perego and Belardinelli (2024)
			JS_item3	Even if I had the opportunity of a better job, it wouldn't be fair to leave my organization (UNIPV)	Perego and Belardinelli (2024)
			JS_item4	I feel the problems that my organization (UNIPV) faces as if they were my own	Perego and Belardinelli (2024)
	Salary	Salary: Competitive and fair wages to prevent financial insecurity	Salary	Considering everything, how satisfied are you with your salary?	Bae and Kim (2016)

(continued)

Table 2 (continued)

	Variable name	Variable definition	Item	Item definition	Adapted from
	Supervision	Supervision: Evaluating the quality of management, that should be supportive and competent	SU_item1	My supervisor is able to prioritize for me and my colleagues during TW	de Miranda et al. (2024)
			SU_item2	My supervisor is able to set actionable goals for me and my colleagues during TW	de Miranda et al. (2024)
			SU_item3	My supervisor is able to distribute/assign tasks to me and my colleagues, considering the skills and working conditions of each one	de Miranda et al. (2024)
			SU_item4	My supervisor is able to locate the information he needs to manage the team efficiently	de Miranda et al. (2024)
			SU_item5	In general, I have a good relationship with my supervisor	Park et al. (2023)
			SU_item6	I have enough confidence in my supervisor/boss to defend and justify his/her decisions	Park et al. (2023)
			SU_item7	My supervisor/boss understands [removed: my problems and] my needs	Park et al. (2023)
			SU_item8	My supervisor/boss supports my need to balance work and other aspects of life	Kim and Lee (2020)
			SU_item9	I have a high level of respect for my organization's (UNIPV) senior leaders	Caillier (2012)
			SU_item10	Regardless of how much power he/she has built into his/her position, my supervisor/boss would be personally inclined to use his/her power to help me solve problems in my work	Park et al. (2023)

Motivator factors	Achievement	Achievement of meaningful results: Recognizing and celebrating successes	AC_item1	TW allows me to better achieve my professional goals	Bonacci et al. (2024)
			AC_item2	My work effectiveness has increased thanks to TW	Bonacci et al. (2024)
			AC_item3	My work performance has improved thanks to TW	Bonacci et al. (2024)
	Acknowledgment	Acknowledgment of results achieved: Regular and sincere acknowledgment of efforts	AK_item1	My supervisor is able to periodically evaluate my results and those of my colleagues, during TW	de Miranda et al. (2024)
			AK_item2	My supervisor/boss recognizes my potential	Park et al. (2023)
	Work_itself	The work itself: Engaging and meaningful tasks that people enjoy	WI_item2	I like the kind of work I do	Caillier (2012)
			WI_item3	My job gives me a sense of personal satisfaction	Caillier (2012)
			WI_item4	Considering everything, how satisfied are you with your job?	Kim and Lee (2020) and Ki and Lee (2024)

(continued)

Table 2 (continued)

	Variable name	Variable definition	Item	Item definition	Adapted from
		Level of responsibility: Empowering employees with ownership of their work		Individuals who work in TW are evaluated/held responsible for their actions as much as those who work in presence	
	Responsibility		RE_item1	Individuals who work in TW are evaluated/held responsible for their actions as much as those who work in presence.	Monroe and Haug (2023)
			RE_item2	I have the opportunity to put my ideas into practice at work	Palumbo et al. (2021)
			RE_item3	I am involved in initiatives that aim to improve the organization (UNIPV)	Palumbo et al. (2021)
			RE_item4	I participate in the definition of organizational objectives	Palumbo et al. (2021)
			RE_item5	I have the ability to influence important decisions	Palumbo et al. (2021)
			RE_item6	I have a say in decisions that affect my work	Giacomini and Palumbo (2023)
			RE_item7	I am asked to give suggestions on how to do my job better	Giacomini and Palumbo (2023)
	Career_advance	Advancement: Opportunity for promotions and career advancements	CA_item3	I would be very happy to continue my career in UNIPV	Perego and Belardinelli (2024)

	Personal_growth	Personal growth: Encouraging development and learning	PG_item1	My supervisor/boss gives me constructive suggestions to improve my work performance	Caillier (2012)
			PG_item2	My supervisor/boss is able to offer constructive feedback to both me and my colleagues (indicating opportunities for improvement)	de Miranda et al. (2024)
Dependent variable	TW_Satisfaction	Factors influencing the level of satisfactions toward TW	TWS_item1	TW make me feel free	Bonacciet al. (2024)
			TWS_item2	Due to TW I can manage my work schedule with more freedom	Bonacciet al. (2024)
			TWS_item3	TW has improved my work-life balance	Bonacci et al. (2024)
			TWS_item4	TW has increased my work motivation	Bonacciet al. (2024)
			TWS_item5	The ability to work in TW is a great benefit for the agency to recruit and retain its workforce	Monroe and Haug (2022)
			TWS_item6	My job satisfaction has increased thanks to TW	Bonacci et al. (2024)

(continued)

Table 3 Covariance matrix

	(1)	(2)	(3)	(3)	(4)	(5)	(6)	(7)	(8)	(9)	(10)	(11)
Policy_procedures (1)	0.409	0.145	0.218	0.251	0.194	0.109	0.212	0.273	0.197	0.295	0.336	0.098
Personal_relations (2)	0.145	0.607	0.113	0.178	0.151	0.322	0.084	0.186	0.111	0.149	0.249	0.320
Work_conditions (3)	0.218	0.113	0.535	0.196	0.276	0.063	0.450	0.171	0.330	0.222	0.218	0.058
Supervision (4)	0.251	0.178	0.196	0.462	0.150	0.122	0.180	0.390	0.195	0.259	0.450	0.146
Salary (5)	0.194	0.151	0.276	0.150	0.941	−0.015	0.270	0.129	0.167	0.160	0.172	0.056
Achievement (6)	0.109	0.322	0.063	0.122	−0.015	0.701	0.073	0.103	0.105	0.113	0.108	0.320
Advancement (7)	0.212	0.084	0.450	0.181	0.270	0.073	0.813	0.195	0.338	0.217	0.232	0.084
Acknowledgment (8)	0.273	0.186	0.171	0.390	0.130	0.103	0.195	0.573	0.209	0.259	0.567	0.141
Work_itself (9)	0.197	0.111	0.330	0.195	0.167	0.105	0.338	0.209	0.547	0.205	0.224	0.071
Responsibility (10)	0.295	0.149	0.222	0.259	0.160	0.113	0.217	0.259	0.205	0.470	0.291	0.089
Personal_growth (11)	0.336	0.249	0.218	0.450	0.172	0.108	0.232	0.567	0.224	0.291	0.780	0.167
TW_Satisfaction (12)	0.098	0.320	0.058	0.146	0.056	0.320	0.084	0.141	0.071	0.089	0.167	0.453

Table 4 Variance inflation factors (VIF)

Hygiene factors	VIF	Motivator factors	VIF
Policy_procedures	2.39	Advancement	1.96
Personal_relations	1.56	Acknowledgment	4.2
Work_conditions	2.59	Work_itself	1.77
Supervision_lat	2.96	Responsibility	2.07
Salary	1.27	Personal_growth	4.29
Achievement	1.41		

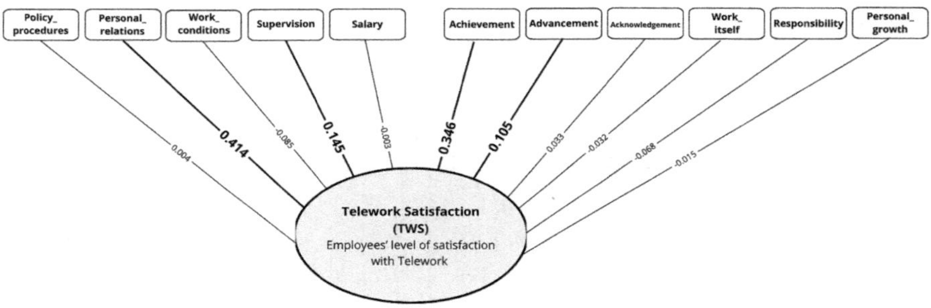

Fig. 2 Path analysis

However, after the item selection process, we found that SEM was not the most suitable approach for our study. This model does not perform well when certain variables are based on a single item, and saturation issues emerged. To address these challenges, we opted for Path Analysis, which allowed us to resolve the overfitting issue and simplify the model by constructing variables using the mean of their corresponding items.

By analyzing the covariance matrix (Table 3) and performing a VIF test (Table 4), we confirmed that all results were still below the accepted threshold of 5 [34], indicating no multicollinearity issues. The Path Analysis model was implemented using R language and RStudio software. The model demonstrated an excellent fit to the data (Table 6). Furthermore, we successfully resolved the saturation and overfitting issue by significantly reducing the number of parameters, resulting in a final model comprising 12 parameters based on 365 complete observations (out of the 373 responses from employees who regularly engage in TW).

The results of the Path Analysis are illustrated in Fig. 2 and summarized in Table 5.

Table 5 Path analysis results (elaborated with R Studio)

	Variables	Estimate	Stand. err.	z-value	P-value	β (Std.all)
Hygiene factors	Policy_procedures	0.004	0.061	0.063	0.950	0.004
	Personal_relations	0.358	0.040	8.853	0.000	0.414
	Work_conditions	−0.079	0.055	−1.418	0.156	−0.085
	Supervision_lat	0.143	0.064	2.243	0.025	0.145
	Salary	−0.002	0.029	−0.069	0.945	−0.003
Motivator factors	Achievement	0.278	0.036	7.778	0.000	0.346
	Advancement	0.078	0.039	1.999	0.046	0.105
	Acknowledgment	0.030	0.068	0.435	0.664	0.033
	Work_itself	−0.029	0.045	−0.650	0.516	−0.032
	Responsibility	−0.067	0.053	−1.258	0.209	−0.068
	Personal_growth	−0.012	0.059	−0.198	0.843	−0.015
Dependent variable	TW_Satisfaction	0.232	0.017	13.509	0.000	0.512

Table 6 Model fit (elaborated with RStudio)

Fit Index	Value
CFI	1000
TLI	1000
RMSEA	0.000
SRMR	0.000

4 Findings

Our model includes all variables representing both hygiene factors and motivators, maintaining even those that did not reach statistical significance (p-value > 0.05). Our analysis identified four variables with a significant impact on TWS. Among the hygiene factors, interpersonal relations emerged as the strongest predictor of TWS (Personal_relations: $\beta = 0.414$), suggesting that maintaining positive relationships and effective collaboration with colleagues, both during in-person work and teleworking, is a fundamental driver of TWS.

Additionally, having trust in and a good relationship with one's supervisor(s) also moderately but positively influences TWS (Supervision: $\beta = 0.145$). Regarding motivators, the sense of achievement—employees' feeling of being capable of achieving meaningful results—has the greatest impact on TWS (Achievement: $\beta = 0.346$). Finally, opportunities for advancement also play a significant, though more moderate, role in enhancing TWS (Advancement: $\beta = 0.105$). An overview of Path Analysis results and overall model fit are provided in Tables 5 and 6, respectively.

4.1 Common Source Bias

Because our study relies on data from a single entity, it may be subject to common source bias. To address this concern, we followed the approach of Metselaar and colleagues (2023) [22]. Although our variables are indeed perceptual and self-reported, employees' perceptions of TW and their level of telework satisfaction are central to our investigation. Therefore, despite the potential bias, we consider this data both valid and relevant for our analysis.

5 Discussion and Implications

Our findings offer several insights that are well-anchored in the existing literature. Notably, the fact that some variables are not significant is, in itself, an interesting finding within the context of our study—the administrative and technical staff of the University of Pavia. In these settings, factors such as job stability and standardized salary progression (e.g., advancement through public competition) are often taken for granted by employees, which may explain why they do not significantly influence telework satisfaction.

Our Path Analysis results reveal mixed findings that partially confirm both H1a and H2a. On the one hand, the strongest predictor of TWS is a hygiene factor, *interpersonal relations* (Personal_relations: β = 0.414). This suggests that maintaining positive and trust-based relationships with colleagues, both in person and remotely, is a fundamental driver of TWS. Additionally, the quality of the relationship with supervisors also exerts a significant yet moderate influence (Supervision: $\beta = 0.145$). From this perspective, our findings align with the existing literature: one of the most significant challenges associated with TW is the risk of isolation and the deterioration of interpersonal relationships and overall sense of belonging [6]. Therefore, having well-established and solid relationships with both supervisors and colleagues helps mitigate these risks, especially considering that the majority of respondents telework only once or twice a week, a pattern shown to reduce feelings of isolation. Indeed, a balanced mix of TW and in-office work fosters a greater sense of connection [4]. The significant role of supervision is also supported by previous studies [26], which highlight the importance of trust-building management as a key determinant of organizational performance when TW is implemented.

On the other hand, among the motivators, the sense of personal achievement (Achievement: $\beta = 0.346$)—meaning that employees feel capable of achieving their work goals, improving performance, and enhancing effectiveness—emerges as an essential factor. The University environment appears to foster a favorable context for TW, enabling employees to feel both productive and accountable, as observed by Monroe and Haug (2021) [24]. Applying Herzberg's two-factor theory (1959) [27] in this context underscores that while hygiene factors establish the necessary baseline for satisfaction, motivators, particularly personal achievement, are essential for telework to be perceived as truly meaningful rather than merely acceptable.

Overall, our findings align with previous studies and reaffirm the relevance of the two-factor theory in understanding modern workplaces [11]. They suggest that both hygiene factors and motivators contribute to TWS, with hygiene factors exerting the strongest influence, yet with a crucial contribution from personal achievement as a motivator. This could imply that, for telework to be truly satisfying, public organizations must first establish a solid foundation of good working conditions (hygiene factors). However, to maximize TWS, they must also cultivate an environment where employees experience a strong sense of achievement and purpose that is also reflected in the employees' desire to continue their career inside the organization (motivators). The interplay between hygiene factors and motivators in determining TWS suggests that telework is a rather complex phenomenon, extending beyond its functional role as a tool for working from a different location.

In essence, our findings suggest that a positive telework experience depends on two key aspects. First, trust-based interpersonal relationships with both colleagues and supervisors are fundamental; telework thrives in environments where strong professional bonds exist, effectively mitigating the risks of isolating people. Second, a strong sense of personal achievement is essential for sustained motivation and satisfaction when working remotely. Employees must feel that their work is meaningful and that they are making significant progress toward their goals; otherwise, engagement may gradually decline.

6 Conclusions and Limitations

Our study contributes to the growing body of research on flexible work arrangements (FWA) with a particular focus on telework satisfaction (TWS). We investigated the key drivers of satisfaction with this work modality by adopting Herzberg's well-established two-factor theory, which has proven valid even in contemporary settings [11].

We argue that a deeper understanding of the factors influencing TWS can help public managers enhance the FWA they implement, thereby enabling organizations to fully leverage the benefits of telework. When properly managed, telework can lead to increased productivity, higher engagement, improved job satisfaction, and a better work-life balance. At the same time, organizations can work to mitigate potential drawbacks, such as reduced socialization and collaboration.

However, our study is not without limitations. First, it is based on data from a single organization, which may limit the generalizability of our findings due to the influence of organization-specific culture and practices. Second, our focus on a public institution, which has distinct characteristics compared to the private sector, means that results may differ in other organizational contexts. To address these limitations, future research should explore and compare insights across diverse settings, including both public and private organizations and various national contexts. Moreover, further studies should investigate additional factors (e.g., digital competencies, gender, or age) that may affect the relationship between individual characteristics and telework satisfaction. Such a broader approach would contribute to a more comprehensive understanding of TWS and its key drivers.

References

1. De Vries, H., Tummers, L., Bekkers, V.: The benefits of teleworking in the public sector: reality or rhetoric? Rev. Publ. Pers. Admin. **39**, 570–593 (2019). https://doi.org/10.1177/0734371X18760124
2. Park, J.W., Park, S., Cho, Y.J.: More isn't always better: exploring the curvilinear effects of telework. Int. Publ. Manage. J. **26**, 744–763 (2023). https://doi.org/10.1080/10967494.2023.2214133
3. Carbonara, N., Pellegrino, R., Scozzi, B.: The impact of smart working on organization performance. EJKM. **20**, 152–166 (2022). https://doi.org/10.34190/ejkm.20.3.2611
4. Perego, A., Belardinelli, P.: Telework and public employees' attitudes post-pandemic: experimental evidence from Italy. Rev. Publ. Pers. Admin. (2024). https://doi.org/10.1177/0734371X241227426

5. Mele, V., Belardinelli, P., Bellé, N.: Telework in public organizations: a systematic review and research agenda. Publ. Admin. Rev. **83**, 1649–1666 (2023). https://doi.org/10.1111/puar.13734
6. Palumbo, R., Flamini, G., Gnan, L., Pellegrini, M.M.: Looking for meanings at work: unraveling the implications of smart working on organizational meaningfulness. IJOA. **31**, 624–645 (2023). https://doi.org/10.1108/IJOA-04-2021-2708
7. Perry, J.L., Engbers, T.A., Jun, S.Y.: Back to the future? Performance-related pay, empirical research, and the perils of persistence. Publ. Admin. Rev. **69**, 39–51 (2009). https://doi.org/10.1111/j.1540-6210.2008.01939_2.x
8. Jung, G., Moon, K.-K.: Examining public service motivation's impact on organizational commitment: focusing on moderating roles of hygiene and motivation factors. Behav. Sci. **14**, 476 (2024). https://doi.org/10.3390/bs14060476
9. Herzberg, F.: Work and the nature of man. World Publ, New York (1966)
10. Herzberg, F.: One more time: how do you motivate employees? In: Gruneberg, M.M. (ed.) Job Satisfaction—A Reader, pp. 17–32. Palgrave Macmillan, London (1976). https://doi.org/10.1007/978-1-349-02701-9_2
11. Mitsakis, M., Galanakis, M.: An empirical examination of Herzberg's theory in the 21st century workplace. Organizational psychology re-examined. Psychology. **13**, 264–272 (2022). https://doi.org/10.4236/psych.2022.132015
12. Mazzucchelli, S.: Flexibility and work-family balance: a win-win solution for companies? The case of Italy. Int. Rev. Sociol., 1–21 (2017). https://doi.org/10.1080/03906701.2017.1377411
13. Angelici, M., Profeta, P.: Smart working: work flexibility without constraints. Manage. Sci. **70**, 1680–1705 (2024). https://doi.org/10.1287/mnsc.2023.4767
14. Bonacci, I., Scarozza, D., Greco, E.: The innovative implications of smart working in a post-pandemic era: a model of smart working satisfaction in public sector organizations. Admin. Soc. **56**, 911–940 (2024). https://doi.org/10.1177/00953997241261614
15. Caillier, J.G.: Satisfaction with work-life benefits and organizational commitment/job involvement: is there a connection? Rev. Publ. Pers. Admin. **33**, 340–364 (2013). https://doi.org/10.1177/0734371X12443266
16. Caillier, J.G.: Do role clarity and job satisfaction mediate the relationship between telework and work effort? Int. J. Publ. Admin. **37**, 193–201 (2014). https://doi.org/10.1080/01900692.2013.798813
17. Kim, S.Y., Lee, D.: Work–life program participation and employee work attitudes: a quasi-experimental analysis using matching methods. Rev. Publ. Pers. Admin. **40**, 468–490 (2020). https://doi.org/10.1177/0734371X18823250
18. Baruch, Y.: The status of research on teleworking and an agenda for future research. Int. J. Manage. Rev. **3**, 113–129 (2001). https://doi.org/10.1111/1468-2370.00058
19. Fleischer, J., Wanckel, C.: Job satisfaction and the digital transformation of the public sector: the mediating role of job autonomy. Rev. Publ. Pers. Admin. **44**, 431–452 (2024). https://doi.org/10.1177/0734371X221148403
20. Bae, K.B., Kim, D.: The Impact of Decoupling of Telework on Job Satisfaction in U.S. Federal Agencies. American Review of Public Administration
21. Kwon, M., Kim-Goh, M.: The impacts of telework options on worker outcomes in local government: social exchange and social exclusion perspectives. Rev. Publ. Pers. Admin. **43**, 754–773 (2023). https://doi.org/10.1177/0734371X221121051
22. Metselaar, S.A., Den Dulk, L., Vermeeren, B.: Teleworking at different locations outside the office: consequences for perceived performance and the mediating role of autonomy and work-life balance satisfaction. Rev. Publ. Pers. Admin. **43**, 456–478 (2023). https://doi.org/10.1177/0734371X221087421
23. Lewis, G.B., Pizarro-Bore, X., Emidy, M.B.: Who gets denied telework in the U.S. Federal Service? Rev. Publ. Pers. Admin. **46**(3) (2024). https://doi.org/10.1177/0734371X241274126
24. Monroe, R.W., Haug, J.C.: Assessment of telework in a Federal Agency at the operational phase. Publ. Org. Rev. **22**, 725–742 (2022). https://doi.org/10.1007/s11115-021-00538-0

25. Mehta, P.: Work from HOME—WORK engagement amid COVID-19 lockdown and employee happiness. J. Publ. Affairs. **21**, e2709 (2021). https://doi.org/10.1002/pa.2709
26. Kim, T., Mullins, L.B., Yoon, T.: Supervision of telework: a key to organizational performance. Am. Rev. Publ. Admin. **51**, 263–277 (2021). https://doi.org/10.1177/0275074021992058
27. Herzberg, F., Mausner, B.: Snyderman: The Motivation to Work, 2nd edn. Wiley, Hoboken, NJ (1959)
28. Thant, Z.M., Chang, Y.: Determinants of public employee job satisfaction in Myanmar: focus on Herzberg's Two Factor Theory. Publ. Org. Rev. **21**, 157–175 (2021). https://doi.org/10.1007/s11115-020-00481-6
29. Aggarwal, A., Sadhna, P., Gupta, S., Mittal, A., Rastogi, S.: Gen Z entering the workforce: restructuring HR policies and practices for fostering the task performance and organizational commitment. J. Publ. Affairs. **22**, e2535 (2022). https://doi.org/10.1002/pa.2535
30. Alshmemri, M., Shahwan-Akl, L., & Maude, P. (2017). Herzberg's two-factor theory. Life Science Journal, 14(5), 12–16.
31. Cellini, M., Pisacane, L., Crescimbene, M., Di Felice, F.: Exploring employee perceptions towards smart working during the COVID-19 pandemic: a comparative analysis of two Italian Public Research Organizations. Publ. Org. Rev. **21**, 815–833 (2021). https://doi.org/10.1007/s11115-021-00559-9
32. FPA Annual Report 2023: la sintesi dei dati. https://www.forumpa.it/riforma-pa/fpa-annual-report-il-2023-della-pa-piu-competente-efficiente-e-digitale/. Accessed 28 Jun 2025
33. Ritrovare l'ambizione e credere nei giovani: l'employer pubblico. https://www.forumpa.it/riforma-pa/ritrovare-lambizione-e-credere-nei-giovani-lemployer-pubblico-come-prima-scelta-per-le-nuove-generazioni/. Accessed 28 Jun 2025
34. Kock, N., Lynn, G.: Lateral collinearity and misleading results in variance-based SEM: an illustration and recommendations. JAIS. **13**, 546–580 (2012). https://doi.org/10.17705/1jais.00302
35. Krosnick, J.A., Fabrigar, L.R.: Designing rating scales for effective measurement in surveys. In: Lyberg, L., Biemer, P., Collins, M., De Leeuw, E., Dippo, C., Schwarz, N., Trewin, D. (eds.) Wiley Series in Probability and Statistics, pp. 141–164. Wiley, Hoboken, NJ (1997). https://doi.org/10.1002/9781118490013.ch6

Navigating Cobot Adoption in Industry 5.0: Exploration of Key Success Factors for the Adoption of Cobots in Manufacturing

Nisar Ahmed Channa, Gian Luca Casali, Claudio Del Regno, Greg Hearn, and Mirko Perano

Abstract Collaborative robots, also known as Cobots, are rapidly evolving as part of the new strategy of Industry 5.0 which advocates cooperative working between human and non-human agents to deliver a more human-centric, resilient, and sustainable future. However, despite these potentials, the adoption of Cobots is challenging precisely because the nature of these technologies involves workforce and innovation issues. This paper aims at locating critical components of the process of firms' adoption of Cobots and discussing key success factors of Cobot adoption that may benefit future research and practice. To this end, we adopted a content analysis approach and analyzed literature from 2020 to 2024 to determine critical components that may impact firms' adoption process. We explored 14 enablement components from a compilation of 155 variables identified in literature and integrated them into key success factors of Cobot adoption. Our study contributes to the theorization of key success factors that influence the adoption of Cobots in manufacturing and how these factors help to understand paradigm shift toward Industry 5.0. This theorization is of vital importance for both industry practitioners and researchers interested in studying Cobots adoption in manufacturing from a paradigm shift approach.

Keywords Cobots · Collaborative Robot · Technological integration · Organizational capabilities · Industry 5.0 · Systematic literature review · Manufacturing

N. A. Channa · G. L. Casali · G. Hearn
Queensland University of Technology, Brisbane, QLD, Australia
e-mail: nisarahmed.channa@hdr.qut.edu.au; luca.casali@qut.edu.au; g.hearn@qut.edu.au

C. Del Regno · M. Perano (✉)
University of Salerno, Fisciano, Italy
e-mail: cldelregno@unisa.it; mperano@unisa.it

N. Omrani et al. (eds.), *Human-Machine Synergy and the Digital Future - Exploring Collaboration and Competition Volume 1*, Springer Proceedings in Business and Economics, https://doi.org/10.1007/978-3-032-21347-1_10

1 Introduction

Collaborative robots or "Cobots" are one of the most innovative technological advancements of the current era which academics and industry experts argue has the potential to revolutionize global manufacturing [1]. A Cobot is a context-aware, AI, and vision-enabled robot that can safely share workspace with both human operators and machines [2].

Industry 5.0 focuses on collaboration between human and non-human agents. The concept was introduced to address evolving industrial dynamics by emphasizing the integration of advanced production systems, machines, and human workers [3]. It highlights the transformation of manufacturing practices through human–machine collaboration while prioritizing workers' well-being [3, 4].

Industry experts and labor economists suggest that not only will Cobots be used as an alternative for human workers for performing repetitive, heavy, and laborious jobs in manufacturing, but this will also enable human workers to focus on more challenging and conceptual tasks [5, 6]. The adoption of Cobots may require restructuring existing manufacturing processes, business models, and workforce skill profiles. There are concerns about a lack of trust in human to work with Cobots and a lack of understanding among managers of significant opportunities and challenges that will arise in the evolution of Industry 5.0.

We argue that identification, categorization, and evaluation of key factors that influence the adoption of Cobots in manufacturing is needed to study these disruptive changes that emerged due to an industry paradigm shift from Industry 4.0 to Industry 5.0 from a firm's perspective. The existing literature on Cobots mainly focuses on engineering, design, and technical factors [1] and there is a paucity of consideration on this topic in literature as well [7–10].

To address these research gaps, we sought precedents from prior studies used for conceptual theory building. We adopted a content analysis approach and analyzed literature content published from 2020 to 2024. Firstly, we identified key components that may impact firms' adoption process. Secondly, we established empirical validity and reliability of identified components through using established procedures suggested in prior studies [11]. Finally, the empirically validated components were categorized into clusters theorizing the key factors that influence Cobot adoption process.

2 Methodology

To identify the key success factors contributing to a firm's adoption of Cobots. We followed precedents of [12] and conducted a content analysis of literature identifying key variables studied by previous Cobotics researchers. We adapted the problem-driven content analysis procedures outlined by the author [13], which include identifying relevant materials, defining the units of analysis, developing recording protocols, presenting findings, drawing conclusions, and validating the results. Each of these steps was carefully selected and executed to derive meaningful insights from the text while maximizing reliability and validity.

This research has been designed in two steps: the first explorative step one aims at identifying core concepts and keywords to be used in a specified query within a Systematic Literature Review (SLR) developed in the step two. Both the steps have been developed by using Scopus database.

2.1 Data

In applying the SLR with the keywords and Boolean operators defined "Cobot" OR "Collaborative Robot AND "Industry 5.0" AND "Adoption" and the settings "2020–2024 timespan" and search field "All fields" in Scopus database, the following string has been generated:

> (ALL ("Cobot") OR ALL ("Collaborative Robot") AND ALL ("Industry 5.0") AND ALL ("Adoption")) AND PUBYEAR>2020 AND PUBYEAR<2025

$N = 292$ documents have collected. We have filtered documents with the following rules: "Article" document type, "Business, Management and Accounting, Social Sciences, Multidisciplinary" subject areas, "English" language. The following string has been generated:

> ((ALL ("Cobot") OR ALL ("Collaborative Robot") AND ALL ("Industry 5.0") AND ALL ("Adoption")) AND PUBYEAR>2019 AND PUBYEAR<2025 AND (LIMIT-TO (SUBJAREA, "BUSI") OR LIMIT-TO (SUBJAREA, "SOCI") OR LIMIT-TO (SUBJAREA, "MULT"))

$N = 124$ documents have been extracted. The nature of scientific articles is structured as follows: $n = 74$ articles, $n = 22$ Book chapters $n = 14$ review papers, $n = 8$ books, $n = 6$ Conference.

3 Findings

Our analysis obtained a total of 155 variables used by various studies included our literature corpus. Abductive inference of contextual phenomena from textual data allows researchers to bridge the gap between the descriptive aspects of the text and the underlying meaning, by identifying unobserved phenomena that are significant to the analysis [14]. At this stage in the content analysis, we compiled a list of considerations without yet interpreting their meaning. We reviewed this data to group identified variables based on autocorrelation functions. After reaching a consensus, we identified 14 components from the initial list of 155 variables as depicted in Table 1. These components include dynamic capabilities, creativity environment, knowledge creation, human–robot collaboration models, technology integration, human–Cobot interaction, advanced technologies environment, workforce issues in relation to technology needs, innovation processes, skills, job redesign, workforce readiness, adoption process, and spectrum of adoption/ adoption issues.

The analytical constructs, referred to as components of the firm's adoption process, were derived from the literature and used to cluster into key success factors of firms' adoption of Cobots based on our knowledge and experience with established technology adoption theories. The extrapolation of these 14 components indicates that these factors encompass the considerations necessary for firms' adoption of Cobots. To validate these results, empirical testing was conducted.

4 Empirical Validity

To assess the convergence and distinction of identified components with existing literature, we endeavor to evaluate current Cobots implementation frameworks and compared the findings of our content analysis with the factors elaborated in prior frameworks. In this section, we outline our literature search procedures for identifying these Cobot implementation frameworks, our assessment of each framework, and our conclusions regarding the reliability and validity of our results.

4.1 Data Collection

The step two starts from the deliverable obtained in the step one outcome. The criteria to select articles for establishing empirical validity of our results simple and straightforward: it had to include a Cobot implementation framework. We used Scopus database to locate articles with the keywords and Boolean operators defined "Cobots Implementation" OR "Cobots Adoption" AND "Industry 5.0 Adoption" OR "Industry 5.0 Implementation" AND "Framework" OR "Model" and the settings "2020–2024 timespan" and search field "All fields." The following string has been generated:

((ALL ("Cobots Implementation") OR ALL ("Cobots Adoption") AND ALL ("Industry 5.0 Adoption") OR ALL ("Industry 5.0 Implication") AND ALL("Framework") OR ALL ("Model")) AND PUBYEAR>2020 AND PUBYEAR<2025

Table 1 Variables used in Cobots adoption research (Step one)

Variables	General factors
Dynamic capability perspective, dynamic capability theory, seizing capability mediates, collaborative capability, digitalization capability, transforming capabilities	Dynamic capabilities
Creativity dimensions, individual creativity, creativity, creativity dimensions, individual creativity, value creation	Creativity environment
Knowledge, green knowledge creation, green knowledge search, knowledge transfer, theoretical knowledge	Knowledge creation
Collaborative, alternating collaboration, anticipated collaboration, bounded collaboration, collaborative applications, collaborative robot applications, collaborative robot solutions, collaborative robotics, collaborative robots classification, collaborative space, collaborative technology, direct-assistance collaboration, human–robot collaborations, industrial collaborative network, industrial collaborative robot, machine collaborations, parallel collaboration, robot collaboration, robotic collaboration implementation, sequential collaboration, socio-ethical collaborative robots	Human–robot collaboration models
Integrating, integrated architecture, integrated work system, integrating Cobots, integrating innovation, integrating perception, integration knowledge, seamless integration, seamlessly integration, vital integration	Technology integration
Interaction, human–machine interaction, human–robot interaction research, human–robot interactions, interaction modeling, man–machine interaction, unique interaction model, work system interactions	Human–Cobot interaction
Technological, blockchain technology, collaborative technology, cutting-edge technologies, digital technologies, emerging technologies, enabling technologies, key technologies, new-age technology adoption, open technologies, technological backwardness, technological development, technological framework, technological innovation, technological innovations, technological instruments, technological measures, technological substitution, technologies utilization, technology adoption, technology advancements, technology assessments, technology elements, technology providers	Advanced technologies environment
Future industry demands, future workforce demands, future workforce requirements, skilled workforce, workforce role, workplace, hybrid workplace, industrial workplaces, shared workplace	Workforce issues in relation to technology needs
Innovation, green innovation activities, green innovation performance, innovation management, innovative solutions, integrating innovation, technological innovation, innovation theory, innovative results, integrating innovation, personal innovativeness, technological innovations	Innovation processes
Evolving skill requirements, multidisciplinary skill mix, skilled workforce, social skills	Skills

(continued)

Table 1 (continued)

Variables	General factors
Tasks, multimode multiprocessor task, multiple work tasks, operational tasks, work, actual work practices, transformation, addressing workers, changed work situation, future work, human workers, integrated work system, multiple work tasks, research work, routine work, smart work cell solution, supportive production workers, work system interactions, work system perspective, worker safety, working life, working rhythms, workforce	Job redesign
Workforce role, workplace, hybrid workplace, industrial workplaces, shared workplace, readiness, enhancing safety readiness, industrial Cobot safety readiness, readiness level	Workforce readiness
Process, adoption process, ambidextrous business process management, food processing industries	Adoption process
Adoption barriers, adoption level, adoption process, adoption theories, cobots adoption, effective adoption, future adoption, future adoption challenges, new-age technology adoption, robotics adoption, successful adoption, technology adoption	Adoption issues

Only n = 3 articles have been obtained. We thoroughly read identified articles and found that only one article is relevant to our analysis. To locate more literature, we again go back to our original literature corpus and tried to locate research studies that proposed an implementation framework or model. Although many articles were retrieved and reviewed, only four met the criteria. Both methods used to locate literature yielded a total of five articles that met our criteria.

4.2 Evaluation of Frameworks

The exhaustive search described above resulted in five studies that met our criteria. To validate our findings, we evaluated the frameworks proposed in these studies to determine the extent of agreement with the components identified in the findings. The results of this comparison are presented in Table 2, showing the considerations covered by each framework.

Similarly, authors elaborated discriminant validity as "the extent to which correlations are absent between results and variables known to be valid but measuring phenomena that are distinctly different" (p. 319) [13]. If an existing framework included all the components identified in our analysis, it would suggest that enablement of firms' readiness to adopt Cobots is not significantly different from other Cobot implementation frameworks. However, our findings did not support this. We compared each framework against the 14 components from our analysis to assess divergence levels. Percent agreement was calculated by dividing the number of components present in each framework by the total number of components identified in our analysis, as shown in the far-right column of Table 2. The results indicate that no single framework includes all components, suggesting sufficient divergence from existing frameworks.

Table 2 Evaluation of existing Cobot implementation frameworks (Step two)

Study	1	2	3	4	5	6	7	8	9	10	11	12	13	14	C. a. in f. (%)
Dornelles et al. (2023)				X		X				X					0.21
Silva et al. (2024)	X		X			X			X						0.28
Liu and Son (2024)	X		X										X		0.21
Simões et al. (2020)			X				X					X	X		0.21
Zemlyak et al. (2022)	X						X		X	X	X				0.35
Framework addressing consideration (%)	0.6	0	0.6	0.2	0	0.4	0.4	0	0.4	0.4	0.2	0.2	0.4	0	

Note: Columns 1–14 represents the variables: 1 = Dynamic capabilities; 2 = Creativity environment; 3 = knowledge creation; 4 = Human–robot collaboration models; 5 = Technology integration; 6 = Human–cobot interaction; 7 = Advanced technologies environment; 8 = Workforce issues in relation to technology needs; 9 = Innovation processes; 10 = Skills; 11 = Job redesign; 12 = Work force readiness; 13 = Adoption processes; 14 = Adoption Issues. Column 15 represents the Components addressed in framework (%)

5 Key Success Factors for the Adoption of Cobots in Manufacturing

The components we discussed in previous sections lay the groundwork for a firm's adoption of Cobots. However, merely identifying and explaining these components is insufficient for theorizing key factors for adoption of Cobots; unless we categorize and put them together in clusters. Thus, the next step is to combine these components into key factors. To put identified components into clusters, we used a two-step two novel approach. Firstly, we used generative AI to categorize identified components into clusters. The use of generative AI tools to cluster or categorize variables into different groups is supported by a number of studies. Generative AI tools such as Chat GPT, Copilot, and Gemini are useful for classification, identification of similarities and differences, and concise definition of characteristics to understand the distinctions among the subjects [15]. Secondly, to validate the clusters identified by generative AI, an expert meeting was organized where all the authors were presented and discussed the findings. The generative AI output was thoroughly discussed and each of the identified cluster and its components were reviewed to ensure that all the components included in the cluster are homogenous and have similarities in their definitions. It was ensured that components in each cluster group represent commonalities in their definition. The authors unanimously concluded that except cluster 3, all the identified clusters (Table 3) are appropriate, and their components positioned closely together. The reason why authors believe cluster 3 is inappropriate and need to be revised is the fact that dynamic capabilities are organizational capabilities that help organizations to remain competitive and resilient during changing market dynamics. Therefore, the authors believe "creativity," "innovation," and "knowledge creation" are the components of dynamic capabilities that help organizations to remain competitive and resilient. Thus, we changed

Table 3 Key factors of influencing Cobot adoption in manufacturing

Key factors	Identified components
Technological integration and interaction	Technology integration
	Advanced technologies environment
	Human–robot collaboration models
	Human–Cobot interaction
Workforce and skills	Workforce issues in relation to technology needs
	Skills
	Job redesign
	Workforce readiness
Innovation and creativity	Dynamic capabilities
	Creativity environment
	Innovation processes
	Knowledge creation
Adoption and implementation	Adoption process
	Spectrum of adoption

the name of cluster 3 from "Innovation and Creativity" to "Organizational Capabilities."

Owing to the potential influence that Cobots can have on the customization and manufacturing of goods and the overall performance of the manufacturing sector, it has become a strategic priority for manufacturing companies [16]. With this increased awareness of Cobots among managers and manufacturing policymakers, we now discuss key success factors for the adoption of Cobots in manufacturing, a relatively new focus. Our findings indicate four key success factors that impact to firms' adoption of this innovative technology.

5.1 Technological Integration and Interaction

Technological integration and interaction refer to the process of incorporating new technologies into existing workflows, systems, or environments and the ways in which humans and technologies interact and collaborate. Our analysis revealed that technological integration and interaction is often affected by human–robot collaboration models, human–robot interaction, and advanced technology environment.

Human–robot collaboration deals with to "integrate the best of two worlds: strength, endurance, repeatability and accuracy of the robots with the intuition, flexibility and versatile problem-solving and sensory skills of the humans" (p. 369:5) [17]. Classifying applications of Cobots, some authors reported that integration of Cobots to perform specific tasks requires safety and well-being of humans collaborating with them and regarded safety one of the key factors affecting efficiency of human–robot collaboration models [18]. In reviewed literature, we identified different human–robot collaboration models.

The reviewed content suggested that the digital transformation fueled by the evolution of Industry 4.0 is crucial to sustain and compete in long term. It plays a key role in competitiveness of global firms and therefore the integration of advanced technologies must surpass short-term management goals [19]. Also, the complexity of integration challenges needs to be addressed in a sustainable manner, without adversely affecting organizational performance [19]. The reviewed content also suggested a notable intersection and co-evolution between Society 5.0 and Industry 5.0 [20]. These complementary visions both promote the integration of advanced technologies with human-centric approaches. Society 5.0 offers a broad framework for societal transformation, while Industry 5.0 provides a roadmap for industrial evolution within this framework. Industry 5.0 brings changes not only to manufacturing but also to sectors like transportation and logistics, marketing, and communication [20]. Also, the literature highlighted that integration of technology cannot be done without alignment of organizational systems and routines [21]. Automating certain tasks is only successful when significant changes are made in organization, design, and production. Other tasks can be effectively automated by integrating advanced equipment with existing machinery and human workers [21].

By integrating and interacting with technology such as Cobots, organizations can stay competitive, improve efficiency by streamlining processes and reducing manual effort, enhance innovation by enabling new ways of working and problem-solving.

5.2 *Workforce and Skills*

Workforce and skills refer to the human aspect of an organization, focusing on the abilities and readiness of employees to adapt to and work with new technologies. It deals with the collective group of employees or workers within an organization their abilities and expertise required to perform tasks effectively, especially in relation to new technologies. Workforce and skills are often affected by workforce issues in relation to technology adoption, skills, job redesign, and workforce readiness.

The adoption of Cobots in manufacturing is expected to enhance the quality of work by providing room for self-development and work autonomy to workers, thus enabling human workers to act as problem-solvers and strategic decision-makers [22]. Human–Cobot collaboration can combine high levels of accuracy, speed, precision, and repeatability of Cobot with cognitive skills, creativity, sensitivity, and flexibility of human workers to achieve sustainable and economically viable manufacturing processes [23, 24].

The adoption of Cobots require organization to focus on development of abilities, skills, and readiness of employees to adapt to and work with new technologies. Organizations need to ensure that workforce can adapt to technological changes to maintain productivity and competitiveness. Organizations also need to equip their workforce with new skills to drive innovation and implement new technologies effectively so that they can work effectively with Cobots and contribute to the long-term sustainability and growth of the organization. By focusing on workforce and skills, organizations can better navigate the challenges and opportunities presented by technological advancements such as Cobots.

5.3 *Organizational Capabilities*

Organizational capabilities refer to the collective skills, abilities, and expertise that an organization possesses, enabling it to achieve its goals and maintain a competitive advantage. These capabilities are developed over time through the combination of resources, processes, and knowledge.

There are various organizational factors that influence the adoption of Cobots. The role of an organization's dynamic capabilities is relevant in determining the success of Cobot adoption [25]. For the authors to reap the benefits of Cobot technology, it is important for manufacturers to possess dynamic capabilities [25]. They empirically tested a framework suggesting that adoption of Cobots improves organizations' human resource, operational, and market performance. Human machine collaboration element of Industry 5.0 put human workers at forefront of production processes using technologies such as AI and Cobots to augment human skills and creativity and create a sustainable industrial landscape [20]. Similarly, the correlation between creativity and employee work behavior in a human–Cobot collaborative work environment was explored [26]. Their findings suggested employee having creativity traits are likely to work in a human–machine collaborative environment due to assumption that advanced technologies such as Cobots will enhance their creative work skills.

Another variable we discovered in our literature corpus is "knowledge management." Various authors highlighted the importance of knowledge in adoption of Cobots and other Industry 5.0 fueled technologies. While arguing about the importance of Cobot safety readiness, While discussing the importance of Cobot safety, it was highlighted that due to lack of knowledge and awareness about safety, the adoption of Cobots is limited [27]. To address this challenge, they developed and tested a tool to enhance safety and knowledge awareness about Cobots using a system-wide perspective.

Organizations with robust capabilities can better respond to market changes, technological advancements, and other external factors caused by industry paradigm shift. By developing and leveraging organizational capabilities, companies can enhance their performance, drive innovation, and achieve long-term success through adoption of technologies like Cobots.

5.4 Adoption and Implementation

Adoption and implementation refer to the processes involved in introducing and integrating new technologies, practices, or innovations within an organization. It deals with the process of accepting, acquiring, and starting to use new technologies or practices, and putting the adopted technology or practice into action within the organization. Proper adoption and implementation can lead to more efficient processes and operations, can provide a competitive edge, can better equipped to adapt to changes in the market and industry. Adoption and implementation are often affected by adoption processes, and adoption issues.

The adoption process refers to the series of steps an organization or individual goes through to accept and begin using a new technology, practice, or innovation. Researchers illuminate that technology adoption is not a single event but a transition [28, 29], where the organization progresses through different stages of adoption characterized by varying levels of readiness, defined as "the willingness and capacity of companies to implement ideas" [28]. At each stage, organizations must address different aspects of technology adoption, with varying implications for workers. Various studies suggest that the perceived benefits of a technology influence their process of adoption. Perceived advantage of a technology (i.e., relative advantage, compatibility, complexity, observability, and trialability) influence the adoption of technology [30].

Understanding and managing the Cobot adoption process, organizations can effectively integrate these advanced technologies and innovations, leading to improved performance and growth; while the adoption and implementation can lead to more efficient Cobot adoption processes and operations. This will also result into enhancement of organization's ability to respond to market changes and technological advancements and development of competitive advantage.

6 Cobot Adoption as Enabler of Industry 5.0

We believe that the adoption of Cobots is closely aligned with the principles and goals of Industry 5.0. It is because Cobots are designed to work alongside humans, enhancing their capabilities rather than replacing them. This aligns with Industry 5.0's emphasis on human-centricity, where the well-being and creativity of workers are prioritized. Cobots can take over repetitive, dangerous, or physically demanding tasks, allowing humans to focus on more complex and creative activities. Cobots facilitate seamless collaboration between humans and machines. They are equipped with advanced sensors and safety features that allow them to operate safely in close proximity to humans. This collaboration enhances productivity and innovation, as humans can leverage the precision and efficiency of Cobots while contributing their unique problem-solving skills. Cobots are highly flexible and can be quickly adapted to different tasks and production environments. This aligns with Industry 5.0's focus on resilience and adaptability. Cobots can be easily integrated into existing workflows and can be reprogrammed to respond to changing production needs, making them ideal for dynamic and unpredictable environments. Cobots are designed with safety in mind, featuring sensors and algorithms that prevent collisions and ensure safe interactions with human workers. This focus on safety aligns with Industry 5.0's goal of creating a safe and supportive work environment. By taking over hazardous tasks, Cobots help reduce workplace injuries and improve overall worker safety. The collaboration between humans and Cobots fosters innovation and allows for greater customization in production. Cobots can assist in tasks that require a high degree of precision and customization, enabling the production of personalized products at scale. This aligns with Industry 5.0's emphasis on creating more personalized and innovative products.

The adoption of Cobots is a key enabler of Industry 5.0, supporting its goals of human-centricity, sustainability and innovation.

7 Conclusion, Implication, and Limitations

In this study, we explored key factors a firm need to consider for adoption of Cobots to exploit the manufacturing opportunities created by Industry 5.0 paradigm shift. We adopted a content analysis approach and analyses literature content published (2020–2024). Firstly, we identified key components that may impact firms' adoption process. Secondly, we established empirical validity and reliability of identified components through using established procedures suggested in prior studies [11]. Finally, the empirically validated components were categorized into clusters to theorize the key factors that influence Cobot adoption process. This theorization of key factors is of vital importance for both industry practitioners and researchers interested in studying Cobots adoption in a more nuanced way.

Our study endeavors to identify key success factors influence adoption of Cobots in manufacturing. Previous studies in this domain are dominated by interaction design, ergonomics, and engineering-related aspects of Cobots. There are few studies on factors that influence firms' adoption of Cobots. Moreover, existing literature lacks a comprehensive discussion on the critical components that may impact firms' adoption process. Other authors called for more studies on human and managerial aspects of Cobots adoption [1]. Furthermore, the need for research on the adoption of digital technologies in the manufacturing sector to improve competitiveness and generate a sustainable competitive advantage was highlighted [31]. We respond to these and various other calls for research and utilized qualitative content analysis approach to identify key success factors of adoption of Cobots in manufacturing. The identified key factors aim at describing the conceptual structure and mechanisms that influence firms to adopt Cobots. Our findings will pave the way for future research addressing the challenges associated with Cobots adoption. Future researchers may use our findings to understand the underlying mechanisms that enable firms to adopt Cobots.

The identified key factors could be promising for manufacturing companies' strategic plans for Cobots adoption. The analysis of components identified in our framework has the potential to highlight what sort of capabilities a firm needs to develop in order to successfully adopt Cobots. It stresses that Cobots cannot simply be integrated like a piece of equipment because they are highly interactive with humans. Our findings provide managers and executives of manufacturing firms with a tool that might help them concentrate on factors they need to work on and assess their firm's readiness to adopt Cobots. Furthermore, our work identifies the strategic importance of technologies powered by Industry 5.0 in advancing manufacturing potential and attaining a sustainable competitive advantage. The adoption of Cobots offers manufacturing companies new ways to strengthen their competitive position, a good knowledge of essential factors and how they contribute to enhance their potential to adopt Cobots is required to reap the benefits of this technology. Manufacturing firms can use our findings to understand adoption factors and alter their organizational policies, practices, and routines as required and highlighted in our work.

This research has inherent limitations. Firstly, there is a chance that some relevant literature data might have been unintentionally missed by the recorder but, given the large number of articles analyzed and the many variables identified, this limitation is unlikely to significantly impact the study's findings. Secondly, despite validating our findings against existing Cobot implementation frameworks, author bias may still influence the results. We attempted to minimize this risk by involving multiple authors in the evaluation process, but some bias may persist. Future research could further refine these results and deepen our understanding of Cobots adoption in manufacturing by testing the concepts presented here. Methods such as Delphi studies or surveys could be used to evaluate the relative impact of each component. Regardless of the methods used in future research, our study lays the groundwork for further exploration in this field.

References

1. Hearn, G., Casali, G.L., Channa, N.A.: "Cobots" and manufacturing: a bibliometric study. In: ACRA 2022 Proceedings, pp. 1–8 (2022) https://ssl.linklings.net/conferences/acra/acra2022_proceedings/views/includes/files/pap118s2.pdf
2. Adriaensen, A., Costantino, F., Di Gravio, G., Patriarca, R.: Teaming with industrial cobots: a socio-technical perspective on safety analysis. Hum. Fact. Ergon. Manuf. **32**(2), 173–198 (2022). https://doi.org/10.1002/hfm.20939
3. Xu, X., Lu, Y., Vogel-Heuser, B., Wang, L.: Industry 4.0 and industry 5.0—inception, conception and perception. J. Manuf. Syst. **61**, 530–535 (2021). https://doi.org/10.1016/j.jmsy.2021.10.006
4. Leng, J., Sha, W., Wang, B., Zheng, P., Zhuang, C., Liu, Q., Wuest, T., Mourtzis, D., Wang, L.: Industry 5.0: prospect and retrospect. J. Manuf. Syst. **65**, 279–295 (2022). https://doi.org/10.1016/j.jmsy.2022.09.017
5. Javaid, M., Haleem, A., Singh, R.P., Rab, S., Suman, R.: Significant applications of Cobots in the field of manufacturing. Cognit. Robot. **2**, 222–233 (2022). https://doi.org/10.1016/j.cogr.2022.10.001

6. Liu, L., Guo, F., Zou, Z., Duffy, V.G.: Application, development and future opportunities of collaborative robots (Cobots) in manufacturing: A literature review. Int. J. Hum. Comput. Interact. **40**(4), 915–932 (2024). https://doi.org/10.1080/10447318.2022.2041907
7. Hearn, G., Williams, P., Rodrigues, J.H.P., Laundon, M.: Education and training for industry 4.0: a case study of a manufacturing ecosystem. Educ. Train. **65**(8–9), 1070–1084 (2023). https://doi.org/10.1108/ET-10-2022-0407
8. Laundon, M., McDonald, P., Greentree, J.: How education and training systems can support a digitally-enabled workforce for the manufacturing industry of the future: an exploratory study. Educ. Train. **65**(6–7), 909–922 (2023). https://doi.org/10.1108/ET-04-2023-0158
9. Pauliková, A., Babel'ová, Z.G., Ubárová, M.: Analysis of the impact of human–cobot collaborative manufacturing implementation on the occupational health and safety and the quality requirements. Int. J. Environ. Res. Publ. Health. **18**(4), 1–15 (2021a). https://doi.org/10.3390/ijerph18041927
10. Rega, A., Vitolo, F., Di Marino, C., Patalano, S.: A knowledge-based approach to the layout optimization of human–robot collaborative workplace. Int. J. Interact. Des. Manuf. **15**(1), 133–135 (2021a). https://doi.org/10.1007/s12008-020-00742-0
11. Krippendorff, K.: Content Analysis: an Introduction to its Methodology, 4th edn. SAGE (2018)
12. Hazen, B.T., Hall, D.J., Hanna, J.B.: Reverse logistics disposition decision-making: developing a decision framework via content analysis. Int. J. Phys. Distrib. Logist. Manag. **42**(3), 244–274 (2012). https://doi.org/10.1108/09600031211225954
13. Krippendorff, K.: Measuring the reliability of qualitative text analysis data. Qual. Quant. **38**, 787–800 (2004). https://doi.org/10.1007/s11135-004-8107-7
14. Krippendorff, K.: The changing landscape of content analysis: reflections on social construction of reality and beyond. Commun. Soc. **47**(1), 1–27 (2019)
15. Kotmungkun, S., Chompurach, W., Thaksanan, P.: OpenAI ChatGPT vs Google Gemini: a study of AI chatbots' writing quality evaluation and plagiarism checking. Eng. Lang. Teach. Educ. J. **7**(2), 90–108 (2024). https://doi.org/10.12928/eltej.v7i2.11572
16. de Dornelles, J., Ayala, N.F., Frank, A.G.: Smart working in industry 4.0: how digital technologies enhance manufacturing workers' activities. Comput. Ind. Eng. **163**, 107804 (2022). https://doi.org/10.1016/j.cie.2021.107804
17. Cheon, E.J., Schneiders, E., Skov, M.B.: Working with bounded collaboration: a qualitative study on how collaboration is co-constructed around collaborative robots in industry. In: Proceedings of the ACM on Human-Computer Interaction, vol. 6, pp. 1–34 (2022). https://doi.org/10.1145/3555094
18. Jocelyn, S., Ledoux, É., Armas Marrero, I., Burlet-Vienney, D., Chinniah, Y., Bonev, I.A., Ben Mosbah, A., Berger, I.: Classification of collaborative applications and key variability factors to support the first step of risk assessment when integrating cobots. Saf. Sci. **166**, 106219 (2023). https://doi.org/10.1016/j.ssci.2023.106219
19. Machado, E.A., Scavarda, L.F., Caiado, R.G.G., Santos, R.S.: Industry 4.0 and sustainability integration in the supply chains of micro, small, and medium enterprises through people, process, and technology within the triple bottom line perspective. Sustainability. **16**(3), 1141 (2024). https://doi.org/10.3390/su16031141
20. Bakator, M., Ćoćkalo, D., Makitan, V., Stanisavljev, S., Nikolić, M.: The three pillars of tomorrow: how marketing 5.0 builds on industry 5.0 and impacts society 5.0? Heliyon. **10**(17), e36543 (2024). https://doi.org/10.1016/j.heliyon.2024.e36543
21. Correia Simões, A., Lucas Soares, A., Barros, A.C.: Factors influencing the intention of managers to adopt collaborative robots (cobots) in manufacturing organizations. J. Eng. Technol. Manag. **57**, 101574 (2020). https://doi.org/10.1016/j.jengtecman.2020.101574
22. Leesakul, N., Oostveen, A.M., Eimontaite, I., Wilson, M.L., Hyde, R.: Workplace 4.0: exploring the implications of technology adoption in digital manufacturing on a sustainable workforce. Sustainability. **14**(6), 3311 (2022). https://doi.org/10.3390/su14063311
23. Michalos, G., Makris, S., Tsarouchi, P., Guasch, T., Kontovrakis, D., Chryssolouris, G.: Design considerations for safe human-robot collaborative workplaces. Procedia CIRP. **37**, 248–253 (2015). https://doi.org/10.1016/j.procir.2015.08.014

24. Villani, V., Pini, F., Leali, F., Secchi, C.: Survey on human–robot collaboration in industrial settings: safety, intuitive interfaces and applications. Mechatronics. **55**, 248–266 (2018a). https://doi.org/10.1016/j.mechatronics.2018.02.009
25. Liu, D., Son, S.: Exploring the impact mechanism of collaborative robot on manufacturing firm performance: a dynamic capability perspective. Sustain. Fut. **8**, 100262 (2024). https://doi.org/10.1016/j.sftr.2024.100262
26. Verma, S., Singh, V.: The employees intention to work in artificial intelligence-based hybrid environments. IEEE Trans. Eng. Manag. **71**, 3266–3277 (2024). https://doi.org/10.1109/TEM.2022.3193664
27. Berx, N., Decré, W., Pintelon, L.: A tool to evaluate industrial cobot safety readiness from a system-wide perspective: an empirical validation. Saf. Sci. **170**, 106380 (2024). https://doi.org/10.1016/j.ssci.2023.106380
28. Lichtblau, K., Stich, V., Bertenrath, R., Blum, M., Bleider, M., Millack, A., Schmitt, K., Schmitz, E., Schröter, M.: Industrie 4.0-Readines. Impuls Stiftung (2015)
29. Machado, C.G., Winroth, M., Carlsson, D., Almström, P., Centerholt, V., Hallin, M.: Industry 4.0 readiness in manufacturing companies: challenges and enablers towards increased digitalization. Procedia CIRP. **81**, 1113–1118 (2019). https://doi.org/10.1016/j.procir.2019.03.262
30. Rogers, E.M.: Diffusion of Innovations, 3rd edn. The Free Press, New York (1983)
31. Luz Martín-Peña, M., Díaz-Garrido, E., Sánchez-López, J.M.: The digitalization and servitization of manufacturing: a review on digital business models. Strateg. Chang. **27**(2), 91–99 (2018). https://doi.org/10.1002/jsc.2184

Artificial Intelligence, Technostress, and Organizational Support in Business Context? What Impact on Productivity Through a Typology Model

Raffaele Silvestre and Mauro Romanelli

Abstract This study aims to model the relationships between independent variables AI-implementation, techno-eustress, techno-distress, and organizational support and the impact on dependent variable productivity to understand if an organization that has, or not has, implemented AI-technologies, are more or less near the ideal organizational typology and to design the possible path to maximize AI-implementation, techno-eustress, and organizational support and to minimize techno-distress impacting positively on productivity. The Methodology used is the Typology Analysis which will allow us to define a Typology Model with theoretical organizational typologies on the basis of the cases described and identified in different contributions emerging from the Literature. The result is a Four-dimensional-Typology-Model identifying 16 different organizational typologies that we named in a particular way for better to represent the situation identified and the distance from the ideal one. These organizational typologies are: "Zen Garden," "Euphoric Mansion," "Orchard Garden," "Euphoric Mansion Carousel," "Haunted Mansion," "Haunted Euphoric Mansion Carousel," "Haunted Mansion Carousel," "Haunted Euphoric Mansion," "Cybernetic Jungle," "Cybernetic Carousel," "Cybernetic Jungle," "Cybernetic Carousel," "Automatic Home," "Cybernetic Carousel," "Cybernetic Jungle," "Futuristic Oasis." This work represents a framework for future research on the topic and offers a theoretical model for managers to understand which organizational typology is closest to their organization noting the level achieved by productivity and having the possibility to understand what actions to realize on independent variables to divert them toward the ideal typology of "Futuristic Oasis" that maximizes productivity.

Keywords AI-technologies · Technostress · Productivity · Typology analysis · Four dimensional-Typology-Model

---

R. Silvestre (✉) · M. Romanelli
Department of Business and Economics, University of Naples "Parthenope", Naples, Italy
e-mail: raffaele.silvestre@collaboratore.uniparthenope.it; mauro.romanelli@uniparthenope.it

N. Omrani et al. (eds.), *Human-Machine Synergy and the Digital Future - Exploring Collaboration and Competition Volume 1*, Springer Proceedings in Business and Economics, https://doi.org/10.1007/978-3-032-21347-1_11

1 Introduction

The use of Artificial Intelligence technologies is growing in numerous sectors such as business, medical-healthcare, educational-training, and consumer, and this evidence requires us to reflect on all present and future changes. Specifically in organizational context, according to Lee, M.C.M., et al. [1], organizations are increasing the inclusion and use of AI-technologies in carrying out their activities. Among the definitions of Artificial Intelligence, emerged the one in the IEEE guide [2], where it is qualified as "the combination of cognitive automation, machine learning, reasoning, hypothesis generation and analysis, natural language processing, and intentional algorithm mutation producing insights and analytics at or above human capability" (p. 12). In the literature, there are numerous studies on AI, all conducted mainly in recent years in all sectors. Analyzing some of these, Zhang, J., et al. [3] considered and analyzed the emotional expressions of chatbots to study and understand their impact on customer satisfaction. While Hashem, R., et al. [4], faced with a progressive and incremental use of Artificial Intelligence technologies in education in the United Arab Emirates, focused on the possible burnout that may arise for teachers from their integration and on the search for possible solutions to address and resolve this problem. Finally, Sjödin, D., Parida, V., Kohtamäki, M. [5] sought to understand whether the AI-technologies can potentially foster the circular business model innovation for industrial manufacturers.

Among the issues related to the use of AI, the phenomenon of technostress is increasingly emerging in various sectors such as business, medical-healthcare, and educational-training. To better understand this phenomenon linked to AI, it is appropriate to clarify, first of all, what technostress means. According to Tarafdar, M., Pullins, E.B., Ragu-Nathan, T.S. [6], technostress is "the stress caused by the use of IS in the workplace" (p. 51). Furthermore, according to Tarafdar, M., Cooper, C.L., Stich, J.-F. [7], techno-eustress explains how "individuals appraise IS as challenging or thrilling, and experience consequent "good" stress which motivates them to engage in coping behaviours that lead to positive outcomes" (p. 13), while techno-distress explains "the processes by which individuals appraise IS as a threat, experience consequent "bad" stress, and are faced largely with detrimental outcomes" (p. 13). With reference to the organizational field, for Tarafdar, M., et al. [8], technostress is activated when an individual, in an organizational context, encounters difficulties in following and dealing with the continuous changes that occur in information and communication technologies and in acquiring the increasingly new physical, social and cognitive requirements necessary for their use. Nayak, S., Budhwar, P [9], considering technostress today as a common problem for many organizations, investigated the technostress deriving from the enterprise social networks and the consequences.

Therefore, if we consider that technostress derives from the use of technologies and if we consider that AI-technologies represent more innovative, complex and still little-known technologies, it is clear how their use contributes to the phenomenon of technostress. In effect, the use of different technologies, especially new and complex, can produce techno-distress and techno-eustress with repercussions also on productivity, job satisfaction, health and well-being of workers and managers, as also highlighted in Tarafdar, M., Pullins, E.B., Ragu-Nathan, T.S. [6], in Tarafdar, M., et al. [8] and in Tarafdar, M., Cooper, C.L., Stich, J.-F. [7], so it is possible to hypothesize that also the use of AI-technologies can produce techno-distress causing job dissatisfaction, low productivity and malaise, and techno-eustress promoting the right enthusiasm toward new opportunities translating all into more efficiency, productivity, job satisfaction and well-being. In particular, with reference to AI-technologies and Responsible Artificial Intelligence, Verma, S., et al. [10] analyzed the stress induced by the principles of responsible artificial intelligence by focusing on the negative and positive consequences that their use can have in terms of technostress, also in psychological terms, and on the impact that this can have on workers' performance and well-being. At this point, it is reasonable to ask whether and how the integration and use of AI can impact this phenomenon especially in business, educational-training, consumer and medical-healthcare sectors. In the literature there are some contributions in this sense. Santos, R., et al. [11], analyzing the use of AI in government and its risks, showed both the existence of positive feelings and a small percentage of negative feelings resulting from the interaction of AI and the consumer. While Pagán-Garbín, I., Méndez, I., Martínez-Ramón, J.P. [12] explored the stress, burnout and technostress of teachers using the artificial neural network. Finally, Kumar, A., Krishnamoorthy, B., Bhattacharyya, S.S. [13] analyzed, with reference to organizations, the technostress resulting from the use of machine learning and artificial intelligence technologies and the coping mechanisms for navigating technostress with success.

Considering the results that emerged, it is evident the scarcity of studies that model the relationships between AI-implementation, techno-distress, and techno-eustress, considering the role played by organizational support and the impact of these variables and relationships on the productivity of workers and managers. This model may be useful for understanding whether organizations that have or have not implemented AI-technologies are more or less near the ideal organizational typology and for designing the possible path to maximize techno-eustress and minimize techno-distress deriving from the use of AI through organizational support, thereby positively on productivity. For these reasons, after an analysis of the papers that emerged in the specific business context, we developed and described a typology model capable of explaining the possible relationships between AI-implementation, techno-distress, techno-eustress, organizational support and productivity and of identifying different theoretical organizational typologies on the basis of these dimensions and their combinations, also the ideal one of maximization of productivity.

In this study, we will consider organizational support as the way in which the organization supports, in material, immaterial, and emotional terms, its workers and managers in achieving their objectives, promoting their well-being, job satisfaction, and productivity. This interpretation was deduced from Eisenberger, R., et al. [14] where the authors, defining the perceived organizational support, considered how it "would be influenced by various aspects of an employee's treatment by the organization and would, in turn, influence the employee's interpretation of or organizational reasons underlying that treatment. This implies that there will be agreement in the degree of support that the employee would expect of the organization in a wide variety of situations" (p. 501). We will define productivity, according to Statt, D.A. [15], as "The rate of output of a worker or a machine" (p. 121).

Therefore, we tried to answer the following research questions:

- RQ1. What are the relationships between AI-technologies, technostress, and organizational support and their impact on productivity in a business context?
- RQ2. What are the emerging organizational typologies considering the independent variables AI-implementation, techno-distress, techno-eustress, and organizational support and the dependent variable productivity?
- RQ3. What is the ideal organizational typology that maximizes productivity?

2 Theoretical Background

In the literature on relationships between AI, techno-distress, techno-eustress, and organizational support in business, medical-healthcare, consumer, and educational-training sectors, there are some contributions that offer interesting insight. Analyzing these works it was possible to summarize them in seven topic clusters in Table 1 identifying a growing interest on the topic.

At this point, considering the specific business context is possible to detect contributions that considered and analyzed the relationships between AI, technostress, and organizational support with some of these that analyzed also the impact on productivity of workers and managers. Among these, Verma, S., et al. [10] described a possible impact that the work exhaustion can have on the work performance and well-being of employees during the use of Responsible artificial intelligence for the various difficulties, concerns and uncertainties that can arise from its excessive use. While, Choudrie, J., et al. [26], in their analysis, identified, among others, some interviewees that in light of the frustration and delays linked to the VPA function, stated that "these delays had a negative impact on productivity and customer relations" (p. 6), while from other interviewees emerged that "When individuals were aware of and actively used smartphones' AI functions, their digital skills and confidence grew, which contributed to enhanced management capabilities, and impacted the way that individuals managed their activities"(p. 6).

Considering, specifically, the positive and/or negative impact of AI and the consequent technostress on productivity, Kumar, A., Krishnamoorthy, B., Bhattacharyya, S.S. [13], analyzing the responses to semi-structured interviews carried out with experts, recorded in particular a response from a senior executive of a travel services company who underlined how the implementation of Artificial Intelligence and Machine Learning technologies has contributed to increasing productivity.

Finally, considering the role of organizational support, its importance emerged in the literature to promote the optimization of AI-implementation and technostress to

Table 1 Summary of the literature

Topic clusters	Contributions of authors
"Use and functions of Artificial Intelligence, Virtual and Augmented Reality and Metaverse in organizational, working and professional context, with possible consideration of the risks associated such as technostress"	1. Verma, S., et al.: Elevating employees' psychological responses and task performance through responsible artificial intelligence. (2024) [10] 2. Alkhayyal, S., Bajaba, S.: Countering technostress in virtual work environments: The role of work-based learning and digital leadership in enhancing employee well-being. (2024) [16]
"Artificial Intelligence and Avatar, Virtual and Augmented Reality and Metaverse in consumer context with consideration of technostress and possible use of the hybrid SEM-ANN approach"	1. Lv, X.F., Li, J., Wang, Q.Y.: The Dark Side of Recommendation Algorithms in Chinese Mass Short Video Apps: Effect of Perceived Over-Recommendation on Users' Cognitive Dissonance and Discontinuance Intention. (2024) [17] 2. Rui Qiao, Cong Liu & Jun Xu: Making algorithmic app use a virtuous cycle: Influence of user gratification and fatigue on algorithmic app dependence. (2024) [18]
"Artificial Intelligence to study and manage technostress and emotions"	1. Doost, E.Z., Zhang, W.: The Impact of Different Interruptions on Perceived Stress: Developing a Multimodal Measurement for Early Detection. (2024) [19] 2. James, G., et al.: Analysis of support vector machine and random forest models for classification of the impact of technostress in covid and post-covid era. (2024) [20]
"Artificial Intelligence, Virtual and Augmented Reality and Metaverse in medical-healthcare context with consideration of AI-responsibility signals and the related disadvantages such as technostress"	1. Issa, H., Jaber, J., Lakkis, H.: Navigating AI unpredictability: Exploring technostress in AI-powered healthcare systems. (2024) [21] 2. Grüning, M., Wolf, T., Trenz, M.: A Stressful Explanation: The Dual Effect of Explainable Artificial Intelligence in Personal Health Management. (2024) [22]
"Artificial Intelligence, Virtual and Augmented Reality, Metaverse and Technostress in the educational-training context with possible consideration of the impact on productivity and performance and with possible use of machine learning algorithms"	1. Pagán-Garbín, I., Méndez, I., Martínez-Ramón, J.P.: Exploration of stress, burnout and technostress levels in teachers. Prediction of their resilience levels using an artificial neuronal network (ANN). (2024) [12] 2. Khan, W., et al.: Opening a new horizon in digitalization for e-learning in Malaysia: Empirical evidence of Covid-19. (2023) [23]
"Use of robots, chatbots and Vrchat and possible technostress and Robostress"	1. Wenzhen Z., Emma L.S., Eleonora P.: Humanlike service robots: A systematic literature review and research agenda. (2024) [24]

(continued)

Table 1 (continued)

Topic clusters	Contributions of authors
"Work from home, Technostress, Techno-stressors, computational metaphor and computer criticism, Artificial Intelligence, other new technologies and the possible impact in terms of productivity, self-efficacy and/or continuance intention	1. Daneshfar, Z., et al.: Work-from-home (WFH) during COVID-19 pandemic–A netnographic investigation using Twitter data. (2023) [25]

produce a positive impact on productivity minimizing techno-distress and maximizing techno-eustress, also considering the possible coping strategies that an individual decides, or could decide, to adopt faced with technostressful situations. In these terms, Cram, W.A., et al. [27], analyzing the way in which the two forms of algorithmic control with reference to drivers of Uber, specifically gatekeeping algorithmic control and guiding algorithmic control, which correspond to the challenge technostressors and the threat technostressors, defined how, at an organizational and managerial support level, "by enhancing challenge technostressors and minimizing threat technostressors, gig economy organizations can contribute to the cultivation of a more committed work-force"(p. 446). Therefore, based on this emerging literature, it was possible to develop a model for identifying the different possible organizational typologies in business context that can arise from a combination of the values of AI-implementation, techno-distress, techno-eustress and organizational support as independent variables, even if technostress in turn depends on AI-implementation as well as on other technologies, and productivity as the dependent variable.

3 Research Methodology

Starting from the literature, we developed a model capable of describing, summarizing, and explaining the possible configurations that an organization could assume in a business sector, considering as independent variables AI-implementation, techno-eustress, techno-distress, and organizational support and, as the dependent variable, productivity to understand the ideal typology that can maximize it. Using Typology Analysis and considering the works of D. Harold Doty and William H. Glick [28] and Valbuena, D., Verburg, P.H., Bregt, A.K. [29], we analyzed the papers on the topic in the business sector; we identified examples of organizations that, with reference to the variables considered and the relationships between them, present regularities; we identified and described independent and dependent variables, and we highlighted all the relationships. Afterward, we developed the typology model, identifying different theoretical organizational typologies in which the dependent variable assume a certain value, but only in ideal one realizes its maximization. Figure 1 shows the flow chart of research methodology.

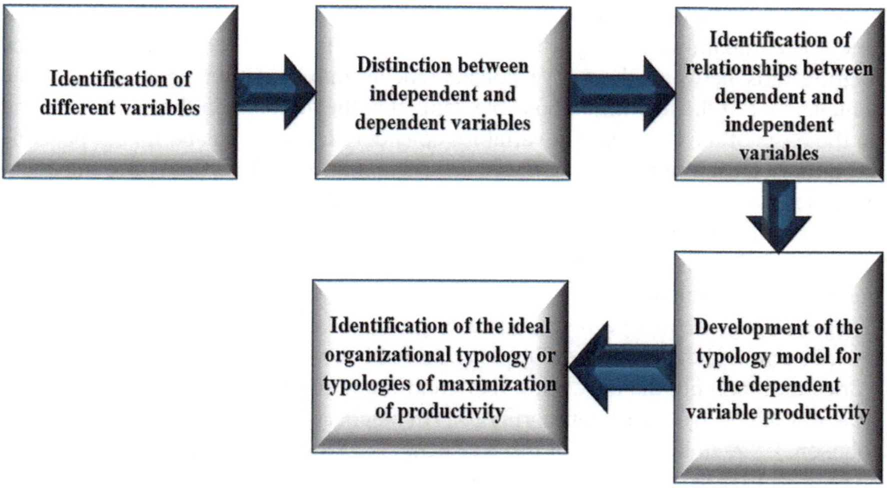

Fig. 1 Flow chart of research methodology

In particular, we analyzed the individual contributions present in the literature on the topic in two databases online, Scopus and Web of Science. Subsequently, after reading and studying them, we identified what are, in our opinion, independent variables whose variations result in variations in the variable that we considered as dependent. Specifically, the independent variables that emerged are AI-implementation, techno-distress, techno-eustress and organizational support while the dependent one is the productivity of workers and managers. At this point, we evaluated and detected, always on the basis of the existing literature, the type of relationships between these variables and their regularities and this information served as a basis for identifying organizational typologies, each of which is characterized by a specific combination of high and low values that these variables can assume precisely on the basis of the relationships identified between them. Finally, after having built a systematizing model representing these typologies, we identified the ideal one that, on the basis of specific values assumed by the independent variables, allows to maximize the dependent variable productivity. It should be noted that each typology doesn't identify an organizational category but a specific typology toward which an organization can approach considering that each will try to aim, through specific organizational policies, at the ideal one.

4 Results

The variables emerged most frequently in the literature, in an organization that operates in business sector and that implemented, or intends to implement, AI-technologies, are: AI-implementation, techno-eustress, techno-distress, and organizational support as independent variables and productivity as dependent variable, to be maximize, among which it was possible to detect regularities also in the relationships between them. We considered, as maximization of a variable, the achievement of the maximum possible value that the variable, in the conditions and on the basis of the independent variables considered, can reach and it isn't possible to go further without modifying the structural conditions. Therefore, once this maximum level is reached, a further maximization could result either in an invariability or even in a reduction of the dependent variable under the same structural conditions, according also to Hal R Varian [30] with reference to the concept of decreasing marginal productivity.

Specifically, we analyzed several cases presented in the literature to identify the independent and dependent variables mentioned above and, in particular, the main works, although not the only ones, that contributed most to our conclusions are the works of Kumar, A., Krishnamoorthy, B., Bhattacharyya, S.S. [13], of Thunberg, S., Johnson, E., Ziemke, T. [31], of Fu, S., Zheng, X., Wong, I.A. [32] and of Choudrie, J., et al. [26] where it was possible, after a careful reading of them, to detect the variables that, according to our interpretation, the Authors consider as independent variables, the one that instead acts as dependent variable, the relationships existing between them and the regularities between these relationships.

Based on these premises, and indicating with β and 1/β how much a variable varies as a function of other variables, the first relationship identified is between AI-implementation and technostress. Technostress depends positively on AI-implementation because these new and still little-known technologies can influence the various technostressors (Techno-overload, Techno-invasion, Techno-complexity, Techno-insecurity, and Techno-uncertainty) from which technostress can arise, as also reported by Tarafdar, M., et al. [8] with reference to technologies in general. The use of these technologies can result in greater techno-distress where individuals perceive AI as a threat, and/or greater techno-eustress where individuals perceive AI as something challenging or thrilling, as also theorized by Tarafdar, M., Cooper, C.L., Stich, J.-F. [7] with reference to the technologies in general. In turn, technostress could influence the AI-implementation where techno-distress could favor a negative attitude toward AI, perceived as a threat, while techno-eustress could favor a positive attitude toward AI perceived as something stimulating or thrilling.

$$\text{Technostress} = \delta + \beta \text{AI implementation} + \varepsilon \quad (1)$$

while the maximization of Technostress is:

$$\max \text{Technostress} = \delta + \left[\max\left(\beta \text{AI implementation}\right)\right] + \varepsilon$$

$$\text{AI implementation} = \delta + \left(1 / \beta \text{Techno} \setminus \text{eustress} - 1 / \beta \text{Techno} \setminus \text{distress}\right) + \varepsilon \quad (2)$$

while, the maximization of AI-implementation is:

$$\max \text{AI implementation} = \delta + \left[\max\left(1/\beta \text{Techno} \setminus \text{eustress}\right)\right] - \left[\min\left(1/\beta \text{Techno} \setminus \text{distress}\right)\right] + \varepsilon$$

The second relationship concerns the variables AI-implementation and organizational support where the second would influence, positively, the first to facilitate the achievement of the desired goals just as the AI-implementation could influence, positively, the extent of organizational support stimulating, precisely, the need to optimize, through greater support, the management of these technologies when their use increases in organization, as emerged in Fu, S., Zheng, X., Wong, I.A. [32].

$$\text{AI implementation} = \delta + 1/\beta \text{Organizational support} + \varepsilon \quad (3)$$

while the maximization of AI-implementation is:

$$\max \text{AI implementation} = \delta + \left[\max\left(1/\beta \text{Organizational support}\right)\right] + \varepsilon$$

$$\text{Organizational support} = \delta + \beta \text{AI} \setminus \text{implementation} + \varepsilon \quad (4)$$

while the maximization of organizational support is:

$$\max \text{Organizational support} = \delta + \left[\max\left(\beta \text{AI implementation}\right)\right] + \varepsilon$$

The third relationship concerns the variables organizational support, techno-distress and techno-eustress during the use of AI. There is a positive relationship between organizational support and techno-eustress and a negative relationship between organizational support and techno-distress, as emerged in Cram, W.A., et al. [27].

$$\text{Techno distress} = \delta + \left(-\beta \text{Organizational support}\right) + \varepsilon \quad (5)$$

while the minimization of techno-distress is:

$$\min \text{Techno distress} = \delta - \left[\max\left(\beta \text{Organizational support}\right)\right] + \varepsilon$$

$$\text{Techno eustress} = \delta + \beta \text{Organizational support} + \varepsilon \quad (6)$$

while the maximization of techno-eustress is:

$$\max \text{Techno eustress} = \delta + \left[\max\left(\beta \text{Organizational support}\right)\right] + \varepsilon$$

$$\text{Organizational support} = \delta + 1/\beta \text{Technostress} + \varepsilon \quad (7)$$

while the maximization of organizational support is:

$$\max \text{Organizational support} = \delta + \left[\max\left(1/\beta \text{Technostress}\right)\right] + \varepsilon$$

Considering, now, the relationship between productivity and AI-implementation, in the literature emerged how productivity depends positively from AI-implementation because they will most likely favor productivity as innovative technologies. Furthermore, if the productivity, detected and attributed to AI, is high there will be greater incentives to further implement it to increase productivity, as also emerged in Kumar, A., Krishnamoorthy, B., Bhattacharyya, S.S. [13] and in Choudrie, J., et al. [26].

$$\text{Productivity} = \delta + \beta \text{AI implementation} + \varepsilon \tag{8}$$

while the maximization of productivity is:

$$\max \text{Productivity} = \delta + \left[\max\left(\beta \text{AI implementation}\right)\right] + \varepsilon$$

$$\text{AI implementation} = \delta + 1/\beta \text{Productivity} + \varepsilon \tag{9}$$

while the maximization of AI-implementation is:

$$\max \text{AI implementation} = \delta + \left[\max\left(1/\beta \text{Productivity}\right)\right] + \varepsilon$$

With reference to the relationship between productivity and technostress, from the literature emerged a link which varies according to the sign of technostress. If we refer to techno-distress the link will be negative because it would demotivate and discourage the actors with negative repercussions on productivity, while techno-eustress, creating a challenge and greater motivation, incentivize the actors with positive effects on productivity, as emerged in Tarafdar, M., et al. [8]. It would be possible, also, to deduce an impact of productivity on technostress because if an organizational actor is productive, could perceive less the impact of technostressors, from which techno-distress could arise, managing it better and instead maximizing techno-eustress.

$$\text{Productivity} = \delta + \left(-\beta \text{Techno} \setminus \text{distress}\right) + \varepsilon \tag{10}$$

while the maximization of productivity is:

$$\max \text{Productivity} = \delta - \left[\min\left(\beta \text{Techno} \setminus \text{distress}\right)\right] + \varepsilon$$

$$\text{Productivity} = \delta + \beta \text{Techno} \setminus \text{eustress} + \varepsilon \tag{11}$$

while the maximization of productivity is:

$$\max \text{Productivity} = \delta + \left[\max\left(\beta \text{Techno} \setminus \text{eustress}\right)\right] + \varepsilon$$

$$\text{Techno distress} = \delta + \left(-1 / \beta \text{Productivity}\right) + \varepsilon \tag{12}$$

while the minimization of techno-distress is:

$$\min \text{Techno distress} = \delta - \left[\max\left(1 / \beta \text{Productivity}\right)\right] + \varepsilon$$

$$\text{Techno eustress} = \delta + 1 / \beta \text{Productivity} + \varepsilon \tag{13}$$

while the maximization of techno-eustress is:

$$\max \text{Techno eustress} = \delta + \left[\max\left(1 / \beta \text{Productivity}\right)\right] + \varepsilon$$

Finally, considering the relationship between productivity and organizational support, emerged in the literature how a support for optimal management of AI and for optimization of possible technostress, impacts positively on productivity of actors that would be incentivized and guided in this sense, as emerged in Cram, W.A., et al. [27]. It would be possible, also, deduce an impact of productivity on organizational support because greater productivity would encourage greater investments in actions which, if effective, would lead to further increase in productivity.

$$\text{Productivity} = \delta + \beta \text{Organizational support} + \varepsilon \tag{14}$$

While, the maximization of productivity is:

$$\max \text{Productivity} = \delta + \left[\max\left(\beta \text{Organizational support}\right)\right] + \varepsilon$$

$$\text{Organizational support} = \delta + 1 / \beta \text{Productivity} + \varepsilon \tag{15}$$

while the maximization of organizational support is:

$$\max \text{Organizational support} = \delta + \left[\max\left(1 / \beta \text{Productivity}\right)\right] + \varepsilon$$

Starting from these relationships, and considering the maximization of productivity in an organization that implemented or intends to implement AI-technologies with possible techno-distress and/or techno-eustress and with organizational support, we considered, in our model, as dependent variable productivity and, as independent variables, AI-implementation, techno-eustress, techno-distress and organizational support. For this reason, considering only these variables, to exemplify a complex reality, we assumed that productivity depends positively from AI-implementation, techno-eustress and organizational support and negatively from techno-distress. So, the multiple regression formula identified is:

$$\text{Productivity} = \delta + \beta_1 \text{AI} \backslash \text{ implementation} \\ + \left(\beta_2 \text{Techno} \backslash \text{ eustress} - \beta_3 \text{Techno} \backslash \text{ distress}\right) \\ + \beta_4 \text{Organizational} \backslash \text{ support} + \varepsilon$$

Where β indicates how much the dependent variable varies as a function of independent variables, the formula for maximization of productivity is:

$$\max \text{Productivity} = \delta \\ + [\max\left(\beta_1 \text{AI} \backslash \text{ implementation}\right) \\ + \max\left(\beta_2 \text{Techno} \backslash \text{ eustress}\right) \\ - \min\left(\beta_3 \text{Techno} \backslash \text{ distress}\right) \\ + \max\left(\beta_4 \text{Organizational} \backslash \text{ support}\right)] + \varepsilon$$

Considering this formula and these relationships, we can define the following hypothesis:

H1: If the organization analyzed wants to maximize productivity must maximize AI-implementation, techno-eustress, and organizational support and minimize techno-distress.

Subsequently, we implemented a typology model that define the different organizational typologies that can arise from the intersection between the theoretical high and low values that independent and dependent variables can assume in a four-dimensional-space, a difficult model to represent graphically being the result a hypercube or tesseract. Therefore, we drew only as geometric figure and described all the possible theoretical combinations between the high and low values of variables, noting the characteristics of the theoretical organizational typologies emerging and the entity of productivity, as shown in Fig. 2.

5 Discussion

In our Typology Model, considering the values that the variables can assume, 16 organizational typologies emerged, each identifying a specific value for productivity, but only one is the ideal typology that maximizes it.

The first theoretical organizational typology, "Zen Garden," sees low AI-implementation, low techno-distress, low techno-eustress and low organizational support. Without new AI-technologies, without the right enthusiasm of techno-eustress, without negative effects deriving from techno-distress and without, or low, organizational support to optimize the three variables, an organization is created that, as in a Zen garden, presents simplicity, minimalism and harmony aiming at the essential, maintaining an acceptable balance without risks. In this case, actors accept a lower level of productivity.

Fig. 2 Hypercube or tesseract of the four-dimensional-model

The second theoretical organizational typology, "Euphoric Mansion," sees low AI-implementation, low techno-distress, high techno-eustress, and low organizational support. We are faced with a traditional house without new AI-technologies, with euphoria and energy to accept new challenges, without the negative climate of techno-distress and without a support to optimize the previous variables. In this case, the level of productivity is medium-low for low AI-implementation, low organizational support, high techno-eustress, and low techno-distress.

The third theoretical organizational typology, "Orchard Garden," sees low AI-implementation, low techno-distress, low techno-eustress, and high organizational support. We are faced with a traditional garden without new technologies but with many orchards ready to grow their fruit also thanks to the high support but without the right enthusiasm for cultivation and harvesting of these fruits. In this case, the level of productivity is low for low AI-implementation, low techno-eustress, low techno-distress, and high organizational support.

The fourth theoretical organizational typology, "Euphoric Mansion Carousel," sees low AI-implementation, low techno-distress, high techno-eustress, and high organizational support. We are faced with a carousel of a traditional house without new AI-technologies and demotivation deriving from techno-distress but with the guidance of high support and the right enthusiasm and energy of actors. In this case, the level of productivity is high for low level of techno-distress, high level of techno-eustress, and high level of organizational support, even if the level of AI-implementation is low.

The fifth theoretical organizational typology, "Haunted Mansion," sees low AI-implementation, high techno-distress, low techno-eustress, and low organizational support. We are faced with a traditional house without new AI-technologies but with ghosts, linked to phantasmagorical techno-distress accepted passively and without intervening through any form of support and without motivation and positive energy. In this case, the level of productivity is low for low AI-implementation, high techno-distress, low techno-eustress and low organizational support.

The sixth theoretical organizational typology, "Haunted Euphoric Mansion Carousel," sees low AI-implementation, high techno-distress, high techno-eustress, and high organizational support. We are faced with a carousel where actors are enthusiastic and full of energy, where there is the right guidance but, at the same time, this carousel is a traditional and phantasmagoric house, without AI-technologies and with demotivation deriving from high techno-distress. In this case, the level of productivity is medium for low AI-implementation, high techno-distress, high techno-eustress and high organizational support.

The seventh theoretical organizational typology, "Haunted Mansion Carousel," sees low AI-implementation, high techno-distress, low techno-eustress, and high organizational support. We are faced with a carousel of a traditional haunted mansion without AI-technologies, with a phantasmagoric presence of high techno-distress, which creates anxiety and demotivation, without the right energy and euphoria and with the right guidance. In this case, the level of productivity is low for low AI-implementation, high techno-distress, and low techno-eustress, even if organizational support is high.

The eighth theoretical organizational typology, "Haunted Euphoric Mansion," sees low AI-implementation, high techno-distress, high techno-eustress, and low organizational support. We are faced with a traditional haunted mansion without AI-technologies, with a phantasmagoric presence of high techno-distress, that creates anxiety and demotivation, with euphoria and energy deriving from techno-eustress but without the right guidance. In this case, the level of productivity is low for low AI-implementation, high techno-distress, and low organizational support, even if the techno-eustress is high.

The ninth theoretical organizational typology, "Cybernetic Jungle," sees high AI-implementation, high techno-distress, low techno-eustress, and low organizational support. The organization lives in a Cybernetic Jungle with AI, the negative effects of high techno-distress, the absence of positive effects of techno-eustress, and low support for the future to optimize other variables. In this case, the level of productivity is low for high techno-distress, low techno-eustress, and low organizational support, even if the AI-implementation is high.

The tenth theoretical organizational typology, "Cybernetic Carousel," sees high AI-implementation, high techno-distress, low techno-eustress, and high organizational support. The organization operates on a carousel that is cybernetic for the use of AI-technologies but sad for confusion and demotivation without the right euphoria, for low techno-eustress, even if there is guidance. In this case, the level of productivity is medium-low for high AI-implementation, high techno-distress, low techno-eustress, and high organizational support.

The eleventh theoretical organizational typology, "Cybernetic Jungle," sees high AI-implementation, high techno-distress, high techno-eustress, and low organizational support. The organization operates in a cybernetic world for the use of AI-technologies but this world is a jungle for the negative impact of techno-distress and for the euphoria and energy deriving from high techno-eustress, without a right support. In this case, the level of productivity is medium for high AI-implementation, high techno-eustress, high techno-distress, and low organizational support.

The twelfth theoretical organizational typology, "Cybernetic Carousel," sees high AI-implementation, high techno-distress, high techno-eustress and high organizational support. The organization operates as a carousel, but cybernetic for the use of AI-technologies, with support but also with confusion and demotivation for high techno-distress, beyond the euphoria and energy deriving from high techno-eustress. In this case, the level of productivity is high for high AI-implementation, high techno-eustress and high organizational support, even if the techno-distress is high.

The thirteenth theoretical organizational typology, "Automatic Home," sees high AI-implementation, low techno-distress, low techno-eustress, and low organizational support. The organization lives in a house with AI and tranquility for low techno-distress, low techno-eustress, and low support that can compromise the optimization of all variables for the future. In this case, the level of productivity is medium-low for low techno-eustress, low techno-distress, and low organizational support, even if the AI-implementation is high.

The fourteenth theoretical organizational typology, "Cybernetic Carousel," sees high AI-implementation, low techno-distress, low techno-eustress, and high organizational support. The organization operates as a carousel that is cybernetic for the use of AI-technologies and for the guidance, with actors that, however, let themselves be guided by the waves, without anxiety, demotivation, euphoria and strength to experience new emotions. In this case, productivity is medium-high for high AI-implementation, low techno-distress, high organizational support, and low techno-eustress.

The fifteenth theoretical organizational typology, "Cybernetic Jungle," sees high AI-implementation, low techno-distress, high techno-eustress, and low organizational support. The organization operates in a cybernetic world, for the use of AI-technologies, without techno-distress, but also in a jungle with euphoria and energy deriving from high techno-eustress without a right support. In this case, the level of productivity is high for high AI-implementation, high techno-eustress, and low techno-distress, even if organizational support is low.

The sixteenth and last theoretical organizational typology, "Futuristic Oasis," sees high AI-implementation, low techno-distress, high techno-eustress, and high organizational support. The organization is located in a futuristic oasis where there is the future in AI-technologies and the oasis in the perfection with high techno-eustress with motivation, energy, euphoria, and enthusiasm without the anxiety and demotivation and with the right support. For this reason, this is the theoretical ideal typology with maximization of productivity for high AI-implementation, high techno-eustress, low techno-distress and high organizational support.

6 Implications, Limitations, and Future Research

This study provides interesting theoretical and practical implications.

Considering that models of organizational typologies able to systematize and describe the relationships between AI-implementation, techno-distress, and techno-eustress, considering also the role played by organizational support and the impact of these variables and relationships on the productivity of workers and managers, the typologies model that we developed represents a step forward to allow future advancement of studies and knowledge on this topic and for the development of new and more effective management and organizational policies.

In particular, starting from this work, scholars can conduct research to modify or expand the model developed because only some variables and factors have been considered to simplify the reality. Furthermore, scholars can conduct field investigations, through questionnaires or interviews, and then use this model. This study considers only organizations that operate in the business sector and assumes a generic cultural context as well as a generic organizational culture; therefore, scholars can extend the work by considering other sectors, cultural contexts, and organizations that present different organizational cultures.

In terms of practical implications, managers can use the model to understand which organizational typology is closest to their organization, on the basis of the values assumed by AI-implementation, techno-distress, techno-eustress, organizational support and productivity. In this way, they can understand what action to take to achieve the ideal typology of "Futuristic Oasis" that maximizes productivity. To give just a few examples, if the organization has a typological configuration that is far from the ideal one, managers can act on organizational levers to encourage the insertion of AI-technologies into the context by reducing techno-distress as much as possible and increasing the techno-eustress and this: through the creation of a specific department with the task of promoting the implementation of AI and managing and resolving all the problems and doubts that may arise from its use; through the organization of periodic training courses to develop greater awareness of the potential of these technologies and to develop greater skills in the organizational actors who will have to use them; acting on specific mechanisms, such as those of rules or of the group, to encourage their harmonious integration without negative consequences; promoting correct communication aimed at bringing out all the problems that actors face in the use of AI-technologies; providing incentives, material or immaterial, to stimulate the motivation of the actors to accept the challenge and to use AI-technologies by looking at them in a positive and no longer negative way; or again, encouraging a generational exchange by ensuring that young technological natives, who have greater skills and familiarity in the use of AI-technologies, provide support and transfer their knowledge to differently young actors who, having lived between two technological eras profoundly different, have greater difficulty in approaching the new that is advancing. It is clear how all these organizational initiatives, together with many others, can have a positive impact on the variables AI-implementation, techno-eustress and organizational support and a negative impact on techno-distress, guaranteeing a notable increase of productivity and, finally, of overall performances.

About limitations, the first is related to the nature of the topic in continuous evolution. So, the contribution will need to be constantly updated. Furthermore, this is an initial work that considers only some variables and contexts. We advise scholars to carry out empirical studies for a better and more extensive understanding of the variables considered with reference to a greater number of organizational contexts. Finally, we advise expanding the study to also consider other factors such as personality traits, personal factors, cultural contexts, and organizational cultures.

AI-technologies are running fast. If we want to collaborate with these technologies, we must learn to know them, to understand their positive and negative effects and to understand how to manage them, identifying and spreading those organizational practices that will help to maximize productivity, creating an explosive fusion between Artificial Intelligence and Human Intelligence.

References

1. Lee, M.C.M., et al.: The implementation of artificial intelligence in organizations: a systematic literature review. Inf. Manage. **60**(5) (2023)
2. IEEE Corporate Advisory Group: IEEE Guide for Terms and Concepts in Intelligent Process Automation, p. 2755 (2017)
3. Zhang, J., et al.: Emotional expression by artificial intelligence chatbots to improve customer satisfaction: Underlying mechanism and boundary conditions. Tour. Manag. (2024)
4. Hashem, R., et al.: AI to the rescue: exploring the potential of ChatGPT as a teacher ally for workload relief and burnout prevention. Res. Pract. Technol. Enhanced Learn. **19** (2024)
5. Sjödin, D., Parida, V., Kohtamäki, M.: Artificial intelligence enabling circular business model innovation in digital servitization: conceptualizing dynamic capabilities, AI capacities, business models and effects. Technol. Forecast. Soc. Change. (2023)
6. Tarafdar, M., Pullins, E.B., Ragu-Nathan, T.S.: Examining impacts of technostress on the professional salesperson's behavioural performance. J. Pers. Sell. Sales Manage. **34**(1), 51–69 (2014)
7. Tarafdar, M., Cooper, C.L., Stich, J.-F.: The technostress trifecta—techno eustress, techno distress and design: theoretical directions and an agenda for research. Inf. Syst. J. **29**(1), 6–42 (2019)
8. Tarafdar, M., et al.: The impact of technostress on role stress and productivity. J. Manage. Inf. Syst. **24**(1), 301–328 (2007)
9. Nayak, S., Budhwar, P.: Negative effects of enterprise social networks (ESNs) and technostress: empirical evidence from R&D centres operating in India. Aslib J. Inf. Manag. **74**, 956–988 (2022)
10. Verma, S., et al.: Elevating employees' psychological responses and task performance through responsible artificial intelligence. Inf. Technol. People. (2024)
11. Santos, R., et al.: The Use of AI in Government and Its Risks: Lessons from the Private Sector. Transforming Government-People Process and Policy (2024)
12. Pagán-Garbín, I., Méndez, I., Martínez-Ramón, J.P.: Exploration of stress, burnout and technostress levels in teachers. Prediction of their resilience levels using an artificial neuronal network (ANN). In: Teaching and Teacher Education (2024)

13. Kumar, A., Krishnamoorthy, B., Bhattacharyya, S.S.: Machine learning and artificial-intelligence-induced technostress in organizations: a study on automation-augmentation paradox with socio-technical systems as coping mechanisms. Int. J. Org. Anal. (2023)
14. Eisenberger, R., et al.: Perceived organizational support. J. Appl. Psychol. **71**(3), 500–507 (1986)
15. Statt, D.A.: The Routledge Dictionary of Business Management, 3rd edn. Routledge Publishing, Detroit (2004)
16. Alkhayyal, S., Bajaba, S.: Countering technostress in virtual work environments: the role of work-based learning and digital leadership in enhancing employee well-being. Acta Psychol. (Amst). (2024)
17. Lv, X.F., Li, J., Wang, Q.Y.: The dark side of recommendation algorithms in Chinese mass short video apps: effect of perceived over-recommendation on users' Cognitive dissonance and discontinuance intention. Int. J. Hum. Comput. Interact. (2024)
18. Qiao, R., Liu, C., Jun, X.: Making algorithmic app use a virtuous cycle: influence of user gratification and fatigue on algorithmic app dependence. Human. Soc. Sci. Commun. (2024)
19. Doost, E.Z., Zhang, W.: The impact of different interruptions on perceived stress: developing a multimodal measurement for early detection. Int. J. Hum. Comput. Interact. (2024)
20. James, G., et al.: Analysis of support vector machine and random forest models for classification of the impact of technostress in COVID and post-COVID era. J. Niger. Soc. Phys. Sci. **6**(3) (2024)
21. Issa, H., Jaber, J., Lakkis, H.: Navigating AI unpredictability: exploring technostress in AI-powered healthcare systems. Technol. Forecast. Soc. Change. (2024)
22. Grüning, M., Wolf, T., Trenz, M.: A stressful explanation: the dual effect of explainable artificial intelligence in personal health management. In: Proceedings of the Annual Hawaii International Conference on System Sciences, pp. 3607–3616 (2024)
23. Khan, W., et al.: Opening a new horizon in digitalization for e-learning in Malaysia: empirical evidence of Covid-19. Educ. Inf. Technol. (2023)
24. Wenzhen, Z., Emma, L.S., Eleonora, P.: Humanlike service robots: a systematic literature review and research agenda. Psychol. Mark. (2024)
25. Daneshfar, Z., et al.: Work-from-home (WFH) during COVID-19 pandemic—a netnographic investigation using Twitter data. Inf. Technol. People. **36**(5), 2161–2186 (2023)
26. Choudrie, J., et. al.: Hey Siri, Google! Can you help me? A qualitative case study of smartphones AI functions in SMEs. Technol. Forecast. Soc. Change. (2023)
27. Cram, W.A., et al.: Examining the impact of algorithmic control on Uber drivers' technostress. J. Manage. Inf. Syst. **39**(2), 426–453 (2022)
28. Harold Doty, D., Glick, W.H.: Typologies as a unique form of theory building: toward improved understanding and modeling. Acad. Manage. **19**(2), 230–251 (1994)
29. Valbuena, D., Verburg, P.H., Bregt, A.K.: A method to define a typology for agent-based analysis in regional land-use research. Agric. Ecosyst. Environ. **128**(1–2), 27–36 (2008)
30. Hal, R.: Varian: Microeconomia. Cafoscarina Editore (2002)
31. Thunberg, S., Johnson, E., Ziemke, T.: Investigating healthcare workers' technostress when welfare technology is introduced in long-term care facilities. Behav. Inf. Technol. (2024)
32. Fu, S., Zheng, X., Wong, I.A.: The perils of hotel technology: the robot usage resistance model. Int. J. Hosp. Manag. (2022)

Artificial Intelligence in the PhD Journey: Transforming Research, Mentorship, and Learning

Giuseppe Ceci, Mauro Gatti, and Michela Iannotta

Abstract This study investigates the impact of artificial intelligence (AI) on doctoral programs across three European countries—Germany, Italy, and the Netherlands—through a multiple-case study approach. By conducting 15 semi-structured interviews with PhD students, the paper explores how AI is transforming research practices, mentor-mentee dynamics, and emotional well-being in PhD education. Key findings highlight AI's role in automating micro-tasks such as data cleaning, literature reviews, and basic analyses, allowing students to focus more on advanced research. AI also reduces the need for regular feedback from supervisors, fostering greater independence but raising concerns about the depth of mentorship. Additionally, AI helps alleviate the emotional isolation often experienced by PhD students by providing real-time support. This paper contributes theoretically by addressing the unexplored impact of AI specifically on PhD programs, a topic not previously studied in depth. Most prior research has focused on AI within higher education institutions (HEIs) at large, making this a novel investigation. This paper also contributes to understanding how AI reshapes academic processes, offering practical implications for students, supervisors, and HEIs in adapting to a technology-driven research environment.

Keywords Artificial Intelligence · Higher Education Institutions · PhD student · PhD program

---

G. Ceci (✉) · M. Gatti · M. Iannotta
Sapienza University of Rome, Rome, Italy
e-mail: Giuseppe.ceci@uniroma1.it

N. Omrani et al. (eds.), *Human-Machine Synergy and the Digital Future - Exploring Collaboration and Competition Volume 1*, Springer Proceedings in Business and Economics, https://doi.org/10.1007/978-3-032-21347-1_12

1 Introduction

Artificial Intelligence (AI) is not only reshaping technologies but also redefining how organizations navigate change as they adapt and evolve. In this context, higher education institutions (HEIs) are deeply involved in this transformation. Indeed, AI is having significant implications for research, teaching, and academic services, making HEIs a crucial area of discussion [1, 2]. The growing presence of AI tools is expected to reshape the research landscape [3, 4] while simultaneously offering new insights to enhance teaching methodologies across various disciplines [5, 6].

AI, broadly defined, refers to the development of computer systems capable of engaging in human-like cognitive processes such as learning, reasoning, and self-correction [7]. As AI technologies advance, the ongoing debate is investigating how humanity is reacting to this disruptive innovation [8, 9]. On one side, some argue that a successful implementation of AI in organizations has a positive effect on their competitiveness [10, 11], while others claim that AI technologies could lead to significant job losses [12]. Similarly, analyzed through the same lens, both opportunities and challenges arise in HEIs. Indeed, one of the most critical transformations AI brings to academia is the potential for automation, which could significantly impact research processes, administrative tasks, and even academic careers [13]. However, this rapid integration of AI raises numerous concerns regarding ethical issues, academic integrity, and the reliability of AI-generated content in research and publishing [14–16]. In this context, while several authors investigated how AI technologies are changing the academic world, a notable gap exists in how AI is specifically reshaping PhD program. We believe that addressing this topic is crucial as PhD programs and publications play a crucial role in both driving the economic development of organizations and contributing to innovation and technology transfer [17, 18]. These challenges highlight an existing research gap and reinforce the importance of further investigation into AI's role in reshaping doctoral programs.

For these reasons, this study aims to address the research question:

How Has AI Changed PhD Programs?

To explore our research question, we conducted a multiple-case study in three universities in different countries—Italy, the Netherlands, and Germany. Data collection involved five semi-structured interviews per case, allowing for an in-depth examination of how AI is influencing PhD research, academic practices, and doctoral training.

This study contributes to the ongoing debate on HEIs by examining how AI-driven transformations are reshaping PhD programs. It highlights the evolving roles of doctoral researchers, supervisors, and academic structures, positioning AI as an increasing integral element in knowledge production and academic training. From a practical viewpoint, this study will be useful for PhD students by enhancing research efficiency, for supervisors by improving mentorship and feedback processes, and for institutions by informing program design and AI integration strategies.

2 Literature Review

The literature on AI's influence in PhD programs remains relatively scarce; however, its role in shaping students' academic journeys has been widely explored. *Since the 1980s, digital writing tools have supported students in their academic work, particularly through the introduction of style and grammar analysis software in word processors* ([19], p. 2). More recently, AI-powered chatbots have proven effective in enhancing student engagement and satisfaction in higher education [20]. While some of these developments can be extended to PhD students, the unique challenges and tasks of doctoral programs require a more specific analysis.

In this context, Jafari and Keykha [21] investigated the opportunities created by AI tools within a HEI, focusing on a single university and interviewing PhD students with expertise in the field. However, their study, based on a single-case approach, primarily highlights the broader challenges and opportunities for HEIs rather than examining how AI is reshaping doctoral programs. In contrast, Pretorius et al. [22] found that AI fosters inclusivity by enabling PhD students to contribute more meaningfully to their academic communities, an aspect particularly relevant in environments where access to resources and academic support is uneven. In this vein, AI-driven tools support PhD students refine their writing, organize research data, and streamline administrative tasks, allowing them to concentrate on their core research contributions. Despite these advantages, AI's role in doctoral studies presents challenges. Samuelsson et al. [23] discuss how PhD supervision is evolving due to AI intervention. Traditionally, doctoral mentorship has relied heavily on in-person guidance, but AI-powered tools now provide automated feedback, suggest research directions, and identify gaps in literature reviews. While these advancements enhance efficiency, they also raise concerns about the diminishing role of direct human interaction in academic mentorship raising concern on the quality of published work (e.g., research paper and doctoral theses) as showed by Lopes et al. [24].

Further research has attempted to assess PhD students' perspectives on AI in academia, yet limitations remain. For example, Firat's [2] study, which examined students from diverse backgrounds, was restricted to only 14 PhD students from the same country, limiting the generalizability of the findings. This suggests that while AI presents global opportunities, its impact varies based on regional and institutional contexts. Despite these challenges, García-Peñalvo [25] argues that criticism of ChatGPT and other AI tools largely stems from resistance to change rather than their disruptive potential. Indeed, AI holds the promise of making research more accessible, improving efficiency, and fostering collaboration among PhD students worldwide.

3 Methods

A multiple-case study methodology was employed in this paper. Case study research allows investigation of phenomena in their general complexity and within their natural environment [26]. This characteristic makes the methodology effective for a paper on an unexplored topic where the main aim is to answer to "*how*" research questions [26, 27]. Multiple-case study methodology is regarded as more robust than single case study, since cross-case comparisons allow a more vigorous explanation and understanding of contextual variables' effects [28]. These properties of the multiple-case study methodology made it particularly appropriate for the aim of the presented paper. We chose to conduct our case studies on three different HEIs that are located in three different countries: Germany, Italy, and the Netherlands. We decided to conduct semi-structured interviews with five PhD students for each HEI as the main source of data analysis. We chose these three different contexts for three reasons: (i) each country offers a distinct academic environment, but all PhD students are highly engaged with AI in research and education; (ii) while the PhD candidates have backgrounds in economics, their research interests vary, allowing us to examine how AI impacts different aspects of their work across these countries under an "economic lens"; (iii) all three countries are part of the European Union, which means they have equal access to funding opportunities and research applications. Data has been collected through documents, business records, and direct observations on the HEIs websites. However, the main source for our study is 15 in-depth semi-structured interviews with PhD students, 5 for each case (Table 1).

To reach a multitude of interviews, the participants were sampled through snowball sampling. This technique was employed for two main reasons: (i) we looked for PhD students enrolled in their third or fourth year to gather insights from individuals who could provide a more comprehensive perspective on the final stages of AI adoption in their doctoral research; (ii) there was a widespread conviction among PhD students that opening up on these topics could have generated repercussions with their supervisors. To this specific aim, through personal connections and friendships, the interviewees felt more comfortable opening up and telling us their impressions. However, together with them, we decided to guarantee anonymity both in terms of the case study (e.g., name of the HEI) and of personal characteristics of the interviewee (e.g., name, department, research topic). The interviews lasted approximately −35 min and they were carried out by one of the authors. They were divided into three main sections.

The interview protocol was built to freeze three main aspects that were mainly divided into the use of AI in (1) research, (2) teaching, (3) other tasks related with PhD programs (e.g., funding applications).

The interviews were conducted in English, recorded and later fully transcribed. Data triangulation has been employed: this technique involves the use of different sources of data to examine phenomena across settings and at different points in time [29].

Table 1 List of interviewees

Age of the interviewees	Country	PhD program	Duration of the interview
29	The Netherlands	Economics	45′
30	The Netherlands	Economics	30′
30	The Netherlands	Management and innovation	30′
31	The Netherlands	Management and innovation	30′
30	The Netherlands	Economics	40′
28	Germany	Management and innovation	35′
29	Germany	Management	40′
29	Germany	Management and innovation	40′
30	Germany	Economics	40′
28	Germany	Management and innovation	35′
28	Italy	Industrial PhD in management	40′
27	Italy	Management	30′
29	Italy	Management	50′
32	Italy	Management	40′
31	Italy	Economics	45′

Finally, a content analysis was realized: this technique makes replicable and valid inferences from data to their context [30]. Both descriptive and interpretive encoding was performed using the software for qualitative analysis MAXQDA 11. This approach was employed to explore emerging factors and to collect our textual data. Also, the authors systematically employed thematic analysis by immersing themselves in the data, generating initial codes organizing these into broader themes, and refining and defining them to ensure a comprehensive and reliable interpretation of the qualitative data [31]. The analysis was first performed separately and then jointly by the authors to compare the results and guarantee intercoder reliability. In this vein, our research group tried to minimize the effect of subjectivity derived from the analysis of the textual matrix. In a qualitative study, intercoder reliability is particularly significant since words may have multiple meanings, may be open to interpretation, and may only be understood in the context of other words, making them harder to work with than numbers [32].

4 Findings

In the following paragraphs, we will explore the changes AI brings to the PhD journey, including task automation, shifts in the supervisor-student relationship, and the emotional impact of AI's availability. In the discussion section, we will summarize the key findings and their implications.

4.1 Speeding Up Micro-Tasks

One of the most significant changes introduced by AI in PhD programs is the automation and acceleration of micro-tasks. In the domain of HEIs, micro-tasks refer to small but time-consuming activities such as data cleaning, preliminary analysis, literature searches, and basic statistical testing. These tasks, while crucial to research, often take up a substantial amount of time, leaving PhD students less time to focus on the core aspects of their research journey.

AI tools, particularly machine learning algorithms and natural language processing systems, are increasingly being employed to assist with these tasks [33]. From automating data extraction from massive datasets to simplifying repetitive tasks like coding qualitative data, AI allows PHD students to focus more on theory development and advanced analysis, which are at the heart of their PhD work. Here we have come examples:

> *AI has drastically reduced the time I spend on repetitive tasks like data cleaning and preparation. What used to take days now takes just hours, which allows me to focus more on theoretical analysis and writing my dissertation. PhD student from the Netherlands - Economics*

The use of AI has had a profound effect on the productivity of PhD students, allowing them to work faster and with greater precision. The increasing use of AI technologies resonates with the "publish or perish" while several concerns about the need to stay proficient in traditional research methods despite the growing reliance on automation.

> *Automated data analysis has allowed me to test multiple hypotheses in a fraction of the time it used to take. It's made my work more dynamic, as I can quickly iterate and refine my models based on real-time data processing. PhD student from Germany – Management and Innovation*

While AI accelerates data analysis, it also encourages students to develop new skills related to AI tools, creating a demand for interdisciplinary knowledge in economics, data science, and computer science.

> *AI has significantly sped up the literature review process. I can use AI-driven tools to scan vast amounts of academic articles, extracting relevant data points and summaries. This has allowed me to focus more on the synthesis of information and theory development. PhD student from Germany – Management and Innovation*

The literature review process, traditionally a labor-intensive part of the PhD journey, has become more efficient thanks to AI-powered tools that summarize articles, identify key trends, and even suggest connections between different theories or studies.

> *Before, I spent countless hours trying to sort through messy data or finding small errors in code. Now, AI tools like code analyzers and automated data validation software help me identify problems quickly, cutting my workflow down dramatically. PhD student from Italy – Management*

AI's role in streamlining these micro-tasks allows students to devote more time to hypothesis testing and econometric modeling, critical components of their research. However, the increased reliance on AI also brings about the question of how to maintain a balance between automation and hands-on research experience.

> *The use of AI for data visualization and exploratory data analysis has saved me hours of work. AI tools can generate advanced plots and charts that would have taken me much longer to do manually. It's made presenting my research more accessible and efficient. PhD student from Italy – Economics*

AI tools' ability to quickly generate insights through data visualization and exploration has been especially useful for PhD students working in areas that require large-scale empirical analysis, such as behavioral economics and econometrics.

4.2 Reduced Need for Feedback from Supervisors

As AI tools increasingly take on tasks that were traditionally handled by PhD supervisors, some PhD students have reported a decrease in their need for regular feedback. AI-driven research tools are becoming increasingly proficient at offering immediate suggestions for improvements or identifying gaps in the student's work. This shift has both positive and negative effects on the PhD student-supervisor relationship.

> *I find that I rely on my supervisor less for minor corrections or clarifications. I can ask AI tools for instant feedback on the logic of my models or the accuracy of my results. This has allowed me to work more independently. PhD student from The Netherlands – Management and Innovation*

While this independence is valued, some PhD students also miss the intellectual exchange with their supervisors, which help refine their thinking and research.

> *... I don't need my supervisor as much for routine tasks. The AI can point out errors in my code or suggest improvements in my theoretical models. The feedback I receive now is more focused on higher-level conceptual discussions. PhD student from Germany – Management and Innovation*

The quote highlights this inner conflict—how even seeking help for seemingly small matters can trigger doubt. Is it the professor's genuine insight, or has technology played a role? It raises important questions about the evolving nature of learning and the role of AI in education.

I often find myself afraid to ask for advice on something that feels minor, because I wonder if AI could answer for me, or if, even asking the professor, their advice might be the result of an algorithm. And so, I end up questioning: is it my own thought, or that of a machine? PhD student from Italy – Management

This quote highlights a growing uncertainty many PhD students face in the age of AI—wondering whether their questions are being answered by technology or genuine human guidance. The student reflects on the *fear* that even when seeking help, it might not be their own thinking or a professor's advice, but an algorithm at work. This concern is particularly relevant in fields like management, where original thought and creativity are key [34, 35]. As AI becomes more integrated into academia, the line between human mentorship and machine-generated responses blurs, leaving students questioning the authenticity of their learning process.

4.3 Less Sense of Isolation Due to AI's Availability

AI also appears to address some of the emotional challenges of PhD life, such as the sense of isolation that can arise when students are left to work alone on their projects [36, 37]. AI's ability to offer real-time feedback and assistance provides a sense of constant support, reducing the emotional burden of solitude.

One of the biggest changes I've noticed is that I feel less isolated. When I'm stuck on a problem or need guidance, I can turn to AI-driven platforms that provide immediate answers. It's like having an assistant at my fingertips all the time. PhD student from The Netherlands – Management and Innovation

While AI can provide immediate responses, it also raises concerns about the loss of human interaction and the potential for students to become overly reliant on machine-generated solutions, rather than thinking through problems on their own.

In the past, I would often feel like I was alone with my research, but now, I can always find something online or get feedback from AI tools that simulate academic discussions. It feels more interactive, even when I'm physically isolated. PhD student from Germany – Management and Innovation

This reflects a shift in the experience of research for a PhD student from Germany, emphasizing how AI tools and online resources have transformed their sense of isolation. In the past, this student felt alone with their research, but now, they mention how they can engage in more interactive ways, despite being physically isolated. The use of AI here is viewed as a means to simulate academic discussions and get continuous feedback, which makes the process feel more dynamic and less solitary. This reflects how technology, particularly AI, helps bridge the gap between isolation and interaction, bringing a sense of connection even without direct human presence

As a PhD student with two supervisors (one supervisor belongs to a foreign university) I often feel divided between two worlds, but thanks to AI, my mentorship knows no boundaries. The technology allows me to feel less isolated, providing constant and timely support, regardless of time zones. In a world where physical distance can feel insurmountable, AI makes my academic journey more connected than ever. PhD student from Italy – Management

In this case this PhD student feels divided between two worlds, but AI helps alleviate that tension by offering continuous and timely support. The emphasis here is not just on academic feedback, but also on the role of AI in enabling real-time communication and mentorship, no matter the geographic distance (and temporal distance). The quote paints AI as a connector, not just in terms research ideas, but also of relationships, making the student's academic journey feel more integrated and connected.

5 Discussion and Implications

This work contributes theoretically to understanding the impact of AI on PhD programs by examining three key aspects.

First, AI is emerging as a catalyst for redefining the research process itself. By automating and accelerating micro-tasks such as data cleaning, literature searches, and preliminary analyses, AI significantly transforms how PhD students approach their work. This shift can be understood within the broader concept of "*cognitive offloading*" [38] where PhD students rely on AI to handle repetitive tasks, freeing up time to focus on higher-level activities such as theory development, complex analysis, and writing. The theoretical implication of this transformation is that AI is not just a tool that supports research as it was mentioned in our discourse on HEIs [3, 4] but it serves as an active force reshaping how knowledge is produced in doctoral programs.

Second, the increasing reliance on AI for feedback and task automation leads to a rethinking of traditional mentor-mentee dynamics. This shift showed that AI complements human interaction by providing immediate, precise feedback. While this has the potential to enhance students' independence, it also raises concerns about the depth and quality of mentorship. Students may feel more autonomous but risk losing the nuanced intellectual exchange that human supervisors provide. The theoretical contribution here is that mentorship in PhD programs is becoming more complex, blending human guidance with machine interaction in ways that challenge conventional ideas about the role of supervisors and the nature of academic mentorship.

Third, AI plays a significant role in reducing the emotional challenges faced by PhD students, particularly the sense of isolation that often accompanies independent research. From a theoretical perspective, AI tools act as virtual companions, offering real-time support and responses that help alleviate the emotional burden of working alone. This aligns with theories of social and emotional well-being in academia [12] suggesting that AI can positively impact mental health by mitigating isolation. However, this shift also raises surprisingly important questions about the potential trade-offs, as students may become overly reliant on AI, potentially reducing important interpersonal interactions that are vital for both intellectual and emotional development.

The practical contribution of this study is threefold. First, it provides valuable insights for **PhD students**, helping them leverage AI tools to enhance research efficiency by automating repetitive tasks and allowing more focus on higher-level academic work. Second, it offers guidance for **supervisors**, demonstrating how AI can improve the feedback process, enhance mentorship, and enable more effective use of time. Finally, it benefits **HEIs** by informing the integration of AI into PhD programs, helping to design curricula and support systems that align with the evolving needs of both students and faculty in a technology-driven research environment.

6 Conclusion and Limitations

This work explores how AI reshape PhD programs by automating research tasks, transforming mentor-mentee dynamics, and alleviating students' emotional isolation. It offers practical insights for students, supervisors, and institutions on using AI to improve research efficiency, mentorship, and curriculum design in response to evolving academic needs. However, it is not free of limitations. First, its focus on a small number of European countries, particularly Germany, the Netherlands, and Italy, limits the generalizability of the findings. The economic and academic contexts of these countries differ significantly, especially between Italy and other nations, which may affect how AI influences PhD programs. Second, the interpretation of results may be subject to bias, as the data relies on self-reported experiences, which may vary based on individual perspectives or familiarity with AI tools. Finally, the relatively small sample size limits the broader applicability of the conclusions, as it may not fully represent the diversity of experiences across all PhD students.

These limitations offer opportunities for future research. First future studies could address these limitations by expanding the sample to include a wider range of countries, disciplines, and PhD student backgrounds. Additionally, investigating the role of industrial PhDs, which combine academic research with industry collaboration, could provide insights into AI's impact in more applied research contexts. Exploring the long-term effects of AI integration, particularly on career outcomes and the development of skills beyond academia, could also offer valuable perspectives on the evolving role of AI in doctoral education.

References

1. Barros, A., Prasad, A., Śliwa, M.: Generative artificial intelligence and academia: implication for research, teaching and service. Manage. Learn. **54**(5), 597–604 (2023)
2. Firat, M.: What ChatGPT means for universities: perceptions of scholars and students. J. Appl. Learn. Teach. **6**(1), 57–63 (2023)
3. Al-Zahrani, A.M.: The impact of generative AI tools on researchers and research: implications for academia in higher education. Innov. Educ. Teach. Int. **61**(5), 1029–1043 (2024)
4. Lai, W.Y.W., Lee, J.S.: A systematic review of conversational AI tools in ELT: publication trends, tools, research methods, learning outcomes, and antecedents. Comput. Educ. Artif. Intell. **7**, 100291 (2024)
5. Chan, C.K.Y.: A comprehensive AI policy education framework for university teaching and learning. Int. J. Educ. Technol. High. Educ. **20**(1), 38 (2023)
6. Huang, K.: Alarmed by AI chatbots, universities start revamping how they teach. The New York Times. **16** (2023)
7. Kok, J.N., Boers, E.J., Kosters, W.A., Van der Putten, P., Poel, M.: Artificial intelligence: definition, trends, techniques, and cases. Artif Intell. **1**, 51–299 (2009)
8. Laukkonen, R., Biddell, H., Gallagher, R.: Preparing Humanity for Change and Artificial Intelligence. (2019)
9. Oldemeyer, L., Jede, A., Teuteberg, F.: Investigation of artificial intelligence in SMEs: a systematic review of the state of the art and the main implementation challenges. Manage. Rev. Q. **75**, 1–43 (2024)
10. Mayer, A.S., Strich, F., Fiedler, M.: Unintended consequences of introducing AI systems for decision making. MIS Q. Exec. **19**(4) (2020)
11. Wamba-Taguimdje, S.L., Wamba, S.F., et al.: Influence of artificial intelligence (AI) on firm performance: the business value of AI-based transformation projects. Bus. Process Manage. J. **26**(7), 1893–1924 (2020)
12. Pataranutaporn, P., Danry, V., Leong, J., et al.: AI-generated characters for supporting personalized learning and well-being. Nat. Mach. Intell. **3**(12), 1013–1022 (2021)
13. Watermeyer, R., Phipps, L., Lanclos, D., Knight, C.: Generative AI and the automating of academia. Postdigit. Sci. Educ. **6**(2), 446–466 (2024)
14. Casal, J.E., Kessler, M.: Can linguists distinguish between ChatGPT/AI and human writing?: a study of research ethics and academic publishing. Res. Meth. Appl. Linguist. **2**(3), 100068 (2023)
15. Gruenhagen, J.H., Sinclair, P.M., Carroll, J.A., Baker, P.R., Wilson, A., Demant, D.: The rapid rise of generative AI and its implications for academic integrity: students' perceptions and use of chatbots for assistance with assessments. Comput. Educ. Artif. Intell. **7**, 100273 (2024)
16. Miao, J., Thongprayoon, C., Suppadungsuk, S., Garcia Valencia, O.A., Qureshi, F., Cheungpasitporn, W.: Ethical dilemmas in using AI for academic writing and an example framework for peer review in nephrology academia: a narrative review. Clin. Pract. **14**(1), 89–105 (2023)
17. Asongu, S.A., Nwachukwu, J.C.: PhD by publication as an argument for innovation and technology transfer: with emphasis on Africa. High. Educ. Q. **72**(1), 15–28 (2018)
18. Casey, B.H.: The economic contribution of PhDs. J. High. Educ. Policy Manag. **31**(3), 219–227 (2009)
19. Perkins, M.: Academic integrity considerations of AI large language models in the post-pandemic era: ChatGPT and beyond. J. Univ. Teach. Learn. Pract. **20**(2) (2023)
20. Sengupta, S., Chakraborty, T.: Use of chatbots in higher education: a study of student engagement and satisfaction. Educ. Inf. Technol. **25**(6) (2020)
21. Jafari, F., Keykha, A.: Identifying the opportunities and challenges of artificial intelligence in higher education: a qualitative study. J. Appl. Res. High. Educ. **16**(4), 1228–1245 (2024)

22. Pretorius, L., Huynh, H., Pudyanti, A., Li, Z., Noori, A. Q., Zhou, Z.: Empowering International PhD Students: Generative AI, Ubuntu, and the Decolonisation of Academic Communication. (2024)
23. Samuelsson, C.R., Polverini, G., Gregorcic, B.: Preparing PhD students for the doctoral defense with generative AI. In: NU2024, 17–19 June 2024, Umeå, Sweden (2024)
24. Lopes, C., Forgas, R.C., Cerdà-Navarr, A.: A PhD dissertation in education written by artificial intelligence? Rev. Bras. Educ. **29**, e290065 (2024)
25. García-Peñalvo, F.J.: The perception of artificial intelligence in educational contexts after the launch of ChatGPT: disruption or panic? Educ. Knowl. Soc. **24**, 1–16 (2023)
26. Yin, R.K.: Designing case studies. Qual. Res. Methods. **5**(14), 359–386 (2003)
27. Siggelkow, N.: Persuasion with case studies. Acad. Manage. J. **50**(1), 20–24 (2007)
28. Chiesa, V., Frattini, F.: Exploring the differences in performance measurement between research and development: evidence from a multiple case study. R&D Manage. **37**(4), 283–301 (2007)
29. Denzin, N.: The Research Act in Sociology. Butterworths, London (2012)
30. Krippendorff, K.: Content Analysis. (1989)
31. Terry, G., Hayfield, N., Clarke, V., Braun, V.: Thematic analysis. In: The SAGE Handbook of Qualitative Research in Psychology, 2nd edn, pp. 17–37. SAGE, London (2017)
32. Miles, M.B., Huberman, A.M.: Qualitative Data Analysis: A Sourcebook of New Methods. Sage, Beverly Hills, CA (1984)
33. Naveed, H., Khan, A. U., Qiu, S., et al.: A comprehensive overview of large language models. arXiv preprint arXiv:2307.06435 (2023)
34. Eloranta, V., Hakanen, E., Shaw, C.: Teaching for Paradigm Shifts. (2024)
35. Xu, F., Rickards, T.: Creative management: a predicted development from research into creativity and management. Creat. Innov. Manag. **16**(3), 216–228 (2007)
36. Bettinson, E., Haven-Tang, C.: Voices of isolation and marginalisation–an investigation into the PhD experience in tourism studies. Int. J. Manage. Educ. **19**(3), 100539 (2021)
37. Cantor, G.: The loneliness of the long-distance (PhD) researcher. Psychodynam. Pract. **26**(1), 56–67 (2020)
38. Risko, E.F., Gilbert, S.J.: Cognitive offloading. Trends Cogn. Sci. **20**(9), 676–688 (2016)

AI in the Service Sector

Exploring the Spectrum of FinTech Innovations Implemented in Microfinance Companies: A Comprehensive Review

Uwakmfon Promise Offiong and Katarzyna Szopik-Depczyńska

Abstract The integration of financial technology into microfinance companies has transformed how these companies deliver services to financially excluded demographics. This study provides a comprehensive review of FinTech innovations most frequently adopted by microfinance companies, with focus on their strategic and managerial implications. Drawing on 67 peer-reviewed articles retrieved from Web of Science, Scopus, and Google Scholar (2010–2024), bibliometric and thematic analyses were conducted using VOS Viewer to identify key innovations, research trends, and influential contributors. Findings reveal that mobile banking, digital lending platforms, and blockchain technology with digital payments made up the most widely adopted tools. These innovations boost organizational effectiveness through improving transparency, automating lending and administrative processes, and expanding financial inclusion, particularly in underserved demographics. Blockchain supports accountability, regulatory compliance, and trust-building; digital lending platforms streamline credit evaluation, risk management, and client experience; while mobile banking facilitates secure transactions, efficient loan disbursement, and accurate record-keeping. Citation analysis highlights England, Sweden, Wales, Malaysia, and China as leading contributors, with a concentration of influential conceptual publications. The study underscores that FinTech implementation is not mainly a technical shift but a managerial transformation affecting decision-making, governance, and strategic orientation in microfinance companies. Practical implications include prioritizing blockchain for compliance, integrating data analytics with lending platforms, and tailoring mobile banking services to local contexts. Policymakers are urged to enable regulatory sandboxes and digital identity systems to support scalability. This review contributes to bridging fragmented research by offering a structured understanding of FinTech-driven transformation in microfinance.

U. P. Offiong (✉) · K. Szopik-Depczyńska
Institute of Management, University of Szczecin, Szczecin, Poland
e-mail: uwakmfon.offiong@phd.usz.edu.pl; katarzyna.szopik-depczynska@usz.edu.pl

N. Omrani et al. (eds.), *Human-Machine Synergy and the Digital Future - Exploring Collaboration and Competition Volume 1*, Springer Proceedings in Business and Economics, https://doi.org/10.1007/978-3-032-21347-1_13

Keywords FinTech · Microfinance companies · Innovation · Literature review

1 Introduction

The increasing integration of digital technologies into financial service delivery has transformed the strategic orientation of organizations, particularly those operating in resource constrained environments [1]. Microfinance companies, which serve low income and financially excluded populations, have become central players in this shift due to their dual mandate of financial inclusion and social impact [2]. Technology adoption has allowed these companies to improve service efficiency, expand outreach, and respond to complex client needs [3]. Through the deployment of modern information and communication systems, microfinance companies have reduced transaction costs, mitigated geographic barriers, and optimized operational workflows [4]. However, despite these advancements, the persistence of client--facing functions requiring interpersonal engagement suggests that technology alone cannot replace all aspects of service delivery [5].

This growing reliance on digital infrastructure has positioned financial technology, or FinTech, as a critical enabler of strategic and operational transformation within microfinance [6]. FinTech encompasses a broad range of tools, including automated lending systems, digital customer relationship management, algorithmic financial advisory services, and mobile transaction platforms [4]. These solutions allow companies to gather and analyze client data more effectively, improve decision-making accuracy, and automate key administrative functions. As microfinance companies implement these technologies, they are increasingly confronted with complex managerial challenges, including the need to ensure regulatory compliance, coordinate across digital platforms, and uphold ethical standards in data usage [5]. This intersection of technological advancement and mission-driven management raises important questions regarding how FinTech reshapes organizational strategy and leadership within microfinance companies.

Despite the increasing importance of FinTech in this domain, the academic literature remains dispersed. Most prior research has concentrated on specific digital tools such as mobile payments or online lending, often treating them in isolation from broader managerial concerns [7]. Moreover, much of this research is situated within the context of commercial banking and large-scale financial entities, with relatively limited attention paid to the distinctive features of microfinance companies. As a result, key managerial dimensions of FinTech implementation including decision-making processes, structural adaptation, and strategy alignment remain underexplored. Existing studies acknowledge both the benefits and challenges of FinTech adoption, including enhanced financial inclusion and increased operational risks [8]. Regional evidence, such as in Vietnam, highlights the practical potential of these innovations in expanding access and scale [9]. Furthermore, digital tools like mobile payments and algorithmic credit scoring have been shown to enhance outreach and data quality in rural contexts [10]. However, these insights have yet to be integrated into a comprehensive study suitable for guiding organizational transformation.

In response to this gap, the present study undertakes a comprehensive review of FinTech innovations implemented in microfinance companies, with a specific emphasis on their strategic and managerial implications. To guide this inquiry, the research is organized around the following core questions:

- What are the most implemented FinTech innovations in microfinance companies, and how do they contribute to organizational effectiveness?
- What are the key contributors within the existing literature, and which areas remain insufficiently explored?

Through addressing these questions, the study seeks to generate a structured and integrated understanding of how FinTech innovations influence the management of microfinance companies. In doing so, it contributes to the Management discourse through theoretical insights into technology-enabled strategy, empirical guidance for future research, and practical implications for top management. Rather than treating FinTech adoption as a purely technical development, this study positions it as a managerial transformation with far-reaching effects on decision-making, operational models, and strategic direction. The paper proceeds through the following structure: introduction, methodology, findings, discussion, and conclusion.

2 Methods

2.1 Collection of Data and Literature Resources

This study relies on the Web of Science and Scopus Core Collection as the primary databases for literature gathering. These databases provide more accurate filtering capabilities and are preferred for their standardized references, which ensure consistency in data analysis. Additionally, Google Scholar was utilized to search for relevant articles. To achieve a comprehensive understanding of the subject, keywords were thoroughly chosen, including Microfinance AND FinTech OR Financial Technology AND FinTech tools OR "FinTech innovation" AND projects. The search was conducted using the "All" field, encompassing the title, abstract, and keywords, to guarantee that the retrieved documents are highly pertinent to the phenomenon being studied. The initial search yielded 309 records from 2010 to 2024. Given the broad scope of FinTech and its implementation across different domains, it was crucial to carefully screen the initial records. Three documents were filtered based on their importance to the research question by reviewing titles, abstracts, and, when needed, full texts. This screening procedure excluded publications that did not offer substantial insights into the types of FinTech tools implemented by microfinance companies, such as those mainly focusing on FinTech trends in general without specific reference to microfinance. The final sample comprised 67 documents, covering peer-reviewed journal articles, book chapters, conference proceedings, and review papers.

2.2 Analysis and Visualization of Data

To address our research questions, a thematic analysis and bibliometric data analysis techniques were employed to analyze the chosen publications. Bibliometric methods can help researchers to map the intellectual structure of a research field [11]. This approach is specifically useful for identifying key themes, influential studies, research gaps, and trends which are essential for our study. The analysis incorporated a descriptive strategy to identify leading publications, countries, and organizations contributing to the domain. Citation analysis was conducted to uncover the most impactful studies and to map the progression of research on this subject over time. For representing the bibliometric data visually, VOS Viewer software was used. This methodology provides a clear and structured approach to conducting a comprehensive literature review on the types of FinTech innovation implemented by microfinance companies.

3 Findings

3.1 Key Innovations in FinTech-Driven Microfinance

This section presents the study's findings and insights, with a particular emphasis on the FinTech solutions that microfinance companies have adopted most frequently. The influence of these four solutions on improving organizational effectiveness is also examined. A thorough analysis of the body of research in this area is necessary, given the crucial role played by these key FinTech tools and the growing necessity to change the way microfinance businesses operate. Three essential tools were found in thematic analysis of reviewed literature, as outlined in Table 1.

Table 1 Thematic analysis of key findings from studies (2010–2024)

Key themes	Impact on organizational processes
Blockchain technology	Automates contract execution, ensures transparency, and reduces manual interventions
Digital lending platforms	Streamline processes and automates loan approvals, reduces administrative burden, efficiency
Mobile banking and digital payment	Digitizes payment collections, automates transactions, and supports financial inclusion in remote areas

Source: Own elaboration

3.1.1 Blockchain Technology

In the quest for organizational effectiveness, the adoption of blockchain technology into microfinance companies represents a crucial advancement. This theme finding describes how blockchain redefines key operational procedures in the areas of personnel management, customer engagement, administrative tasks, and general managerial oversight, hence breaking down conventional barriers within microfinance companies. Significant advancements are made in each of these areas not just by using new tools but also by radically altering organizational procedures [12]. Within the microfinance company, employee operations sometimes entail decentralized, field-based tasks that call for thorough tracking and reporting. The use of blockchain technology presents a fresh way to guarantee accountability and accuracy in these procedures [13]. Blockchain eliminates the problems of inconsistent data, false reporting, and inefficiencies that often-beset manual tracking systems by creating an unchangeable and transparent mechanism for documenting all employee--related activity [14]. Another study [15] emphasizes that blockchain can minimize information asymmetry within Islamic microfinance companies and support this finding. Their study broadens our understanding by indicating that blockchain not only enhances internal procedures but also aligns with Islamic financial principles, like risk-sharing and transparency, which are essential to the decentralized operations of personnel in microfinance. This alignment highlights the fact that integrating blockchain involves more than just a technology upgrade; rather, it involves a deliberate reorganization of staff management to meet larger organizational objectives. Moreover, relationships with microfinance customers depend on openness, trust, and consistent communication, all of which blockchain improves as corroborated by [16], who suggested a blockchain-based strategy that uses smart contracts to enforce terms and dynamically change loans, guaranteeing compliance and minimizing abuse. Their results are consistent with important elements of fostering trust. To sum up, blockchain integration can improve the administrative processes of microfinance companies, which are frequently ineffective because of manual processes. Maintaining correct records is made easier with blockchain's decentralized, digital record-keeping system. According to research [17], administrative procedures in decentralized KYC and lending systems are made simpler by cutting expenses and eliminating middlemen. This demonstrates how blockchain can improve security and efficiency. Furthermore, blockchain's transparency facilitates decision-making and lowers errors, while its immutability guarantees consistency and supports regulatory compliance. The importance of blockchain in advancing sustainability and financial inclusion in microfinance is further highlighted [18].

3.1.2 Digital Lending Platforms

The incorporation of digital lending platforms within microfinance companies signifies a noteworthy progression in streamlining and augmenting the overall performance of the organization. These platforms, which are distinguished by attributes like data analytics, automated loan processing, and user-friendly interfaces, play a crucial role in changing the way microfinance companies offer their lending services [19]. Through the smooth implementation of these digital technologies, the company scales up its capacity and flexibility in efficient service delivery to their customers. It is noteworthy that microfinance companies expedite loan processing by leveraging advanced automation tools integrated into digital lending platforms, which manage the entire loan cycle from application receipt to credit evaluation and approval while significantly reducing the need for manual labor [20]. According to [21], the application of artificial intelligence and other digital technologies in P2P lending increases the accuracy of funding success predictions and lowers the likelihood of six defaults, indicating the importance of this automation. Through the implementation of comparable technologies, microfinance companies enhance their overall lending processing efficiency, thereby reducing human error and achieving speedier processing times. Additionally, user-friendly interfaces provided by digital lending platforms enhance client experience. These platforms usually offer users convenient access to financial services through a variety of channels, such as web portals and mobile applications. This is consistent with [22] observations, which show that the growth of local digital lending in Kenya significantly reduces wellness insecurity in rural areas. This underscores the potential of digital platforms to improve welfare in marginalized communities and increase financial inclusion. Additionally, other findings [23] pointed out that risks might be reduced and peer screening's efficacy increased by improving the visibility and accuracy of socially relevant soft information on P2P lending platforms. The frameworks for compliance and risk management are strengthened when digital lending platforms are implemented into microfinance companies. Because these platforms are made to meet strict regulatory requirements, all lending operations are guaranteed to abide by national and international financial legislation. FinTech and BigTech lending exert a dual influence on the stability of the microfinance business sphere, simultaneously promoting financial resilience while posing risks such as increased nonperforming loans, which can be mitigated through the application of advanced risk assessment models, thereby preserving stability and strengthening the credibility of microfinance companies among stakeholders and investors [24].

3.1.3 Mobile Banking and Digital Payments

A major advancement in the optimization of microfinance operations is the introduction of digital payment and mobile banking technologies by microfinance companies. The ability of these digital tools to improve client interactions, enable safe, real-time financial transactions, and expedite general business procedures makes them indispensable for streamlining business operations and guaranteeing that microfinance companies can sustainably grow their customer base [25]. A revolutionary method that profoundly alters the way Microfinance carry out their primary tasks is introduced by the combination of these technologies. Mobile banking platforms, which offer features such as automated payment reminders, real-time fund transfers, and remotely accessible transaction histories, enhance the functionality of microfinance companies by providing a seamless experience for both the organization and its customers [26]. Moreover, digital payment systems enable secure and cashless transactions through various channels, including digital tokens, direct bank transfers, and mobile wallets. These services are connected to an integrated financial ecosystem designed to support efficient, secure, and seamless financial transactions [27]. The study conducted by other authors [28] revealed that some parameters, including financial expenses, company size, and deposit share, had a noteworthy impact on microfinances' adoption of mobile financial services. Larger organizations and banks are more likely to implement mobile technology without sacrificing their social goal, according to their analysis. This result emphasizes how mobile banking technology may be scaled up, particularly in larger Microfinance companies that have the capacity to use their resources to put these systems in place efficiently Enhancing organizational effectiveness in microfinance companies requires the optimization of critical processes by aligning digital tools with business operations to accelerate loan approvals and fund delivery, which in turn enables prompt disbursements, improves cash flow management and loan distribution, increases client satisfaction, and strengthens both client services and operational capabilities through more efficient fund allocation [8]. Moreover, combining mobile banking with information and communication technology enhances the effectiveness, scalability, and outreach of microfinance services [29]. ICT adoption increases loan payback rates and financial inclusion despite obstacles like inadequate infrastructure and low understanding. Repayments are also made easier by automated payment methods.

Overall, customers no longer need to rely on in-person branch visits or cash transactions because digital platforms enable them to make payments straight from their smartphones. Repayment schedule predictability is improved, and cash-handling risks are reduced because of this change. Microfinance companies are able to keep more accurate financial records using automated systems, which is essential for doing financial audits and keeping track of portfolio performance. With this degree of operational accuracy, digital tools play a critical role in bolstering Microfinance companies' financial management system.

3.2 Descriptive Bibliometric Analysis

The examination of influential documents as they are presented illustrates how important citation metrics are for determining the significance of scholarly publications. Citations indicate how much later research builds upon or interacts with a particular work, which is a commonly accepted measure of a publication's impact in the academic world. In this context, the quantity of citations a publication obtains is frequently indicative of its influence. Based on citation counts, Table 2 lists the top five publications that have the greatest influence. With 336 citations, [1] is the

Table 2 Top five most cited documents

Documents	Type of research	Document type	Citations
Gabor [2017] The digital revolution in financial inclusion: International development in the FinTech era	Conceptual	Article	336
Demir [2022] FinTech, financial inclusion and income inequality: a quantile regression approach	Empirical	Article	220
Hasan [2021] Determinants of Financial Sustainability for Microfinance Institutions: Lessons for Islamic Microfinance Banks in Nigeria	Conceptual	Article	68
Banna [2021] FinTech-based Financial Inclusion and Risk-taking of Microfinance Institutions. Evidence from Sub-Saharan Africa	Empirical	Article	52
Kong [2021] Digitally Down to the Countryside: FinTech and Rural Development in China	Conceptual	Article	25

Source: Own elaboration

most cited paper. It looks at how the FinTech era's financial inclusion is being impacted by the digital revolution in microfinance.

Then, using a quantile regression technique, Demir et al. [30] investigated FinTech, financial inclusion, and income inequality and received 220 citations. A noteworthy study [31] with 68 citations, evaluated the factors that contribute to microfinance organizations' financial sustainability and offered guidance to Nigeria's Islamic microfinance banks. Surprisingly, three of the top five papers [1, 30, 31] concentrate on FinTech-driven systems that advance financial inclusion in the microfinance industry. Furthermore, two highly influential studies [31, 32] highlight the importance that FinTech solutions play in promoting financial inclusiveness while addressing the sustainability element of microfinance. These results highlight the prominence of FinTech solutions and financial inclusion in the microfinance space, as demonstrated by these important contributors. Additionally, a higher proportion of the most prominent papers are conceptual studies (3) as opposed to empirical studies (2), suggesting that these researchers frequently use conceptual approaches in their work. It is also significant that articles make up most of the most prominent publications. In terms of intellectual input, the countries with the highest total number of publications and citations on the topic under review include England, Sweden, Wales, Malaysia and People's republic of China, with 9 (615), 3 (260), 1 (220), 6 (93), and 9 (84), respectively (Table 3).

This brings us to our final point: the Web of Science and Scopus databases classify all of the most prominent publications as papers that are under the management, business, and economics category. The publications' thematic concentration on microfinance, FinTech, and financial inclusion—all major topics in the larger scholarly discourse—aligns with this classification. These seminal texts' analysis highlights the relevance of sustainability in FinTech solutions, the role of FinTech and financial inclusion in current microfinance research, and the continued development of conceptual frameworks in this dynamic field. Figure 1 illustrates a network

Table 3 Top five most cited countries

Country	Total publications	Total citations
England	9	615
Sweden	3	260
Wales	1	220
Malaysia	6	93
People's republic of China	9	84

Source: Own elaboration

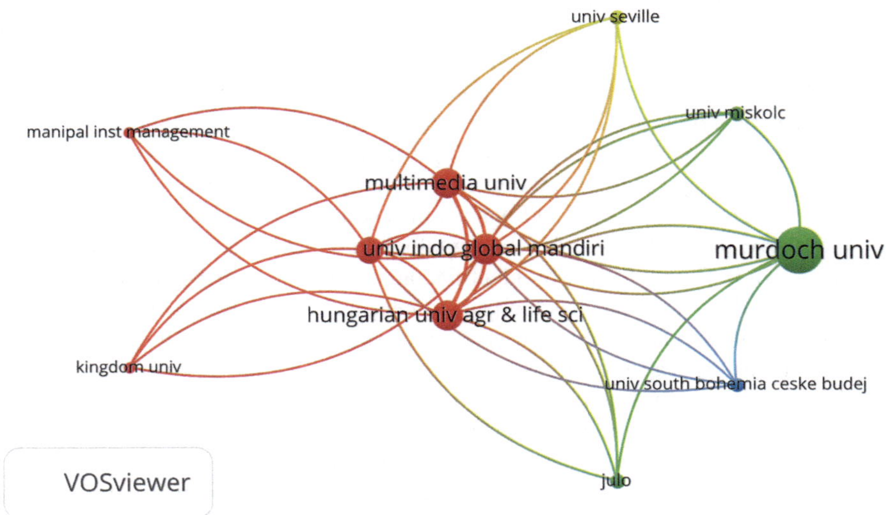

Fig. 1 Organizations' citation network extracted from VOSviewer software

visualization of top-cited documents by organizations about the analyzed phenomenon, generated using VOSviewer. Each node represents an organization, with the size indicating the number of citations received. The most influential organizations include University of West England, University of New York, Stockholm School of Economics, Bangor University, and SOAS University of London with 336, 336, 235, 220, and 220, respectively.

Color-coded clusters indicate groups of closely related organizations, reflecting thematic or regional collaboration patterns. Central nodes, such as Multimedia University and the Hungarian University of Agriculture and Life Sciences, are prominent contributors within their clusters. This network visualization is a useful tool for comprehending the academic landscape around the study of subject under review. It illustrates the interconnectedness of research in this field, identifies important organizations that have had a major scholarly impact, and exposes patterns of collaboration. These kinds of insights are vital for researchers and practitioners who are trying to find their way through the body of literature, find possible partners, or pinpoint important centers of research in the subject.

4 Discussion

This study has demonstrated that blockchain technology, digital lending platforms, and mobile banking solutions are among the most widely adopted FinTech innovations in microfinance companies. These technologies collectively influence organizational effectiveness by enhancing operational transparency, automating service delivery processes, and expanding financial access. When compared with prior studies, several key patterns emerge that underscore both the consistency and novelty of this research.

The findings concerning blockchain technology confirm earlier insights [12, 13], which emphasized the potential of blockchain to minimize information asymmetry and improve compliance in microfinance operations. However, the current study extends these contributions by mapping blockchain's utility beyond regulatory alignment. It details its influence on internal management structures, personnel accountability, and customer relationship transparency. This extension highlights the broader managerial implications of blockchain adoption, positioning it as a governance tool rather than solely a financial infrastructure.

Similarly, the study's insights on digital lending platforms reinforce the conclusions drawn by Tetteh [22], who identified automation and artificial intelligence as pivotal to reducing default risks in peer-to-peer lending environments. The present research confirms the operational benefits of such platforms but moves further to address their implications for strategic management, including organizational scalability and risk management capacity. In contrast to prior work focused on technology performance, this study situates digital lending within broader decision-making frameworks, offering a management-specific perspective.

Findings on mobile banking and digital payments are consistent with [8], who observed that mobile financial services improve outreach and operational efficiency. However, this study refines that understanding by illustrating how mobile platforms enhance financial record accuracy, improve cash flow visibility, and support customer retention in rural and underserved areas. This underscores the strategic value of mobile technologies in strengthening internal processes and client-facing services simultaneously.

Interestingly, several significant publications have looked at risk-taking [32], rural development [31], and sustainability factors [31], although they frequently stay isolated within certain contexts. To incorporate these viewpoints, the current study frames the adoption of FinTech as a component of a larger management transition. With blockchain, digital lending, and mobile platforms identified as the most important advances, the analysis brings together many research streams and places them in a strategic framework that may direct organizational adaptation. This synthesis contributes new ideas through connecting the strategic and operational areas of microfinance research.

Additionally, the bibliometric results showed that research output and influence are concentrated geographically, with China, Malaysia, Sweden, and England emerging as major contributors. This focus brings up significant issues about the creation of knowledge and the findings' contextual relevance. There is a chance that local managerial realities in other locations will continue to be underrepresented if the most cited books come primarily from those regions. This asymmetry and the necessity of more extensive empirical engagement with various organizational contexts are what make the current work unique.

The organizational network visualization, which reinforces patterns of concentrated academic influence, shows that prestigious universities and research organizations control the conversation. These institutions offer useful conceptual frameworks, but the preponderance of conceptual research over empirical research indicates that more practical lessons from microfinance operations need to be included in the area. The current study advances this direction by synthesizing previous studies and pointing out unexplored fields that require empirical investigation, especially those pertaining to managerial collaboration, the ethical use of data, and strategic leadership in FinTech implementation.

5 Conclusion, Implication, and Limitation

This study has provided a comprehensive examination of the spectrum of FinTech innovations adopted within microfinance companies, with particular attention to their influence on organizational effectiveness and managerial practice. Addressing the research objectives, the study identified blockchain technology, digital lending platforms, and mobile banking solutions as the most frequently implemented tools, each contributing in distinct ways to transparency, operational efficiency, customer engagement, and risk management. Through bibliometric analysis, the research also revealed key scholarly trends, influential contributors, and thematic concentrations within the literature, thereby advancing understanding of the intellectual structure of this evolving domain.

From a theoretical perspective, the study contributes to Management scholarship by positioning FinTech adoption not merely as a technological evolution but as a driver of strategic and organizational transformation. The integration of digital tools was shown to impact managerial decision-making, organizational design, and operational frameworks, offering new insights into how mission-driven financial organizations navigate innovation. These findings extend existing theories on technological adoption in hybrid organizations and underline the importance of contextualizing FinTech implementation within company goals, stakeholder dynamics, and regulatory constraints.

In practical terms, the study offers actionable recommendations for managers of microfinance companies, including strategies for deploying blockchain in administrative operations, leveraging digital lending platforms for enhanced credit assessment, and designing customer-centric mobile interfaces to increase adoption and retention. Policymakers and regulators are encouraged to create enabling environments that support responsible experimentation, infrastructure development, and the alignment of digital tools with inclusion goals.

The original contribution of this study lies in its integrative and management-oriented analysis of FinTech applications in microfinance. Unlike prior research that often isolates technological tools or prioritizes financial performance, this work adopts a holistic perspective that links innovation with organizational capabilities, strategic goals, and managerial implications. This approach offers a valuable foundation for both academic inquiry and practice in the evolving intersection of FinTech and inclusive finance.

Nevertheless, the study is subject to several limitations. Firstly, the study relies exclusively on secondary data drawn from bibliometric data and thematic review of published sources, which constrains the ability to capture emergent innovations in microfinance operating in diverse contexts. Moreover, while the review identifies the most widely adopted technologies, it does not measure their relative effectiveness across different organizational settings, leaving inquiries about contextual contingencies such as client demographics and company size. Lastly, while the bibliometric approach enabled the identification of thematic and citation patterns, it did not capture the full depth of theoretical arguments or methodological nuances within individual studies. Future research could benefit from mixed methods approaches that combine bibliometric mapping with in-depth case studies of microfinance actively deploying FinTech solutions.

Acknowledgments Cofinanced by the Minister of Science under the "Regional Excellence Initiative" Program.

References

1. Gabor, D., Brooks, S.: The digital revolution in financial inclusion: International development in the fintech era. New Polit. Econ. **22**(4), 423–436 (2017)
2. Fersi, M., Boujelbéne, M., Arous, F.: Microfinance's digital transformation for sustainable inclusion. Eur. J. Manag. Bus. Econ. **32**(5), 525–559 (2023)
3. Ali, A., Ramakrishnan, S., Faisal, F., Ullah, Z.: Bibliometric analysis of global research trends on microfinance institutions and microfinance: suggesting new research agendas. Int. J. Financ. Econ. **28**(4) (2023)
4. Jarvis, R., Han, H.: Fintech innovation: review and future research directions. Int. J. Bank Financ. Ins. Technol. **1**(1), 79–102 (2021)
5. Banna, H., Mia, M.A., Nourani, M., Yarovaya, L.: Fintech-based financial inclusion and Risk-taking of microfinance institutions (MFIs): evidence from sub-Saharan Africa. Financ. Res. Lett. **45**(5) (2022)
6. Timbula, M.A., Marvadi, C.: Digital transformation: acceptance and use of technology among microfinance institutions in developing country: an application of UTAUT2 mode. Int. J. Inf. Technol. **15**(8), 4459–4468 (2023)
7. Mia, M.A.: Technological change and innovations in microfinance institutions: what matters? Glob. Bus. Rev. **24**(6), 1454–1467 (2023)
8. Ndungu, J.M., Moturi, C.A.: Determinants of Mobile Fintech uptake in Kenyan microfinance sector. Curr. J. Appl. Sci. Technol. **102**, 114 (2020)
9. Dang, T.T., Vu, H.Q.: Fintech in microfinance: a new direction for microfinance institutions in Vietnam. J. Bus. Econ. Environ. Stud. **10**(3), 13–22 (2020)

10. Benami, E., Carter, M.R.: Can digital technologies reshape rural microfinance? Implications for savings, credit, insurance. Appl. Econ. Perspect. Policy. **43**(4), 1196–1220 (2021)
11. Župič, I., Čater, T.: Bibliometric methods in management and organization. Organ. Res. Methods. **18**(3), 429–472 (2015)
12. Kovács, D., Molnár, B., Weininger, V.: Blockchain-driven transparency and efficiency in small loan processing: a case of microfinance integration. SEFBIS J. **46**(1), 33–49 (2025)
13. Hoffmann, H.C.: Blockchain use cases revisited: micro-lending solutions for retail banking. J. Syst. Sci. Inf. **9**(2), 145–158 (2021)
14. Zahari, A., Nordin, R., Lee, M.: An adaptive utility ranking algorithm (AURA) for evaluating blockchain applications in microfinance. Int. J. Eng. Sci. **14**(1), 77–91 (2025)
15. Wanke, P., Hassan, M.K., Azad, M.A.K., Rahman, M.A., Akther, N.: Application of a distributed verification in Islamic microfinance institutions: a sustainable model. Financ. Innov. **8**(1) (2022)
16. Kumarathunga, M., Calheiros, R.N., Ginige, A.: Sustainable microfinance outreach for farmers with Blockchain cryptocurrency and smart contracts. Int. J. Comput. Theory Eng. **14**(1), 9–14 (2022)
17. Sai, B.D.S., Nikhil, R., Prasad, S., Naik, N.S.: A decentralised KYC based approach for microfinance using blockchain technology. Cyber Secur. Appl. **1**(9) (2023)
18. Liu, A., Urquía-Grande, E., López-Sánchez, P., Rodríguez-López, Á.: Research into microfinance and ICTs: a bibliometric analysis. Eval. Program Plann. **97**(November), 0–2 (2023)
19. Katsamakas, E., Sánchez-Cartas, J.M.: Network formation and financial inclusion in P2P lending: a computational model. Systems. **10**(5) (2022)
20. Basha, S., Elgammal, M.M., Abuzayed, B.: Online peer-to-peer lending: a review of the literature. Electron. Commer. Res. Appl. **48**(6), 101069 (2021)
21. Ashta, A., Herrmann, H.: Artificial intelligence and fintech: an overview of opportunities and risks for banking, investments, and microfinance. Strateg. Chang. **30**(3), 211–222 (2021)
22. Tetteh, G.K.: Local digital lending development and the incidence of deprivation in Kenya. Financ. Innov. **9**(1), 102 (2023)
23. Wang, Y., Drabek, Z.: Adverse selection in P2P lending: does peer screening work efficiently?—Empirical evidence from a P2P platform. Int. J. Financ. Stud. **9**(4), 73 (2021)
24. Ozili, P.K., Reporting, F., Risk, M.: Determinants of FinTech and BigTech lending: the role of financial inclusion and financial development. J. Econ. Anal. **2**(3), 66–79 (2023)
25. Shaikh, A.A., Hanafizadeh, P., Karjaluoto, H.: Mobile banking and payment system: a conceptual standpoint. Int. J. E-Bus. Res. **13**(2), 14–27 (2017)
26. Ammar, A., Ahmed, E.M.: Factors influencing Sudanese microfinance intention to adopt mobile banking. Cogent Bus. Manag. **3**(1), 1186312 (2016)
27. Ahmed, E.M., Ammar, A., Ali, A.E.L.S.: Sudanese microfinance services providers drivers for intention to adopt mobile banking. J. Internet Bank. Commer. **21**(3), 1–25 (2016)
28. Dorfleitner, G., Nguyen, Q.A., Röhe, M.: Microfinance institutions and the provision of mobile financial services: first empirical evidence. Financ. Res. Lett. **31**, 357–362 (2019)
29. Liu, R., Wang, Z., Sindakis, S., Showkat, S.: Unlocking financial inclusion through ICT and Mobile banking: a knowledge-based analysis of microfinance institutions in Ghana. J. Knowl. Econ. **15**(2), 1–33 (2023)
30. Demir, A., Pesqué-Cela, V., Altunbaş, Y., Murinde, V.: Fintech, financial inclusion and income inequality: a quantile regression approach. Eur. J. Financ. **28**(1), 86–107 (2022)
31. Abdullahi, A., Othman, A.H.A.: Determinants of financial sustainability for microfinance institutions: lessons for Islamic microfinance banks in Nigeria. Turk. J. Islam. Econ. **8**(Special Issue), 301–320 (2021)
32. Kong, S.T., Loubere, N.: Digitally down to the countryside: Fintech and rural development in China. J. Dev. Stud. **57**(10), 1739–1754 (2021)

AI and Platform Models in Communication Agencies Transforming Business Architecture Through Organizational and Revenue Model Innovation

Stefan Kemp

Abstract This study explores how generative artificial intelligence (AI) and platform-based models are transforming the business architecture of communication agencies. It focuses on the dual impact of these technological drivers on organizational structures and revenue models. The study design involved multi-perspective triangulation, with four research groups independently examining the same organizational case of a German communication agency. Findings reveal that AI enables workflow integration and automation, supporting a transition from siloed operations to process-oriented logic. Simultaneously, platform models facilitate ecosystem coordination and support modular services. The research identifies the emergence of hybrid revenue models that blend traditional human-led services with AI-powered solutions. The study concludes that AI and platform models represent transformative forces that require agencies to strategically realign business models to remain competitive in an increasingly digitized B2B environment.

Keywords AI · Platform business models · Communication agencies

1 Introduction

Traditional services of communication agencies, such as campaign development and visual and textual content production, are increasingly supported by AI technologies like generative pre-trained transformers (GPTs) [1, 2]. For instance, AI tools such as Lumen5 or Pictory can automate visual content creation, while tools

S. Kemp (✉)
Macromedia University, Berlin, Germany
e-mail: s.kemp@macromedia.de

N. Omrani et al. (eds.), *Human-Machine Synergy and the Digital Future - Exploring Collaboration and Competition Volume 1*, Springer Proceedings in Business and Economics, https://doi.org/10.1007/978-3-032-21347-1_14

like ChatGPT, PaLM, or Azure can generate textual content, often rivaling or surpassing human-created work in speed and cost-efficiency [3, 4]. These technologies allow for greater personalization and faster iteration in creative outputs. Experts see a rapid rise of AI and an increasingly widespread availability of self-service tools [5]. The advancements promise significant productivity gains, but they also lead to heightened client expectations, with many demanding that these efficiencies translate into reduced communication agency service costs and faster delivery timelines. AI technologies can alter how agencies deliver value to their clients.

The rise of the platform economy is fundamentally reshaping industries across the globe. Among the most valuable companies are several that operate based on the organizational principle of the platform [6–8]. The platform organizational model uses a digital infrastructure to facilitate interactions and value exchanges between multiple user groups. A platform is a more recent organizational paradigm, enabling unprecedented scalability, efficiency, and connectivity [9, 10]. Platforms are evolving further by embedding AI-driven capabilities that optimize processes, analyze vast datasets in real time, and deliver hyper-personalized user experiences [11, 12].

Communication agencies are at a critical juncture when faced with the transformative pressures deriving from AI technologies and platform models. These technological drivers put the traditional business architecture of agencies, encompassing their revenue model and organizational model, under threat. In its place, new agency models are beginning to emerge, driven by AI integration and platform-based approaches [13]. Both technological drivers, AI and platform models, extend the firm's boundaries beyond internal production to a decentralized network [14]. However, this shift also introduces challenges, such as the risk of commoditization, ethical concerns surrounding AI-generated content, and the need for agencies to upskill their workforces to remain competitive in an AI-powered landscape [15].

This study pursues two main research objectives. First, it investigates how AI technologies affect the organizational and revenue models of communication agencies. Second, it explores the role of platform-based models in reshaping both organizational structures and revenue generation mechanisms. Given the limited research in this area, a qualitative case-study approach is adopted to examine how technological drivers incur potential shifts in business architecture. The study starts with a theoretical background that draws on three aspects. First, it examines the role of AI in business transformation. Second, it considers platform business models, emphasizing their role in commercially oriented business-to-business (B2B) environments of communication agencies. Third, it explores how these developments drive business-model innovation regarding organizational and revenue models of communication agencies.

2 Theoretical Background

2.1 AI and Business Transformation

AI encompasses a broad range of technologies, making it challenging to provide a concrete definition [16]. Enholm et al. [17] suggest that AI is an applied discipline that enables systems to identify, interpret, make inferences, and learn from data to achieve predetermined organizational and societal goals. One common consideration is that AI involves computers simulating human behavior, allowing machines to acquire skills related to decision-making, judgment, and the emulation of human behavior [16]. A core feature of all definitions seems to be the ability to mimic human cognitive functions such as problem-solving and learning [18]. As an innovative and often disruptive technology, AI enables organizations to innovate and transform business processes [19, 20]. It redraws the frontier of commercial possibilities and incites the redefinition of strategic approaches and organizational cultures, anticipating a business future shaped by unprecedented synergies between technology and entrepreneurial innovation [21]. AI disrupts business processes and generates new entrepreneurial opportunities [22].

Perifanis and Kitsios [23] emphasize the strategic value of AI in contemporary business ecosystems, suggesting that AI can establish a competitive advantage for businesses. Other authors see AI as the core technology driving automation and connectivity, thus "ushering in the fourth industrial revolution" [24].

2.2 Platform Business Models in B2B Contexts

In their recent work, Zeamari and Laurier [25] conducted a systematic literature review, gathering and analyzing 64 definitions from 58 scholarly sources using qualitative content analysis. As a result, digital platforms are described as organizational forms that facilitate interactions between independent users through digital interfaces. Platform-based models generate revenue through transaction fees, subscription models, and premium service tiers [26]. This study focuses on communication agencies operating within business-to-business models oriented toward commercial objectives, so more specific definitions of digital platforms are useful. Marr [27] reviewed and summarized definitions of industrial digital platforms in the literature. Industrial digital platforms are defined as a "foundational technological architecture and data upon which a [...] firm organizes a diverse set of interdependent actors, activities, and interfaces to create, deliver, and capture value" [p. 13]. The core difference between the definitions lies in the ontological framing of platforms. Zeamari and Laurier [25] shift focus to the platform as an organizational field or ecosystem, coordinating external, autonomous actors through digital means. This perspective draws from the platform economy and multi-sided market theory, emphasizing decentralized orchestration. Platforms enable new forms of market-based coordination rather than referring to the internal management of an organization. The definition proposed by Madanaguli et al. [28] conceptualizes the platform as a firm-centric technological system that manages actors and processes within a value chain. Platforms are viewed as institutional infrastructures that enable new forms of market-based coordination. This aligns with the internal organizational design and platform governance from the perspective of the platform owner. As such, this reflects a broader duality in platform research [29, 30] that is important for understanding and analyzing platform innovation and dynamics.

Both definitions offer distinct perspectives on digital platforms. However, this study adopts the definition proposed by Madanaguli et al. [28]. Their firm-centric view, which conceptualizes platforms as technological systems designed to manage actors and processes within a value chain, aligns more closely with the purpose of this investigation. By emphasizing internal organizational design and platform governance from the perspective of the platform owner, this definition provides a more suitable foundation for analyzing platform dynamics within communication agencies operating in commercially-oriented B2B environments.

2.3 *Business Model Innovation: Organizational and Revenue Dimensions*

Generally, digital platforms are viewed as drivers of innovation, enabling companies to modernize their business models and create new value [25]. Their significance reflects this: "Platform companies have become increasingly important to the global economy and are some of the largest and most valued companies today" [31], [00:19]. Digital platforms may allow communication agencies operating within B2B contexts to scale their services more efficiently by minimizing traditional operational costs. Unlike linear business models, platforms do not require proportional labor or increases in physical infrastructure as they grow [32]. Platforms reduce marginal costs to enhance value creation. For instance, a communication agency using a proprietary platform to connect freelance creatives with client projects can expand its service offerings without hiring full-time staff or establishing new offices, thereby reducing overhead. This benefits commercially-driven agency environments where responsiveness, cost-efficiency, and adaptability are critical to competitive advantage. Digital platforms are driving fundamental changes in business models across industries, including the field of communication agencies. According to O'Reilly [33], the transformation is driven by brand self-service tools, automation, and extensive networks that enable them to reduce or eliminate reliance on traditional agencies. Marr [27] notes that adopting digital platforms supports the refinement of business models, allowing firms to remain agile and competitive. Integrating new technologies into agency workflows enhances service delivery and reshapes revenue models. Veling and Sellappan [34] suggest that implementing AI technologies reduces operational costs for marketing and communication agencies.

AI enhances efficiency in various marketing processes, such as customer segmentation and campaign management, leading to substantial cost savings.

Enholm et al. [17] examined how AI contributes to competitive performance by analyzing its effects at two levels: First, on the level of the organization's business processes, denoted as first-order impacts, and second, on the level of overall firm performance, denoted as second-order impacts. The first-order impacts of AI use are related to the changes it causes at the process level of an organization. Process efficiency refers to enhancing business performance through AI-driven task automation and support of human decision-making. This reduces errors, increases speed and precision, and allows employees to focus on higher-value activities. As a result, organizational workflows become more productive and transparent [17]. This reflects considerations of [20], suggesting that AI is a driver of business process innovation, proposing "that organizations achieve performance through AI capabilities [...] when they use their features [...] to reconfigure their processes" [p. 1893]. The second-order impacts of AI are related to the firm-level effects of AI use in operations, such as financial performance [17]. Financial performance refers to the gains achieved through AI adoption, such as increased revenue and cost reduction, mainly when organizations develop structured AI capabilities and integrate them into core activities. This directly relates to an organization's revenue model, reflecting enhanced value creation and more efficient monetization of services and processes [35, 36].

The convergence of AI and digital platform technologies fundamentally reshapes business model innovation, particularly within communication agencies operating in B2B contexts. AI, a transformative technology capable of mimicking human cognitive functions, enables organizations to optimize processes, create new services, and redefine strategic orientations [17, 21]. Simultaneously, platform-based business models provide technological architecture for coordinating actors and activities across value chains, fostering scalability and cost-efficiency [28].

This study adopts a firm-centric perspective. As platform infrastructures integrate AI-driven capabilities, such as automation, data analytics, and self-service tools, enhancing service delivery, enabling agencies to reconfigure their revenue models, and remaining agile in increasingly digitally mediated markets [27, 32]. Together, these developments could mark a paradigm shift in how communication agencies innovate and compete. The underlying assumption is that AI and platform technologies act as transformative forces that drive innovation in business models, specifically influencing organizational and revenue models.

Technological drivers, AI, and platforms can potentially drive organizational and revenue model innovation. In this study, these two dimensions—organizational model and revenue model—are understood as the core components of what is referred to as business architecture. Building on these considerations, the following chapter outlines the research questions that guide this study.

3 Research Areas

The investigation is divided into two research areas. Each area is examined concerning its first-order impact on the organizational model and its second-order impact on the revenue model [17].

3.1 *Research Area 1: AI as a Technological Driver*

The first research area (denoted as research area 1) explores the implications of AI technologies on the organizational and revenue models of communication agencies. The emphasis is on identifying opportunities to optimize workflows and enhance automation. It is assumed that (a) AI can improve the productivity of the organizational model and (b) AI affects the revenue model.

3.2 *Research Area 2: Platforms as Technological Drivers*

Another research area (denoted as research area 2) focuses on platforms. The exploratory premise is that connecting the agency to the external value-chain ecosystem creates opportunities for service innovations in communication agencies, with implications for (a) organizational and (b) revenue models.

The following table presents the research approach, outlining the relationship between technological drivers, AI, and platform models in the context of communication agencies. It examines their impact on key business architecture elements, organizational structures, and revenue models. The research areas are positioned at the interfaces between technological drivers and business architecture elements.

3.3 *Overview of Research Areas*

The following table presents the research approach, outlining the relationship between technological drivers, AI, and platform models in the context of communication agencies. It examines their impact on key business architecture elements, organizational structures, and revenue models. The research areas are positioned at the interfaces between technological drivers and business architecture elements (Fig. 1).

	Business Architecture Elements	
Technological Drivers	Organizational Model	Revenue Model
AI	*Research area 1(a)*	*Research area 1(b)*
Platform models	*Research area 2(a)*	*Research area 2(b)*

Fig. 1 Business architecture elements, technological drivers, and research areas

4 Methodology

This study adopts an in-depth qualitative case study approach. The explorative method is particularly appropriate due to the limited existing evidence and case studies in the research area [37]. The case study examines a Germany-based communication agency with several hundred employees that operates within a global agency network and collaborates with international brands.

Using a multi-perspective triangulation, the research integrates various analytical angles to comprehensively understand the agency's operations related to the research areas [38]. Four independent groups of researchers addressed these areas over 5 months and produced academic reports [39–42]. The observations from all groups were collected from a current international flagship project of the agency. Analyses rely on secondary sources from within the agency, which include confidential business-critical information. Additionally, several series of personal semi-structured group interviews were conducted with executives at the first and second management levels. A semi-structured interview is a qualitative data collection method that combines pre-determined topics with the flexibility to explore emerging subjects during the conversation [43]. This approach allowed the research groups to delve deeper into respondents' perspectives to understand the dynamic and unexplored areas of research while maintaining a consistent framework across interviews and the broader project.

5 Case Description

5.1 Organizational Model

The agency's traditional and current organizational model comprises four competence units, each specializing in a specific area of expertise: Concept & Creation, Visual Communication and Brand Spaces, Video, Audio, Virtual Motion Design, and Live Experiences. However, the competence units do not reflect the process model for client work. They operate in a coordinated manner within a sequential workflow encompassing five phases: Basic concept, Concept development and pre-planning, Implementation planning, Execution, and Evaluation of results and documentation. Each of the five phases features a specific spec sheet detailing services and deliverables. This approach establishes a vertical or silo perspective on the five elements of the workflow. Each phase has a distinct beginning and end. The phases proceed sequentially, with each subsequent phase building on the previous one.

5.2 Revenue Model

The agency's revenue model accounts for areas of expertise, job grades, and the hours engaged in the five phases. It reflects communications agencies' traditional billing model [44]. This traditional agency model typically relies on time-based billing, where clients are charged according to the hours spent by professionals at varying levels of seniority. This approach delineates roles and responsibilities across strategy, creation, production, distribution, and evaluation phases. Another aspect of this model is the role of the human factor. Both expertise and job grade are significant elements in the equation determining revenue. According to the agency's senior leadership, the organization's digital maturity aligns with its peer groups. The agency does not significantly utilize AI [45]. However, awareness of its potential strategic implications exists. The senior leadership believes that "AI is challenging established systems" [40, p. 1].

6 Analysis and Findings

The research questions place the organizational model as a critical area of investigation. Considerations are made in the context of the current sequential agency workflow, which consists of five phases, as illustrated in the case description. A defining feature of the workflow is that each of the five phases operates as a distinct unit with a defined description of services. In-depth investigations of the services included in each phase revealed horizontal relationships between work items across different phases, particularly in phases one, two, and three (basic concept, concept development and pre-planning, and implementation planning). Inductive reasoning based on these observations suggests the existence of processual and workflow interdependencies among these phases. Phases one, two, and three focus on iterative development of the concept, text, and imagery. These findings indicate end-to-end relations within the early project stages. This corresponds to the views of [19] or [20] proposing AI as an enabler to transform and innovate business processes to unlock unprecedented synergies [21]. Phases one, two, and three relate to phase five, which evaluates results and documentation. This observation suggests that decisions made in the initial phases directly influence later efforts and highlights the potential for stronger integration. Adopting a cross-phase perspective reveals relationships that could lead to process innovations, allowing clients to access AI-supported workflow tools for monitoring, analysis, or instant intervention. Such connectivity might be perceived as a revolution at the agency level or the level of the communication agency industry [24].

This study also investigates the agency's revenue model, using its traditional revenue approach as a starting point. This model considers the value of professional expertise and seniority within the team, as reflected by the job grade. A systematic evaluation of eight alternative agency revenue models revealed that a monthly retainer model offers the most suitable option and opportunities for additional services. This perspective aligns with subscription usage models popular in platform economics [26]. Usage-based subscriptions allow clients to engage with a core offering while flexibly accessing additional services. These services may include access to experts and the manual processing of revision cycles in line with traditional models. An alternative feature could be a model with reduced human-to-human interaction and automated workflows, based on respective GPTs. This might lead to faster turnaround times and lower production costs [32, 34]. A middle ground between traditional models and AI-supported workflow infrastructure could be hybrid models emphasizing either traditional service elements or automated workflows in line with the view of [27], assuming that agility is a success factor. The considerations reflect client relationships based on adaptable, tiered service offerings. Incorporating platform-economic principles into agency revenue strategies enhances responsiveness to differentiated client demand in a changing market environment.

The business model innovations observed in this case study align with [17], who suggest levels of impact. First-order impacts from AI use drive innovation at the organizational process level, while second-order impacts affect financial performance. The following table connects the case-study evidence to the assumptions made regarding the specific research areas. It illustrates the potential implications of technological drivers for the business architecture of communication agencies (Fig. 2).

7 Discussion

This study indicates that AI and platform models significantly transform communication agencies' business architecture by reshaping organizational and revenue structures. However, this transformation does not seem to be uniformly distributed. At the strategic level, leading firms are already responding with large-scale realignments, such as the $10 billion acquisition announced by a significant industry player in late 2024 [5]. These developments could underscore a growing divide between technology-enabled communication agencies and smaller competitors, which face the risk of exclusion due to limited resources and an inability to match the speed or scale of digital integration. However, technological readiness does not equate to organizational readiness. Integrating AI into agency workflows remains a complex

	Business Architecture Elements	
Technological Drivers	Organizational Model	Revenue Model
AI	*Research area 1(a)* • Potential for AI-supported cross-phase tools • Transition from siloed to processual logic	*Research area 1(b)* • Packages defined by factors such as human involvement or AI integration • Transition from hourly, expertise-based to usage-based billing • Potential hybrid pricing models that combine manual and automated service tiers
Platform models	*Research area 2(a)* • Coordination across external value chain ecosystems of creators and clients • Modular service offerings based on platform logic	*Research area 2(b)* • Enhanced scalability, reduced marginal costs, and increased responsiveness to client needs • Shift towards subscription and tiered pricing models

Fig. 2 Technological drivers and business architecture elements

challenge. As Bauwe [46] notes, many firms are still in the early stages of digital maturity. This study confirms that AI-supported process innovation might be technically feasible but requires internal coordination, sequencing, and rethinking of service delivery models.

An additional challenge could be AI governance. As AI becomes embedded in content creation and strategic outputs, agencies must address emerging concerns around transparency, accountability, and ethical boundaries. Existing frameworks, such as the European Commission's Ethics Guidelines for Trustworthy AI [47], offer orientation for responsible AI implementation. However, many agencies may lack formal governance mechanisms. Without governance structures, they may risk reputational damage, client mistrust, and potential regulatory consequences. Governance should evolve from reactive compliance to a proactive, strategic function that ensures the alignment of technological innovation with ethical and organizational integrity.

Together, these findings reveal a double challenge: How can we seize the opportunities of technological transformation while managing the systemic and ethical complexities it introduces?

8 Limitations

Its exploratory, qualitative design limits this study, focusing on one communication agency within the German market. Consequently, the findings are not generalizable across various organizational contexts or geographic regions. Further research is needed to validate results through comparative or multi-case analyses.

References

1. Kaput, M.: Marketing Artificial Intelligence: AI, Marketing, and the Future of Business. BenBella Books, Dallas, TX (2023)
2. Morapeli, S., Khemisi, M.: The influence of artificial intelligence on the strategic communication industry. Communicare. **43**(1), 48–58 (2024). https://doi.org/10.36615/jcsa.v43i1.1432
3. Aljanabi, A.: Generative AI in marketing: efficiency or disruption? J. Digit. Strateg. **12**(2), 45–58 (2023)
4. BotPenguin: The top 10 best LLM as a service providers in 2024. BotPenguin. https://botpenguin.com/blogs/top-best-llm-as-a-service-providers (2024)
5. Wang, Z.: Omnicom agrees to acquire IPG and take the AI fight to Big Tech. The Current. https://www.thecurrent.com/omnicom-acquires-ipg-ai-big-tech (2024)
6. Holler, J., Wang, L., Perez, A.: Platforms and the future of work. Strateg. Manag. Rev. **18**(3), 210–225 (2022)
7. Pomykalski, P.: Revenue and valuation of companies with digital platform business models. Manag. Sci. **24**(1), 15–23 (2019)
8. Ruggieri, R., Savastano, M., Scalingi, A., D'Ascenzo, F.: The impact of digital platforms on business models: An empirical investigation on innovative start-ups. Manag. Market. **13**(4), 1210–1225 (2018)
9. Choudary, S.P.: Platform Scale: How An Emerging Business Model Helps Startups Build Large Empires with Minimum Investment. Platform Thinking Labs (2022)
10. Takagi, M.: The platform paradigm: a new business model for the digital age. J. Digit. Bus. Models. **6**(1), 12–35 (2020)
11. Brynjolfsson, E., McAfee, A.: The Second Machine Age: Work, Progress, and Prosperity in a Time of Brilliant Technologies. W.W. Norton, New York (2017)
12. Parker, G., Van Alstyne, M., Jiang, X.: Platform ecosystems: how developers invert the firm. MIS Q. **41**(1), 255–266 (2017)
13. Sophia, D.M., Dugar, U.M.: Ad Giant Omnicom Takes Aim at Big Tech, AI Era with $13 Billion Interpublic Deal. Reuters. https://www.reuters.com/ (2024)
14. Zenger, T.R., Felin, T., Bigelow, L.: Theories of the firm–market boundary: a review and future directions. J. Manag. **37**(4), 1135–1168 (2011)
15. Jha, R., Verma, K.: Redefining advertising: AI and the future of communication agencies. J. Market. Innov. **9**(4), 98–113 (2023)
16. Da Xu, L., Lu, Y., Li, L.: Embedding blockchain technology into IoT for security: a survey. IEEE Internet Things J. **8**(13), 10452–10473 (2021)
17. Enholm, I.M., Papagiannidis, E., Mikalef, P., et al.: Artificial intelligence and business value: a literature review. Inf. Syst. Front. **24**, 1709–1734 (2022). https://doi.org/10.1007/s10796-021-10186-w
18. Lee, J., Suh, T., Roy, D., Baucus, M.: Emerging technology and business model Innovation: the case of artificial intelligence. J. Open Innov. Technol. Mark. Complex. **5**(3), 44 (2019)
19. Christensen, C.M., Raynor, M.E., McDonald, R.: What is disruptive innovation? Harvard Bus. Rev. https://hbr.org/2015/12/what-is-disruptive-innovation (2015)

20. Wamba-Taguimdje, S.L., Wamba, S.F., Kamdjoug, J.R.K., Wanko, C.E.T.: Influence of artificial intelligence (AI) on firm performance: the business value of AI-based transformation projects. Bus. Process Manag. J. **26**(7), 1893–1924 (2020). https://doi.org/10.1108/BPMJ-10-2019-041
21. Del Val Núñez, M.T., Yela Aránega, A., Ribeiro-Soriano, D.: Artificial Intelligence and Business Transformation. Springer, Berlin (2024)
22. Del Olmo-García, F., Crecente-Romero, F.J., Sarabia-Alegría, M., del Val Núñez, M.T.: Artificial intelligence, business activity and entrepreneurial opportunities: the European case. In: Peña-Sánchez, J.A., Torelli, C.J. (eds.) Artificial intelligence and business transformation. Springer, Berlin (2024). https://doi.org/10.1007/978-3-031-58704-7_8
23. Perifanis, N.-A., Kitsios, F.: Investigating the influence of artificial intelligence on business value in the digital era of strategy: a literature review. Information. **14**(2), 85 (2023). https://doi.org/10.3390/info14020085
24. Costa-Climent, R., Haftor, D.M., Staniewski, M.W.: Intelligent transformation: navigating the AI revolution in business and technology. In: Del Val Núñez, M.T., Yela Aránega, A., Ribeiro-Soriano, D. (eds.) Artificial Intelligence and Business Transformation: Impact in HR Management, Innovation and Technology Challenges, pp. 3–20. Springer, Berlin (2024). https://doi.org/10.1007/978-3-031-51753-0_1
25. Zeamari, I., Laurier, W.: Defining digital platforms: a systematic literature review. In: Bach Tobji, M.A., Jallouli, R., Sadok, H., Lajfari, K., Mafamane, D., Mahboub, H. (eds.) Digital Economy. Emerging Technologies and Business Innovation. ICDEc 2024. Lecture Notes in Business Information Processing, vol. 530. Springer, Cham (2025). https://doi.org/10.1007/978-3-031-76365-6_4
26. Evans, P.C., Gawer, A.: The Rise of the Platform Enterprise: A Global Survey. The Center for Global Enterprise, New York (2016)
27. Marr, B.: The impact of digital transformation on business models: opportunities and challenges. Forbes. https://www.forbes.com/sites/bernard-marr/2023/10/12/the-impact-of-digital-transformation-on-business-models-opportunities-and-challenges/ (2023
28. Madanaguli, A., Parida, V., Sjödin, D., Oghazi, P.: Literature review on industrial digital platforms: a business model perspective and suggestions for future research. Technol. Forecast. Soc. Change. **194**, 122606 (2023). https://doi.org/10.1016/j.techfore.2023.122606
29. Constantinides, P., Henfridsson, O., Parker, G.G.: Introduction—platforms and infrastructures in the digital age. Inf. Syst. Res. **29**(2), 381–400 (2018). https://doi.org/10.1287/isre.2018.0794
30. Gawer, A.: Bridging differing perspectives on technological platforms: toward an integrative framework. Res. Policy. **43**(7), 1239–1249 (2014). https://doi.org/10.1016/j.re-spol.2014.03.006
31. Zhu, F.: 5 Benefits of Platform Business Models [Video]. Harvard Business School Online. https://online.hbs.edu/blog/post/platform-business (2023)
32. Gibson, K.: 5 Benefits of Platform Business Models. Harvard Business School Online. https://online.hbs.edu/blog/post/platform-business (2024)
33. O'Reilly, L.: An Nvidia exec explains how CMOs are using AI to get the most out of their ad budgets. Business Insider. https://www.businessinsider.com/nvidia-brands-using-ai-boost-marketing-delta-unilever-mars-2025-3 (2025)
34. Veling, P., Sellappan, P.: The role of artificial intelligence in cost reduction of marketing agencies. In: 2024 2nd DMIHER International Conference on Artificial Intelligence in Healthcare, Education and Industry (IDICAIEI), pp. 1–6 (2024)
35. PR-Report: Werden Vergütungsmodelle aus der Software-Branche sehen. https://www.prreport.de/singlenews/uid-960823/werden-verguetungsmodelle-aus-der-software-branche-sehen/v (2024)
36. StarsMedia: Automatisierte Marketingkampagnen: Wie KI-Technologie die Effizienz steigern kann. https://www.starsmedia.com/ki/automatisierte-marketingkampagnen-wie-ki-technologie-die-effizienz-steigern-kann/ (n.d.)
37. Eisenhardt, K.M.: Building theories from case study research. Acad. Manage. Rev. **14**(4), 532–550 (1989)

38. Paltridge, B.: Multi-perspective research. In: Paltridge, B. (ed.) The Routledge Handbook of Research Methods in Applied Linguistics, pp. 9–21. Routledge, London (2015)
39. Buchbinder, L., Goergen, V.: Designing the Competitive Future of Communication Agencies (unpublished academic report). Macromedia University of Applied Sciences (2025)
40. Kliemt, A., Negash, M.: Designing the Competitive Future of Communication Agencies (Unpublished Academic Report). Macromedia University of Applied Sciences (2025)
41. Schäfer, K., Genesi, C.: Designing the Competitive Future of Communication Agencies (Unpublished Academic Report). Macromedia University of Applied Sciences (2025)
42. Van Lier, F., Starke, J., Pantelmann, L.: Designing the Competitive Future of Communication Agencies (Unpublished Academic Report). Macromedia University of Applied Sciences (2025)
43. Given, L.M.: Semi-structured interview. In: Given, L.M. (ed.) The SAGE Encyclopedia of Qualitative Research Methods, pp. 811–812. SAGE, Thousand Oaks (2008)
44. ACC (Association of Communication Companies): Remunerating for Success. https://www.acc.be/tool/remunerating-for-success (2022). Accessed 10 Apr 2025
45. Project Briefing: Designing the Competitive Future of Communication Agencies (Unpublished Internal Document). Macromedia University of Applied Sciences (2024)
46. Bauwe, H.: KI in Marketing & Vertrieb (B2B) [Vortrag]. BIG BANG KI-Festival, KPMG AG Wirtschaftsprüfungsgesellschaft (2024)
47. European Commission: Ethics guidelines for trustworthy AI. In: High-Level Expert Group on Artificial Intelligence. https://ec.europa.eu (2019)

Graph-Based Sentiment Analysis: An AI-Driven Approach to Mapping Customer Feedback in Retail

Jérôme Baray

Abstract His study proposes a novel method for analyzing customer feedback using graph-based semantic clustering. By leveraging 3000 Google Maps reviews of Costco Wholesale Los Angeles, a graph of 261 sentiment adjectives was constructed using semantic proximity coefficients generated via the Mistral 7B LLM. Dimensionality reduction with PCA and hierarchical clustering revealed six sentiment clusters. Further, customer feedback was processed to extract attribute-sentiment pairs as well as attribute-opinion pairs, which were integrated into the graph to identify semantic clusters highlighting retail strengths and weaknesses. Results underline the potential of AI-driven sentiment analysis for enhancing customer satisfaction in retail. Implications for retail technology and service improvement are discussed.

Keywords Sentiment analysis · Retail technology · AI in retail · Semantic clustering · Customer satisfaction

1 Introduction

1.1 Context and Challenges in Retail Technology

The retail industry is undergoing a profound transformation, driven by a wave of technological advancements that are reshaping the way businesses operate and how consumers shop. The convergence of cutting-edge technologies, such as artificial intelligence (AI), machine learning, big data analytics, and digital innovations, has created unprecedented opportunities for retailers [1]. These opportunities are further supported by research demonstrating the transformative impact of technology

J. Baray (✉)
Le Mans Université, ARGUMans—EA 7505, Le Mans Cedex 9, France
e-mail: jerome.baray@univ-lemans.fr

N. Omrani et al. (eds.), *Human-Machine Synergy and the Digital Future - Exploring Collaboration and Competition Volume 1*, Springer Proceedings in Business and Economics, https://doi.org/10.1007/978-3-032-21347-1_15

on retail operations and customer satisfaction [2]. These advancements prioritize convenience, personalization, and efficiency, catering to evolving consumer expectations in a competitive marketplace.

AI and machine learning, in particular, have revolutionized demand forecasting, personalized marketing, and customer service strategies. Predictive analytics enables retailers to anticipate customer needs and market trends, ensuring proactive decision-making in areas such as pricing and inventory management. Simultaneously, digital innovations, such as augmented reality (AR), virtual reality (VR), and cashierless payment systems, have enhanced the shopping experience, offering immersive and seamless interactions for consumers [3]. Studies like Roy et al. have further highlighted how these technologies contribute to smarter customer experiences, enhancing both engagement and satisfaction [4].

Despite these advancements, understanding and addressing consumer satisfaction remains a pivotal goal. Customer feedback provides retailers with a critical lens to evaluate their performance, identify areas for improvement, and build stronger relationships with their clientele. Analyzing this feedback helps retailers not only address specific grievances but also anticipate customer needs, fostering long-term loyalty and competitive advantage. At the same time, the integration of technology into retail operations poses several challenges. Retailers must manage the complexity of data-driven systems, address cybersecurity risks, and ensure compliance with ethical standards while implementing AI-driven solutions. Furthermore, achieving a balance between automation and the human touch in customer service remains a critical concern. These challenges underscore the need for robust research and practical frameworks to help retailers leverage technology effectively.

1.2 Objectives of the Study

This study aims to address the growing need for innovative methods to analyze customer feedback in the retail sector. Specifically, the objectives are to develop a novel graph-based approach for analyzing customer sentiments and feedback, leveraging advanced AI techniques such as semantic clustering and modularity algorithms. This approach is applied to a real-world dataset of 3000 customer reviews from Costco Wholesale in Los Angeles, providing actionable insights into customer perceptions of retail services. The ultimate goal is to highlight the practical implications of this methodology for improving retail operations, enhancing customer satisfaction, and driving strategic decision-making. Ultimately, the study emphasizes the central role of consumer satisfaction as both a metric and a driver of success in the modern retail landscape. By achieving these objectives, the study contributes to the broader discourse on how technological innovations can address the challenges faced by modern retailers.

1.3 Contributions to Retail Sentiment Analysis

The role of technological innovations in enhancing retail practices is increasingly acknowledged. Research, such as [5], emphasizes the critical importance of customer feedback analysis as a driver of improved service quality and operational excellence.

This research significantly advances the field of retail sentiment analysis through a comprehensive approach that integrates methodological, practical, and academic innovations. A key contribution is the ability to model and map sentiments using a graph-based framework informed by the Mistral Large Language Model (LLM). By leveraging its extensive knowledge base, the LLM evaluates semantic relationships between adjectives, generating a rational and structured representation of sentiments. This allows for the creation of classifications rooted in semantic proximity and contrast, which stand out from conventional heuristic or intuitive approaches. By introducing a graph-based sentiment analysis framework, this study builds on traditional methods to rationally structure and capture nuanced relationships between sentiments and their contexts. This approach provides a systematic way to analyze and visualize sentiment classifications, offering insights that surpass conventional methodologies. Unlike keyword-based or rule-based approaches, this methodology leverages advanced AI techniques, including the Mistral Large Language Model (LLM), to explore customer emotions and feedback patterns more effectively.

The application of this framework to a dataset of 3000 customer reviews from Costco Wholesale demonstrates its practical utility. Insights derived from this analysis provide actionable recommendations for retail managers, focusing on enhancing service quality and addressing customer grievances. Furthermore, these findings contribute to bridging the gap between theoretical advancements in AI-driven sentiment analysis and their practical implications, making a notable impact on both academic discourse and industry practices.

Overall, this study addresses the role of technological innovations in retail, particularly AI-driven tools, in transforming customer feedback into actionable insights. By providing normative decision support for practitioners, this study highlights the integration of advanced analytics into competitive retail strategies, echoing the emphasis on efficiency and personalization in the context of retail innovation.

2 Literature Review

2.1 Sentiment Analysis and Customer Feedback in Retail

Sentiment analysis has emerged as a critical tool in retail for understanding customer perceptions and enhancing service quality. Beyond its technical capabilities, sentiment analysis provides insights into the behavioral underpinnings of customer satisfaction. Oliver [6] emphasizes that customer satisfaction is not solely a transactional outcome but is deeply influenced by consumer emotions and expectations, making sentiment analysis an indispensable tool for decoding these factors.

The dynamic nature of customer satisfaction, as discussed by Wirtz, highlights the "satisfaction paradox," which directly influences operational strategies in retail [7]. For instance, as businesses strive to exceed evolving customer expectations, they often face the challenge of diminishing returns on investment in service enhancements. This paradox necessitates innovative approaches, such as leveraging sentiment analysis, to identify critical areas for improvement while optimizing resources. Retailers can use these insights to fine-tune their service offerings and maintain customer satisfaction without overextending operational capacities. Wherein rising customer expectations make it increasingly challenging for businesses to sustain high satisfaction levels despite continuous service improvements. This paradox underscores the need for tools like sentiment analysis to track and adapt to evolving consumer demands. Similarly, Bordalo, Gennaioli, and Shleifer introduce the concept of "competition for attention," which provides a framework for understanding how customers prioritize certain aspects of service quality when forming satisfaction judgments [8]. By capturing these nuanced perspectives, sentiment analysis enables businesses to target key drivers of customer satisfaction effectively.

Organizational structure also plays a significant role in shaping customer experiences. Bradach examines the influence of franchised operations and structural designs on delivering consistent service quality, particularly in multi-unit retail contexts [9]. Bingham, Howell, and Ott further emphasize the importance of adaptive learning and organizational agility in meeting customer expectations [10]. By leveraging sentiment data, retailers can align operational strategies with customer-centric goals, ensuring both consistency and responsiveness.

Modern Applications and Implications The integration of advanced AI and machine learning techniques, such as the Mistral Large Language Model (LLM), has enhanced the capacity of sentiment analysis to capture contextual relationships and subtle nuances in feedback [1, 4]. These advancements allow businesses to transition from descriptive to predictive and prescriptive analytics, offering actionable insights that directly address customer concerns and improve satisfaction. Grewal et al. and Guha et al. further illustrate how sentiment analysis informs strategic decisions, shaping customer-centric policies and fostering long-term loyalty [3, 5].

By bridging behavioral insights, organizational strategies, and technological advancements, sentiment analysis stands as a cornerstone of modern retail practices, enabling businesses to adapt to the complexities of evolving customer expectations while driving satisfaction and operational excellence.

The evolution of artificial intelligence (AI) and natural language processing (NLP) has significantly enhanced the accuracy and scalability of sentiment analysis methods. For example, Huang and Rust discuss the transformative potential of AI in automating sentiment classification tasks, reducing human bias and improving efficiency [1]. Similarly, the integration of machine learning models, such as the Mistral Large Language Model (LLM), has enabled more nuanced analyses, capturing the contextual relationships between words and sentiments [4].

Despite its advantages, sentiment analysis is not without challenges. One significant limitation is the difficulty in interpreting complex or ambiguous feedback, which may include sarcasm, mixed emotions, or cultural nuances. As Inman and Nikolova (2017) point out, understanding these subtleties requires advanced models capable of recognizing contextual and linguistic variations [11]. Emerging technologies such as graph-based sentiment analysis and transformer models, like the Mistral LLM, are addressing these issues by improving contextual understanding and providing deeper insights into nuanced feedback. Additionally, frameworks emphasizing ethical AI practices, including transparent data handling and algorithmic fairness, can help mitigate concerns about data privacy and ensure the responsible use of customer data.

Effective sentiment analysis directly influences customer satisfaction by enabling retailers to respond proactively to feedback. Research by Roy et al. demonstrates how businesses can utilize sentiment data to refine their service offerings and address common complaints, thereby fostering loyalty and trust [4]. Furthermore, studies like those by Guha et al. underline the strategic value of sentiment insights in shaping customer-centric policies and enhancing the overall shopping experience [3].

Sentiment analysis represents a cornerstone of modern retail strategies, providing retailers with the tools to decode customer feedback and translate it into actionable improvements. By leveraging advanced AI-driven methodologies and addressing existing challenges, retailers can unlock the full potential of sentiment analysis to drive customer satisfaction and operational excellence.

2.2 Advances in AI-Driven Sentiment Classification

The field of sentiment classification has undergone significant advancements in recent years, driven by the rapid development of artificial intelligence (AI) and natural language processing (NLP) technologies. These innovations have revolutionized how customer feedback is analyzed, providing retailers with tools to extract deeper insights and make data-driven decisions to enhance customer satisfaction. Furthermore, these advancements contribute to the evolving classification frameworks of emotions, bridging existing discrete and dimensional models with AI-driven techniques. Recent surveys, such as Chakriswaran et al., Keivandarian and Taherdoost, emphasize the growing importance of hybrid approaches, including ontology-based, lexicon-based, and machine learning models, in improving sentiment classification accuracy [12, 13].

Traditional Approaches and Their Limitations Traditional sentiment analysis methods, such as rule-based systems and basic machine learning algorithms, often relied on predefined lexicons and limited feature sets. These lexicons, while offering a structured vocabulary for sentiment identification, struggled with interpreting the context of words in sentences, especially in cases involving sarcasm, idiomatic expressions, or ambiguous phrasing. For instance, a phrase like "just great" could be interpreted as positive in isolation but carries a negative connotation when used sarcastically. This inability to discern nuanced meanings highlighted a critical limitation of early sentiment analysis approaches. While effective to a degree, these approaches struggled with understanding context, sarcasm, and nuanced expressions. Additionally, dimensional and discrete emotion classification models, such as Ekman's basic emotion categories [14] and Russell's circumplex model [15], were limited in capturing complex emotional states in real-world data. These frameworks laid a strong theoretical foundation but lacked the flexibility needed to handle the vast and diverse nature of modern customer feedback.

Large Language Models (LLMs) and Their Applications The emergence of advanced AI models, particularly transformer-based architectures, has addressed these limitations. Models like Bidirectional Encoder Representations from Transformers (BERT) and Generative Pre-trained Transformers (GPT) enable a more nuanced analysis of textual data by capturing context and semantic relationships between words. These advancements have significantly enhanced the granularity and scalability of sentiment classification, allowing for improved performance in both general and domain-specific applications [15, 16]. Transformer models are particularly effective in identifying latent sentiment patterns across large datasets, making them invaluable for retail applications.

Large language models (LLMs) have further expanded the capabilities of sentiment classification. These models leverage extensive training data and advanced algorithms to understand and generate human-like text. Their ability to perform zero-shot and few-shot learning allows for sentiment classification with minimal labeled data. LLMs excel at extracting object-sentiment pairs from textual data, offering actionable insights into specific aspects of customer feedback, such as identifying pain points or service strengths. Recent advancements in hybrid deep-learning architectures showcase the potential of combining multiple AI techniques for enhanced sentiment analysis performance [17]. For example, these models can connect qualitative sentiments, such as "affordable," with quantitative trends in customer behavior.

The application of these AI-driven advancements in retail has led to significant improvements in customer experience management. By analyzing sentiment trends, retailers can identify emerging issues and address them proactively. AI-driven sentiment classification also supports personalized marketing strategies, helping businesses tailor their offerings to individual customer preferences. Moreover, these techniques enable real-time analysis of customer feedback, allowing retailers to adapt quickly to changing consumer sentiments and maintain a competitive edge. For instance, integrating sentiment data with inventory management systems can optimize product availability based on customer demand and preferences [18].

Despite these advancements, AI-driven sentiment classification faces ongoing challenges. Issues such as data privacy, ethical AI implementation, and computational resource requirements remain critical concerns. Additionally, the need for domain-specific training data to improve model accuracy in niche markets continues to be a limitation. Future research is expected to focus on developing more efficient models that balance accuracy with computational efficiency as well as frameworks that ensure ethical and transparent AI applications. Emerging approaches, such as integrating multimodal sentiment analysis (e.g., combining text, video, and audio data), hold promise for providing richer insights into customer feedback. For instance, audio cues in customer service calls combined with textual feedback can offer a more holistic understanding of consumer sentiment [19].

Advances in AI-driven sentiment classification have transformed the landscape of customer feedback analysis. By integrating cutting-edge technologies, retailers can unlock valuable insights, drive customer satisfaction, and gain a competitive edge in an increasingly data-driven marketplace.

2.3 Graph-Based Approaches to Semantic Analysis

Graph-based approaches to semantic analysis have gained significant traction in recent years, particularly in the fields of natural language processing (NLP) and sentiment analysis. These methods leverage the inherent relational structure of language to uncover deeper insights into textual data. Unlike traditional linear models, graph-based techniques represent words, phrases, or concepts as nodes in a graph, with edges denoting their semantic relationships [20, 21]. This approach allows for the modeling of complex dependencies and contextual nuances, making it particularly well-suited for analyzing customer feedback.

The use of graphs in semantic analysis draws heavily on theories of network science and graph theory. Early works by Newman and Girvan demonstrated the potential of community detection algorithms to uncover hidden structures within complex networks [22]. Building on this foundation, Lancichinetti and Fortunato developed modularity optimization techniques that have become a cornerstone for identifying semantic clusters within textual data [15]. Recent advancements, such as those described by Buehler, emphasize how generative AI and graph-based methods can reveal hidden connections and enable novel discoveries through knowledge graphs [23]. These advancements have paved the way for the integration of graph-based methods into sentiment analysis workflows.

Graph-based approaches have been particularly effective in capturing the semantic relationships between words and phrases, enabling a more nuanced understanding of sentiment. For instance, sentiment graphs constructed using co-occurrence patterns or syntactic dependencies can reveal the contextual polarity of sentiments expressed in customer reviews [19]. Recent studies have also explored the use of graph embeddings to enhance the scalability and accuracy of sentiment classification tasks [21].

One notable application is the use of semantic graphs to analyze customer feedback in the retail sector. By mapping adjectives and sentiments to graph nodes and connecting them based on their semantic proximity, researchers can identify key themes and areas of concern. This approach aligns with the findings of García-Torres et al. [18], who utilized graph-based methods to evaluate customer satisfaction in the hospitality industry. Additionally, multimodal graph representation techniques, as discussed by Ektefaie et al. [24], further expand the capabilities of these methods by incorporating heterogeneous data sources.

The integration of graph neural networks (GNNs) has further expanded the capabilities of graph-based semantic analysis. GNNs leverage deep learning techniques to learn node representations that capture both local and global graph structures, enabling more accurate sentiment predictions [25]. Moreover, the concept of Graph XAI (Explainable AI), as highlighted by Sun et al. [26], focuses on improving the explainability of graph-based models, which is particularly important for applications requiring transparency and interpretability. These innovations have opened new avenues for real-time sentiment analysis and the dynamic modeling of customer feedback.

2.4 *Retail Applications: Enhancing Customer Satisfaction Through Sentiment Analysis*

The application of sentiment analysis in retail has transformed how businesses understand and respond to customer feedback. By leveraging advanced analytical tools, retailers can gain actionable insights into customer preferences, pain points, and overall satisfaction levels. This section explores the role of sentiment analysis in enhancing customer satisfaction and driving business success.

Customer satisfaction is a critical determinant of retail success, influencing factors such as brand loyalty, customer retention, and revenue growth. Traditional methods of gaging satisfaction, such as surveys and focus groups, often suffer from biases and limited sample sizes. Sentiment analysis addresses these limitations by analyzing large volumes of unstructured data, such as online reviews and social media posts, to provide a more comprehensive understanding of customer perceptions [6] ADDIN ZOTERO_ITEM CSL_CITATION {"citationID":"hJHsKGJp","properties":{"formattedCitation":"[22]","plainCitation":"[22]","noteIndex":0},"citationItems":[{"id":32,"uris":["http://zotero.org/users/local/BqDxWKoN/items/4KHLQJ6M"],"itemData":{"id":32,"type":"article-journal","container-title":"Journal of Classification","DOI":"10.1007/s00357-014-9161-z","issue":"3","page":"274–295 ","title":"Ward’s hierarchical clustering method: Clustering criterion and agglomerative algorithm","volume":"31","author":[{"family":"Murtagh","given":"F."},{"family":"Legendre","given":"P."}],"issued":{"date-parts":[["2014"]]}}}],"schema": "https://github.com/citation-style-language/schema/raw/master/csl-citation.json"} [22].

One of the primary benefits of sentiment analysis in retail is its ability to identify specific aspects of the customer experience that drive satisfaction or dissatisfaction. For example, by analyzing sentiment trends in product reviews, retailers can pinpoint issues related to product quality, pricing, or customer service [27]. This aligns with the findings of [28], who highlighted the strategic value of sentiment analysis in enhancing customer experience management.

Another key application is in personalized marketing. By understanding individual customer sentiments, retailers can tailor their marketing strategies to address specific needs and preferences. This approach has been shown to improve customer engagement and conversion rates [29]. Furthermore, Johnson et al. emphasize the role of graph-based AI models in capturing intricate customer relationships, facilitating more effective personalization strategies [30].

Recent advancements in sentiment analysis, such as the use of transformer models and graph-based methods, have further enhanced its applicability in retail. For instance, the integration of sentiment graphs with customer feedback allows for the dynamic clustering of sentiments, providing retailers with real-time insights into emerging trends [31]. Similarly, the use of hybrid models that combine machine learning and rule-based approaches has been shown to improve the accuracy of sentiment predictions [32]. The work of Buehler also highlights how generative knowledge extraction in graph-based systems can offer deeper insights into customer sentiment by leveraging multimodal data [23].

Despite its benefits, the application of sentiment analysis in retail is not without challenges. Issues such as data privacy, algorithmic biases, and the need for domain-specific training data remain significant hurdles. Future research is expected to focus on addressing these challenges through the development of more robust and ethical analytical frameworks [16, 17].

Sentiment analysis represents a powerful tool for enhancing customer satisfaction in retail. By leveraging advanced analytical techniques, businesses can gain deeper insights into customer needs and preferences, enabling them to deliver more personalized and effective services.

3 Methodology

This study employed a multi-step methodological framework to analyze customer sentiment from Costco Los Angeles reviews. The approach integrates advanced AI techniques, graph theory, and clustering algorithms to generate actionable insights. Below, each step is briefly introduced and will be elaborated in subsequent sections. A summary of these steps is also provided in Table 1.

- Preliminary Step: General Semantic Sentiment Mapping. A general semantic mapping of sentiment terms was created to establish a foundational framework for sentiment analysis. Using an adjective dictionary of 261 terms, semantic relationships were calculated with the Mistral 7B LLM, producing coefficients ranging from −10 (antonyms) to +10 (synonyms). These relationships were visu-

Table 1 Overview of the methodological steps employed in the sentiment analysis of customer reviews, summarizing key techniques and resulting outcomes

Step	Description	Key techniques	Outcome
Preliminary Step: General Semantic Sentiment Mapping	Creation of a semantic mapping of 261 sentiment terms and their relationships using Mistral LLM. Semantic graph visualization and clustering into emotional units	Mistral LLM, Semantic Graph, PCA, HAC	Clusters of sentiment terms forming cohesive emotional units
Step 1: Data Collection	Collection of 3000 Google Maps reviews for Costco Los Angeles, ensuring ethical data scraping practices	Web Scraping, Ethical Standards	Dataset of customer feedback ready for analysis
Step 2: Object-Sentiment and Object-Opinion Extraction	Extraction of object-sentiment (e.g., "price/unsatisfied") and object-opinion pairs (e.g., "price/expensive") to enrich the semantic graph	Mistral LLM, Semantic Graph Enrichment	Integration of real-world feedback into the semantic graph
Step 3: Modularity Algorithm Application	Application of modularity algorithms to detect thematic clusters in the graph, identifying strengths and weaknesses in customer feedback	Modularity Algorithm, Graph Analysis	Actionable insights into service strengths and weaknesses

alized in a semantic graph, clustering terms into cohesive emotional units or "bags of words." Dimensionality-reduction techniques, including Principal Component Analysis (PCA), were employed to preserve critical variance, and Hierarchical Agglomerative Clustering (HAC) was used to organize sentiment data into meaningful clusters.

- Step 1: Data Collection. Customer feedback was sourced from 3000 publicly available Google Maps reviews of Costco Los Angeles. Web scraping techniques ensured accurate data extraction while adhering to ethical and privacy standards.
- Step 2: Object-Sentiment and Object-Opinion Extraction. Object-sentiment pairs (e.g., "price/unsatisfied") and object-opinion pairs (e.g., "price/expensive") were extracted from customer reviews using the Mistral LLM. These pairs enriched the semantic graph by linking specific feedback to sentiment clusters, providing a richer understanding of the interplay between customer feedback and emotional responses.
- Step 3: Modularity Algorithm Application. A modularity algorithm was applied to the enriched semantic graph to detect thematic clusters of customer feedback. These clusters provided a nuanced understanding of Costco's service strengths and weaknesses, facilitating targeted managerial interventions.

3.1 Preliminary Step: General Semantic Sentiment Mapping

A comprehensive semantic mapping of sentiment terms and their relationships was constructed as a foundational framework for the analysis. This mapping represents a detailed model of how terms describing sentiments interrelate, forming the basis for further analysis. Terms were grouped into cohesive emotional units or "bags of words," each tied to a specific sentiment domain, enhancing the granularity and interpretability of the analysis. The sentiment graph was constructed using semantic relationships calculated by querying the Mistral 7B LLM model, generating coefficients ranging from −10 (antonyms) to +10 (synonyms). These relationships allowed for the clustering of terms based on their contextual similarities and differences, forming a network of sentiment terms. This graph forms the backbone of the analysis, as it organizes sentiments into meaningful groups to be further explored.

To refine and validate the robustness of this graph, dimensionality reduction techniques such as Principal Component Analysis (PCA) were applied. PCA, while not strictly necessary for the construction of the graph, served as a verification tool to ensure that the graph effectively captured the variance in the dataset. Hierarchical Agglomerative Clustering (HAC) was subsequently applied, also as an optional step, to further validate the organization of sentiment data into distinct clusters. HAC allowed for the identification of both broad categories and more detailed subclusters, providing a nuanced understanding of the data and aligning well with foundational clustering methodologies [33].

Following this validation, specific object-sentiment and object-opinion pairs were extracted from 3000 customer reviews of Costco Los Angeles using the Mistral 7B LLM. These pairs (e.g., "price/unsatisfied" or "price/expensive") were then overlaid onto the sentiment graph, enriching it by linking specific customer feedback to sentiment clusters. This step was critical for bridging abstract sentiment analysis with tangible customer insights.

3.2 Step 1: Data Collection

Customer feedback was sourced from 3000 publicly available Google Maps reviews of Costco Los Angeles. Web scraping techniques ensured accurate data extraction while adhering to ethical and privacy standards, as recommended by industry guidelines and academic literature on ethical data scraping [34]. Google Maps reviews were selected as the data source for their breadth, diversity, and real-time updates, offering a comprehensive representation of customer experiences across various service dimensions.

These reviews are particularly advantageous due to their high volume, detailed narratives, and global user base, making them more reliable compared to other platforms. The platform's extensive user engagement ensures diverse perspectives, while its real-time updates provide an up-to-date reflection of customer sentiment. This reliability has been noted in academic studies highlighting the platform's effectiveness for sentiment analysis in retail contexts. This platform is particularly advantageous due to its high volume of detailed narratives and broad user base, making it a reliable and versatile tool for sentiment analysis. These reviews are widely regarded as reliable indicators of customer sentiment due to their real-time nature, high volume, and detailed narratives, making them particularly well-suited for sentiment analysis.

Costco Wholesale in Los Angeles was chosen as the focus of the study due to its large customer base and diverse range of services. The retail giant's prominence in the wholesale market ensures a substantial amount of feedback that covers multiple aspects of the shopping experience, such as pricing, product quality, and customer service. This diversity provides a robust foundation for exploring complex sentiment dynamics in a retail context.

3.3 Step 2: Attribute/Sentiment Pair Extraction

To ensure consistency and depth in analyzing customer reviews, a standardized approach was adopted to link sentiments and opinions to specific attributes even when the attributes were not explicitly mentioned. For example, a review such as "Expensive" is interpreted as "Price/Expensive," allowing the analysis to infer the context and avoid ambiguity. This process involved several enhancements to standardize opinions and deduce implicit attributes while preserving the diversity of customer feedback.

The methodology included:

- Clear and Rigorous Standardization Logic: Synonyms and related expressions were grouped to reduce linguistic variations while maintaining the richness of feedback. For instance, "not polite," "impolite," and "very rude" were all standardized to "Rude." Similarly, "filthy," "very dirty," and "disgusting" were categorized under "Dirty."
- Expanded Prompt Examples for the AI Model: The Mistral LLM was guided by providing explicit examples in the prompts, ensuring a clear transformation of varied expressions into standardized opinions.
- Robust Inference of Attributes: When an opinion was mentioned without a clear attribute (e.g., "Expensive"), the AI model deduced the attribute based on contextual cues. If no clear attribute was identifiable, the system defaulted to "Store" to maintain the integrity of the analysis.
- Key Steps in the Extraction Process.
- Attribute-Sentiment Mapping: A dictionary of opinions and their corresponding attributes was developed to guide the inference process, ensuring precision and alignment with customer context.
- Integration into Semantic Graphs: Extracted pairs, such as "price/expensive" or "service/rude," were integrated into the pre-constructed semantic sentiment graph, enriching it with actionable connections and real-world feedback patterns.
- Reinforcement with Examples: Clear prompts were designed to demonstrate the mapping of varied opinions to standardized terms, improving the AI model's accuracy and reliability.

Table 2 Examples of customer reviews and extracted attribute/sentiment and attribute/opinion pairs

Customer review	Attribute/sentiment pair	Attribute/opinion pair
"Very slow checkout process"	Checkout/frustrated	Checkout/slow
"The prices here are way too expensive"	Price/dissatisfied	Price/expensive
"Dirty floors and broken chairs in the cafe"	Floor/disgusted	Floor/dirty
	Chairs/annoyed	Chairs/broken
"Staff was extremely friendly and helpful!"	Staff/appreciative	Staff/friendly
"Overpriced items but great service."	Price/dissatisfied	Price/expensive
	Service/satisfied	Service/great
"The waiting time is unacceptable—Too slow!"	Waiting/annoyed	Waiting/slow
"The store was clean, but parking was a mess."	Store/satisfied	Store/clean
	Parking/frustrated	Parking/unorganized

In practice, reviews were processed systematically to align with the standardized framework. For instance, a review like "Very slow checkout" was interpreted with the attribute "Checkout" and the standardized opinion "Slow." Similarly, a review such as "Overpriced items" was mapped to the attribute "Price" and the standardized opinion "Expensive." This structured approach ensured that linguistic variations in customer language did not dilute the insights gained from the analysis. To illustrate the standardization and extraction process, a selection of customer reviews and their corresponding attribute/sentiment and attribute/opinion pairs is provided in Table 2.

This process ensured that variations in customer language did not dilute the insights derived from the reviews, enabling cohesive and actionable clusters in the sentiment analysis. The result is a refined dataset that accurately captures customer sentiments, supports detailed analysis, and integrates seamlessly into subsequent graph-based clustering methodologies.

3.4 Step 3: Modularity Algorithm Application

A modularity algorithm was employed to detect semantic clusters within the enriched graph, highlighting thematic groupings of customer feedback. This choice was guided by its proven effectiveness in uncovering community structures within complex networks, as described by Newman and Girvan [22] and further elaborated in Lancichinetti and Fortunato [35]. By analyzing interconnected nodes representing sentiment and opinion pairs, the algorithm facilitated the identification of cohesive clusters that reflect distinct themes or concerns expressed by customers. This methodological choice aligns with its successful application in diverse fields requiring network analysis, thus ensuring robustness and relevance in extracting actionable insights. By analyzing the interconnected nodes representing sentiment and opinion pairs, the algorithm identified distinct clusters that correspond to specific themes or issues raised by customers.

The identified clusters provided actionable insights into the strengths and weaknesses of Costco's retail services. For instance, clusters highlighting positive sentiments, such as "service/friendly," indicated areas of customer satisfaction, while clusters dominated by negative sentiments, such as "price/terrible," pinpointed areas requiring improvement. These insights are invaluable for retailers aiming to enhance customer satisfaction and operational efficiency.

4 Results

4.1 Overview of Sentiment Graph Clusters

A semantic graph was constructed to map relationships between sentiment terms extracted from customer reviews. Using semantic proximity coefficients generated by the Mistral 7B LLM, 261 adjectives were grouped into cohesive emotional units or "bags of words." While Principal Component Analysis (PCA) and Hierarchical Agglomerative Clustering (HAC) were not required for graph construction, these methods validated its structure and interpretability. The resulting graph provided a robust framework for analyzing customer sentiment and enabled the identification of six thematic clusters.

The PCA results revealed eigenvalues distributed across key axes, with the first axis accounting for 17.61% of the total variance and a cumulative variance of 38.31% across the first five axes. Global critical values were used to confirm these results, with thresholds set at 1 for Kaiser-Guttman and 3 for Karlis-Saporta-Spinaki. This validation process simplified the relationships between terms, ensuring that the graph structure was sound and interpretable.

The modularity algorithm applied to the enriched graph resulted in the detection of six thematic clusters, which represent distinct emotional domains. These clusters provide insights into Costco's service strengths and weaknesses by capturing recurring themes in customer sentiment. Each cluster is described in detail below, focusing on the adjectives and sentiments that define its semantic boundaries.

Cluster 1: Anxiety and Disorientation This cluster represents states of emotional turbulence and uncertainty. Adjectives such as "anxious" and "disturbed" convey a sense of mental unease and heightened worry, potentially triggered by external stressors. "Confused" indicates cognitive disarray, where individuals struggle to make sense of their circumstances, while "islanded" metaphorically portrays isolation, as though being emotionally or socially cut off from support networks. Together, these adjectives point to experiences of anxiety, vulnerability, and a fragmented sense of stability.

Cluster 2: Despair and Devaluation This cluster is characterized by profoundly negative emotions, reflecting a sense of hopelessness and personal inadequacy. Key adjectives such as "hopeless" and "rejected" evoke a perception of abandonment and a lack of agency. The presence of "pitiful" and "miserable" suggests a deep sense of self-deprecation or being looked down upon by others. Finally, "patronized" highlights feelings of condescension, where individuals may perceive themselves as treated with false sympathy or diminished respect. Overall, this cluster encapsulates themes of despair, alienation, and diminished self-worth.

Cluster 3: Exhaustion and Tension The adjectives in this cluster highlight emotional and physical fatigue, alongside heightened sensitivity to stress. "Wornout" reflects a state of prolonged exhaustion, whether from overwork, emotional strain, or other factors. "Onedge" suggests an acute sense of tension, as though constantly bracing for something adverse to happen. "Shaken" indicates being unsettled or destabilized, whether due to a specific traumatic event or cumulative stress. This cluster captures a broader theme of burnout, fragility, and chronic stress.

Cluster 4: Resilience and Fulfillment In contrast to clusters dominated by negativity, this cluster conveys themes of personal growth, motivation, and emotional satisfaction. "Encouraged" reflects a sense of external or internal reinforcement, inspiring individuals to persevere. "Fulfilled" suggests a deep-seated contentment arising from the achievement of meaningful goals. "Fortunate" emphasizes gratitude and the acknowledgment of positive circumstances or outcomes. Collectively, these adjectives encapsulate a narrative of resilience, where individuals overcome adversity and find purpose or satisfaction in their experiences.

Cluster 5: Intellectual and Emotional Stimulation This cluster captures emotions associated with curiosity, creativity, and excitement. "Interested" and "inspired" highlight the engagement of intellectual and emotional faculties, suggesting an openness to learning or discovering new ideas. "Fascinated" amplifies this sense of intrigue, reflecting intense focus and admiration for something novel or compelling. Finally, "expectant" adds a forward-looking dimension, implying anticipation of a positive or stimulating outcome. Together, these adjectives illustrate a mindset of intellectual curiosity and emotional vitality.

Cluster 6: Gratitude and Contentment This cluster is centered around positive emotional states associated with peace and satisfaction. "Thankful" reflects an appreciation for favorable circumstances or the actions of others. "Satisfied" and "pleased" denote a sense of achievement or alignment between expectations and outcomes, suggesting that personal or external goals have been met. Lastly, "peaceful" conveys an inner tranquility and emotional balance, often the result of a harmonious environment or personal well-being. This cluster embodies gratitude, stability, and a sense of wholeness.

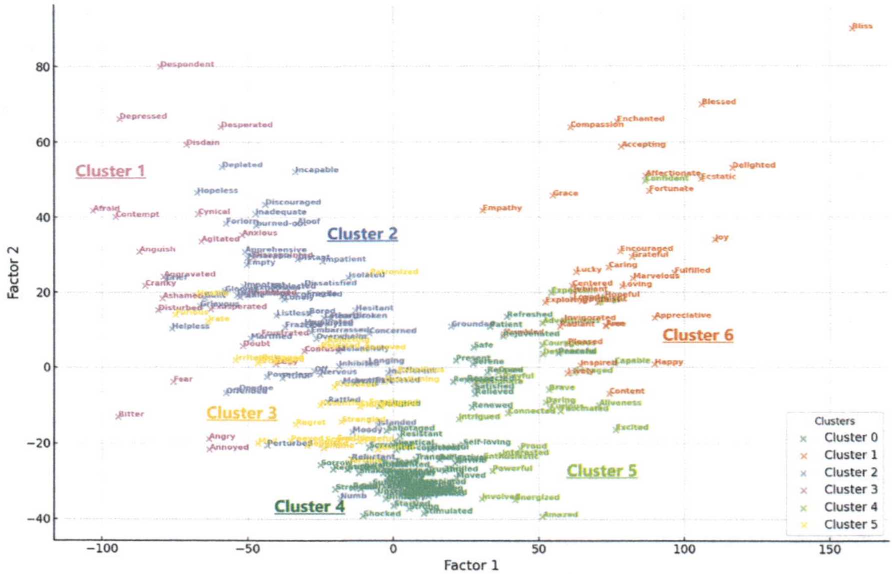

Fig. 1 Semantic clusters of interconnected sentiments mapped on factorial axes 1 and 2

Figure 1 illustrates the factorial axes 1 and 2 derived from the Principal Component Analysis (PCA), showcasing the six thematic clusters. The adjectives within each cluster are color-coded to highlight their semantic relationships and emotional nuances.

4.2 Object-Sentiment Integration and Semantic Modularity

The classification of positive and negative aspects is guided by the modularity classes detected in the semantic graph (Fig. 2). Each modularity class groups objects, sentiments, and opinions into thematic clusters based on their relationships. Positive aspects or service attributes are identified through connections to positive sentiments (e.g., Satisfied, Delighted) or favorable opinions (e.g., Cheap), while negative aspects are identified through associations with negative sentiments (e.g., Frustrated, Annoyed) or unfavorable opinions (e.g., Dirty, Broken). This modularity analysis performed on the network provides a structured way to interpret customer feedback. 5 clusters have been detected and each class reflects a distinct thematic grouping:

- Modularity Class 1 (Overall Store Experience): Encompasses both positive and negative sentiments tied to the general Costco experience.
- Modularity Class 2 (Price and Affordability): Focused exclusively on Price and its positive evaluation as Cheap.

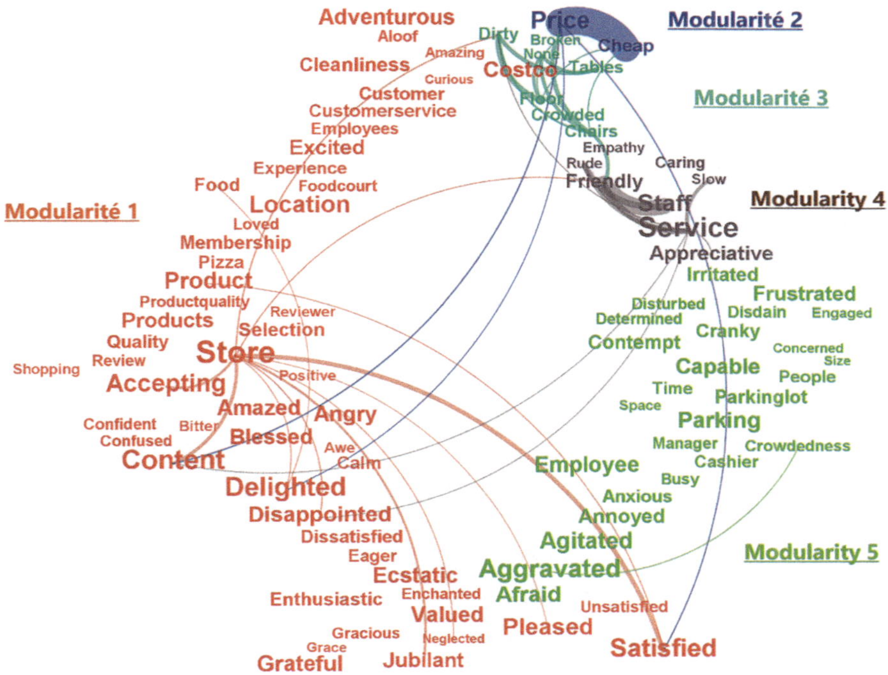

Fig. 2 Thematic modularity classes in the semantic graph: Positive and negative aspects of customer feedback

- Modularity Class 3 (Cleanliness and Maintenance): Captures dissatisfaction with physical environment attributes like floor, chairs, and tables.
- Modularity Class 4 (Service and Staff Interactions): Balances positive feedback on friendliness with criticisms about rudeness or inefficiencies.
- Modularity Class 5 (Operational Issues): Highlights logistical frustrations related to parking, crowding, and time management.

Figure 2 visually represents the thematic modularity classes detected in the semantic graph, illustrating the clustering of objects, sentiments, and opinions into distinct positive and negative domains based on their interconnections.

Figure 3 also visualizes the same relationships between attributes, sentiments, and opinions extracted from customer feedback. Nodes are this time organized into three distinct groups—attributes, sentiments, and opinions—highlighting the connections and interactions within the semantic graph and providing a clearer understanding of how specific service aspects are evaluated by customers.

Positive Aspects of Costco Services The analysis of the graph highlights several key strengths in Costco's service offering:

1. Affordable Pricing (Modularity Class 2):

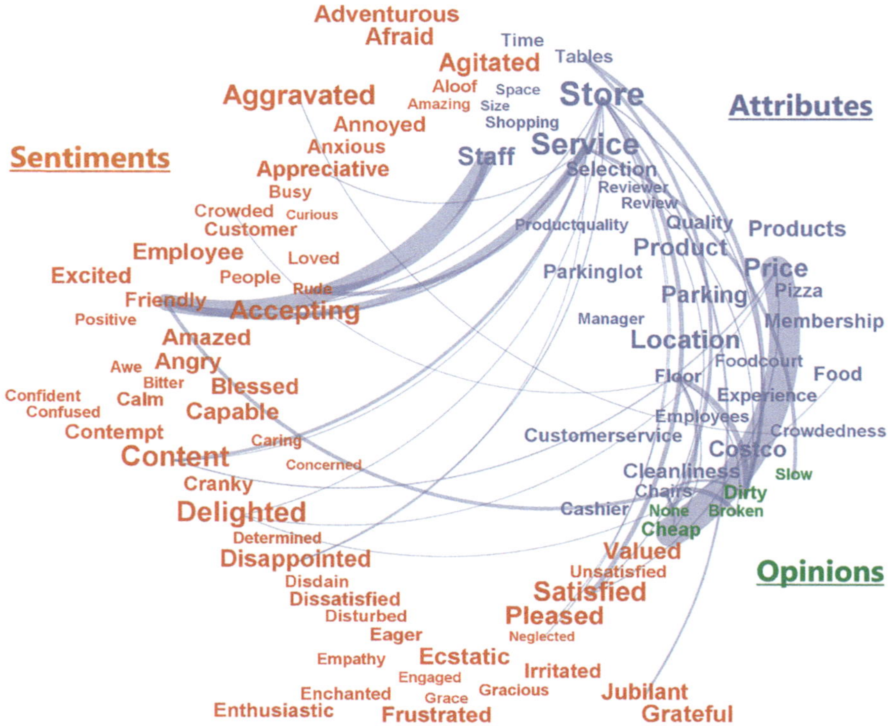

Fig. 3 Semantic graph with interconnected nodes grouped by attributes, sentiments, and opinions

One of the strongest themes emerging from the graph is Costco's affordability, as reflected in the dominant edge Price → Cheap (weight = 2306). This pairing alone accounts for the highest edge weight in the entire network, underscoring how central low prices are to customer satisfaction. Additional connections, such as Price → Satisfied (59), Price → Content (77), and Price → Delighted (38), further reinforce that Costco's pricing strategy is a core driver of positive sentiment.

This result aligns with established theories in consumer behavior, where price perceptions strongly influence value judgments [36]. Costco's ability to maintain low prices while delivering quality products is a key element of its competitive advantage.

2. Friendly Staff and Service (Modularity Class 4):

The positive sentiment Friendly is strongly associated with both Staff and Service, as evidenced by the edges Staff → Friendly (1293) and Service → Friendly (491). These relationships indicate that interactions with Costco employees frequently leave a positive impression on customers.

Additionally, the presence of Appreciative within the same cluster suggests that customers often express gratitude for the helpfulness and courteousness of the staff. This finding suggests that Costco's investment in employee training and customer service excellence pays dividends in terms of customer satisfaction.

3. Overall Store Experience (Modularity Class 1):

   The general experience of shopping at Costco is reflected in positive associations with Store, as evidenced by edges such as Store → Satisfied (321), Store → Content (222), and Store → Delighted (43). These sentiments highlight that many customers find the overall shopping experience fulfilling, further cementing Costco's reputation as a reliable retailer.

4. Food and Membership Quality (Modularity Class 1):

   The attributes Food and Membership are linked to positive sentiments such as Satisfied and Delighted, indicating that Costco's food offerings and its membership model resonate well with customers. These elements contribute to a sense of exclusivity and value, which are key components of customer loyalty.

Negative Aspects of Costco Services While the graph reveals many positive aspects, it also sheds light on areas where Costco could improve. The negative aspects primarily center around cleanliness, staff interactions, and operational challenges:

1. Cleanliness and Maintenance Issues (Modularity Class 3):

   A significant portion of negative feedback relates to the cleanliness and upkeep of the physical environment. The strong connections Floor → Dirty (409), Tables → Dirty (289), and Chairs → Broken (324) indicate recurring complaints about these specific aspects of the store. Customers perceive unclean or poorly maintained areas as detracting from the overall experience.

   This issue is particularly prominent in the seating and dining areas, where customers expect higher standards of cleanliness and comfort. Addressing these concerns could enhance customer perceptions and mitigate negative feedback.

2. Staff and Service Inconsistencies (Modularity Class 4):

   While staff friendliness is a notable strength, the graph also reveals inconsistencies in service quality. Edges such as Staff → Rude (470) and Service → Rude (300) highlight that a subset of customers experience negative interactions with employees. Additional sentiments such as Slow and Disappointed connect to Service, indicating frustrations with delays or inefficiencies in service delivery.

   These inconsistencies suggest the need for enhanced training and accountability measures to ensure a consistently positive service experience across all customer interactions.

3. Crowding and Parking Challenges (Modularity Class 5):

   Attributes such as Parking and Crowdedness are associated with negative sentiments like Frustrated, Aggravated, and Annoyed. For example, Parking → Frustrated represents a frequent pain point for customers, particularly during peak hours. Similarly, Crowdedness is linked to logistical challenges within the store, such as long queues or limited space.

Table 3 Positives and negatives opinions by theme in relation to the modularity classes

Aspect	Type	Description	Cluster
Affordable pricing	Positive	Strong association between Price and cheap (weight: 2306). Reinforced by connections to satisfied, content, and delighted	Modularity class 2
Friendly staff and service	Positive	Staff and service nodes strongly linked to friendly (weights: 1293 and 491). Customers appreciate courteous employees	Modularity class 4
Overall store experience	Positive	Store is positively associated with satisfied, content, and delighted. Reflects a fulfilling shopping experience	Modularity class 1
Food and membership quality	Positive	Attributes like food and membership linked to positive sentiments (satisfied, delighted). Adds value to customer experience	Modularity class 2
Cleanliness and maintenance issues	Negative	Frequent complaints about floor, chairs, and tables being dirty or broken (weights: 409, 324, 289)	Modularity class 3
Staff and service inconsistencies	Negative	Rude interactions linked to staff and service (weights: 470, 300). Delays and inefficiencies also noted	Modularity class 4
Crowding and parking challenges	Negative	Parking and crowdedness linked to frustrated, annoyed, and aggravated sentiments. Operational challenges	Modularity class 5
Perceived neglect	Negative	Store linked to neglected and disappointed sentiments (weights: 41, 65). Reflects unmet customer expectations	Modularity class 1

These operational challenges detract from the overall customer experience and warrant targeted interventions, such as better parking management or optimized store layouts to reduce congestion.

4. Perceived Neglect (Modularity Class 1):

   Sentiments such as Neglected and Disappointed are connected to Store in Modularity Class 1, indicating that a subset of customers feels their expectations are not met. This feedback may stem from unmet needs in terms of cleanliness, service quality, or availability of products.

The positive and negative opinions by theme and in relation to the modularity classes are summarized in Table 3.

5 Discussion

5.1 Implications for Retail Technology

The application of AI-driven sentiment analysis, as demonstrated in this study, has significant implications for retail technology. By leveraging advanced techniques such as semantic clustering and graph-based modularity algorithms, this methodology goes beyond traditional sentiment analysis, offering a more precise and interconnected approach to understanding customer feedback. A critical innovation lies in the preparation of a network of interrelated sentiments, which is constructed in the preliminary stages of the analysis. This semantic graph interconnects 261 sentiment terms using advanced AI techniques, enabling a deeper and more cohesive understanding of customer emotions.

Unlike traditional methods where adjectives such as dissatisfied and unhappy might remain isolated, the semantic graph links them based on their contextual and semantic proximity. This pre-established network ensures that even when different customers use distinct expressions, the sentiments are captured as part of a cohesive cluster. For instance, dissatisfied and unhappy are treated as part of a unified sentiment group, avoiding the fragmentation that would occur in a standard graph where terms are not semantically connected. This innovation strengthens the precision of the analysis by integrating linguistic variations into a unified framework, ensuring that subtle relationships between sentiments are not lost.

The sentiment graph serves as a foundation for clustering customer feedback into thematic domains while also linking these sentiments to specific service attributes and opinions. This interconnected structure allows for the detection of nuanced patterns in customer feedback, such as identifying recurring associations between attributes like "cleanliness" and sentiments such as frustrated or pleased. By revealing the relationships between sentiments themselves and their connections to other elements (attributes and opinions), this methodology enables a more granular and interpretable analysis.

Table 4 illustrates the comparative advantages of this approach over existing methods. Traditional techniques such as rule-based or lexicon-based approaches fail to establish these connections and cannot account for the semantic proximity between terms. Even transformer models like BERT, while powerful in capturing word embeddings, focus on isolated word-level relationships rather than integrating sentiments into a broader semantic network. By contrast, the proposed graph-based framework not only constructs a network of interrelated sentiments but also enhances it with object-sentiment-opinion triples extracted from customer reviews, validated through dimensionality reduction techniques such as PCA and clustering algorithms like HAC.

The preparation of this semantic network in advance also enhances the interpretability of customer feedback analysis. For example, a customer review mentioning "dirty floors" may be connected to another review describing "filthy tables," ensuring that both are understood as part of a broader theme of dissatisfaction with cleanliness. This allows for the identification of actionable clusters that are semantically meaningful, even when linguistic variations exist among the feedback. Retailers can then prioritize operational improvements based on these clusters, such as addressing cleanliness issues or improving customer interactions.

Additionally, the modularity clustering applied to the enriched graph provides a thematic segmentation of customer feedback, enabling retailers to detect specific strengths and weaknesses. Positive clusters, such as those emphasizing "affordable prices," allow retailers to reinforce competitive advantages, while negative clusters,

Table 4 Comparative analysis of sentiment analysis methods: key features, limitations, and advantages of the proposed graph-based framework

Method	Key features	Limitations	Advantages of proposed method	Key references
Rule-based systems	– Relies on predefined lexicons	– Inability to capture context	– Overcomes contextual limitations by leveraging semantic relationships in a graph structure	Liu (2012) and Cambria et al. (2013)
	– Simple implementation	– Poor handling of nuanced expressions (e.g., sarcasm, ambiguity)		
Lexicon-based approaches	– Utilizes word dictionaries to identify sentiments	– Fails to capture semantic nuances	– Dynamically captures semantic relationships between words using Mistral LLM	Mohammad et al. (2013) and Hu and Liu (2004)
	– Structured vocabulary	– Inflexibility for domain-specific language		
Traditional machine learning	– Uses supervised learning for classification	– Requires large labeled datasets	– Eliminates need for extensive labeled datasets through zero-shot and multilingual capabilities	Pang and Lee (2008) and Sebastiani (2002)
	– Effective with structured training datasets	– Limited in handling multilingual feedback		
Transformer models (e.g., BERT)	– Context-aware sentiment classification	– Computationally intensive	– Enhances transformer outputs by structuring word relationships within an interpretable graph	Devlin et al. (2019) and Radford et al. (2019)
	– Captures semantic relationships through advanced embeddings	– Focused on word-level rather than relational patterns		
Graph-based methods	– Models semantic relationships as nodes and edges	– Limited adoption of advanced language models	– Your method goes beyond isolated term interconnections by linking sentiments to specific objects and opinions for deeper analysis	Hamilton et al. (2017) and Kipf and Welling (2017)
	– Highlights interconnected patterns between terms	– Focuses on isolated term relationships rather than integrating broader sentiment contexts		

Table 4 (continued)

Method	Key features	Limitations	Advantages of proposed method	Key references
Proposed graph-based framework	– Builds a semantic graph interconnecting 261 sentiment terms using IA LLM	– High computational requirements for modularity clustering	– Models relational patterns between sentiments while linking them to objects and opinions	This study (2024), Newman and Girvan (2004) and Lancichinetti and Fortunato (2009)
	– Validated through PCA and HAC for robustness		– Enables thematic clustering within multilingual customer feedback	
	– Enriches these clusters with object-sentiment-opinion triples extracted from reviews	Requires advanced expertise in network theory and AI implementation	Combines network modularity with semantic precision to reveal actionable insights	
	– Incorporates clustering through modularity to identify thematic communities			

such as those highlighting "crowded parking," help identify areas for improvement. The semantic graph's ability to link sentiments across languages further enhances its utility in multilingual settings, making it a powerful tool for global retailers.

The automation enabled by AI tools, such as the Mistral LLM, further enhances scalability. By extracting object-sentiment-opinion triples and organizing them into cohesive clusters, this framework reduces manual effort while delivering precise insights. This is particularly advantageous for large datasets, such as the customer feedback analyzed in this study, which spans diverse operational dimensions, including pricing, service quality, and the physical shopping environment.

This study's methodology addresses a significant gap in traditional sentiment analysis by introducing a network of interconnected sentiments prepared in advance, ensuring that linguistic variations and semantic nuances are captured. This advancement not only enhances precision but also enables the identification of actionable patterns in customer feedback, positioning the proposed graph-based framework as a transformative tool for modern retail sentiment analysis.

5.2 Recommendations for Retail Management

The insights derived from this study offer clear and actionable recommendations for improving customer satisfaction at Costco and similar retail environments. These recommendations are based on the visualization and analysis of semantic clusters, which highlight both strengths and weaknesses in the retail experience.

Leverage Strengths:

- Promote and maintain competitive pricing: The strong association between "Price" and "Cheap" highlights Costco's success in delivering value to its customers [36]. Zeithaml's model demonstrates how customer perceptions of value are directly tied to price competitiveness, making this a critical focus for retail managers. Retail managers should continue to emphasize this strength in marketing and operational strategies, ensuring that pricing remains a key differentiator.
- Continue staff training to sustain and improve friendliness and service quality: Positive sentiments associated with staff and service interactions, such as "Friendly" and "Appreciative," suggest that Costco's employees are a valuable asset [37]. The SERVQUAL framework emphasizes the importance of consistent service quality in driving customer satisfaction and loyalty. Enhancing training programs to ensure consistency in service quality can further reinforce this strength.

Address Weaknesses:

- Prioritize cleaning and maintenance: The strong negative associations with attributes such as "Floor," "Tables," and "Chairs" (e.g., "Dirty," "Broken") [38]. Wakefield and Blodgett emphasize that a clean and well-maintained environment is crucial for fostering customer trust and repeat visits, particularly in retail and hospitality sectors. Indicate a pressing need to improve cleanliness and maintenance [39]. Their research highlights the critical role of cleanliness as a driver of repeat patronage in service environments, directly impacting customer satisfaction and trust. In the context of retail, maintaining cleanliness across high-traffic areas such as floors and tables ensures positive customer experiences and loyalty. Their study highlights how cleanliness is a fundamental expectation in service environments, directly impacting repeat patronage and customer trust. Investments in regular cleaning schedules and preventive maintenance programs can mitigate these concerns.
- Explore solutions for parking capacity and crowd management: Feedback related to "Parking" and "Crowdedness" underscores the importance of addressing logistical challenges. Bitner's research on servicescapes highlights how physical surroundings, including parking and crowd management, directly influence customer perceptions and satisfaction [40]. Their exploration of the service-profit chain identifies operational efficiencies, such as parking and spatial management, as key contributors to improved customer satisfaction and profitability. Retail managers can consider technology-driven solutions, such as real-time

parking availability updates, optimized store layouts, or scheduling incentives to reduce peak-hour congestion.

By implementing these recommendations, Costco and similar retailers can enhance their operational efficiency and customer satisfaction, ultimately driving long-term loyalty and competitive advantage.

5.3 Limitations and Future Research

While this study provides valuable insights, it is important to acknowledge its limitations. The analysis is based on customer reviews from a single retailer (Costco) in a specific geographical location (Los Angeles). Consequently, the findings may not be fully generalizable to other retail contexts or regions. Future research should extend this methodology to diverse datasets and retail environments to validate its broader applicability.

Another limitation lies in the static nature of the dataset analyzed. Customer feedback is inherently dynamic, with sentiments evolving over time in response to changes in retail operations, market conditions, and consumer preferences. Future research could explore the integration of real-time feedback analysis to capture these temporal dynamics and provide even more actionable insights. Real-time systems, such as those highlighted in the broader literature on real-time sentiment analysis and natural language processing, could be adapted for retail contexts to enable dynamic monitoring of customer sentiments and opinions. Advanced systems can address the challenges of processing high-volume feedback by leveraging streaming data pipelines and scalable cloud computing infrastructure. This would allow retailers to identify shifting customer preferences in real-time, rapidly address service issues, and even predict future trends based on sentiment trajectories or frameworks like MOA for streaming data analysis [41], could be adapted for retail contexts to enable dynamic monitoring of customer sentiments and opinions.

Finally, while this study demonstrates the utility of AI-driven sentiment analysis, it also highlights the need for ongoing refinement of AI models to account for nuances such as sarcasm, cultural differences, and mixed emotions. Future research could also test larger language models on advanced hardware, as this study utilized the Mistral-7B-Instruct-v0.1.Q4_0 model, optimized to run on a PC with 16 GB of GPU memory. More powerful systems could potentially enable deeper and more nuanced sentiment analysis, offering enhanced accuracy and insights. The model used in this study, Mistral-7B-Instruct-v0.1.Q4_0, was chosen for its ability to run efficiently on a PC with 16 GB of GPU memory. However, future research could explore the application of larger and more powerful models on advanced hardware to improve performance and the depth of analysis. Advancements in natural language processing and machine learning, including multimodal sentiment analysis that incorporates textual, visual, and audio data, represent promising avenues for future research. Additionally, dynamic sentiment analysis approaches, such as those highlighted by Ghiassi et al. [42] for hybrid systems, could be explored to enhance the precision and adaptability of real-time opinion mining.

Addressing these limitations and exploring new research directions will allow future studies to build on the findings of this study. This can further enhance the utility and impact of AI-driven sentiment analysis in retail, paving the way for more comprehensive and actionable insights in the ever-evolving retail landscape.

6 Conclusion

This study highlights the transformative potential of AI-driven sentiment analysis for the retail sector, providing actionable insights into customer perceptions and operational priorities. By leveraging semantic graphs and modularity algorithms, the proposed approach advances beyond traditional methodologies, offering a structured framework to link and analyze customer sentiments, opinions, and attributes.

The findings demonstrate how advanced technologies like large language models (e.g., Mistral-7B-Instruct) can effectively process high volumes of unstructured customer feedback, delivering precise and actionable insights. For instance, semantic clusters revealed key strengths, such as Costco's competitive pricing and staff friendliness, alongside operational challenges related to cleanliness and crowd management. These insights are pivotal for guiding data-driven strategies aimed at enhancing customer satisfaction and operational efficiency.

Future research can further expand on this methodology by exploring the integration of larger, more powerful AI models and multimodal sentiment analysis to account for diverse data sources, including audio, video, and textual feedback. Additionally, the potential for real-time feedback analysis using streaming data frameworks could enable dynamic monitoring of customer sentiments, allowing retailers to adapt proactively to evolving consumer expectations.

In conclusion, this research underscores the critical role of AI in navigating the complexities of modern retail environments. By combining advanced technologies with actionable insights, retailers can not only meet but exceed customer expectations, fostering long-term loyalty and competitiveness in an increasingly dynamic market.

References

1. Huang, M.-H., Rust, R.T.: Artificial intelligence in service. J. Serv. Res. **21**(2), 155–172 (2018). https://doi.org/10.1177/1094670517752459
2. Pantano, E., Di Pietro, L.: Understanding consumer's acceptance of technology-based innovations in retailing. J. Retail. Consum. Serv. **19**(3), 245–252 (2012). https://doi.org/10.1016/j.jretconser.2012.01.001
3. Guha, S., Grewal, D., Kopalle, P.K., Roberts, J.: How artificial intelligence will affect the future of retailing. J. Retail. **97**(1), 28–41 (2021). https://doi.org/10.1016/j.jretai.2020.10.007

4. Roy, S.K., Balaji, M.S., Sadeque, S., Nguyen, B., Melewar, T.C.: Constituents and consequences of smart customer experience in retailing. J. Retail. Consum. Serv. **39**, 101–111 (2017). https://doi.org/10.1016/j.jretconser.2017.07.010
5. Grewal, D., Roggeveen, A.L., Nordfält, J.: The future of retailing. J. Retail. **93**(1), 1–6 (2017). https://doi.org/10.1016/j.jretai.2016.12.008
6. Oliver, R.L.: Satisfaction: A Behavioral Perspective on the Consumer. Routledge, London (2014)
7. Wirtz, J., Zeithaml, V.A., Kwan, L.: Cost-effective service excellence. J. Acad. Market Sci. **46**(1), 59–80 (2018). https://doi.org/10.1007/s11747-017-0560-7
8. Bordalo, P., Gennaioli, N., Shleifer, A.: Competition for attention. Rev. Econ. Stud. **83**(2), 481–513 (2016). https://doi.org/10.1093/restud/rdv048
9. Bradach, J.L.: Using the plural form in the management of restaurant chains. Adm. Sci. Q. **42**(2), 276–303 (1997). https://doi.org/10.2307/2393921
10. Bingham, C.B., Howell, T., Ott, T.E.: Capability creation: heuristics as microfoundations. Strateg. Entrepr. J. **13**(2), 121–153 (2019). https://doi.org/10.1002/sej.1312
11. Inman, J.J., Nikolova, H.: Shopper-facing retail technology: a retailer adoption decision framework incorporating shopper attitudes and privacy concerns. J. Retail. **93**(1), 7–28 (2017). https://doi.org/10.1016/j.jretai.2016.12.006
12. Chakriswaran, P., Vincent, D.R., Srinivasan, K., Sharma, V., Chang, C.-Y., Reina, D.G.: Emotion AI-driven sentiment analysis: a survey, future research directions, and open issues. Appl. Sci. **9**(24), 5462 (2019). https://doi.org/10.3390/app9245462
13. Keivandarian, N., Taherdoost, H.: A Survey on Sentiment Classification Methods and Challenges. Florida AI Research Society (2023)
14. Ekman, P.: An argument for basic emotions. Cognit. Emot. **6**(3), 169–200 (1992)
15. Devlin, J., Chang, M.-W., Lee, K., Toutanova, K.: BERT: pre-training of deep bidirectional transformers for language understanding. In: NAACL-HLT (2019)
16. Radford, A., Wu, J., Child, R., Luan, D., Amodei, D., Sutskever, I.: Language models are unsupervised multitask learners. OpenAI Blog. **1**(8) (2019)
17. Ghosh, R., Ravi, K., Ravi, V.: A novel deep learning architecture for sentiment classification. In: 3rd International Conference on Recent Advances in Information Technology (RAIT), pp. 511–516 (2016). https://doi.org/10.1109/RAIT.2016.7507953
18. García-Torres, M.A., Marchante-Lara, M., Palacios-Marqués, D.: Evolution of customer satisfaction with hotel services in Spain: a sentiment analysis approach. Tour. Manag. **77**, 104008 (2020). https://doi.org/10.1016/j.tourman.2019.104008
19. Chakraborty, P., Kim, Y., Sudhir, K.: Attribute sentiment scoring with online text reviews: accounting for language structure and missing attributes. J. Market. Res. **59**(3), 600–622 (2022). https://doi.org/10.1177/00222437221094134
20. Hamilton, W., Ying, Z., Leskovec, J.: Inductive representation learning on large graphs. Adv. Neural Inf. Proces. Syst. **30**, 1024–1034 (2017)
21. Kipf, T.N., Welling, M.: Semi-supervised classification with graph convolutional networks. In: International Conference on Learning Representations (2017)
22. Newman, M., Girvan, M.: Finding and evaluating community structure in networks. Phys. Rev. E. **69**, 026113 (2004). https://doi.org/10.1103/PhysRevE.69.026113
23. Buehler, M.J.: Accelerating scientific discovery with generative knowledge extraction, graph-based representation, and multimodal intelligent graph reasoning. arXiv, [Online]. https://arxiv.org/abs/2401.00000 (2024)
24. Ektefaie, Y., Dasoulas, G., Noori, A., Farhat, M., Zitnik, M.: Multimodal learning with graphs. arXiv (2022). https://doi.org/10.48550/arXiv.2209.03299
25. Veličković, P., Cucurull, G., Casanova, A., Romero, A., Lió, P., Bengio, Y.: Graph attention networks. In: International Conference on Learning Representations (2018)
26. Sun, R., Simione, Y., Zhang, J., Wang, V.: Graph XAI: graph-augmented AI with accuracy, depth, explainability, and velocity. In: 26th International Workshop on Design, Optimization, Languages and Analytical Processing of Big Data (DOLAP), pp. 55–62. ACM, Singapore (2024)

27. Chen, J., Hong, Z., Liu, X.: Multi-dimensional rating systems: a natural experiment comparison. Mar. Sci. **36**(4), 513–531 (2017)
28. Mishra, N., Gupta, P.: A review of sentiment analysis techniques in social media. J. Inf. Sci. Theory Pract. **7**(1), 1–14 (2019)
29. Peng, L., Cui, G., Chung, Y., Li, C.: A multi-facet item response theory approach to improve customer satisfaction using online product ratings. J. Acad. Market Sci. **47**, 960–976 (2019). https://doi.org/10.1007/s11747-019-00675-7
30. Johnson, R., Li, M.M., Noori, A., Queen, O., Zitnik, M.: Graph artificial intelligence in medicine. Annu. Rev. Biomed. Data Sci. **7**, 345–368 (2024). https://doi.org/10.1146/annurev-biodatasci-110723-024625
31. Wang, J., Zhou, L., Lin, H.: Sentiment analysis with BERT and Kismet emotional recognition. Inf. Process. Manag. **58**(4), 102525 (2021). https://doi.org/10.1016/j.ipm.2021.102525
32. Hu, H.-W., Chen, Y.-L., Hsu, P.-T.: A novel approach to rate and summarize online reviews according to user-specified aspects. J. Electron. Commer. Res. **17**(2), 132–152 (2016)
33. Murtagh, F., Legendre, P.: Ward's hierarchical clustering method: clustering criterion and agglomerative algorithm. J. Classif. **31**(3), 274–295 (2014). https://doi.org/10.1007/s00357-014-9161-z
34. Munoz, E., Smith, A.: Navigating the ethics of web scraping: frameworks and best practices. J. Inf. Ethics. **29**(1), 65–81 (2020). https://doi.org/10.1007/s11673-020-1002-1
35. Lancichinetti, A., Fortunato, S.: Community detection algorithms: a comparative analysis. Phys. Rev. E. **80**(5), 056117 (2009). https://doi.org/10.1103/PhysRevE.80.056117
36. Zeithaml, V.A.: Consumer perceptions of price, quality, and value: a means-end model and synthesis of evidence. J. Market. **52**(3), 2–22 (1988). https://doi.org/10.1177/002224298805200302
37. Parasuraman, A., Zeithaml, V.A., Berry, L.L.: SERVQUAL: a multiple-item scale for measuring consumer perceptions of service quality. J. Retail. **64**(1), 12–40 (1988)
38. Wakefield, K.L., Blodgett, J.G.: The effect of the servicescape on customers' behavioral intentions in leisure service settings. J. Serv. Market. **10**(6), 45–61 (1996). https://doi.org/10.1108/08876049610148594
39. Barber, N., Goodman, R.J., Goh, B.K.: Restaurant consumers repeat patronage: a service quality concern. Int. J. Hosp. Manag. **30**(2), 329–336 (2011). https://doi.org/10.1016/j.ijhm.2010.08.008
40. Bitner, M.J.: Servicescapes: the impact of physical surroundings on customers and employees. J. Market. **56**(2), 57–71 (1992). https://doi.org/10.1177/002224299205600205
41. Bifet, A., Kirkby, R.: Data Stream Mining: A Practical Approach. Cambridge University Press, Cambridge (2009)
42. Ghiassi, M., Skinner, J., Zimbra, D.: Twitter brand sentiment analysis: a hybrid system using n-gram analysis and dynamic artificial neural network. Expert Syst. Appl. **40**(16), 6266–6282 (2013). https://doi.org/10.1016/j.eswa.2013.05.057

AI for Sustainability

Artificial Intelligence and Circular Business Model Innovation: A Dynamic Capabilities Perspective

Mauro Sciarelli, Lorenzo Turriziani, and Anna Prisco

Abstract This study explores the transformative role of Artificial Intelligence (AI) in enabling dynamic capabilities—sensing, seizing, and reconfiguring—to foster Circular Business Model Innovation (CBMI). As sustainability imperatives demand a shift from linear to circular models, incumbent firms often encounter rigid path dependencies rooted in routines, industry norms, and institutional lock-ins. AI emerges not only as a tool for operational efficiency but also as a strategic enabler that facilitates the transition toward circularity.

Adopting an interpretivist, narrative-based multi-case study approach, this article analyzes three cases from the agri-food, textile/polymer, and waste management sectors. The findings reveal that AI-driven platforms significantly enhance firms' ability to sense emerging sustainability signals, identify hidden circular opportunities, and model alternative futures. Seizing capabilities are augmented by AI's capacity to support agile experimentation, while reconfiguring capabilities are triggered through systemic transformation in processes, partnerships, and value creation logics.

Crucially, AI acts as a boundary-spanning infrastructure, fostering ecosystem collaboration, data transparency, and cross-sectoral knowledge recombination. The cross-case analysis illustrates how AI enables double-loop learning and institutional entrepreneurship, allowing firms to challenge entrenched assumptions and reorient their business models toward circularity.

Theoretically, the paper extends dynamic capabilities theory by integrating AI as an enabler of ecosystem co-evolution and organizational transformation. From a managerial perspective, it offers insights into leveraging AI to unlock sustainable innovation, orchestrate partnerships, and shape institutional fields. The study concludes with a discussion of its limitations and outlines future research directions further to explore the socio-technical dynamics of AI in circular economy transitions.

M. Sciarelli · L. Turriziani (✉) · A. Prisco
Department of Economics, Management, Institutions, University of Naples Federico II, Naples, Italy
e-mail: mauro.sciarelli@unina.it; lorenzo.turriziani@unina.it; anna.prisco@unina.it

N. Omrani et al. (eds.), *Human-Machine Synergy and the Digital Future - Exploring Collaboration and Competition Volume 1*, Springer Proceedings in Business and Economics, https://doi.org/10.1007/978-3-032-21347-1_16

Keywords Artificial intelligence · Circular business model · Dynamic capabilities

1 Introduction

The shift toward a Circular Economy (CE) is widely regarded as a crucial response to the growing environmental harm, resource shortages, and the unsustainability of linear economic systems [1]. Circular Business Models (CBMs) represent a strategic move toward sustainability, focusing on resource efficiency, waste reduction, extending product life, and regeneration [2, 3]. Although the benefits of circular models are clear, moving from linear to circular practices remains very challenging for established companies due to path dependency [4, 5]. Path dependency involves ingrained routines, cognitive biases, industry norms, and regulations that lock organizations into existing ways of working, making radical innovation and strategic change difficult [6, 7].

Recently, scholars have stressed the importance of understanding how organizations can overcome these path dependencies to enable sustainable transitions [5, 8]. Key to this is the concept of dynamic capabilities [4, 9], which suggests that organizations can strategically manage change by sensing opportunities, acting on them effectively, and continuously reconfiguring their internal and external capabilities. These capabilities are exceptionally vital for sustainability efforts, as they help organizations break free from old patterns and develop new business models aligned with circularity [10].

In this context, Artificial Intelligence (AI) has emerged as a potentially transformative technological tool to build dynamic capabilities [11]. AI's ability to process vast and diverse datasets, provide predictive insights, and automate complex decisions offers the potential to enhance strategic innovation significantly [12]. Specifically, AI can uncover hidden inefficiencies and opportunities, improve managerial agility through experimentation, and facilitate the redesign of processes and ecosystems [10]. Despite its growing recognition, there is still limited empirical understanding of how AI concretely supports dynamic capabilities within circular business models [3].

To address this gap, this study employs an interpretivist, narrative-based, multicase approach to explore how AI-driven CBMs enhance organizational dynamic capabilities. We focus on three research questions derived from the identified gaps:

RQ1: How does AI enhance firms' dynamic capabilities (sensing, seizing, reconfiguring) to support the transition from linear to circular business models?
RQ2: How do firms use AI to overcome path dependencies in their production and innovation routines?
RQ3: How do ecosystems and institutional contexts facilitate or hinder AI-enabled circular transformations?

These questions guide an in-depth qualitative analysis of three cases of AI-enabled CBM innovation: a multinational agri-food company aiming for zero waste; a polymer and textile producer shifting R&D toward eco-design and recycling; and a government-private waste utility leading community-wide circular efforts. Each case offers unique insights into its context, ecosystem factors, and institutional hurdles, illustrating how AI is strategically employed to challenge entrenched routines.

Through this qualitative research, we aim to deepen our theoretical understanding of dynamic capabilities in circular settings and provide practical insights into AI's strategic role in sustainability transitions. Our findings contribute to the literature on dynamic capabilities [4, 10], the implementation of circular economy [1–3], and institutional entrepreneurship in sustainable innovation [13, 14]. Additionally, the study offers managerial implications on how organizations can leverage AI not only for efficiency but also as a strategic driver of circular innovation, ecosystem collaboration, and regulatory change.

The article is structured as follows: the next section reviews key theoretical concepts; the third discusses the methodology justifying our interpretivist, multi-case approach; the fourth presents detailed empirical case narratives; the fifth offers an integrated discussion linking evidence to theory; and the final section concludes with contributions, practical implications, limitations, and directions for future research.

2 Literature Review

2.1 Circular Business Models and the Challenge of Path Dependency

The shift toward sustainable business practices has led to increased interest in Circular Business Models (CBMs) as a strategic way to tackle environmental and social issues [15, 16]. CBMs represent a fundamental change in how companies create, deliver, and capture value, emphasizing durability, reuse, regeneration, and closed-loop systems. They challenge the traditional linear model of production and consumption, which is inherently extractive [5].

However, adopting circular principles often requires substantial changes in internal processes, inter-company relationships, and core value systems. Despite growing awareness, many firms remain caught in traditional routines and linear resource flows, mainly due to path dependency—a concept rooted in evolutionary economics and institutional theory [17–19]. Path dependency involves mechanisms that reinforce current practices, technologies, and routines, thereby limiting a firm's flexibility over time. Moving toward circularity, path dependency manifests in sunk costs associated with linear production, KPIs focused on short-term throughput, supply chain lock-ins, and regulations that favor compliance over innovation [4, 7].

Recent research indicates that failures of CBMs are more often caused by structural inertia, cognitive conservatism, and institutional misalignment than by technological issues [3]. In resource-intensive sectors, existing practices hinder experimentation with circular strategies. Companies often lack the skills to identify alternative circular options or face difficulties in reshaping supplier relationships, pricing, or product design standards. These transitions are complex because circular strategies usually involve multiple functions and stakeholders, including regulators, customers, and competitors [20]. Consequently, CBMs are not simple solutions; they require profound organizational and cognitive changes as well as systemic coordination across institutions.

The expanding literature emphasizes the need for conceptual frameworks that explain how firms can overcome linear lock-ins and promote circular innovation. Among these, the dynamic capabilities framework provides a strong theoretical foundation, as it describes how companies identify and exploit opportunities and reconfigure resources to remain competitive in changing environments [4, 9]. Although CBMs and dynamic capabilities have been studied separately for some time, scholars have only recently begun exploring their connection, particularly in relation to digital technologies like AI and their role in facilitating this integration.

2.2 Dynamic Capabilities and the Strategic Role of AI in Circular Innovation

The concept of dynamic capabilities (DCs) was developed to explain how companies adapt their skills and strategic resources in response to rapid technological and market changes [4, 21]. DCs are not routine operations, but rather relatively higher-level skills that enable firms to develop, expand, and change their resource base intentionally. Teece identified three key aspects of DCs: sensing, which is the ability to spot emerging opportunities and risks; seizing, the capacity to mobilize resources and implement strategies; and reconfiguring, which involves ongoing transformation of organizational structures, processes, and assets [4]. These aspects are especially relevant in uncertain situations, such as during sustainability transitions and digital transformations [9, 22].

In the case of Circular Business Models (CBMs), dynamic capabilities are critical. Sensing involves monitoring environmental trends, regulations, and technological advancements that may uncover opportunities for resource circularity. Seizing includes creating new value propositions and aligning internal processes to support circular offerings. Reconfiguring often requires rethinking product design, logistics, sourcing, and customer engagement—all of which can differ significantly from traditional routines and demand significant organizational change.

Recent research highlights AI as a key enabler of dynamic capabilities in sustainability contexts. AI systems, through machine learning, predictive analytics, and automation, offer unique opportunities to enhance managerial understanding, expedite decision-making, and improve responsiveness to complexity [23, 24]. Specifically, AI helps sensing by detecting weak signals and hidden patterns in large datasets; enhances seizing by supporting rapid prototyping and testing; and facilitates reconfiguring through adaptive learning, feedback, and ongoing optimization [10].

Sjödin, Parida, and Kohtamäki [10] offer a theoretical integration of AI into the DCs framework, particularly in digital servitization and circularity. They suggest that AI capabilities map onto the three DCs as: value discovery (sensing), value realization (seizing), and value optimization (reconfiguring). This demonstrates that AI is not only about increasing efficiency but also about driving strategic change. These AI-enabled DCs are interconnected; for example, improved sensing can lead to more informed seizure, which then provides feedback to enhance sensing and reconfiguration. This creates a dynamic feedback system that supports organizational learning and transformation beyond isolated innovation projects.

However, integrating AI into CBM contexts is a complex process. It requires organizational readiness, cultural acceptance, proper data infrastructure, and governance aligned with strategic goals [11]. Moreover, AI's role in dynamic capabilities depends on how it is embedded within socio-technical systems, including networks and institutional contexts. Therefore, understanding how AI facilitates CBM transitions involves examining both internal processes and the broader ecosystem and knowledge dynamics.

2.3 Knowledge Recombination, Ecosystem Co-Evolution, and Institutional Embeddedness

A central feature of CBMs is that they necessitate cross-boundary collaboration and knowledge recombination. Firms do not transition to circularity in isolation; they must interact with suppliers, customers, competitors, policymakers, and civil society actors in reconfiguring value creation and delivery [20]. These interactions often involve integrating heterogeneous knowledge domains—such as materials science, data analytics, design thinking, and environmental regulation—into new configurations that enable circular value propositions. This dynamic process of knowledge recombination has long been recognized in innovation literature as a key driver of novelty and performance [21, 25].

AI plays a catalytic role in enabling such recombination by serving as a boundary-spanning technology. Through its capacity to process unstructured data from multiple sources, AI allows firms to integrate insights across silos and translate them into actionable intelligence. Moreover, AI platforms often function as boundary objects—artifacts that mediate collaboration among actors with different perspectives and expertise [26, 27]. In this sense, AI is not only a computational tool but also a social infrastructure that facilitates the alignment of interpretive frames and the co-production of knowledge across organizations.

From an ecosystem perspective, the implementation of AI-enabled CBMs can be seen as a process of co-evolution between firms and their external environments [28, 29]. Firms deploying AI tools to coordinate circular initiatives often reshape the behaviors and expectations of ecosystem participants, including suppliers, municipalities, or regulators. In turn, these ecosystem responses influence the firm's trajectory, creating a recursive dynamic of mutual adaptation. This co-evolutionary perspective challenges the traditional firm-centric view of strategy, instead emphasizing relational and systemic forms of value creation.

Furthermore, the institutional context in which CBMs unfold has a significant influence on how AI is adopted and operationalized. Drawing on neo-institutional theory [14, 30], we acknowledge that organizations are subject to coercive, normative, and mimetic pressures that influence their responses to environmental challenges. In our cases, firms were not merely passive recipients of institutional pressures; instead, they acted as institutional entrepreneurs [13], leveraging AI-enabled practices to shape new norms, gain legitimacy, and influence policy discourses.

Therefore, the intersection of AI, CBMs, and dynamic capabilities must be understood within a multi-level framework that accounts for organizational routines, inter-firm collaboration, and institutional transformation. By examining these interdependencies through qualitative case narratives, this study aims to contribute to a more comprehensive understanding of how AI enables dynamic capabilities, supporting firms in navigating the transition to the circular economy.

3 Methodology

3.1 Research Design

This research is anchored in an interpretivist epistemological paradigm and employs a qualitative, inductive, and narrative-based multiple-case study design. The interpretivist approach is particularly well-suited for exploring how firms conceptualize and enact transitions toward circularity through digital technologies, such as AI, as it emphasizes the situated meanings and sense-making processes of organizational actors. In contexts characterized by high complexity, institutional ambiguity, and path-dependent trajectories—such as those typical of circular transformations—the interpretive lens enables a nuanced reconstruction of how firms navigate uncertainty, redefine strategic priorities, and develop new capabilities. Rather than seeking statistical generalizability, this study aims for theoretical insight through analytical generalization, relying on the depth and richness of empirical narratives to develop context-sensitive understandings [22, 31].

The adoption of a narrative-based multi-case study design responds to the need for methodological sensitivity to temporality, causality, and relationality. Narratives, as theorized by organizational scholars, are not simply stories or anecdotal accounts; they are structured ways through which organizations make sense of disruptive events, reconstruct past decisions, and envision future trajectories [32, 33]. Through this lens, AI-enabled circular transitions are treated not as discrete technical interventions but as complex, path-breaking episodes that unfold over time, mediated by cognitive frames, routines, and institutional structures. The comparative nature of the multi-case approach enables the identification of recurring patterns across diverse industrial and organizational settings, as well as the theorization of context-contingent mechanisms.

3.2 *Case Selection*

The empirical foundation of this study is built on three embedded case studies of Italian firms operating in sectors marked by high material intensity, regulatory exposure, and growing societal pressure for sustainability. These include a multinational agri-food company headquartered in Emilia-Romagna (Case A), a vertically integrated polymer and textile manufacturer based in Lombardy (Case B), and a regional waste management utility governed through a public-private partnership in central and northern Italy (Case C). Each of these organizations had engaged in explicit efforts to implement AI technologies within broader strategies of circular business model innovation. Their relevance to the study derives from the richness of their transformation processes, the accessibility of informants and internal documents, and the presence of interorganizational and institutional interactions that shape the dynamics under investigation.

The selection of cases followed theoretical sampling principles, aiming to maximize variation in organizational size, sector, ownership, and ecosystem configuration. This heterogeneity enabled us to explore how AI-enabled dynamic capabilities manifest across distinct contexts and how firms overcome different forms of path dependency. Importantly, all three firms had reached an intermediate to advanced level of maturity in both AI implementation and circular strategy, ensuring the empirical robustness of the narratives. Access to the cases was facilitated through professional networks and previous academic collaborations, with participation formalized through confidentiality agreements and the commitment to anonymize all data and identifiers.

3.3 *Data Collection*

The research was conducted between January and April 2025 and relied on a combination of semi-structured interviews and documentary analysis. A total of 20 interviews were carried out with key informants involved in the design, implementation, and management of AI and sustainability initiatives. Informants included innovation managers, sustainability officers, digital transformation leads, operations directors, and AI engineers, as well as external consultants embedded in the firms' transformation journeys. Interviews lasted between 45 and 90 minutes, were conducted in Italian or English depending on the participant's preference, and were fully transcribed and translated where necessary.

The interview guide was designed to elicit rich, reflective accounts of the transformation processes underway. Topics included the origins and motivations for AI adoption in the context of sustainability, the nature of internal debates and tensions, the reconfiguration of operational practices and routines, and the role of external factors such as supply chain partners, customers, regulators, or local institutions. Rather than adhering to a rigid script, interviews were conducted as open-ended conversations in which respondents were encouraged to narrate the evolution of their strategies, technologies, and collaborations over time.

In addition to interviews, extensive documentary data was collected, including internal reports, sustainability plans, AI implementation roadmaps, internal presentations, and white papers. These were complemented by external materials, including company press releases, conference proceedings, and publicly available regulatory documents. This multi-source approach enabled methodological triangulation, thereby reinforcing the credibility and contextual richness of the findings.

3.4 Data Analysis and Theoretical Framing

Data analysis proceeded through an iterative and abductive process that combined inductive coding with theoretical elaboration. The initial phase involved open coding of interview transcripts and documents to identify recurrent themes, practices, and interpretive frames associated with AI adoption, circular strategy, organizational learning, and ecosystem interaction. Coding remained close to the language of the participants in this phase, to preserve the specificity and granularity of their situated narratives.

As the analysis progressed, emergent codes were organized into second-order categories aligned with the study's conceptual framework. Particular attention was given to identifying processes that exemplified the development of dynamic capabilities, such as the ability to detect previously invisible opportunities (sensing), to experiment with novel circular configurations (seizing), and to transform routines and organizational roles (reconfiguring). In parallel, we tracked cross-boundary interactions and moments of knowledge recombination that signaled broader ecosystem engagement. The data was analyzed using NVivo software, which facilitated coding consistency and cross-case comparison.

For each case, we constructed a narrative synthesis that reconstructed the trajectory of AI-enabled circular transformation over time. These narratives were structured around critical junctures, including cognitive shifts, strategic inflection points, implementation milestones, and collaborative experiments. The aim was not only to describe what happened but to reconstruct how organizational actors made sense of, responded to, and influenced the unfolding process. These rich case reconstructions served as the basis for a cross-case comparison that sought to identify both converging patterns and context-specific dynamics.

Throughout the analysis, we engaged in regular peer debriefings within the research team to discuss emergent interpretations, assess the coherence of coding decisions, and reflect on potential researcher biases. Analytic memos were maintained to document insights, methodological choices, and evolving theoretical propositions. This reflexive stance, combined with the triangulation of sources and the depth of empirical material, enhances the credibility and transferability of the findings, supporting the study's aim of making a theoretical contribution through empirical elaboration.

4 Case A: AI for Waste Valorization and Data-Driven Circularity in the Agri-Food Sector

Case A concerns a multinational agri-food company headquartered in the Emilia-Romagna region, operating in the production and distribution of large-scale packaged food products. Traditionally embedded in a linear business model based on volume, scale, and efficiency, the firm had long relied on standardization, high-throughput processes, and centralized control systems.

The strategic shift toward circularity was not initially motivated by ethical concerns or regulatory pressure. Still, it emerged from growing operational inefficiencies, reputational vulnerabilities, and, crucially, a new strategic vision articulated by a forward-looking innovation unit within the firm. Artificial Intelligence was introduced not as an isolated technological experiment but as a central pillar in a broader transformation strategy aimed at redesigning both product flows and value generation logics. Over the course of 3 years, the firm gradually deployed AI capabilities across several organizational layers, with a particular focus on waste valorization, demand forecasting, and product lifecycle optimization.

4.1 Enhancing Sensing Capabilities Through AI-Driven Analytics

The first and most immediate impact of AI implementation in Case A was the expansion of the firm's sensing capability. Before the transformation, organizational routines were heavily focused on short-term production efficiency, with limited visibility on upstream waste generation or downstream product obsolescence. Data was collected primarily for compliance and quality assurance, but it was rarely integrated or interpreted across silos. The deployment of AI-based analytics platforms marked a radical departure from this fragmented knowledge regime. Through machine learning models trained on historical production data, supply chain metrics, and external variables such as weather patterns and consumer behavior, the firm began to identify underexplored inefficiencies, particularly in the form of overproduction, mismatch between demand and packaging size, and early spoilage of perishable goods.

AI thus enabled the emergence of a new epistemic infrastructure, whereby information was no longer passively stored but actively recombined to generate actionable insights. These insights, in turn, challenged the validity of long-standing assumptions about production scheduling, packaging logic, and distribution priorities. Notably, the sensing capability extended beyond internal operations to encompass ecosystem-level dynamics: AI models were used to simulate alternative packaging designs in terms of customer reuse potential and local recycling rates, leading to more context-sensitive product strategies. The firm's capacity to detect latent environmental and economic inefficiencies increased substantially, paving the way for the next stage of transformation.

4.2 Seizing Circular Opportunities Through Cross-Functional Experimentation

The sensing stage catalyzed a new phase of internal experimentation and cross-functional collaboration, through which the firm sought to translate data-driven insights into strategic initiatives. Here, the seizing capability was not merely technical but also organizational, involving the reallocation of resources, revisiting product development logics, and forging new alliances within and beyond the firm. One particularly transformative initiative was the redesign of packaging for one of the company's best-selling food lines. Using AI simulations that modeled consumer usage behavior and return patterns, the firm developed a modular, reusable packaging system with significantly reduced material intensity. The project required coordination across R&D, logistics, marketing, and external partners, including local waste cooperatives and municipalities.

AI acted as a mediating device across these heterogeneous domains, facilitating a shared understanding of objectives, risks, and trade-offs. The ability to simulate multiple scenarios in real time empowered managers to take calculated risks and test configurations that would have previously been dismissed as too complex or too costly. Moreover, the integration of AI with external data sources—such as municipal recycling statistics and consumer mobility trends—enabled the firm to assess the viability of circular strategies in different urban and regional contexts. Seizing, in this case, was deeply tied to the ability to mobilize and align diverse knowledge domains and to reframe uncertainty as an opportunity for innovation rather than a barrier to be minimized.

4.3 Reconfiguring Processes, Roles, and Ecosystem Relationships

The most profound and institutionally disruptive change emerged through the reconfiguring capability, which involved the structural transformation of organizational processes, role boundaries, and value network configurations. AI-enabled insights and cross-functional experiments revealed that existing performance metrics and incentive systems were poorly aligned with circular goals. In response, the firm initiated a comprehensive redesign of its internal governance structures, including the introduction of circularity KPIs, the establishment of a cross-departmental innovation office, and the creation of a dedicated AI and Sustainability steering committee. These changes signaled a reconfiguration not only of operations but of the organizational identity itself, shifting from a "production-centered" to a "resource stewardship" paradigm.

At the ecosystem level, reconfiguration involved a shift from transactional to collaborative modes of engagement with external stakeholders. The firm co-developed circular pilot projects with logistics providers, local governments, and NGOs, utilizing AI platforms to coordinate the flow of goods, waste, and information. For instance, one initiative focused on closing the loop for food packaging through an innovative return system linked to consumer reward schemes, enabled by AI-powered tracking. In this context, AI served as both an informational infrastructure and a trust-building mechanism, facilitating transparency, accountability, and mutual learning among actors with diverse institutional logics.

Importantly, these reconfigurations were not devoid of tensions. Internal resistance emerged around the reallocation of decision rights and resource priorities, particularly from middle management accustomed to efficiency-based KPIs. Similarly, some external partners struggled to adapt to the firm's increasing data-driven requirements and coordination expectations. Nevertheless, the momentum generated by early successes and the credibility of AI-derived insights gradually legitimized the transformation, both internally and in the eyes of ecosystem partners. Over time, the firm began to be recognized not only as a producer of food products but as a platform orchestrator of regional circular ecosystems.

5 Case B: Artificial Intelligence and Circular Process Innovation in the Polymer-Textile Industry

Case B focuses on a vertically integrated firm operating in the polymer and technical textile sector, headquartered in northern Italy. The company has historically built its competitiveness on innovation in synthetic materials, especially in durability and high-performance applications for automotive and industrial clients. In recent years, the firm has been under increasing pressure to transition toward more sustainable materials and processes, driven by evolving European regulations, client expectations, and internal generational turnover within the ownership structure. The decision to adopt Artificial Intelligence was catalyzed by a strategic need to monitor and reduce environmental impact across the product lifecycle, while maintaining the firm's technological leadership. Unlike Case A, where AI was initially framed as a decision-support tool, in this case, AI became a core element of materials informatics, process redesign, and innovation-oriented cultural transformation.

5.1 Sensing Emerging Opportunities Through AI-Enhanced Material Intelligence

The development of dynamic sensing capabilities in Case B was deeply intertwined with the firm's historical investment in R&D and its identity as a materials innovator. However, before the implementation of AI, the firm's data landscape was characterized by fragmentation across departments, with process engineers, quality control experts, and sustainability teams relying on disconnected data sources. The integration of AI enabled the creation of a unified data infrastructure that can correlate real-time production variables, material performance metrics, and environmental impact indicators. Through deep learning algorithms and process mining techniques, the firm began to uncover complex relationships between polymer formulations, energy consumption, waste generation, and recyclability rates.

This new form of material intelligence enabled the firm not only to improve operational control but to redefine what counts as innovation. AI revealed that certain legacy materials—once considered optimal in terms of mechanical performance—were significantly less circular when lifecycle metrics were considered holistically. Moreover, sensing was extended to encompass external signals from clients and regulatory bodies. By analyzing customer specifications and upcoming EU directives, AI helped the firm anticipate shifts in demand for biodegradable polymers, modular fabrics, and closed-loop supply chains. The ability to detect and make sense of weak signals in both technological and institutional domains marked a significant departure from prior routines, opening new strategic avenues for innovation.

5.2 Seizing Circular Innovation Pathways Through Digital-Physical Integration

Building on the insights generated by AI, the firm undertook a series of initiatives aimed at redesigning products and processes to align with circular economy principles. Central to this seizing phase was the integration of AI with physical experimentation in the pilot plant, where new polymer blends were developed and tested. AI did not replace traditional R&D; instead, it accelerated it, enabling real-time feedback loops between digital simulations and material prototyping. The co-development of circular solutions involved close collaboration between data scientists, process engineers, and sustainability experts—teams that had traditionally operated in silos.

One of the most emblematic projects involved the development of a textile made from post-industrial polymer waste that met stringent performance standards while being fully recyclable. The AI models played a crucial role in optimizing the balance between durability and recyclability, a challenge that had previously been addressed through trial and error. The project also involved coordination with downstream partners to ensure that design-for-recycling principles were integrated across the value chain.

Seizing, in this context, was also an organizational effort: the firm restructured its innovation pipeline to include sustainability and circularity criteria from the earliest design stages. Decision-making processes were altered to incorporate AI-derived sustainability indicators as part of investment appraisal. The traditional divide between technological feasibility and environmental desirability was progressively bridged by data-driven deliberation, which fostered greater alignment between strategic intent and operational execution.

5.3 Reconfiguring Organizational Routines and Institutional Relationships

The reconfiguring phase in Case B revealed the depth of the transformation underway. As the firm increasingly relied on AI to guide its circular innovation trajectory, it began to rearticulate its internal identity, from that of a high-tech materials supplier to a sustainability-driven ecosystem partner. This shift required changes not only in discourse but in institutionalized routines, accountability structures, and external relationships.

Internally, the firm created a new cross-functional "Circular Lab" that combined digital, environmental, and production expertise. This unit operated with semi-autonomous governance and was tasked with identifying scalable circular innovations that could be integrated across product lines. Moreover, the traditional KPI system was revised to include metrics related to resource circularity, carbon footprint reduction, and innovation velocity—metrics that were continuously fed by AI systems. These changes altered how performance was understood and rewarded, prompting middle managers to adopt a more proactive approach, embracing uncertainty, experimentation, and interdependence.

Externally, the firm repositioned itself within the broader industrial ecosystem by engaging in public-private consortia focused on polymer circularity, innovative materials, and digital traceability. AI became a bridge between the firm and its institutional environment, enabling the transparent communication of sustainability performance and the co-design of compliance pathways with regulatory agencies. For instance, the firm collaborated with a regional innovation hub to develop a blockchain-integrated AI platform capable of tracing recycled content from raw input to final textile product. This project not only enhanced supply chain transparency but also increased the firm's legitimacy in the eyes of clients and public stakeholders.

Despite these advances, reconfiguration was not devoid of contradictions. Tensions arose between the firm's legacy business model, which remained partially dependent on virgin fossil-based polymers, and the ambitions for full circularity. Additionally, the cultural shift required to fully embrace AI-guided decision-making encountered resistance, particularly among senior engineers trained in intuition-based heuristics. Nevertheless, the organizational momentum toward circular reconfiguration, reinforced by the credibility of AI insights and the legitimacy granted by ecosystem alliances, enabled the firm to sustain its transformation trajectory.

6 Case C: Orchestrating Ecosystem Transitions Through AI in the Circular Waste Management Sector

Case C examines a regional public-private utility operating in the field of integrated waste management and environmental services. The company serves a densely populated area in central and northern Italy and operates under a hybrid governance model, with strategic oversight shared between public municipalities and private industrial actors. Policy mandates and regional sustainability targets have historically influenced the firm's circularity agenda; however, in recent years, it has actively repositioned itself as an innovation leader, leveraging digital technologies to transform waste collection, valorization, and citizen engagement. Artificial Intelligence has become a cornerstone of this repositioning, enabling the firm to both optimize existing infrastructures and enact systemic change across its urban ecosystem. The case illustrates how AI-enabled dynamic capabilities can emerge not only within firms but also through multilateral interactions that transcend institutional and operational boundaries.

6.1 Sensing Socio-Technical Change Through Real-Time Ecosystem Intelligence

In Case C, the development of sensing capabilities was driven by the need to move beyond reactive compliance and toward a proactive understanding of circular potential across the urban territory. The firm historically relied on periodic reporting and manual data entry to monitor service efficiency and environmental performance. With the deployment of AI, a suite of real-time analytics tools was developed that aggregated data from heterogeneous sources, including smart bins, IoT-enabled collection vehicles, geospatial mapping, citizen apps, and regional environmental sensors. These data streams were processed through machine learning algorithms capable of identifying patterns of waste generation, illegal dumping, seasonal fluctuation, and socio-demographic behaviors at the neighborhood level.

This AI-based intelligence infrastructure enabled the firm to recognize previously hidden inefficiencies, such as mismatches between bin placement and actual waste flows, underperformance in specific collection routes, and low citizen participation in composting schemes. It also revealed opportunities for targeted interventions, such as nudging behavioral change through feedback loops or dynamically reallocating resources in response to predicted anomalies. Importantly, sensing extended to ecosystem actors: by integrating datasets from local schools, businesses, and environmental NGOs, the firm was able to detect emerging needs, community expectations, and potential partnerships for shared value creation.

AI thus acted not only as a data processing engine but as a socio-technical sensorium, making visible the distributed dynamics of circularity across the urban ecosystem. This capability fundamentally reoriented the firm's strategic horizon, shifting its mission from "waste collection" to "urban resource orchestration."

6.2 *Seizing Collective Innovation Opportunities Through Participatory Platforms*

Building on this ecosystemic awareness, the firm initiated a series of collaborative innovation projects aimed at translating data-driven insights into transformative actions. These initiatives reflected an evolved seizing capability, one that went beyond internal experimentation and involved distributed agency among multiple stakeholders. One flagship project involved the co-design of a citizen-facing app that gamified recycling behaviors, providing real-time feedback, ecological scores, and incentive-based rewards. The AI engine behind the app personalized messages based on user behavior, location, and environmental impact, creating a continuous feedback loop between the utility and urban inhabitants.

In parallel, the firm launched a digital marketplace for secondary raw materials derived from municipal waste streams. The platform, enabled by AI matching algorithms, connected local SMEs with residual flows of plastic, metal, and organics, thereby fostering industrial symbiosis at the regional level. The project required not only technological infrastructure but also the alignment of regulatory frameworks, procurement practices, and stakeholder expectations. AI played a key role in simulating scenarios, assessing risk, and designing incentive mechanisms that could make such exchanges economically viable.

Crucially, the firm reframed its role from service provider to ecosystem facilitator. A strategic commitment to inclusion, experimentation, and the co-creation of shared value marked the seizing phase. These actions were made possible by AI's capacity to model complex systems, anticipate behavioral patterns, and support decision-making across distributed actors. Rather than centralizing control, AI became a vehicle for decentralized innovation and strategic alignment.

6.3 Reconfiguring Governance, Legitimacy, and Value Co-Creation Logics

The most profound transformation observed in Case C occurred at the institutional and organizational levels. The firm undertook a deliberate effort to redesign its governance architecture in line with the affordances of AI and the ambitions of circularity. Internally, this involved the creation of an "Innovation and Inclusion Office," tasked with managing cross-sectoral projects, overseeing data ethics, and ensuring alignment with public values. The office operated as a hybrid interface between technological, environmental, and civic domains, signaling a shift toward more reflexive and participatory governance practices.

Externally, the firm developed new relational infrastructures to embed itself more deeply within the urban circular economy. It formalized partnerships with universities, social enterprises, and regulatory bodies, co-developing guidelines for the ethical use of AI, data-sharing agreements, and sustainability reporting standards. One particularly innovative initiative was the co-creation of a municipal AI observatory, where public administrators, citizen representatives, and experts could deliberate on the use, boundaries, and risks of AI in the context of the circular economy. This participatory mechanism not only enhanced transparency but also generated trust and legitimacy, critical resources in a context marked by diverse interests and institutional complexity.

The reconfiguring process also entailed a redefinition of value. Whereas value was previously measured in terms of tons of waste collected or percentage of material recovered, the firm began to conceptualize value in terms of community engagement, environmental literacy, and ecosystem resilience. These shifts were reinforced by AI-generated indicators that captured qualitative dimensions such as citizen satisfaction, behavioral change trajectories, and social inclusion outcomes.

Nevertheless, the transformation was not linear. The hybrid nature of the firm's governance created friction, particularly between public mandates and the profit-driven logics of private stakeholders. Some municipalities resisted the increased reliance on algorithmic systems, citing concerns over surveillance and loss of discretion. Similarly, internal tensions emerged around the allocation of resources and the pace of change. However, the firm's commitment to participatory experimentation, coupled with the credibility of its AI-enabled outcomes, allowed it to navigate these tensions and progressively consolidate a new institutional identity.

7 Discussion

This study set out to explore how Artificial Intelligence can enable dynamic capabilities within firms transitioning toward circular business models, with a focus on overcoming path dependencies, fostering ecosystem collaborations, and reconfiguring strategic orientations. Through a qualitative, narrative-based multiple-case study design, we examined three Italian firms—each embedded in distinct industrial and governance contexts—engaged in AI-driven circular transformations. The findings reveal both converging patterns and context-specific articulations, from which a novel conceptual model of AI-enabled Circular Business Transformation can be inductively derived. This model synthesizes the role of AI across three interrelated processes—sensing, seizing, and reconfiguring—while anchoring these processes within a broader ecosystemic logic of co-evolution, knowledge recombination, and institutional reframing.

7.1 Dynamic Capabilities and the Role of AI in Circular Transformation

The analysis confirms and extends the foundational propositions of dynamic capabilities theory [4, 34] by demonstrating how AI operates not simply as a technological enabler but as a cognitive and organizational infrastructure that catalyzes capability development in a circular economy context. Across all three cases, AI augmented firms' sensing capabilities by enabling them to detect latent inefficiencies, emerging opportunities, and weak signals across both internal operations and external ecosystems. Significantly, this was not limited to technical sensing (e.g., of material flows) but included institutional and behavioral sensing, such as the capacity to anticipate regulatory changes or shifts in consumer expectations. In Case A, for instance, AI illuminated overlooked patterns in product spoilage and packaging misuse, revealing opportunities for circular design. In Case B, AI exposed trade-offs between material performance and recyclability, prompting a fundamental rethinking of what constitutes innovation. In Case C, AI-enabled real-time mapping of urban waste behavior facilitated proactive interventions in ecosystem-wide resource flows.

In terms of seizing opportunities, AI-enabled firms translate sensed insights into actionable strategies by enhancing scenario modeling, cross-functional coordination, and stakeholder alignment. In all three cases, AI reduced the cognitive load and uncertainty typically associated with experimentation, thereby lowering the threshold for strategic risk-taking. In Case A, AI simulations supported the development of modular, reusable packaging systems. In Case B, AI accelerated the co-development of novel polymers with improved circular properties. In Case C, AI empowered citizens to engage in circular behaviors through personalized nudges and gamified platforms. These examples highlight how AI can serve as a boundary object, mediating between organizational domains, epistemic communities, and external actors, thereby fostering a more systemic and participatory logic of innovation [26].

The most radical effects of AI were observed at the level of reconfiguring, where it supported the institutional and organizational transformations necessary to embed circularity into the firm's structure and identity. In each case, AI-derived insights triggered a reevaluation of KPIs, the formation of new cross-functional units, and the redesign of governance architectures. AI acted not merely as an optimizer of existing routines but as a disruptor of taken-for-granted logics, facilitating the transition from linear to circular value creation paradigms. Particularly in Case C, the co-creation of an AI observatory and the redesign of value metrics signaled a profound reframing of the firm's societal role and legitimacy claims.

7.2 Toward a Conceptual Model of AI-Enabled Circular Business Transformation

Drawing from the three case studies, we propose a conceptual model of AI-enabled Circular Business Transformation that synthesizes the empirical patterns observed and articulates them within a unified systemic framework. The model, represented in Fig. 1, illustrates how Artificial Intelligence enables the development and interaction of dynamic capabilities within firms, while embedding them in a broader ecosystemic environment characterized by collaborative flows, institutional responsiveness, and iterative adaptation.

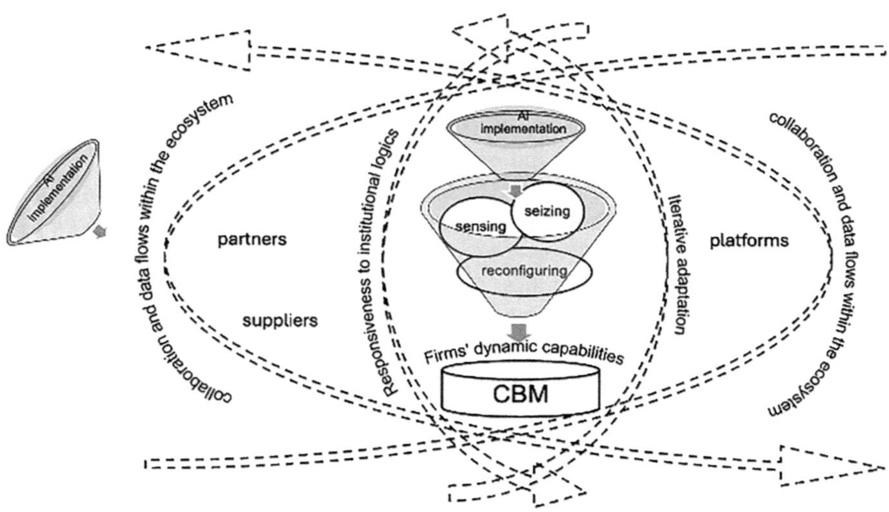

Fig. 1 Conceptual Model: AI-Enabled Circular Business Transformation

At the core of the model lies the canonical triad of sensing, seizing, and reconfiguring, conceptualized as interdependent and recursive processes that collectively shape a firm's ability to innovate its Circular Business Model (CBM). These dynamic capabilities are not linear stages but overlapping domains of organizational cognition, coordination, and transformation. AI implementation serves as the initial and enabling layer, feeding into these capabilities by providing the infrastructure for data integration, pattern recognition, real-time analytics, and predictive modeling.

The sensing function is enhanced through AI's ability to capture, process, and contextualize large volumes of internal and external data. Firms use AI to detect subtle signals in customer behavior, regulatory changes, environmental metrics, and supply chain dynamics. Seizing emerges as firms translate these sensed opportunities into strategic initiatives—such as the development of circular products, digital marketplaces, or citizen engagement platforms—supported by AI's capacity to simulate scenarios, optimize decisions, and coordinate distributed actors. Reconfiguring involves the realignment of organizational structures, governance mechanisms, and value logics, often catalyzed and sustained by the legitimacy and transparency afforded by AI-generated insights.

These dynamic capabilities, however, do not operate in isolation. The model explicitly embeds them within a dual-layered ecosystemic context. On one side, we observe collaboration and data flows with partners and suppliers, facilitated by platforms and interoperable systems where AI enables transparency, traceability, and knowledge recombination. On the other side, there is a continuous responsiveness to institutional logics, including environmental norms, social expectations, and regulatory standards. AI functions here as an interface, translating institutional signals into actionable intelligence and facilitating proactive compliance and value co-creation.

A further key dimension of the model is iterative adaptation. Circular business transformation is not a one-shot strategic move but a process of continuous experimentation, learning, and recalibration. AI's adaptive learning capabilities allow firms to update their models, metrics, and practices dynamically, feeding back into the sensing-seizing-reconfiguring cycle. This recursion is what ultimately reinforces the firm's ability to sustain innovation over time and across changing institutional and market conditions.

Importantly, the model underscores the co-evolutionary nature of circular business innovation. Firms are not merely adapting to external pressures but are actively shaping their ecosystems through new governance roles, data architectures, and collaborative infrastructures. In this light, AI becomes not only a functional enabler but a structural mediator that allows for the realignment of institutional fields, the orchestration of multi-actor platforms, and the unlocking of path-dependent trajectories.

In sum, the conceptual model we propose encapsulates AI-enabled circular business transformation as a nested and dynamic system, where firm-level capabilities are both enabled by and contributors to broader systemic change. It provides a theoretical and analytical lens through which to understand how digital technologies and sustainability imperatives can intersect to produce new forms of organizational agency, value creation, and ecosystem governance.

8 Theoretical and Managerial Implications

This study provides several relevant contributions to ongoing debates at the intersection of digital transformation, circular economy, and organizational theory, particularly with respect to the dynamic capabilities framework. From a theoretical standpoint, our conceptualization of AI-enabled circular business transformation offers a nuanced and empirically grounded extension of dynamic capabilities theory into the sustainability domain, with implications for both foundational constructs and emergent research trajectories.

First, the findings advance the understanding of dynamic capabilities in sustainability-oriented contexts by demonstrating how AI not only supports sensing, seizing, and reconfiguring, but also transforms their ontological and operational dimensions. In traditional conceptualizations, dynamic capabilities have often been discussed in terms of internal learning and resource reallocation [4, 35]. Our study shows that in the context of circular innovation, these capabilities acquire a networked and systemic nature, in which AI acts as a transversal enabler of ecosystemic cognition and coordination. This reframes dynamic capabilities not simply as firm-bound processes, but as relational and infrastructural dynamics that unfold across platforms, institutions, and stakeholder interfaces.

Second, the research contributes to literature on circular business model innovation (CBMI) by introducing the role of AI as both a technical enabler and institutional disruptor. While prior studies have focused on design principles, value loops, or performance metrics in CBMs [1, 36], our model emphasizes the transformative interplay between digital infrastructures and circular logics. Specifically, it demonstrates how AI facilitates not only optimization (e.g., in waste flows or material efficiency) but paradigm shifts in how value is defined, who co-creates it, and how legitimacy is constructed. This shifts the debate from circular design to circular governance—a dimension still underexplored in current scholarship.

Third, the study enriches the growing body of work on ecosystem-oriented management and institutional theory. It shows how AI contributes to the reconfiguration of firms' roles within institutional fields [30], allowing them to act as orchestrators, brokers, or even institutional entrepreneurs. Particularly in Case C, we observed how AI supported the emergence of new governance arrangements that transcended traditional hierarchies and fostered participatory, inclusive, and transparent modalities of interaction. This suggests that AI can be theorized as an institutional actor in itself—one that conditions the field, configures relationships, and stabilizes new normative frames.

Finally, our findings offer methodological implications for qualitative research in management and sustainability. By adopting a narrative and abductive case study approach, we highlight the value of rich, contextualized insights in unpacking the complex, recursive, and often ambiguous processes of transformation. In doing so, we respond to calls for more interpretive and processual studies in organizational sustainability [37, 38], and demonstrate how conceptual models can emerge inductively from grounded fieldwork rather than deductively from theoretical assumptions alone.

From a managerial perspective, the study underscores the necessity of aligning AI deployment with broader strategic, organizational, and cultural transformations. Firms seeking to engage in circular business innovation cannot treat AI as a plug-and-play solution; rather, its successful integration requires new forms of cross-functional collaboration, a culture of experimentation, and inclusive governance structures capable of mediating between technological opportunities and societal expectations.

In particular, managers must cultivate reflexive leadership capabilities that allow them to question prevailing assumptions, reframe performance metrics, and engage with external stakeholders in a transparent and participatory manner. AI tools should be seen not merely as cost-reduction instruments but as platforms for strategic dialog, interorganizational learning, and ecosystem orchestration. As the cases illustrate, it is precisely through this dialogic use of AI that firms can co-create shared value and position themselves as trusted actors in circular transitions.

Moreover, the study reveals that data governance and ethical infrastructure are not ancillary but central to the success of AI in circular contexts. Issues such as data sovereignty, algorithmic bias, and stakeholder inclusion need to be addressed upfront and not as afterthoughts. The experience of Case C, with its municipal AI observatory and citizen engagement mechanisms, exemplifies how AI implementation must be embedded in deliberative and accountable governance frameworks.

For policymakers and institutional actors, the findings suggest the importance of designing supportive regulatory and funding environments that incentivize experimentation, interorganizational data sharing, and circular ecosystem building. AI's potential in enabling sustainability will remain underrealized unless there is an institutional scaffolding that legitimizes its use, aligns it with public interest, and mitigates risks of concentration, opacity, and exclusion.

In this regard, policy frameworks such as the EU's Green Deal, the Circular Economy Action Plan, and the Artificial Intelligence Act can play a crucial role in setting the direction of innovation. However, they must be complemented by local-level experimentation platforms, multi-stakeholder innovation hubs, and capacity-building programs that equip firms and public actors with the skills, tools, and mindsets required to navigate the AI–circularity nexus.

9 Conclusions

This paper examines how Artificial Intelligence supports firms' dynamic capabilities to drive circular business model innovation. Using a qualitative, narrative-driven multiple-case study approach, the research offers both conceptual and empirical insights into how AI enables organizations to break free from path dependencies, reconfigure routines and value logics, and integrate circularity into their strategic and operational frameworks. The analysis shows that AI functions across all three areas of dynamic capabilities—sensing, seizing, and reconfiguring—not just as a technology but also as a catalyst for knowledge, organization, and institutional change.

Based on three Italian case studies in manufacturing and public services, we developed a comprehensive model of AI-enabled Circular Business Transformation. This model highlights the recursive, ecosystemic, and co-evolutionary nature of the transition. It illustrates that successful circular innovation depends not only on technology but on the synergy between digital infrastructure, organizational agility, and governance across the ecosystem. AI plays a key role in this process by managing real-time data, supporting cross-boundary collaboration, and fostering continuous learning.

Our findings emphasize that circular transformation is a profound systemic shift rather than a simple move from "less bad" to "more efficient" models. It involves rethinking how value is created, shared, and validated. In this sense, AI can be a powerful driver of sustainability-driven innovation, especially when embedded within inclusive, participatory, and reflective governance structures. Overall, the study offers both a theoretical perspective and practical guidance for scholars, managers, and policymakers seeking to leverage AI's transformative potential for advancing the circular economy.

10 Limitations and Future Research Directions

Like any qualitative research, the findings of this study should be interpreted within the limitations of its methodology and scope. Firstly, it examines a small number of cases within the Italian industrial ecosystem. While selecting diverse organizations from different sectors adds variation and insight, it also limits the broad applicability of the results. Future studies could test or expand the model in other countries, industries, or cultural contexts to evaluate its wider relevance. Secondly, the narrative approach—effective at capturing the complexity and timelines of transformation—relies on interpretive reconstructions of events, practices, and meanings.

Despite using triangulation and member checks to ensure trustworthiness, the findings remain influenced by the researcher's interpretation and may reflect specific organizational perspectives. Additional studies using mixed methods or longitudinal ethnography could provide deeper insights. Thirdly, while AI is identified as a key enabler of circular transformation, the study does not analyze the technical architectures, data governance, or algorithmic designs behind the AI systems. Future research could explore the micro-level configurations of AI tools and their socio-technical interactions, examining how technological choices influence organizational dynamics and sustainability outcomes.

Lastly, the focus is on internal and ecosystem-level dynamics, with less emphasis on global value chains, geopolitical power, or planetary boundaries. Although the conceptual model addresses institutional responsiveness and ecosystem adaptation, it does not fully consider macro-structural conditions that impact or limit circular innovation. Incorporating these factors could enhance the theoretical framework.

The study's findings suggest several paths for further research, both theoretical and empirical. One area of exploration is the relationship between AI capabilities and organizational learning in circular innovation—how firms develop absorptive capacity and dynamic routines to translate AI insights into action, and how leadership, culture, and change management influence this process.

Another important direction is examining the temporal aspects of AI-driven transformation through longitudinal case studies, which can reveal how AI affects not just the pace but also the evolution of firm identity, stakeholder relations, and legitimacy over time. Such research might adopt process or practice-based approaches to better understand AI's performative role. Comparative research could analyze how different institutional setups and policies influence the adoption and impact of AI in circular transitions. For example, the role of regional innovation ecosystems, digital infrastructure, or circular economy regulations can be studied across countries, sectors, or governance models. Investigating the ethical and political dimensions of AI use—such as data justice, bias, and inclusion—is also crucial to ensure digital sustainability is equitable and transparent. How firms and policymakers design AI systems that are both effective and fair is an important question.

Lastly, interdisciplinary collaboration among management scholars, computer scientists, sustainability experts, and public officials could produce practical frameworks and tools—like diagnostic instruments, participatory design methods, or AI ethics protocols—that support sustainable, AI-enabled circular practices.

Acknowledgments This study was funded by the European Union—NextGenerationEu, in the framework of the GRINS—Growing, Resilient, INclusive and Sustainable project (Codice Progetto MUR: PE00000018—CUP E63C22002140007). The views and opinions expressed in this study are solely those of the authors and do not necessarily reflect those of the European Union. The European Union is not responsible for them.

References

1. Geissdoerfer, M., Morioka, S.N., de Carvalho, M.M., Evans, S.: Business models and supply chains for the circular economy. J. Clean. Prod. **190**, 712–721 (2018)
2. Bocken, N.M.P., Rana, P., Short, S.W.: Value mapping for sustainable business thinking. J. Ind. Prod. Eng. **33**(5), 308–320 (2016)
3. Frishammar, J., Parida, V., Inigo, E.A.: Circular business model transformation: a roadmap for incumbent firms. Calif. Manage. Rev. **63**(2), 53–77 (2021)
4. Teece, D.J.: Explicating dynamic capabilities: the nature and microfoundations of (sustainable) enterprise performance. Strateg. Manag. J. **28**(13), 1319–1350 (2007)
5. Lewandowski, M.: Designing the business models for circular economy—toward the conceptual framework. Sustainability. **8**(1), 43 (2016)

6. Vergne, J.P., Durand, R.: The missing link between the theory and empirics of path dependence. J. Manag. Stud. **47**(4), 736–759 (2010)
7. Lehtimäki, H., Piispanen, V.V., Henttonen, K.: Strategic decisions related to circular business model in a forerunner company. South Asian J. Bus. Manag. Cases. **9**(3), 402–412 (2020)
8. Ritala, P., Aarikka-Stenroos, L., Thomas, L.D.W.: Ecosystem perspective on the circular economy: conceptual foundations and implications. J. Bus. Res. **148**, 599–613 (2023)
9. Sjödin, D., Parida, V., Kohtamäki, M.: Artificial intelligence enabling circular business model innovation in digital servitization. Technol. Forecast. Soc. Change. **197**, 122903 (2023)
10. Kohtamäki, M., Rabetino, R., Einola, S., Parida, V.: Managing digital servitization toward smart solutions. Ind. Market. Manag. **105**, 253–269 (2022)
11. Dubey, R., Gunasekaran, A., Childe, S.J.: Big data analytics and artificial intelligence pathway to operational performance under the effects of entrepreneurial orientation and environmental dynamism. Br. J. Manag. **30**(2), 341–361 (2019)
12. Maguire, S., Hardy, C., Lawrence, T.B.: Institutional entrepreneurship in emerging fields. Acad. Manage. J. **47**(5), 657–679 (2004)
13. Greenwood, R., Raynard, M., Kodeih, F., Micelotta, E.R., Lounsbury, M.: Institutional complexity and organizational responses. Acad. Manag. Ann. **5**(1), 317–371 (2011)
14. David, P.A.: Clio and the economics of QWERTY. Am. Econ. Rev. **75**(2), 332–337 (1985)
15. Arthur, W.B.: Competing technologies, increasing returns, and lock-in by historical events. Econ. J. **99**(394), 116–131 (1989)
16. Sydow, J., Schreyögg, G., Koch, J.: Organizational path dependence: opening the black box. Acad. Manage. Rev. **34**(4), 689–709 (2009)
17. Ranta, V., Aarikka-Stenroos, L., Ritala, P., Mäkinen, S.J.: Exploring institutional drivers and barriers of the circular economy: a cross-regional comparison. J. Clean. Prod. **286**, 125484 (2021)
18. Teece, D.J.: Business models and dynamic capabilities. Long Range Plann. **51**(1), 40–49 (2018)
19. Teece, D.J., Pisano, G., Shuen, A.: Dynamic capabilities and strategic management. Strateg. Manag. J. **18**(7), 509–533 (1997)
20. Kindström, D., Kowalkowski, C.: Service innovation in product-centric firms: a multidimensional business model perspective. J. Bus. Ind. Market. **29**(2), 96–111 (2013)
21. Nonaka, I., Takeuchi, H.: The Knowledge-Creating Company: How Japanese Companies Create the Dynamics of Innovation. Oxford University Press, Oxford (1995)
22. Czarniawska, B.: Narrating the Organization: Dramas of Institutional Identity. University of Chicago Press, Chicago (1997)
23. Gabriel, Y.: Storytelling in Organizations: Facts, Fictions, and Fantasies. Oxford University Press, Oxford (2000)
24. Langley, A.: Strategies for theorizing from process data. Acad. Manage. Rev. **24**(4), 691–710 (1999)
25. Wamba, S.F., Dubey, R., Gunasekaran, A., Akter, S.: The performance effects of big data analytics and supply chain ambidexterity: the moderating effect of environmental dynamism. Int. J. Prod. Econ. **222**, 107498 (2020)
26. Dubey, R., Gunasekaran, A., Childe, S.J., Bryde, D.J., Roubaud, D.: Big data analytics and artificial intelligence pathway to business performance. Ann. Oper. Res. **293**, 287–322 (2020)
27. Dubey, R., Bryde, D.J., Roubaud, D., et al.: Artificial intelligence and big data analytics in humanitarian supply chains: Enabling visibility and coordination under conditions of risk and uncertainty. Int. J. Prod. Res. **59**(11), 3439–3467 (2021)
28. Geissdoerfer, M., Savaget, P., Bocken, N.M.P., Hultink, E.J.: The circular economy—a new sustainability paradigm? J. Clean. Prod. **143**, 757–768 (2017)
29. Barney, J.B.: Firm resources and sustained competitive advantage. J. Manag. **17**(1), 99–120 (1991)
30. Porter, M.E., Kramer, M.R.: Creating shared value. Harv. Bus. Rev. **89**(1–2), 62–77 (2011)
31. Jacobides, M.G., Cennamo, C., Gawer, A.: Towards a theory of ecosystems. Strateg. Manag. J. **39**(8), 2255–2276 (2018)

32. Lichtenthaler, U.: Beyond open innovation: the shifting frontier of innovation management. R&D Manag. **47**(3), 371–389 (2017)
33. George, G., Merrill, R.K., Schillebeeckx, S.J.D.: Digital sustainability and entrepreneurship: How digital innovations are helping tackle climate change and sustainable development. Entrepr. Theory Pract. **45**(5), 999–1027 (2021)
34. Ghobakhloo, M.: Industry 4.0, digitization, and opportunities for sustainability. J. Clean. Prod. **252**, 119869 (2020)
35. Shrestha, Y.R., Ben-Menahem, S.M., Krogh, G.V.: Organizational decision-making structures in the age of artificial intelligence. Calif. Manage. Rev. **63**(4), 85–113 (2021)
36. Lüdeke-Freund, F., Gold, S., Bocken, N.M.P.: A review and typology of circular business model patterns. J. Ind. Ecol. **23**(1), 36–61 (2019)
37. Langley, A.: Process studies of change in organization and management: unveiling temporality, activity, and flow. Acad. Manage. J. **50**(1), 1–13 (2007)
38. Cornelissen, J.P.: Editor's comments: developing propositions, a process perspective. Acad. Manage. Rev. **42**(1), 1–9 (2017)

Leveraging AI for Automation in ESG Reporting

Arnesh Telukdarie, Musawenkosi H. L. Nyathi, and Maddubailu Suresh Sai Vinod

Abstract Environmental, Social, and Governance (ESG) reporting has become a cornerstone for fostering sustainable business practices and improving transparency. However, manual ESG data collection, inconsistent reporting standards and risks of greenwashing undermine the efforts to achieve global sustainability. This study explores the transformative role of Artificial Intelligence (AI) in automating ESG reporting by standardizing and automating the extraction of ESG metrics from company reports listed on the Johannesburg Stock Exchange (JSE) and the National Stock Exchange of India (NSE). Using advanced Natural Language Processing (NLP) techniques and a fine-tuned DistilRoBERTa model, the research demonstrates high accuracy in categorizing ESG disclosures. The findings highlight how an AI-driven approach can facilitate uniform ESG reporting, reduce bias, and enhance the reliability of sustainability assessments. These advancements offer potential to guide investments toward responsible businesses and achieve the Sustainable Development Goals (SDGs). Standardized automation in ESG disclosures ensures equitable evaluation of companies worldwide, promoting accountability and transparency.

Keywords Artificial Intelligence (AI) · ESG automation · NLP · Standardization · Sustainable Development Goals (SDGs) · Sustainability Reporting

A. Telukdarie (✉) · M. H. L. Nyathi
Johannesburg Business School, University of Johannesburg, Johannesburg, South Africa
e-mail: arnesht@uj.ac.za; musawenkosin@uj.ac.za

M. S. S. Vinod
Sri Sathya Institute of Higher Learning, Brindavan Campus, Kadugodi, Bengaluru, India
e-mail: mssaivinod@sssihl.edu.in

N. Omrani et al. (eds.), *Human-Machine Synergy and the Digital Future - Exploring Collaboration and Competition Volume 1*, Springer Proceedings in Business and Economics, https://doi.org/10.1007/978-3-032-21347-1_17

1 Introduction

The increasing urgency of addressing global environmental and social challenges has increased the significance of Environmental, Social and Governance (ESG) principles in promoting sustainable development [1]. ESG metrics provide a framework for evaluating corporate sustainability, enabling investors and stakeholders to hold businesses accountable for their environmental and social impacts while promoting responsible governance. Despite their importance, ESG reporting remains plagued by challenges and inconsistencies, with data often being fragmented, incomplete, or prone to manipulation through practices such as greenwashing. This lack of standardization poses significant challenges to achieving global sustainability goals and assessing corporate contributions equitably [2]. Artificial Intelligence (AI) has emerged as a transformative tool to address these limitations by automating ESG data collection and analysis [3]. Through advanced technologies such as Natural Language Processing (NLP), AI systems can extract, organize, and standardize ESG data from diverse sources with precision and efficiency. Such capabilities reduce subjectivity in assessments, improve comparability across industries, and minimize the risks of greenwashing [4]. This study focuses on developing an AI-driven system to enhance ESG reporting by utilizing a centralized data management framework. Specifically, the research applies NLP techniques to extract and process ESG disclosures from corporate reports of companies listed on the Johannesburg Stock Exchange (JSE) and the National Stock Exchange of India (NSE). By employing the DistilRoBERTa model for ESG classification, this system aims to ensure transparency, consistency, and comparability in ESG disclosures. The paper explores the current state of ESG reporting and the role of AI in overcoming the challenges associated with ESG reporting, furthermore, the processes for data collection, model fine-tuning, and automated system development are also outlined. The findings present the outcomes of the AI-based ESG framework, followed by a discussion and implications on its impact. Finally, in conclusion, a highlight of the study's contributions and areas for future exploration, it executed.

2 Literature Review

2.1 *Sustainability and ESG Principles*

Sustainability has become a pivotal concept shaping policies, business strategies, and technological innovations to address global socio-economic challenges. ESG principles, derived from sustainability goals, serve as a framework to guide organizations toward ethical practices, responsible governance, and positive social and environmental impacts [5]. These principles align closely with the SDGs, emphasizing areas such as climate change mitigation action, social justice, and economic inclusivity [6]. Investor preferences have increasingly shifted toward companies that demonstrate strong ESG performance, as sustainable practices are seen as critical for long-term resilience and profitability. However, interpreting these principles into actionable metrics remains challenging [7]. Organizations must define clear, measurable indicators, in alignment with their sustainability goals while also addressing the evolving expectations of stakeholders and regulators. The double materiality concept that considers both societal and financial, offers a comprehensive approach for integrating ESG principles into business strategies, enabling companies to meet stakeholder expectations and contribute toward global sustainability efforts [8].

2.2 Challenges in ESG Data Collection, Analysis, and Standardization

The current state of ESG data collection poses significant challenges, due to its reliance on manual methods, which are time-intensive, human error prone, and often fail to collect all the information required for meaningful sustainability assessments [9]. Additionally, the lack of standardized metrics across industries and regions further complicates the process, leading to inconsistencies and potential biases in ESG evaluations [10]. The integrity of ESG reporting is seriously threatened by greenwashing, which is the practice of emphasizing positive data while hiding negative effects. Without standardized and automated processes, companies may manipulate disclosures to create a false impression of sustainability, weakening stakeholder trust [11]. Unlike financial reporting, which adheres to standardized global frameworks, ESG reporting lacks a universal standard, leading to significant variations in data quality, transparency, and comparability. Multiple frameworks, inclusive of the Global Reporting Initiative (GRI), Sustainability Accounting Standards Board (SASB), and Task Force on Climate-Related Financial Disclosures (TCFD), provide guidelines for ESG disclosures, but their varying methodologies make it more cumbersome for business organizations to provide consistent and useful data [10, 12].

2.3 Role of Artificial Intelligence in ESG Reporting

AI has emerged as a revolutionary technology for addressing the shortcomings and inconsistencies in ESG reporting [13]. By automating the extraction and analysis of ESG data, AI systems can significantly enhance the accuracy, transparency, and comparability of disclosures [14, 15]. Techniques such as NLP are particularly effective in processing unstructured data from diverse sources, including sustainability reports, corporate disclosures, and social media content. These applications address challenges such as standardization, bias reduction, and efficiency in processing large datasets [14, 16, 17]. For instance, Visalli et al. (2023) demonstrated how AI workflows could extract ESG data from diverse document formats, including PDFs and unstructured text, reducing manual effort and error rates. Furthermore, AI-driven systems facilitate the identification of key performance indicators (KPIs) and quantification of ESG metrics, enabling comparability across organizations and industries. By automating repetitive and labor-intensive tasks, these tools free up resources for deeper analysis and strategic decision-making [18]. Pre-trained transformer models such as BERT, RoBERTa, and DistilRoBERTa have been shown to perform well in ESG classification tasks [19]. DistilRoBERTa is a streamlined version of the RoBERTa model that provides a faster and lighter architecture while retaining most of its predictive potential. It is well-suited for ESG categorization because of its computational efficiency and good performance on small- to medium-sized text datasets, making it ideal for corporate sustainability scenarios with unstructured report formats. Companies can standardize their reporting procedures due to these models' ability to collect and classify ESG indicators [20].

2.4 Research Gap

Despite the advancements in AI applications for ESG reporting, significant research gaps remain. Current systems on ESG reporting often focus on historical data analysis, lacking capabilities for real-time monitoring or predictive analytics [21]. Additionally, most studies prioritize the development of AI models over addressing the integration challenges posed by disparate ESG frameworks [22]. Another critical gap lies in the automation of verification processes. While third-party verification enhances the credibility of ESG data, integrating such capabilities into AI-driven systems remains understudied. Furthermore, expanding the scope of automated systems to include non-traditional data sources, such as social media and news articles, could improve the scope of ESG analytics [23]. Thus, by addressing these gaps, future research can leverage AI to create more robust, adaptable, and reliable ESG reporting systems, fostering greater transparency and accountability in corporate sustainability practices [21, 22].

2.5 Theoretical Frameworks

The integration of AI into ESG reporting draws upon several theoretical frameworks that provide a foundation to understand the intersection of technology, stakeholder engagement, and corporate sustainability. These frameworks guide the design and application of automated ESG systems and offer insights into their implications for corporate strategy and sustainable development. These frameworks are outlined in the following paragraphs' sections.

Stakeholder Theory Stakeholder theory places emphasis on knowledge that businesses must balance the different stakeholders' interests, including investors, employees, customers, regulators, and communities, to achieve long-term value creation [24]. This theory is particularly relevant to ESG reporting, as stakeholders increasingly demand transparent and reliable disclosures about a company's sustainability performance. By automating ESG data collection and standardization, the proposed system supports informed decision-making and strengthens stakeholder trust [25]. For example, the system's ability to extract and classify indicators such as carbon emissions, employee diversity, and board governance aligns with the priorities of various stakeholder groups. This fosters accountability and ensures that businesses remain aligned with societal expectations and regulatory requirements.

Dynamic Capabilities Theory Dynamic capabilities theory refers to the importance of an organization's ability to adapt and transform in response to changing environmental conditions [26]. In the context of ESG reporting, this theory underscores the need for businesses to develop systems that can efficiently manage and respond to evolving sustainability metrics and regulatory demands [27]. The proposed AI-driven ESG system reflects this adaptability by automating the extraction and processing of data from multiple sources, including annual reports, sustainability disclosures, and external frameworks. Its flexibility to integrate new indicators and frameworks enables organizations to remain responsive to emerging trends, such as climate action and social equity.

Technology Acceptance Model (TAM) The TAM explores how users perceive and adopt new technologies based on factors such as ease of use and perceived usefulness [28]. In the case of AI-driven ESG reporting, the model's automation capabilities reduce the manual workload associated with data collection and processing, making it more appealing to corporate users and sustainability analysts [14]. The system incorporating SQL databases and Python-based automation scripts ensures accessibility and efficiency. Moreover, its predictive capabilities enhance perceived usefulness by providing forward-looking insights into corporate sustainability performance, enabling users to anticipate and mitigate risks effectively.

Therefore, by integrating these theoretical foundations, the study provides a comprehensive understanding of how AI-driven systems can transform ESG reporting. These frameworks not only validate the system's design but also emphasize its potential to enhance corporate accountability, stakeholder engagement, and sustainable development. Additionally, by providing a lens through which corporate transparency, adaptability, and technology adoption may be critically evaluated in the ESG space, these theoretical foundations help to explain the interpretation of results. They enhance the study's conceptual rigor and practical usefulness by explicitly connecting the theories to the methods and anticipated results.

3 Methods

3.1 Research Design

The research methodology used for implementing AI techniques for automating ESG reporting utilizes the above-mentioned theoretical frameworks, which collectively reinforce the alignment of the AI-driven ESG system with the Stakeholder theory supporting the system's role in addressing societal and environmental expectations; while dynamic capabilities theory ensures its adaptability to changing sustainability challenges. TAM enhances its usability and adoption, promoting widespread application across industries and regions. Thus, the method adopted a mixed-methods approach, integrating qualitative and quantitative methods to develop and evaluate the ESG reporting system. The development of the ESG reporting system is outlined in detail through the sequential steps of the research methodology below.

3.2 Methodology

The quantitative methodology process (see Fig. 1) involved data collection, processing, and ESG data integration from different sources to develop an automated system for efficient data extraction and standardization. The qualitative method (see Fig. 2) highlights the fine-tuning of AI transformer models to improve classification accuracy for ESG metrics.

3.3 Data Collection

The dataset included ESG disclosures from companies listed on the JSE and the NSE. Primary sources included sustainability reports, annual integrated reports, and publicly available disclosures from corporate websites. Secondary sources, such as rating agencies for example MSCI, Sustainalytics, and Bloomberg, were utilized to validate KPIs and ensure comprehensive coverage of ESG metrics. Automated web-scraping techniques (see Fig. 3) were used to extract data from online sources. Ethical scraping practices were followed, including adherence to website policies and implementation of rate limiting to avoid overloading servers. NLP libraries, such as SpaCy and PDFPlumber, were used to process and extract text data from reports. The extracted data was organized into structured tables containing columns for company name, ESG category, indicators, KPI values, units, and reporting year. These tables were stored in a SQL database for efficient data management and subsequent analysis.

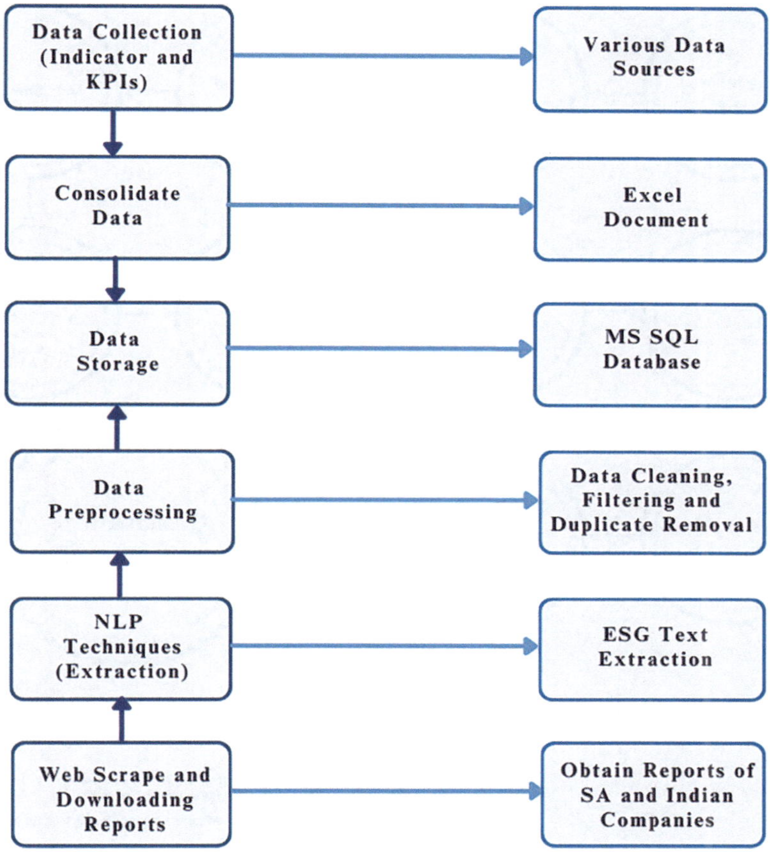

Fig. 1 ESG automation methodology

3.4 Data Processing, Standardization and Automated System Development

A crucial step in the methodology involved standardizing the extracted ESG metrics to ensure comparability across companies and industries. Units of measurement, such as kilowatt-hours (kWh) and tons of CO_2, were converted into standardized formats to eliminate discrepancies. Duplicate entries were removed to maintain data integrity. The consolidated data was categorized into three ESG pillars: Environmental, Social, and Governance. Each pillar contained specific indicators and their associated KPIs, with relationships represented using an entity-relationship diagram. This structured representation facilitated the organization of data into SQL tables, enabling efficient querying and analysis. To develop the automated system, a Python-based system was developed to automate ESG data management, utilizing Pandas and Pyodbc libraries for data manipulation and SQL integration. The system

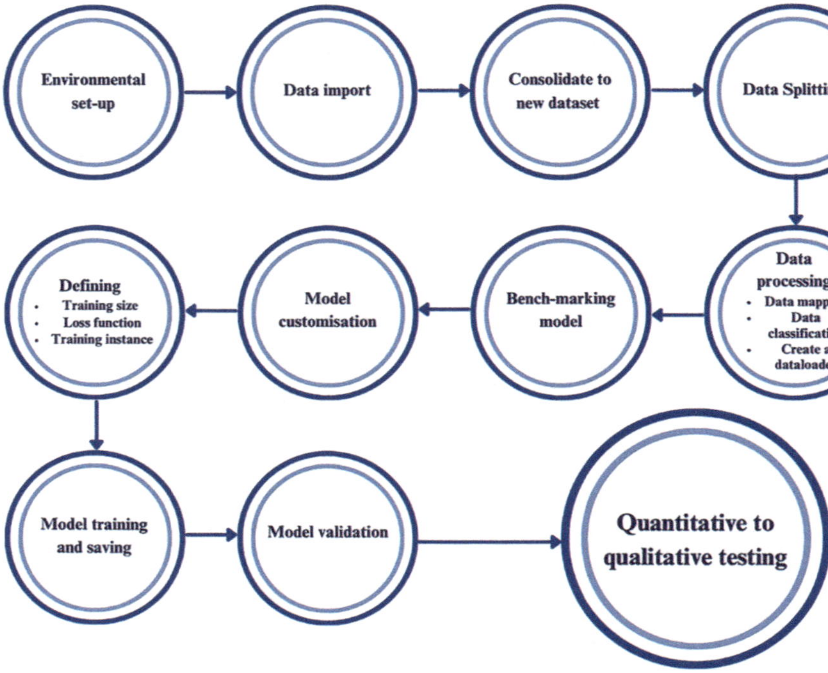

Fig. 2 ESG category transformer models training and fine-tuning

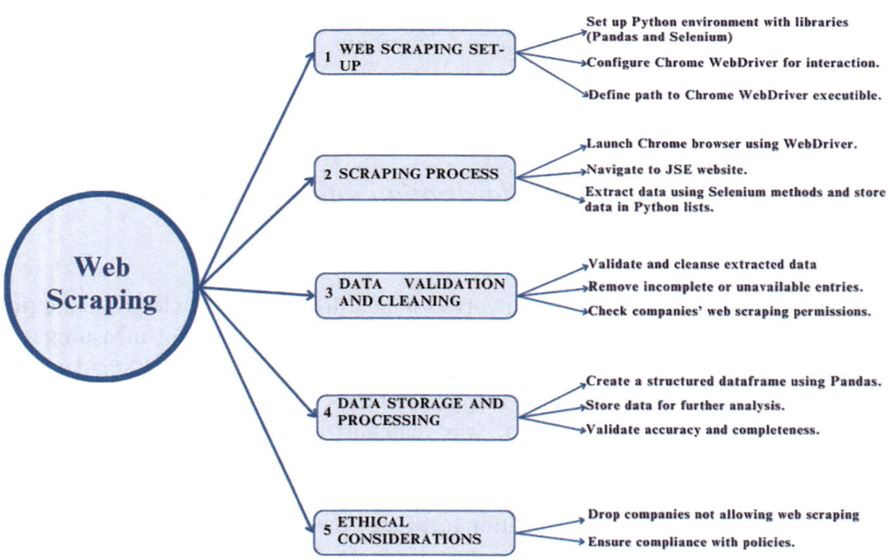

Fig. 3 Automated web-scraping method

Table 1 Model fine-tuning process

Model step	Process
Data preparation	ESG data was split into training (90%) and validation (10%) sets. Each record was labeled based on the presence of predefined ESG keywords derived from frameworks like GRI and SASB
Hyperparameter optimization	Parameters such as learning rate, batch size, and training epochs were optimized to enhance model performance
Keyword expansion	Keywords were expanded by consolidating predefined ESG indicators with those extracted from the data. This ensured comprehensive coverage of ESG-related terms

was designed to extract ESG data from various sources using web scraping. Data to store various entities such as sectors, companies, indicators, KPIs, units, countries and regions were processed and stored in a centralized MS SQL database.

3.5 Model Fine-Tuning

The DistilRoBERTa model, a pre-trained transformer-based NLP model, was fine-tuned for ESG classification and its process is outlined in Table 1. The fine-tuning process included tokenization of categorical variables, such as company names and KPIs, to enable the model to process textual inputs effectively. Batch processing techniques were employed to handle large datasets efficiently, with performance metrics including accuracy, precision, recall, and F1-score used to evaluate model performance.

Validation of the automated system involved two stages to include model validation whereby the performance of the fine-tuned model was assessed on unseen validation data. Confusion matrices were generated to evaluate true positives, true negatives, false positives, and false negatives. Metrics such as precision and F1-score provided insights into classification accuracy. Then, test the end-to-end system using web-scraped ESG data to evaluate its ability to classify and quantify ESG indicators. Results were cross verified with manually curated datasets to ensure reliability and accuracy.

4 Findings

4.1 Automated EG Data Extraction

Using web-scraping techniques and NLP tools such as regular expressions, the study successfully extracted ESG-related data from sustainability and annual integrated reports of 128 companies listed on the JSE and the NSE. The extracted data included 3023 KPIs across the Environmental, Social, and Governance pillars.

CompanyID	CompanyName	Indicator	KPI	KPIValue	Unit	Year
39	Adcock Ingram	Natural capital	Electricity generation - Generators	3 374 972	kWh	2023
40	Adcock Ingram	Natural capital	Electricity generation - Total electricity usage	56 388 770	kWh	2023
41	Adcock Ingram	Waste	Waste to landfill - Non-hazardous	672	tonnes	2023
42	Adcock Ingram	Waste	Recycled waste - Non-hazardous	3 501	tonnes	2023
43	Adcock Ingram	Waste	Recycled waste - Non-hazardous	84	%	2023
44	African Rainbow Minerals (ARM)	Emissions	Scope 1 and 2 emissions	1.80	tCO2e	2023
45	African Rainbow Minerals (ARM)	Energy	Operational energy consumption	7 693 348	GJ	2023
46	African Rainbow Minerals (ARM)	Energy	Electricity consumption	1 331 000 000	kWh	2023
47	African Rainbow Minerals (ARM)	Energy	Group diesel consumption	79 200 000	litres	2023
48	African Rainbow Minerals (ARM)	Water	Operational water withdrawal	18 300 000 000	litres	2023
49	African Rainbow Minerals (ARM)	Water	Water reuse efficiency	78	%	2023
50	African Rainbow Minerals (ARM)	Water	Water consumption	733 063 000	litres	2023
51	African Rainbow Minerals (ARM)	Material	Hazardous waste disposed	4 091	tonnes	2023
52	African Rainbow Minerals (ARM)	Waste	Recycled waste (excluding slag recycled)	5 869	tonnes	2023
53	AfroCentric Group	Environmental	Water consumption	31 751 000	litres	2023
54	AfroCentric Group	Environmental	Electricity consumption	7 803 000	kWh	2023
55	AfroCentric Group	Environmental	Diesel (used in generators)	290 497	litres	2023
56	AfroCentric Group	GHG	Calculated total GHG inventory	15 246	tCO2e	2023
57	AfroCentric Group	Emissions	Direct GHG emissions	813	tCO2e	2023

Fig. 4 Sample of the extracted Environmental data

These KPIs were categorized and stored in a centralized SQL database for further processing. Figure 4 shows a sample of the extracted data from the Environmental section.

For the Environmental pillar, 68 indicators such as energy consumption, emissions, and water usage were identified. The Social pillar included 78 indicators covering employee diversity, health and safety, and community engagement. The Governance pillar comprised 48 indicators, focusing on board diversity, executive compensation, and regulatory compliance (Table 2).

4.2 Standardization of ESG Metrics

Standardization efforts ensured consistency in units of measurement, allowing for seamless comparison across industries and regions. For example, emissions data reported in various units, such as metric tons of CO2 or kilotons of CO2 equivalent, was converted into a uniform format. Similarly, employee diversity metrics were standardized by aligning data across companies and ensuring consistent definitions for indicators such as gender representation and inclusion of differently abled individuals.

4.3 Model Performance and Predictive Insights

The fine-tuned DistilRoBERTa model demonstrated robust performance in classifying ESG data. Key results from the model's training and validation process demonstrated that the Environmental Model achieved an accuracy of 99.1% with an F1-score of 98.9%. The model effectively identified indicators such as emissions reduction and renewable energy usage. Social Model performed moderately with an

Table 2 ESG indicators used to extract data from annual and sustainability reports

Social		Environmental		Governance
Age	Discrimination	Adaptation	Impacts	Board of Directors
Culture	Diversity	Agricultural	Land Use	Corporate Governance
Race	Donation	Air Quality	Methane	Executive Compensation
Access	Education	Animal	Mitigation	Shareholder Rights
Accessibility	Emotion	Atmosphere	N_2O	Audit Committee
Accident	Employee benefit	Biodiversity	Nature	Transparency
Accountability	Employee development	Biomass	Nitrogen	Disclosure
Awareness	Employment benefit	Capture	Ocean	Ethics
Behavior	Empower	CH_4	Ozone	Anti-Corruption
Charity	Equal	Climate	Plant	Code of Conduct
Civil	ESG	CO_2	Pollution	Whistleblower Protection
Code of conduct	Ethics	Coastal	Rainfall	Risk Management
Community	Ethnic	Concentration	Renewable	Compliance
Consumer protection	Fairness	Conservation	Resource	Legal compliance
Cyber security	Family	Consumption	Seasonal	Regulatory Compliance
Data privacy	Female	Degree	Sediment	Data Privacy
Data protection	Financial protection	Depletion	Snow	Cybersecurity
Data security	Gap	Dioxide	Soil	Diversity and Inclusion
Demographic	Gender	Diversity	Solar	Gender Diversity
Disability	Health	Drought	Sources	Employee Relations
Human	Respecting	Ecology	Sustainability	Human Rights
Inclusion	Retirement benefit	Ecosystems	Temperature	Labor Practices
Information security	Safety	Emission	Thermal	Health and Safety
Injury	Salary	Emissions	Environmental Impact	Supply Chain Management
Leave	Social	Energy	Tropical	Stakeholder Engagement
LGBT	Society	Environment	Waste	Community Relations
Mental well-being	Supply chain transparency	Environmental	Water	Philanthropy
Parity	Supportive	Flood	Environments	Political Contributions
Pay equity	Talent	Trees		Lobbying

(continued)

Table 2 (continued)

Social		Environmental		Governance
Peace	Volunteer	Forest	Circular Economy	Sustainable Development Goals (SDGs)
Pension benefit	Wage	Fossil	Sustainable Sourcing	Climate Change Governance
Philanthropy	Welfare	Fuel		Intellectual Property Rights
Poverty	Well-being	Fuels		Energy Efficiency
Privacy	Well-being	Gas		Fair Competition
Product quality	Wellness	Gases		Product Responsibility
Product safety	Women	GHG		Supply Chain Ethics
Promotion	Workforce	Global Warming		Responsible Investment
Quality of life	Working conditions	Green		Quality Management
Religion	Customer Satisfaction	Greenhouse		
Respectful		Hydrogen		

accuracy of 63.7% and an F1-score of 38.9%. Challenges included variations in reporting practices and limited data for certain indicators, such as employee well-being and community engagement. The Governance Model recorded an accuracy of 99.2% and an F1-score of 98.8%, successfully identifying indicators such as board diversity and compliance metrics. Confusion matrices of the models are shown below to demonstrate their validity of the model's accuracy in its predictions (see Fig. 5).

The trained models were tested on previously unseen web-scraped data, enabling accurate predictions of ESG metrics. For instance, the environmental model predicted the amount of CO2 emissions for companies in the basic materials sector, while the governance model accurately quantified board diversity for companies in the financial services sector. These predictive capabilities demonstrate the system's potential to handle real-world ESG data challenges, including the absence of explicit reporting standards and variations in disclosure practices.

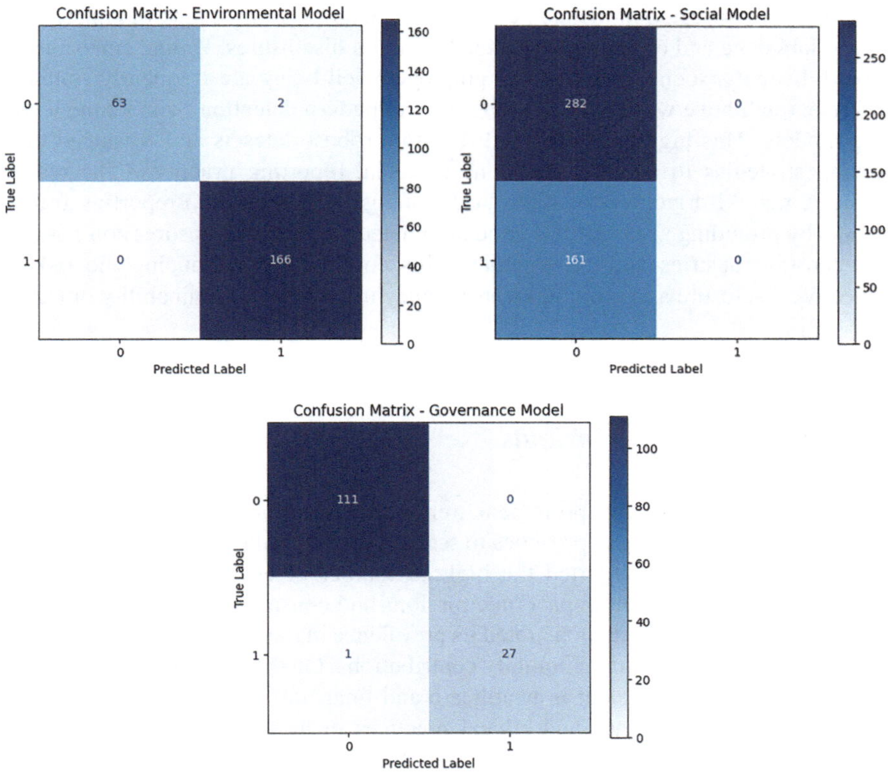

Fig. 5 Confusion matrices of the ESG models

5 Discussion and Implications

5.1 Addressing ESG Reporting Challenges Classification of ESG Data

This study demonstrates how AI may be used to address critical challenges in ESG reporting such as data fragmentation, inconsistent metrics, and risks of greenwashing. The system categorized KPIs into the three ESG pillars with high precision, enabling organized and insightful analysis. The automated system demonstrated scalability by efficiently processing large volumes of ESG data across diverse industries and regions. The integration of web scraping and NLP reduced manual data collection efforts, enabling timely updates to the ESG database. Furthermore, SQL-based storage and querying streamlined data access, making the system suitable for large-scale implementation. The fine-tuned DistilRoBERTa model demonstrated high accuracy in classifying Environmental and Governance indicators, showcasing its effectiveness in processing complex ESG disclosures. However, the

Social model revealed moderate performance, demonstrating a lack of consistency in the language and organization utilized in social disclosures. Unlike emissions or board diversity, social KPIs such as employee well-being are frequently stated in diverse, qualitative ways, posing a difficulty to pattern detection by machine learning models. This highlights the need for more robust datasets and advanced fine-tuning strategies to address variations in social reporting practices. The results indicate that AI-driven systems can bridge the gap between ESG reporting frameworks by providing a standardized and automated solution that ensures comparability across industries and geographies. This contributes to reducing the risk of selective disclosure and promotes transparency in corporate sustainability practices [13, 29].

5.2 Sector-Specific Insights

Sectoral analysis revealed prominent trends in ESG practices, underscoring the importance of modifying approaches to sector-specific challenges. For instance, the basic materials sector reported the highest number of environmental indicators, reflecting their significant impact on emissions and consumption of resources. The financial services sector demonstrated its prevalence in the social metrics, highlighting employee welfare and community contributions. On the other hand, governance metrics were most prevalent in healthcare and financial services, highlighting the critical role of compliance and ethical practices in these sectors. These insights underscore the need for sector-specific ESG frameworks to ensure significance and applicability.

5.3 Advancing AI in ESG Reporting

The incorporation of AI into ESG reporting represents a fundamental change in sustainability analytics. Processing unstructured data from various sources is enabled by the use of NLP and machine learning models which can enable real-time analysis and reducing reliance on static and delayed reports. By incorporating predictive capabilities, AI-driven systems can forecast future sustainability trends, empowering businesses and stakeholders to proactively address emerging challenges [15]. Despite these advancements, there is a need for further research to enhance AI models' capabilities, particularly in addressing social indicators where reporting practices are less uniform. Expanding the dataset to include non-traditional data sources, such as news articles and social media, can improve model accuracy and relevance. Additionally, incorporating third-party verification into the automated system can strengthen the credibility and reliability of ESG data.

5.4 Implementation Challenges

While the results show great promise, implementing AI-powered ESG reporting systems involves several challenges. First, integrating NLP techniques into various company reports necessitates substantial pre-processing and domain-specific customization. The layout, phrasing, and level of disclosures differ throughout reports, making consistent extraction difficult. Second, predictive analytics is strongly reliant on the availability of historical and structured ESG data, which are scarce or inconsistent across many organizations, particularly in emerging markets. Model training and fine-tuning necessitate careful management of skewed data, particularly in the social category. Finally, incorporating such AI systems into current business IT infrastructures may present interoperability, privacy, and data governance issues. Addressing these problems is critical for scaled uptake and long-term impact.

6 Implications

The system's ability to standardize and quantify ESG data has broader implications for global sustainability goals. By aligning corporate ESG practices with SDG indicators, the system facilitates the tracking of progress toward climate action, social equity, and board inclusivity. Standardized reporting ensures that all companies are evaluated on a same level, encouraging global adoption of sustainable practices and greater accountability.

The proposed system offers a scalable solution for monitoring corporate compliance with ESG standards. For regulators, it can utilize the standardized database to assess industry-wide adherence to sustainability principles, reducing the reliance on fragmented and inconsistent reporting practices. For investors, it can enhance ESG data transparency allowing them to make informed decisions by identifying companies with actual commitments to sustainability. The predictive capabilities of the system can also provide insights into corporate performance, enabling better risk assessment and alignment with long-term investment goals. Lastly, for organizations, the system can provide them with actionable insights into their sustainability performance by benchmarking against industry peers. Companies can use these insights to identify areas for improvement, build trust with stakeholders and enhance accountability.

7 Conclusion and Limitations

In conclusion, this study highlights the transformative potential of AI in transforming ESG reporting. By leveraging NLP techniques and a fine-tuned DistilRoBERTa model, the research developed a robust, scalable, and automated system capable of extracting, standardizing, and classifying ESG data. The system successfully addressed significant challenges in ESG reporting, including fragmented data, inconsistent metrics, and risks of greenwashing, thereby promoting transparency, accountability, and comparability in sustainability practices. Key findings demonstrated the system's ability to provide accurate classifications of Environmental and Governance indicators, with success in processing data from high-impact industries such as basic materials, healthcare, and financial services. While the Social model achieved moderate results, and identified areas for improvement, particularly in addressing inconsistencies in social reporting practices.

The study faced limitations, particularly in the availability and quality of social data, which affected the performance of the social model. Additionally, variations in reporting standards across regions posed challenges in achieving universal standardization. Future research must focus on integrating third-party verification systems and expanding datasets to include alternative data sources for a more comprehensive analysis. To improve the system's impact and applicability, the interpretation capabilities and incorporating real-time updates can be enhanced. By aligning corporate ESG metrics with global sustainability frameworks such as the SDGs, the developed system can facilitate more informed decision-making for regulators, investors, and corporations and respond effectively to emerging sustainability challenges.

References

1. Wu, Y., Tham, J.: The impact of environmental regulation, environment, social and government performance, and technological innovation on enterprise resilience under a green recovery. Heliyon. **9**, 10 (2023). https://doi.org/10.1016/j.heliyon.2023.e20278
2. Tînjală, D.-M., Pantea, L.M., Buglea, A.: 2010-2014: a comparative evolution of sustainability reporting and its Assurance in Europe and the U.S.A. Timis. J. Econ. Bus. **8**(s1), 48–69 (2015). https://doi.org/10.1515/tjeb-2015-0004
3. Patil, S.R., Jadhav, S.N., Nimbagal, S.: A study on ethical implications of using technology in ESG investing and ensuring unbiased decision making. Multidiscip. Sci. J. **6**(8) (2024). https://doi.org/10.31893/multiscience.2024153
4. Luccioni, A., Baylor, E., Duchene, N.: Analyzing sustainability reports using natural language processing. arXiv. preprint arXiv:2011.08073, Nov. 2020, [Online]. Available: http://arxiv.org/abs/2011.08073
5. Ahmad, H., Yaqub, M., Lee, S.H.: Environmental-, Social-, and Governance-Related Factors for Business Investment and Sustainability: a Scientometric Review of Global Trends. Feb. 01, 2024, Springer Science and Business Media B.V. https://doi.org/10.1007/s10668-023-02921-x
6. Junaedi, J.: Understanding the role of finance in sustainable development: a qualitative study on environmental, social, and governance (ESG) practices. Golden Ratio Finance Manag. **4**(2), 113–130 (2024). https://doi.org/10.52970/grfm.v4i2.422
7. Adams, C.A., Alhamood, A., He, X., Tian, J., Wang, L., Wang, Y.: The double-materiality concept: application and issues (2021), Global Reporting Initiative, https://www.globalreporting.org/media/jrbntbyv/griwhitepaper-publications.pdf

8. Delgado-Ceballos, J., Ortiz-De-Mandojana, N., Antolín-López, R., Montiel, I.: Connecting the sustainable development goals to firm-level sustainability and ESG factors: the need for double materiality. BRQ Bus. Res. Q. **26**(1), 2–10 (2023). https://doi.org/10.1177/23409444221140919
9. Dwivedi, P.P.: Role of environmental, social and governance (ESG) in the achieving sustainable development goals: a brief review. Public Health Open Access. **7**(2), 1–8 (2023). https://doi.org/10.23880/phoa-16000259
10. Isokulova, M.: Review of the global state of sustainability accounting practices. Policetecnico di Torino. (2024)
11. Moodaley, W., Telukdarie, A.: Greenwashing, Sustainability Reporting, and Artificial Intelligence: A Systematic Literature Review. Jan. 01, 2023, MDPI. doi: https://doi.org/10.3390/su15021481
12. Cort, T., Esty, D.: ESG standards: looming challenges and pathways forward. Organ. Environ. **33**(4), 491–510 (2020). https://doi.org/10.1177/1086026620945342
13. Božić, V.: Environmental, Social, and Governance (ESG) & Artifical Intelligence (AI) (2025), https://doi.org/10.13140/RG.2.2.21345.42087
14. Adelakun, B.O., Antwi, B.O., Ntiakoh, A., Eziefule, A.O.: Leveraging AI for sustainable accounting: developing models for environmental impact assessment and reporting. Finance Account. Res. J. **6**(6), 1017–1048 (2024). https://doi.org/10.51594/farj.v6i6.1234
15. Selvaraj, J.T.: Aligning AI Systems with Corporate Sustainability and CSR Strategies: Providing Actionable Insights and Guidelines for Enhanced Integration. LUT University (2024)
16. Rane, N.L., Choudhary, S.P., Rane, J.: Artificial intelligence driven approaches to strengthening environmental, social, and governance (ESG) criteria in sustainable business practices: a review. In: Social, and Governance (ESG) Criteria in Sustainable Business Practices: a Review, pp. 1–20 (2024) [Online]. Available: https://ssrn.com/abstract=4843215
17. Ruberg, N., Torroni, P., Almeida, V.: BERT Goes Sustainable: an NLP Approach to ESG Financing. Università Di Bologna (2021)
18. Xu, J.: AI in ESG for Financial Institutions: An Industrial Survey (2024), Preprint, https://doi.org/10.48550/arXiv.2403.05541
19. Lee, H., Lee, S.H., Park, H., Kim, J.H., Jung, H.S.: ESG2PreEM: automated ESG grade assessment framework using pre-trained ensemble models. Heliyon. **10**(4) (2024). https://doi.org/10.1016/j.heliyon.2024.e26404
20. Xia, L., Yang, M., Liu, Q.: Using pre-trained language model for accurate ESG prediction. In: Proceedings of the Eighth Financial Technology and Natural Language Processing and the 1st Agent AI for Scenario Planning, pp. 1–22 (2024) [Online]. Available: https://huggingface.co/
21. Lim, T.: Environmental, social, and governance (ESG) and artificial intelligence in finance: state-of-the-art and research takeaways. Artif. Intell. Rev. **57**, 4 (2024). https://doi.org/10.1007/s10462-024-10708-3
22. Feng, S.: Leveraging artificial intelligence to enhance ESG models: transformative impacts and implementation challenges. Appl. Comput. Eng. **69**(1), 37–42 (2024). https://doi.org/10.54254/2755-2721/69/20241473
23. Rupanya, K.: Enhancing Corporate Sustainability Reporting Practices Under the CSRD Framework: An IT Industry Case Study.," Thesis. LUT University (2024)
24. Huang, D.Z.X.: An integrated theory of the firm approach to environmental, social and governance performance. Account. Finance. **62**(S1), 1567–1598 (2022). https://doi.org/10.1111/acfi.12832
25. Telukdarie, A., Mahure, H., Sishi, M.: The digitization of ESG matrix. In: Procedia Computer Science, pp. 808–815. Elsevier B.V (2024). https://doi.org/10.1016/j.procs.2024.06.436
26. Martínez-Peláez, R., et al.: Role of digital transformation for achieving sustainability: mediated role of stakeholders, key capabilities, and technology. Sustainability (Switzerland). **15**(14) (2023). https://doi.org/10.3390/su151411221

27. Liang, Y., Lee, M.J., Jung, J.S.: Dynamic capabilities and an ESG strategy for sustainable management performance. Front. Psychol. **13** (2022). https://doi.org/10.3389/fpsyg.2022.887776
28. Na, S., Heo, S., Han, S., Shin, Y., Roh, Y.: Acceptance model of artificial intelligence (AI)-based technologies in construction firms: applying the technology acceptance model (TAM) in combination with the technology–organisation–environment (TOE) framework. Buildings. **12**, 2 (2022). https://doi.org/10.3390/buildings12020090
29. Nair, P., Venter, F.: Bridging the ESG Data Gap: How AI Can Turn Information into Impact. 4Sight—Business Environment

Sustainable AI-Driven Business Model Innovation: A Theoretical Framework

Rosario Faraci and Rosaria Ferlito

Abstract The integration of artificial intelligence (AI) into business practices holds significant potential to transform industries. However, it simultaneously raises pressing concerns regarding the ethical and responsible use of these advanced technologies. Existing research typically investigates AI-driven business models (AI-BMs) and sustainability-driven business models (SBMs) independently, overlooking their combined capacity for driving innovation. In response to this research gap, the present study examines how firms can responsibly integrate AI to foster sustainable business model innovation (SBMI). Through a systematic literature review of AI-BM and SBM scholarship, we identify the strengths, weaknesses, synergies, gaps, and tensions that emerge when these paradigms intersect. Building on the insights, we introduce a novel theoretical framework grounded in four interrelated pillars: (1) sustainable AI vision, (2) technology-driven sustainable dynamics, (3) ecosystem value flows, and (4) sustainable AI monetization. By bridging technological advancement and environmental, social, and governance (ESG) imperatives, this framework offers guidelines for researchers and practitioners seeking to achieve sustainability objectives amid ongoing digital transformation.

Keywords AI-driven business models · Sustainability-driven business models · Business model innovation · Sustainable AI · Theoretical framework · Literature review

R. Faraci
University of Catania, Catania, Italy
e-mail: faraci@unict.it

R. Ferlito (✉)
University of Enna "Kore", Enna, Italy
e-mail: rosaria.ferlito@unikore.it

N. Omrani et al. (eds.), *Human-Machine Synergy and the Digital Future - Exploring Collaboration and Competition Volume 1*, Springer Proceedings in Business and Economics, https://doi.org/10.1007/978-3-032-21347-1_18

1 Introduction

Digital sustainability—the ethical application of digital technologies to advance environmental, social, and economic objectives [1, 2] has emerged as a critical paradigm in contemporary business strategy. Feroz et al. (2021) [3] delineate technology's pivotal role in enabling pollution control, waste management, sustainable production, and urban sustainability. Within this context, artificial intelligence (AI) represents a disruptive force, defined as "the engineering of intelligent machines capable of adaptive, foresight-driven operation within complex environments" [4, p.13].

Despite growing interest, the literature often treats AI-driven business model and sustainable one as distinct areas of study without addressing their convergence. A few scholars have begun to bridge this gap [5, 6] focusing on specific dimensions of sustainable AI applications without offering a holistic perspective on how these elements can be effectively combined. For instance, Mhlanga (2022) [7] underscores the importance of a human-centered approach to AI that aligns with sustainable development goals.

Consequently, this paper aims to answer the following research question: *How can organizations systematically integrate AI technologies into their business models to concurrently stimulate innovation and realize sustainability objectives?*

Through a theoretical lens, we develop a framework to guide both academic inquiry and managerial practice in this emerging domain.

2 Literature Review

2.1 AI-Driven Business Models

AI-BMs are characterized by data-driven decision-making processes that leverage predictive analytics and machine learning to optimize value creation [8]. Reim et al. (2015) [9] emphasize organizational adaptation as critical to realizing AI's potential, requiring strategic alignment of technological capabilities with existing business architectures, a transformation heavily contingent on executive leadership [10]. Applications span predictive consumer analytics [11], supply chain optimization [12] and cross-industry innovation in sectors from healthcare to agriculture [13, 14].

Furthermore, Menzies et al. (2024) [15] examined the impact of AI on international business, including market selection and entry modes.

2.2 Sustainability-Driven Business Models

SBM represents a new paradigm of business that aims to minimize negative externalities while generating a positive impact on both the environment and society [16]. This means integrating sustainability goals into existing value propositions, and shifting value creation from a purely economic focus to a shared value lens [17, 18].

Scholars converge on several essential elements for SBMs, including operational efficiency, stakeholder engagement, and risk mitigation [19, 20].

3 Methods

3.1 Data Collection

This study employs a systematic literature review of peer-reviewed articles from the SCOPUS database, structured as follows:

- *AI-BMs literature*: the search included articles with the terms "AI" or "artificial intelligence" in the title, and "business model*" in the title, abstract, or keywords. It was limited to the subject areas of "Business, Management, and Accounting" and "Economics, Econometrics, and Finance." Only articles written in English and published between 2018 and 2025 were considered. This search resulted in 129 documents. After reading the abstract, articles inconsistent with the research topics were removed (47 documents). This step resulted in 82 selected documents that we proceeded to analyze.
- *SBMs literature*: the search included articles with the term "sustainab*" in the title and "business model*" in the title, abstract, or keywords. The same subject areas, publication years, and language criteria were applied. Initially, this search yielded 910 documents.
  However, since many articles did not specifically address BMs, the search was refined to include "business model*" only in the title, resulting in 387 relevant documents. After reading the abstract, articles inconsistent with the research topics were removed (104 documents). This step resulted in 283 selected documents that we proceeded to analyze.

3.2 Data Analysis

A comparative analysis identified strengths, weaknesses, synergies, gaps, and tensions, forming the basis for our theoretical framework. The analytical process was structured into four iterative steps:

1. The authors independently analyzed the selected literature. Each author was assigned an equal portion of the papers, which were read to extract relevant passages that referred to strengths and weaknesses. These steps were manually coded using the software NVivo 15, which facilitated the organization and

retrieval of coded segments. Then, the authors discuss interpretations, and resolve any discrepancies.

2. The second phase focused on examining the categorized strengths and weaknesses to identify emerging synergies, gaps, and tensions. This analytical phase moved from descriptive coding to a more interpretive level of abstraction. To strengthen the analytical rigor, the authors involved three additional researchers with different disciplinary backgrounds:
   - a computer science researcher (for technical validation),
   - an engineering researcher (to address technological feasibility), and,
   - a legal philosopher (to assess ethical implications of AI systems).

These researchers acted as critical reviewers and "devil's advocates", continuously questioning the interpretations and requiring explicit justifications for each conceptual grouping.

3. Based on the interpretive synthesis from the previous phase, the authors distilled the emerging concepts into a set of core theoretical pillars underpinning a new framework.
4. The framework and discussion elements were further refined through the engagement of two experienced practitioners from a software company operating in Catania, Milan and Switzerland, with a long experience in R&D projects involving AI. Specifically, the CEO provided insights on the managerial dimensions, while the Head of IT provided feedback on the technical and implementation aspects.

4 Findings

4.1 Strengths and Weaknesses

4.1.1 Strengths of AI-Driven Business Models

AI-BM offer significant strengths that can enhance performance.

1. Operational Efficiency: Firms adopting AI technologies can achieve operational efficiencies that translate into higher profit margins [8]. For instance, AI can streamline processes by reducing the time and resources required for tasks traditionally performed by humans.
2. Enhanced Decision-Making: AI systems can quickly and accurately analyze a large amount of data to predict market trends and consumer behavior [21].
3. Customer-centered value propositions: AI enables businesses to deliver personalized experiences to customers that enhance customer satisfaction, loyalty and retention [22, 23].
4. Innovation: AI foster innovation by enabling organizations to experiment with new products and processes rapidly. The ability to analyze insights allows firms to identify new opportunities [12].

5. Proactive Risk Mitigation: AI mitigates risks through real-time monitoring. By employing AI, firms can assess risks associated with new BM [24].

4.1.2 Strengths of Sustainability-Driven Business Models

The SBM presents several key strengths that contribute to enhanced value created.

1. Shared Value: SBMs are designed to generate shared value by addressing societal challenges through their core operations [17]. This approach contributes to the well-being of communities [25].
2. Innovation: Firms are often motivated to invest in R&D, leading to the creation of eco-friendly products and services [16].
3. Operational Efficiency: SBMs promote practices that reduce waste, conserve resources, and optimize processes, thereby enhancing overall business performance [26].
4. Stakeholder Engagement: These models promote active involvement of stakeholders, aligning business objectives with societal needs and fostering collaboration [27].
5. Enhanced Risk Management: By proactively addressing environmental and social risks, organizations can mitigate potential negative impacts [28].
6. Improved Organizational Culture: SBMs foster a culture of sustainability within organizations, empowering employees to contribute to sustainability initiatives, which can lead to increased job satisfaction and retention [29].
7. Market Differentiation: Firms with an SBM can differentiate themselves and attract customers who prioritize sustainability [25]. Additionally, it can facilitate entry into new niche segments that prioritize sustainability [27].

4.1.3 Weaknesses of AI-Driven Business Models

The adoption of AI-BM is not without challenges.

1. Ethical Considerations: The deployment of AI raises significant ethical concerns, particularly regarding data privacy, algorithmic bias, and transparency. Firms must ensure that their AI systems are designed to be transparent, minimizing the risk of discrimination [30, 31].
2. Regulatory Compliance: As AI technologies evolve, so do its regulations, making it crucial for businesses to stay updated to ensure compliance [8].
3. Skill Shortage: The successful implementation of AI-BM requires skilled staffs. Often, SME lack the necessary core competencies [8].
4. Operational integration: AI-based solutions require dedicated internal and external processes to design, develop, and maintain products, services, and IT systems [11].

5. Resistance to Change: Employees may resist the adoption of AI technologies due to fears of job displacement or a lack of understanding of how AI can augment their roles [32].
6. High energy consumption: AI-driven technologies, particularly those involving machine learning and deep learning, are characterized by high energy demands [33].

4.1.4 Weaknesses of Sustainability-Driven Business Models

SBMs face a range of challenges that hinder their effective implementation.

1. High investment: the high initial investment associated with sustainable technologies, employee training, and supply chain reconfiguration act as barriers, especially for SMEs [34].
2. Complexity of Implementation: Firms must align operational processes, stakeholder expectations, and sustainability goals [19]. The complexity can be particularly challenging for firms lacking the expertise necessary [35].
3. Measurement and Evaluation Challenges: despite advancements in sustainability metrics, inconsistencies in standards result in fragmented reporting practices, making it challenging for stakeholders to assess progress [35].
4. Technological Limitations: while advanced technologies hold great potential for enhancing sustainability, organizations frequently lack the infrastructure to deploy these innovations. The gap between technological potential and practical application often results in the underutilization of technological resources [35, 36].

4.2 Comparative Analysis

This study has been developed by analyzing the elements of convergence, complementarity, and conflict that emerge from a comparative analysis of the strengths and weaknesses of both models. We identify synergies, gaps, and tensions.

4.2.1 Convergence Elements: Synergies

Convergence occurs when individual elements, such as perceptions, feelings, or behaviors, interact in ways that produce similarity or shared meaning, ultimately reinforcing and enhancing one another toward the emergence of a collective property [37]. These elements are grouped by their capacity to generate synergies (Table 1).

Table 1 Convergence elements

	AI-driven business model elements	Sustainability-driven business model elements	Synergy/ Gap/ Tension	Description
Convercence elements	**[S]Operational Efficiency**: AI technologies streamline processes, reducing time and resources	**[S]Operational Efficiency**: Sustainable practices reduce waste and preserve resources	**Synergy**	[S1]Operational efficiency, resource optimization: Both models enhance operational efficiency, reducing costs and optimizing resources
	[S] Enhanced Decision-Making: AI systems provide insights for decision--making using predictive analytics	**[S] Shared Value Creation**: SBMs aim to address societal challenges while achieving economic progress	**Synergy**	[S2] AI-driven shared value decisions: AI can improve and facilitate decision-making for shared value initiatives
	[S] Customer-Centered Value Propositions: AI delivers personalized customer experiences by analyzing preferences and behaviors	**[S] Market Differentiation**: SBMs create value through sustainability-driven differentiation	**Synergy**	[S3] Unique value propositions: AI strengthens the ability of SBMs to create unique customer value propositions
	[S] Innovation: AI enables rapid experimentation and identification of new opportunities	**[S] Innovation**: SBMs drive eco-friendly innovation through investments in sustainable technologies	**Synergy**	[S4] innovation supported by R&D: Both models encourage innovation, with AI supporting R&D in sustainability
	[S] Proactive Risk Mitigation: AI enables real-time monitoring and systematic risk assessment	**[S] Enhanced Risk Management**: SBMs integrate environmental and social risk considerations into strategy	**Synergy**	[S5] real-time risk management:AI strengthens risk management in SBMs by providing real-time insights

4.2.2 Complementary Elements: Gaps

As Carst and Hu (2023) [38] discussed, the fragmentation among complementary constructs highlights the conceptual gaps that may be resolved through integrative exploration. Thus, complementary elements enhance value and expose underlying gaps, pointing to opportunities for integration and mutual reinforcement (Table 2).

4.2.3 Conflicting Elements: Tensions

Conflicting elements refer to inherent or structural tensions that arise when the goals, processes, or outcomes of one model diverge from those of another, potentially requiring coordination or negotiation [39] (Table 3).

4.3 Sustainable AI-Driven Business Model Innovation Framework

The proposed four pillars are based on the theoretical classification of the BM's components [40]: value proposition, value creation, value delivery, and value capture.

4.3.1 Sustainable AI Vision

AI redefines the sustainable value proposition.

1. Customers' focus.

Synergies: [S3]—Gaps: [G2]—Tensions: [T5].

AI-driven predictive analytics leverage machine learning to anticipate behaviors and customer needs by analyzing purchases, preferences, feedback, and reviews [22]. Integrating sustainable considerations [25] through collaboration with some entities, like Fair Trade or B Lab, can be instrumental. Some techniques that can integrate AI are recommendation systems, time series forecasting and sentiment analysis [12]. Therefore, the external stakeholders can foster support [27].

2. Intelligent modular design for flexibility and savings.

Synergies: [S1]—Gaps: [G8]—Tensions: [T2].

AI can support modular design through generative algorithms (Generative Design models), predictive models for lifecycle management and maintenance, material traceability, and reverse logistics planning [8, 16, 41]. This approach enables the pursuit of both sustainability and innovation in a resource-constrained context [34, 36].

Table 2 Complementary elements

	AI-driven business model elements	Sustainability-driven business model elements	Synergy/ Gap/ Tension	Description
Complementary elements	**[W] Skill Shortage**: The lack of skilled personnel to implement AI systems	**[S] Stakeholder Engagement:** SBMs foster the creation of an ecosystem where diverse stakeholders collaborate to address shared goals and challenges, leveraging collective expertise and resources	**Gap**	[G1] Stakeholder-driven AI skill development: Stakeholders can actively contribute to the development and dissemination of the skills required for successful AI integration to achieve shared value
	[W] Operational Integration: Integrating AI with existing systems is complex. The development of complex AI-based solutions requires dedicated internal and external processes, as well as the design, engineering, operation, and maintenance of systems	**[S] Stakeholder Engagement**: SBMs align stakeholder interests to foster collaboration. SBMs emphasize co-creation and participatory approaches, involving stakeholders such as suppliers, IT specialists, and customers early in the process to address challenges collaboratively	**Gap**	[G2] Stakeholder engagement ensures compatibility: Effective stakeholder engagement can support the integration of AI by ensuring the compatibility of AI solutions with current infrastructures, pooling expertise, and minimizing risks associated with delays and cost overruns. The external stakeholders can foster support
	[W] Resistance to Change: Employees are also resisting the introduction of AI due to fears of job displacement	**[S] Improved Organizational Culture**: SBMs cultivate a culture of trust, transparency, and inclusivity, where employees are actively engaged in decision-making processes	**Gap**	[G3] Collaboration aligns AI adoption: By fostering an environment of collaboration and shared benefits, SBMs can address fears associated with AI adoption, emphasizing opportunities for upskilling and aligning AI implementation with employee well-being and organizational goals

(continued)

Table 2 (continued)

	AI-driven business model elements	Sustainability-driven business model elements	Synergy/ Gap/ Tension	Description
	[W] Ethical Considerations: Concerns about data privacy, bias, and transparency in AI systems	**[S] Shared Value Creation**: SBMs focus on addressing societal challenges through business practices	**Gap**	[G4] Ethical AI for societal alignment: SBMs' focus on shared value creation provides a framework to address ethical concerns in AI by integrating societal and environmental priorities into business strategies. This approach can also guide organizations in developing AI systems that prioritize transparency, fairness, and accountability, aligning technological innovation with societal needs
	[S] Enhanced Decision-Making: AI provides predictive analytics	**[W] Complexity of Implementation**: SBMs face challenges in integrating social, environmental, and economic goals	**Gap**	[G5] Simplified sustainability complexity balance: Simplified sustainability complexity balance: AI's decision-making capabilities simplify the complexity of balancing sustainability's multiple dimensions
	[S] Proactive Risk Mitigation: AI enables real-time monitoring and assessment and offers AI reporting tools	**[W] Measurement and Evaluation Challenges**: SBMs struggle to measure sustainability outcomes consistently	**Gap**	[G6] reliable sustainability measurement frameworks: AI'S capacity to analyze large datasets improves sustainability measurements' reliability and consistency, supporting SBMs in achieving more robust evaluation frameworks
	[S] Operational Efficiency: AI enhances optimization of resource allocation	**[W] High Investment**: Sustainable practices require significant upfront investment	**Gap**	[G7] Offsetting high investment burdens: AI-driven efficiency can offset the financial burdens associated with the high initial investments of SBMs
	[S] Innovation: AI-driven business models foster innovative products and processes rapidly by the ability to analyze data and derive insights	**[W] Technological Limitations**: SBMs often lack the infrastructure, expertise, and financial resources to implement technologies	**Gap**	[G8] Optimized resource allocation priorities: AI helps identify technological investment priorities and optimize resource allocation, directly addressing infrastructure and expertise gaps

Table 3 Conflicting elements

	AI-driven business model elements	Sustainability-driven business model elements	Synergy/Gap/ Tension	Description
Conflicting elements	**[W] High Energy Consumption**: AI-driven systems require significant computational resources	**[S] Operational Efficiency**: SBMs focus on preserving resources	**Tension**	[T1] Energy-intensive AI vs sustainability: The energy-intensive nature of AI systems creates a direct conflict with sustainability's resource efficiency goals
	[W] High Energy Consumption: AI-driven systems require significant computational resources	**[W] High Investment:** SBMs demand high initial investments in sustainable technologies and practices, which can strain resources, particularly for SMEs	**Tension**	[T2] financial and operational pressures: The combined resource demands of AI and sustainable practices create financial and operational pressures, limiting the feasibility of pursuing both simultaneously, especially for resource-constrained firms
	[W] Regulatory Compliance: The rapid evolution of AI makes adapting to regulations difficult	**[W] Complexity of Implementation**: SBMs face challenges in integrating multiple dimensions	**Tension**	[T3] regulatory challenges for AI-SBM: The evolving regulations for AI exacerbate the implementation challenges faced by SBM models
	[W] Operational Integration Issues: The implementation of AI-based solutions requires significant resources for the design, engineering, and maintenance of products, services, and IT systems	**[W] Complexity of Implementation:** SBMs require the integration of economic, social, and environmental dimensions, which adds layers of complexity. Balancing these aspects often overwhelms organizations lacking adequate expertise and resources	**Tension**	[T4] Integration barriers. AI-sustainability alignment: The operational challenges of integrating AI systems, combined with the multidimensional requirements of SBMs, create significant barriers to alignment. Firms face compounded difficulties in synchronizing the technical demands of AI with the holistic, resource-intensive goals of sustainability
	[S] Innovation: AI-driven business models foster rapid innovation by experimenting with new products and processes	**[W] Enhanced Risk Management:** SBMs integrate sustainability considerations into strategic planning to proactively address environmental and social risks	**Tension**	[T5] Innovation speed vs risk assessment: The speed of AI-driven innovation may outpace the risk assessment capabilities of SBMs, leading to unintended social or environmental consequences that contradict sustainability goals
	[W] Ethical Considerations: The deployment of AI raises concerns about transparency and accountability	**[S] Stakeholder Engagement:** SBMs emphasize inclusivity and trasparency with stakeholders	**Tension**	[T6] Biased AI undermines stakeholder trust: The potential for biased algorithms and lack of transparency in AI systems conflicts with the stakeholder-centric perspective of SBMs undermining trust

3. Trust, equity and transparency.

Synergies: [S2]; [S5]—Gaps: [G4]—Tensions: [T6].

AI enables real-time analysis and communication of ESG data, enhancing transparency and strengthening stakeholder trust [23, 24]. By minimizing biases in decision-making processes and providing explainable models [21], it fosters fairness in stakeholder interactions, aligning with an ethically driven approach [30].

4.3.2 Tech-Driven Sustainable Dynamics

This pillar focuses on using AI to create value by driving operational efficiency, fostering sustainable innovation, and enhancing customer engagement.

1. Development of Green AI Algorithms.

Synergies: [S1]—Tensions: [T1]; [T4].

AI algorithms can reduce the environmental impact using techniques like edge computing and compressed models [42]. Edge computing processes data closer to its source, minimizing transmission to central servers and optimizing energy consumption [43]. Compressed models reduce computational complexity through pruning and quantization, enabling more efficient hardware use [44].

2. Development of Digital Twins to Reduce Operational Risks.

Synergies: [S1]; [S4]—Gaps: [G7]—Tensions: [T3]; [T4].

Digital twins can simulate production processes and identify operational inefficiencies before real-world implementation [12]. This "digital replica" leverages data collected from sensors or IoT devices to monitor, and optimize the performance of its physical twin [45]. Therefore, it supports sustainable design [26].

3. Implement Real-Time Monitoring Systems to Support Decision-Making Process.

Synergies: [S2]—Gaps: [G2]—Tensions: [T3].

AI-driven real-time monitoring systems use data to continuously track and analyze critical variables along the supply chain [21], such as CO2 emissions, natural resource use and working conditions [35]. This monitoring capability supports decision-making by enabling predictive analysis and aligning operations with global standards (e.g., ISO 14001) [8].

4. AI-Powered CRM for Customer Engagement.

Synergies: [S2]; [S3]—Gaps: [G2]; [G3]—Tensions: [T4]; [T6].

AI systems analyze customer data to identify preferences and offer personalized recommendations based on sustainability attributes like carbon footprint, ethical sourcing, or recyclability [22, 23, 27]. Additionally, AI CRM platforms engage customers with real-time updates on the environmental and social impact of their purchases, fostering co-responsibility [30, 35]. Gamification elements incentivize repeat purchases [46].

5. The Integration of AI Explainability.

Synergies: [S2]; [S5]—Gaps: [G4]—Tensions: [T6].

AI "explainability" provides clear explanations of how a model work and decisions are made [47]. Key elements for increasing stakeholder trust include interpretable models (e.g., decision trees, linear regression) combined with complex algorithms like deep learning to reveal decision-making mechanisms, measuring input variables' influence on AI decisions, ensuring local and global interpretability, auditing AI-driven decisions for compliance, and mitigating biases in input data [27, 30].

6. AI-Powered Internal Sustainability Auditing Systems.

Synergies: [S2]; [S3]; [S5]—Gaps: [G3]; [G4]; [G5]; [G6]—Tensions: [T3]; [T5]; [T6].

AI-based algorithmic auditing tools enable companies to verify ESG compliance in real time, improving data quality and reducing the time and costs of audits [27, 30]. This technology quickly identifies and addresses potential issues, preventing non-compliance risks [8, 24, 28].

4.3.3 Ecosystem Value Flow

The pillar focuses on how companies can use AI to distribute value. We identified the following key elements:

1. Interactive Platforms to spread ESG business information.

Synergies: [S2]; [S5]—Gaps: [G4]—Tensions: [T6].

AI-powered platforms deliver ESG insights to customers and partners through personalized dashboards, simulations, and visual tools (maps, charts) [27, 36]. Interactive tools like simulations and filters increase user confidence [12, 22]. By simplifying complex data, these platforms engage users and build trust [30].

2. Blockchain-Enabled Transparency.

Synergies: [S2]; [S4]; [S5]—Gaps: [G2]; [G4]; [G5]—Tensions: [T1]; [T3]; [T4].

Blockchain eliminates opacity by creating a transparent register of transactions [8, 12, 35, 48]. It records product origins, emissions, and resource use, while AI predicts non-compliance risks, and automates certification [8]. Customers verify product sustainability via blockchain-based digital passports, suppliers meet shared ESG standards through real-time insights, and regulatory bodies access verifiable compliance data [30].

3. Creation of an "Living Lab".

Synergies: [S2]—Gaps: [G1]; [G2]; [G3]; [G4]; [G5]—Tensions: [T4].

Innovation ecosystems enable real-world pilot projects, fostering a test-and-learn approach that reduces risks and accelerates sustainable technology adoption [12]. Acting as "living labs," they promote iterative development and stakeholder involvement [8, 11, 27, 49]. AI enhances sustainable initiative customization through data-driven decisions, while collaboration supports resource sharing and stakeholder alignment [27].

4. AI-Driven Collaboration Platforms to Co-creation.

Synergies: [S2]; [S5]—Gaps: [G4]—Tensions: [T6].

AI-driven collaborative platforms integrate intelligent crowdsourcing methods like NLP-based feedback analysis, actively involving stakeholders in sustainability initiatives [50]. These platforms enable suppliers, customers, and regulatory bodies to share insights and ideas. Virtual prototyping and simulation models transform input into actions, fostering real-time co-creation [51].

5. AI-driven ESG training programs.

Synergies: [S3]—Gaps: [G1]; [G2]; [G3]—Tensions: [T3]; [T4].

AI-driven sustainability training programs enable employees, suppliers, and partners to integrate sustainable practices and AI technologies [29, 32]. The platforms use adaptive learning algorithms and immersive simulations to transfer knowledge across the value chain [12, 36].

6. AI-Powered incentive mechanisms for shared impact.

Synergies: [S1]; [S4]; [S5]—Gaps: [G1]; [G2]; [G4]; [G6]—Tensions: [T1]; [T4]; [T5].

AI-driven incentive mechanisms promote sustainable behaviors by providing economic rewards to stakeholders [52]. Suppliers are incentivized to meet ESG standards through financial bonuses or preferential partnerships [27]. Customers receive discounts for ESG-certified products, while communities benefit from sustainable local business practices [53]. Using real-time data and machine learning, AI ensures incentives align with stakeholder performance [54].

4.3.4 Sustainable AI Monetization

This pillar explores how firm can create new streams of revenue.

1. "Pay-Per-Impact" Contracts

Synergies: [S2]; [S4]; [S5]—Gaps: [G4]; [G5]; [G6]; [G7]—Tensions: [T2]; [T3]; [T5]; [T6].

"Pay-per-impact" contracts link corporate revenues directly to the effectiveness of achieving verified ESG outcomes [55]. For instance, revenues can depend on meeting objectives such as reducing CO2 emissions, improving water usage, soil quality, or using recycled materials. By integrating AI, companies can measure impact in real-time, providing an objective basis for payments [21, 24, 35].

2. Licensing and Subscription Model of AI-Driven ESG Platform.

Synergies: [S2]; [S4]; [S5]—Gaps: [G2]—Tensions: [T4].

AI modular platforms for real-time ESG analysis, initially developed for internal optimization, can create value if shared with ecosystem partners via licensing or subscriptions [8, 16, 41]. For example, companies can use the platform to identify ESG risks and share access with suppliers, customers, or stakeholders [30].

3. Licensing and Subscription Model of other AI-as-a-Service for SME Sustainability Integration.

Synergies: [S2]; [S3]; [S4]; [S5]—Gaps: [G1]; [G2] [G4]; [G6]; [G8]—Tensions: [T2]; [T4]; [T6].

Through AI-as-a-service, offered via subscription or pay-per-use models, SMEs access solutions to monitor emissions, optimize resource use, and provide operational forecasts based on data [12, 36, 56]. This model enables the service provider to capture financial value by promoting sustainable practices among smaller businesses.

4. ESG Data Marketplaces.

Synergies: [S2]; [S3]; [S4]; [S5]—Gaps: [G3]; [G6]; [G8]—Tensions: [T3]; [T5]; [T6].

AI-based ESG data marketplaces are open platforms enabling many firms to share, purchase, and use ESG data [11, 28]. AI ensures standardization, verification, and usability. Firms utilize this data to identify improvement business opportunities and partner. Access fees, subscriptions, and personalized services allow marketplace developers to capture financial value [57].

5 Discussion and Implication

Our framework advances the theoretical debate on SBMI by integrating the transformative potential of AI with the principles of sustainability. It identifies the following key aspects (Fig. 1):

AI-Driven Governance Mechanisms In corporate governance research, AI has recently emerged as a catalyst for board-level decision-making [58]. AI-powered systems monitor key variables, enhance traceability, and ensure alignment with global standards. They support compliance and foster trust by using explainability to reduce algorithmic bias [27, 30]. Enhancing stakeholder confidence makes governance more responsive to sustainability challenges. Another key aspect is redefining incentives for value delivery. Traditional governance, based on fixed mechanisms to align behavior with goals [59], struggles to enable large-scale sustainable actions due to rigidity [60]. The new framework uses dynamic AI systems to personalize incentives and equitably reward stakeholders.

Operational Optimization The study explores AI-driven operational optimization. Customers shift from passive recipients to active participants in sustainability [19, 35]. AI-powered CRM systems analyze behavioral data, enhancing engagement through gamification and real-time impact updates. These mechanisms extend shared value [17] into a technological context, fostering co-creation of sustainable practices.

It also addresses the AI–environmental sustainability trade-off [33]. Green AI, edge computing, and compressed models cut energy use, optimizing efficiency without compromising environmental goals. Digital twins, once operational tools, now help design and simulate sustainable processes.

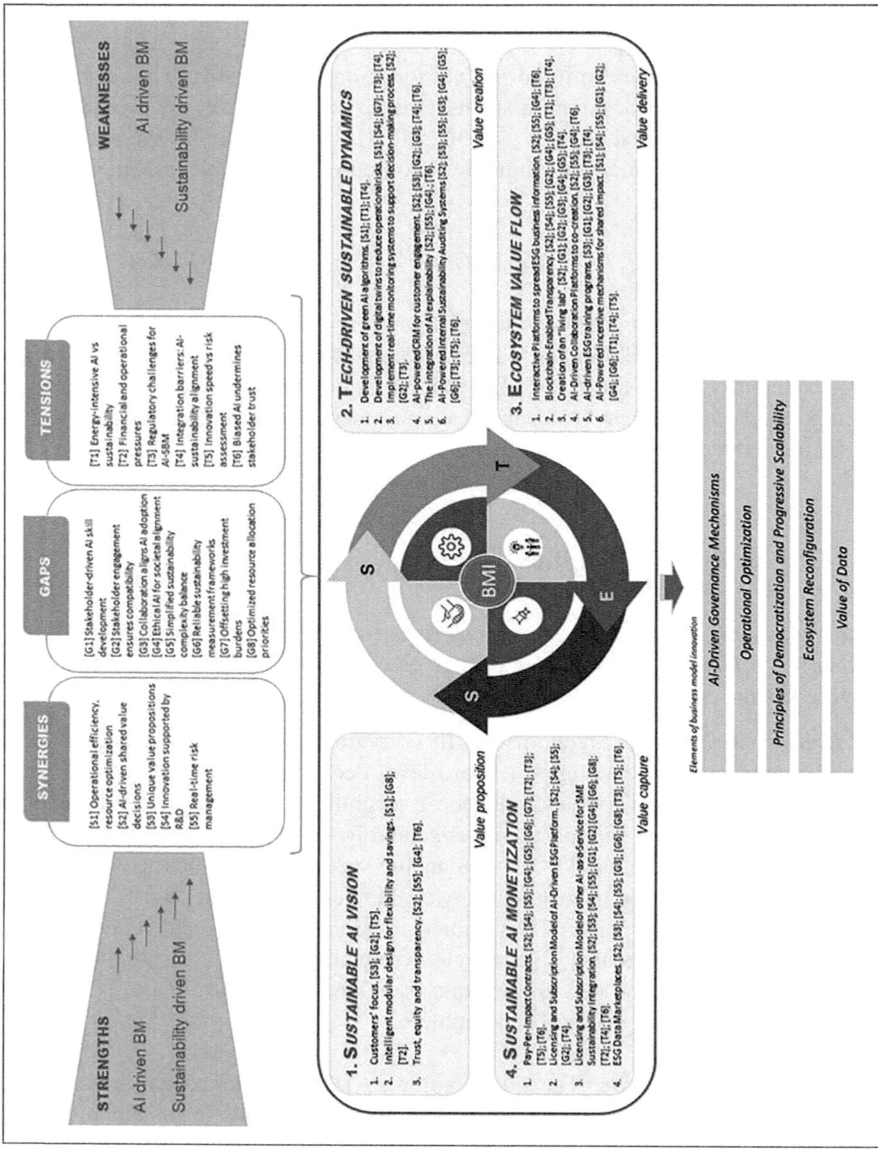

Fig. 1 Sustainable AI-driven business model innovation framework

Additionally, the framework bridges skill gaps [5, 6] through adaptive learning algorithms and immersive simulations, enabling large-scale knowledge transfer and empowering stakeholders to adopt sustainable practices.

Principles of Democratization and Progressive Scalability The framework redefines the principles of BMI by emphasizing progressive scalability and democratization.

At its core is the development of modular, replicable solutions addressing financial, operational, and infrastructural gaps often identified in the literature [6, 41]. These solutions allow businesses to adopt sustainable practices incrementally, lowering entry barriers for SMEs. Another key element is the democratization of advanced tools and services. Traditionally confined to large corporations with substantial resources [6], such tools are now shared with stakeholders via flexible licensing or subscription models, reducing technological inequalities [61]. This democratization fosters uniform ESG metrics, supporting standardization, inclusiveness, and consistent benchmarking across industries.

Ecosystem Reconfiguration Although the literature has recognized the importance of ecosystems for sustainable value distribution [62], the framework goes further by showing how integrating AI and sustainability enhances these ecosystems' ability to adapt solutions to stakeholders' needs. Distributed value delivery is enabled by collaborative platforms, AI–blockchain interconnection, and digital living labs. Traditionally seen as local experimental environments [61], living labs are redefined as digital hubs, empowered by AI to accelerate personalization and scalability of developed solutions.

Value of Data The literature often portrays sustainability and AI as constraints that SMEs struggle to overcome [8, 19]. This study shows how combining them can catalyze economic value creation. AI enhances impact measurement reliability, enabling pay-per-impact contracts that incentivize firms to achieve sustainable outcomes. These contracts align economic interests with sustainability goals, enriching debates on the interconnectedness of social, environmental, and economic sustainability. The framework also introduces the AI-driven ESG data marketplace, redefining data within SBMs from passive repositories [20, 30] to valuable economic resources.

Therefore, this study contributes to the literature on BMI addressing some challenges:

1. Need for BMs to balance technological innovation and sustainability [16],
2. Difficulties in building AI capabilities into existing SBMs [5],
3. The trade-off between AI, ESG and economic sustainability [7],
4. The exploration and exploitation of a re-configurate value proposition [63].

It also provides a practical framework to integrate AI and sustainability into BMs. For example, innovative monetization models, AI-driven training programs and gamified customer engagement.

6 Conclusion and Limitation

This study introduces a theoretically grounded framework designed to guide the integration of AI and sustainability principles within business models. Despite this, it also presents some limitations linked to the methodology that open pathways for future research. The theoretical approach provides a strong conceptual foundation, but the absence of empirical data restricts the ability to assess the framework's operational feasibility. Indeed, it has not been empirically validated through case studies. Moreover, future research should test the framework across industries to evaluate its adaptability and effectiveness in different contexts. Moreover, future studies should focus on dynamic capability development, and should conduct longitudinal studies for evaluating the long-term effects of AI-SBM integration.

References

1. Rosário, A.T., Dias, J.C.: The new digital economy and sustainability: challenges and opportunities. Sustainability. **15**(14), 10902 (2023)
2. Böttcher, T.P., Empelmann, S., Weking, J., Hein, A., Krcmar, H.: Digital sustainable business models: using digital technology to integrate ecological sustainability into the core of business models. Inf. Syst. J. **34**(3), 736–761 (2024)
3. Feroz, A.K., Zo, H., Chiravuri, A.: Digital transformation and environmental sustainability: a review and research agenda. Sustainability. **13**(3), 1530 (2021)
4. Nilsson, N.J.: The Quest for Artificial Intelligence. Cambridge University Press (2009)
5. Di Vaio, A., Palladino, R., Hassan, R., Escobar, O.: Artificial intelligence and business models in the sustainable development goals perspective: a systematic literature review. J. Bus. Res. **121**, 283–314 (2020)
6. Shaik, A.S., Alshibani, S.M., Jain, G., Gupta, B., Mehrotra, A.: Artificial intelligence (AI)-driven strategic business model innovations in small-and medium-sized enterprises. Insights on technological and strategic enablers for carbon neutral businesses. Bus. Strateg. Environ. **33**(4), 2731–2751 (2021)
7. Mhlanga, D.: Human-centered artificial intelligence: the superlative approach to achieve sustainable development goals in the fourth industrial revolution. Sustainability. **14**(13), 7804 (2022)
8. Farayola, O.A., Abdul, A.A., Irabor, B.O., Okeleke, E.C.: Innovative business models driven by AI technologies: a review. Comput. Sci. IT Res. J. **4**(2), 85–110 (2023)
9. Reim, W., Parida, V., Örtqvist, D.: Product-service systems (PSS) business models and tactics–a systematic literature review. J. Clean. Prod. **97**, 61–75 (2015)
10. Jorzik, P., Yigit, A., Kanbach, D.K., Kraus, S., Dabić, M.: Artificial intelligence-enabled business model innovation: competencies and roles of top management. IEEE Trans. Eng. Manag. **71**, 7044–7056 (2023)
11. Mishra, S., Tripathi, A.R.: AI business model: an integrative business approach. J. Innov. Entrep. **10**(1), 18 (2021)
12. Roy, V., Schoenherr, T., Jayaram, J.: Digital enabled agility: industry 4.0 unlocking real-time information processing, traceability, and visibility to unleash the next extent of agility. Int. J. Prod. Res. **62**(14), 5127–5148 (2024)
13. Garbuio, M., Lin, N.: Artificial intelligence as a growth engine for health care startups: emerging business models. Calif. Manag. Rev. **61**(2), 59–83 (2019)

14. D'Amore, G., Di Vaio, A., Balsalobre-Lorente, D., Boccia, F.: Artificial intelligence in the water–energy–food model: a holistic approach towards sustainable development goals. Sustainability. **14**(2), 867 (2022)
15. Menzies, J., Sabert, B., Hassan, R., Mensah, P.K.: Artificial intelligence for international business: its use, challenges, and suggestions for future research and practice. Thunderbird Int. Bus. Rev. **66**(2), 185–200 (2024)
16. Evans, S., Vladimirova, D., Holgado, M., Van Fossen, K., Yang, M., Silva, E.A., Barlow, C.Y.: Business model innovation for sustainability: towards a unified perspective for creation of sustainable business models. Bus. Strateg. Environ. **26**(5), 597–608 (2017)
17. Porter, M.E., Kramer, M.R.: Creating shared value. Harv. Bus. Rev. **89**(1–2), 62–77 (2011)
18. Nosratabadi, S., Mosavi, A., Shamshirband, S., Zavadskas, E.K., Rakotonirainy, A., Chau, K.W.: Sustainable business models: a review. Sustainability. **11**(6), 1663 (2019)
19. Geissdoerfer, M., Vladimirova, D., Evans, S.: Sustainable business model innovation: a review. J. Clean. Prod. **198**, 401–416 (2018)
20. Lüdeke-Freund, F., Bohnsack, R., Breuer, H., Massa, L.: Research on sustainable business model patterns: status quo, methodological issues, and a research agenda. Sustain. Bus. Models Innov. Implement. Success. **25-60** (2018)
21. Olaniyi, O., Abalaka, A., Olabanji, S.O.: Utilizing big data analytics and business intelligence for improved decision-making at leading fortune company. J. Sci. Res. Rep. **29**(9), 64–72 (2023)
22. Potwora, M., Vdovichena, O., Semchuk, D., Lipych, L., Saienko, V.: The use of artificial intelligence in marketing strategies: automation, personalization and forecasting. J. Manag. World. **2024**(2), 41–49 (2024)
23. Desta, E., Amantie, C.: The role of artificial intelligence on market performance: Evidence from scientific review. J. Econ. Behav. Stud. **16**(1 (J)), 82–93 (2024)
24. Farahani, M.S., Ghasemi, G.: How AI changes the game in finance business models. Int. J. Innov. Manag. Econ. Soc. Sci. **4**(1), 35–46 (2024)
25. Bocken, N.M., Short, S.W., Rana, P., Evans, S.: A value mapping tool for sustainable business modelling. Corp. Gov. **13**(5), 482–497 (2013)
26. Heikkurinen, P., Young, C.W., Morgan, E.: Business for sustainable change: extending eco-efficiency and eco-sufficiency strategies to consumers. J. Clean. Prod. **218**, 656–664 (2019)
27. Bellucci, M., Bini, L., Giunta, F.: Implementing environmental sustainability engagement into business: sustainability management, innovation, and sustainable business models. In: Innovation Strategies in Environmental Science, pp. 107–143. Elsevier (2020)
28. Shad, M.K., Lai, F.W., Fatt, C.L., Klemeš, J.J., Bokhari, A.: Integrating sustainability reporting into enterprise risk management and its relationship with business performance: a conceptual framework. J. Clean. Prod. **208**, 415–425 (2019)
29. Assoratgoon, W., Kantabutra, S.: Toward a sustainability organizational culture model. J. Clean. Prod. **400**, 136666 (2023)
30. Akter, S., McCarthy, G., Sajib, S., Michael, K., Dwivedi, Y.K., D'Ambra, J., Shen, K.N.: Algorithmic bias in data-driven innovation in the age of AI. Int. J. Inf. Manag. **60**, 102387 (2021)
31. Attard-Frost, B., De los Ríos, A., Walters, D.R.: The ethics of AI business practices: a review of 47 AI ethics guidelines. AI Ethics. **3**(2), 389–406 (2023)
32. Olutimehin, D.O., Ofodile, O.C., Ejibe, I., Odunaiya, O.G., Soyombo, O.T.: Implementing ai in business models: strategies for efficiency and innovation. Int. J. Manag. Entrep. Res. **6**(3), 863–877 (2024)
33. Toniolo, K., Masiero, E., Massaro, M., Bagnoli, C.: Sustainable business models and artificial intelligence: opportunities and challenges. In: Knowledge, People, and Digital Transformation: Approaches for a Sustainable Future, pp. 103–117 (2020)
34. Lozano, R.: Sustainable business models: providing a more holistic perspective. Bus. Strateg. Environ. **27**(8), 1159–1166 (2018)
35. Bocken, N.M., Geradts, T.H.: Barriers and drivers to sustainable business model innovation: organization design and dynamic capabilities. Long Range Plan. **53**(4), 101950 (2020)

36. Ritala, P., Almpanopoulou, A.: In defense of 'eco' in ecosystem: toward a more sustainable innovation ecosystem. Technovation. **60**, 39–42 (2017)
37. Fulmer, C.A., Ostroff, C.: Convergence and emergence in organizations: an integrative framework and review. J. Organ. Behav. **37**, 122–145 (2016)
38. Carst, A.E., Hu, Y.: Complementors as ecosystem actors: a systematic review. Manag. Rev. Q. **1-57** (2023)
39. Strauss, E., Tessier, S., Väisänen, M.: Exploring the tensions within and among management control elements from a paradox perspective. Manag. Account. Res. **66**, 100925 (2025)
40. Teece, D.J.: Business models, business strategy and innovation. Long Range Plan. **43**(2–3), 172–194 (2010)
41. Bhosekar, A., Ierapetritou, M.: Modular design optimization using machine learning-based flexibility analysis. J. Process Control. **90**, 18–34 (2020)
42. Matsubara, Y., Yang, R., Levorato, M., Mandt, S.: Supervised compression for resource-constrained edge computing systems. In: Proceedings of the IEEE/CVF Winter Conference on Applications of Computer Vision, pp. 2685–2695 (2022)
43. Shi, W., Cao, J., Zhang, Q., Li, Y., Xu, L.: Edge computing: vision and challenges. IEEE Internet Things J. **3**(5), 637–646 (2016)
44. Li, Z., Li, H., Meng, L.: Model compression for deep neural networks: a survey. Computers. **12**(3), 60 (2023)
45. Al-Qudah, A.A., Abdalmuttaleb, M.A., Al-Sartawi, M., Shihadeh, F. (eds.): Artificial Intelligence-Augmented Digital Twins: Transforming Industrial Operations for Innovation and Sustainability. Springer International Publishing AG (2025)
46. Elmashhara, M.G., De Cicco, R., Silva, S.C., Hammerschmidt, M., Silva, M.L.: How gamifying AI shapes customer motivation, engagement, and purchase behavior. Psychol. Mark. **41**(1), 134–150 (2024)
47. Rai, A.: Explainable AI: from black box to glass box. J. Acad. Mark. Sci. **48**, 137–141 (2020)
48. Laroiya, C., Saxena, D., Komalavalli, C.: Applications of blockchain technology. In: Handbook of Research on Blockchain Technology, pp. 213–243. Academic press (2020)
49. Dickinger, A., Kolomoyets, Y.: Value co-creation in tourism living labs. J. Bus. Res. **183**, 114820 (2024)
50. Veshne, N., Jamnani, J.: Enhancing employee engagement through artificial intelligence. In: Industry 4.0 and People Analytics, pp. 131–152. Apple Academic Press (2024)
51. Perna, A., O'Toole, T., Baraldi, E., Gregori, G.L.: The value co-creation journey: a longitudinal process unfolding in a network through collaboration. J. Bus. Ind. Mark. **37**(13), 182–196 (2022)
52. Jia, X., Hou, Y.: Architecting the future: exploring the synergy of AI-driven sustainable HRM, conscientiousness, and employee engagement. Discov. Sustain. **5**(1), 30 (2024)
53. Cao, P., Liu, S.: The impact of artificial intelligence technology stimuli on sustainable consumption behavior: evidence from ant forest users in China. Behav. Sci. **13**(7), 604 (2023)
54. Nayem, Z., Uddin, M.A.: Unbiased employee performance evaluation using machine learning. J. Open Innov.: Technol. Mark. Complex. **10**(1), 100243 (2024)
55. Elisabetta, D., Iannuzzi, A.P.: Incentive plans, pay-for-non-financial performance and ESG criteria: evidence from the European banking sector. Int. Bus. Res. **10**(10), 169–181 (2017)
56. Heinis, T.B., Loy, C.L., Meboldt, M.: Improving usage metrics for pay-per-use pricing with IoT technology and machine learning: IoT technology and machine learning can identify and capture advanced metrics that make pay-per-use servitization models viable for a wider range of applications. Res. Technol. Manag. **61**(5), 32–40 (2018)
57. Hein, A., Schreieck, M., Riasanow, T., Setzke, D.S., Wiesche, M., Böhm, M., Krcmar, H.: Digital platform ecosystems. Electron. Mark. **30**, 87–98 (2020)
58. Schneider, J., Abraham, R., Meske, C., Vom Brocke, J.: Artificial intelligence governance for businesses. Inf. Syst. Manag. **40**(3), 229–249 (2023)

59. Shaikh, I., Randhawa, K.: Managing the risks and motivations of technology managers in open innovation: bringing stakeholder-centric corporate governance into focus. Technovation. **114**, 102437 (2022)
60. Velte, P.: Archival research on sustainability-related executive compensation. A literature review of the status quo and future improvements. Corporate Social Responsibility and Environmental Management (2024)
61. Hossain, M., Leminen, S., Westerlund, M.: A systematic review of living lab literature. J. Clean. Prod. **213**, 976–988 (2019)
62. Granstrand, O., Holgersson, M.: Innovation ecosystems: a conceptual review and a new definition. Technovation. **90**, 102098 (2020)
63. Breuer, H., Lüdeke-Freund, F.: Values-based network and business model innovation. Int. J. Innov. Manag. **21**(03), 1750028 (2017)

Exploring the Role of AI and ML in the Evolution of Green Finance: A Systematic Bibliometric Review

Hossein Habibinejad, Paul Reaidy, and Morteza Alaeddini

Abstract Artificial intelligence (AI) and machine learning (ML) are increasingly enabling green finance by improved ESG scoring, carbon pricing, and climate risk modeling. This study takes a systematic approach to bibliometrically review peer-reviewed publications from 2019 to early 2025. The review was conducted using the PRISMA method across academic and regulatory databases. The analysis identifies six thematic clusters of 48 keywords, along with evolving publication trends. While interest in AI has steadily grown, machine learning, fintech, and impact investing show signs of stagnation. Meanwhile, newer topics such as selection mechanisms and efficiency metrics are emerging, reflecting a shift toward more technical and data-driven research. Findings highlight AI/ML's potential to improve transparency, decision quality, and sustainable investment evaluation. However, significant challenges remain, including data inconsistency, algorithmic bias, energy intensity, limited explainable AI, and poor alignment with climate policies. The paper concludes with a call for interdisciplinary integration of AI, finance, and sustainability to ensure the responsible and policy-aligned adoption of AI in green finance.

Keywords Green Finance · ESG Scoring · Artificial Intelligence · Machine Learning · Explainable AI · Systematic Literature Review

H. Habibinejad (✉) · P. Reaidy
Université Grenoble Alpes, Grenoble-INP, CERAG, Grenoble, France
e-mail: hossein.habibinejad@univ-grenoble-alpes.fr; paul.reaidy@univ-grenoble-alpes.fr

M. Alaeddini
ICN Business School, Université de Lorraine, CEREFIGE, Nancy, France
e-mail: morteza.alaeddini@icn-artem.com

N. Omrani et al. (eds.), *Human-Machine Synergy and the Digital Future - Exploring Collaboration and Competition Volume 1*, Springer Proceedings in Business and Economics, https://doi.org/10.1007/978-3-032-21347-1_19

1 Introduction

Escalating climate threats make sustainability a paramount global concern [1]. Green finance plays a vital role in addressing these challenges by directing capital toward environmentally responsible initiatives such as renewable energy projects and green bonds [2]. Within this context, environmental, social, and governance (ESG) criteria have become essential for evaluating investments and mitigating risks [3]. To improve the reliability and effectiveness of these frameworks, there is increasing attention being paid to digital technologies, particularly artificial intelligence (AI) and machine learning (ML) [4]. AI and ML have the potential to transform green finance by improving forecasting accuracy, supporting real-time risk assessment, and enhancing financial risk evaluation through ESG-related signals [5, 6]. These technologies enable scalable data processing, anomaly detection, and predictive modeling, assisting financial institutions in aligning investment portfolios with climate goals.

Despite these promises, the implementation of AI and ML in sustainable finance is fragmented and poorly understood due to the lack of a comprehensive synthesis of current research. While some studies have focused on narrow applications or proprietary models, there is, to the best of our knowledge, limited visibility into overarching patterns, research clusters, or evolving trends. Moreover, critical challenges persist, including data inconsistencies, algorithmic opacity, ethical concerns, and the high energy consumption of large-scale AI systems [7]. The absence of standardized evaluation frameworks and widely adopted explainability mechanisms further limits the effective deployment of AI/ML tools in sustainable investing [7].

In response to these gaps, this study conducts a systematic bibliometric review to evaluate academic research at the intersection of AI/ML and green finance. Specifically, the study explores how AI and ML technologies contribute to key activities such as ESG performance evaluation, carbon pricing, and climate-related risk assessment. It also identifies major barriers to the technologies' broader adoption. From a policy perspective, growing concerns about greenwashing and unreliable ESG scoring have led to regulatory demands for transparency, algorithmic accountability, and alignment with frameworks such as the EU Sustainable Finance Disclosure Regulation (SFDR) and the Paris Agreement [8]. Understanding how AI and ML technologies align—or fail to align—with these expectations is essential for building trustworthy and effective green financial systems.

This paper aims to bridge the current research gap by mapping the academic landscape, identifying thematic clusters and emerging trends, and offering research and policy recommendations for the responsible integration of AI/ML into climate-aligned finance. By doing so, the paper contributes to the ongoing discourse on sustainable digital transformation and fosters interdisciplinary alignment between technology, finance, and environmental policy. The rest of the paper is organized as follows: Section 2 reviews the literature in the field to provide an overview of green finance and AI/ML integration and to identify key research themes and gaps. Section 3 briefly explains the data and method used for this study. Section 4 presents the results of the bibliometric analysis, as well as future gaps and trends. Section 5 discusses the findings, and Sect. 6 concludes the paper by highlighting limitations and future work.

2 Related Work

2.1 Overview of Green Finance and AI/ML Integration

Financial institutions and investors increasingly require advanced tools to mitigate risks, assess opportunities and optimize portfolio allocation in green finance. Traditional financial models, which often rely on historical data and assume linear relationships, are insufficient to capture the complexities of green finance [9]. These models struggle to incorporate the dynamic interplay between fluctuating policy environments, emerging technologies, and the volatile market conditions of renewable energy investments. As such, innovative approaches are needed to provide reliable forecasting, risk assessment, and decision-making frameworks in this evolving financial landscape [10]. Recent advances in AI and ML offer promising solutions to these challenges.

The integration of AI/ML into green finance has attracted growing scholarly interest in recent years. Green finance broadly refers to financial strategies aimed at supporting environmental sustainability through tools such as green bonds, ESG-focused investment portfolios, and climate-aligned risk assessments [11]. The increasing demand for the robust and transparent evaluation of sustainability indicators has positioned AI/ML as a transformative solution across various stages of financial decision-making [7]. Early studies emphasized the predictive power of ML for ESG score modeling and climate-related financial risks, demonstrating computational advantages over traditional analytical frameworks [12]. However, many of these contributions are narrow in scope, focusing on specific applications without a unified regulatory or conceptual framework, resulting in fragmented insights across the field [7, 12].

2.2 Key Research Themes in the Literature

Recent literature has highlighted four key areas in which AI and ML have been applied to green finance. One major area is *ESG scoring and corporate sustainability evaluation*. AI tools are increasingly being used to process unstructured ESG data, reduce inconsistencies in sustainability ratings, and improve the granularity of firm-level assessments [5, 13]. These applications provide deeper insights into corporate sustainability and enable more precise comparisons and evaluations. However, despite these advancements, there are still substantial concerns about the transparency of these systems, potential algorithmic bias, and the replicability of their outputs. These limitations remain critical to their broader adoption. Another prominent application lies in *carbon pricing and climate risk modeling*. ML techniques, including deep learning, are used to forecast carbon prices and evaluate transition risks across various climate scenarios. While these models offer advanced capabilities for scenario planning and risk assessment, they also raise concerns around explainability and energy efficiency, especially considering the computational intensity of large-scale ML simulations [14].

AI has also shown promise in *detecting greenwashing and managing ethical risks*. AI systems are designed to detect inconsistencies between company's public ESG disclosures and its actual practices. These systems aim to improve accountability and transparency [15]. However, the reliability of these tools heavily depends on the quality of the input data and the development of interpretable models capable of justifying their outputs. The final area of focus is *optimizing sustainable investment portfolios*. Here, AI and ML are used to construct investment strategies that consider multiple objectives, such as maximizing financial return while aligning with ESG principles and minimizing environmental impact [16]. This integration enables more dynamic and adaptive investment planning. However, the absence of standardized evaluation criteria poses a major obstacle, limiting the ability to compare approaches across different studies or investment contexts.

2.3 Identified Gaps in Existing Research

Despite notable developments, the current body of literature on AI and ML in green finance is fragmented and lacks integration across disciplines. Much of the existing research is siloed, with limited attempts to connect technological innovations with financial practices and policy frameworks. One critical area that remains insufficiently explored is the role of explainable AI (XAI) in promoting stakeholder trust, particularly regarding ESG scoring and sustainable investment decisions [17]. This gap is significant given that transparency and interpretability are central to the responsible use of AI in high-stakes financial applications. Similarly, there is a lack of in-depth analysis regarding the alignment of AI-driven tools with emerging regulatory frameworks, such as the EU SFDR, as well as with international climate goals outlined in the Paris Agreement [7, 8]. Without a clear understanding of how AI applications conform to these policies, their legitimacy and effectiveness in sustainable finance are questionable.

Furthermore, existing reviews often have a narrow focus. Some emphasize algorithmic innovations, overlooking the sustainability implications and contextual relevance of the tools in question (e.g., [18]). Others prioritize environmental or social objectives, neglecting the methodological robustness and reliability of the AI models being applied (e.g., [19]). These imbalances underscore the need for integrative, interdisciplinary reviews that categorize thematic clusters and critically evaluate research quality and alignment with evolving regulatory and ethical standards. In response to these deficiencies, this paper conducts a systematic bibliometric analysis to synthesize recent findings, trace emerging trends, and evaluate the integration of AI and ML into green finance. The paper also investigates whether this integration adequately supports policy compliance and ethical integrity, offering a more cohesive, policy-aware understanding of the field.

3 Methodology

This study employs a systematic approach based on the PRISMA 2020 guidelines for transparent and reproducible reviews [20]. The objective was to synthesize peer-reviewed research on the intersection of AI/ML and green finance to capture the scope, trends, and gaps within the existing literature. First, a conceptual mind map was initially created to reflect key themes from exploratory readings and to guide the formulation of search queries. A systematic search was conducted across three major databases—Web of Science, IEEE Xplore, and ScienceDirect—covering the period from 2019 to early 2025. The search strategy combined keywords related to artificial intelligence, machine learning, ESG, green finance, carbon markets, and sustainability analytics.

The initial database search yielded 864 records. After removing duplicates and screening titles and abstracts, full-text assessments—based only on the introduction and conclusion— were conducted to ensure thematic relevance and methodological quality. Ultimately, 109 studies were included in the final analysis, as illustrated in Fig. 1.

To enrich the analysis beyond qualitative synthesis, a bibliometric analysis was performed using VOSviewer on the final pool of selected articles. This enabled the identification of major keyword clusters, thematic proximities, and potential research topics. Additionally, trend analysis was performed in Python to track the evolution of high-frequency terms over time. This offered insights into the maturation and shifting priorities within the field. Text mining techniques were also applied to generate a word cloud of dominant terms to identify research gaps and recurring challenges in the AI–green finance nexus.

4 Findings

4.1 Bibliometric Mapping and Keyword Clustering

Using VOSviewer, we performed a co-occurrence mapping analysis of author keywords on the selected articles and identified 48 relevant terms. These terms were then grouped into six distinct thematic clusters, as shown in Fig. 2.

Fig. 1 PRISMA flow diagram of study selection process

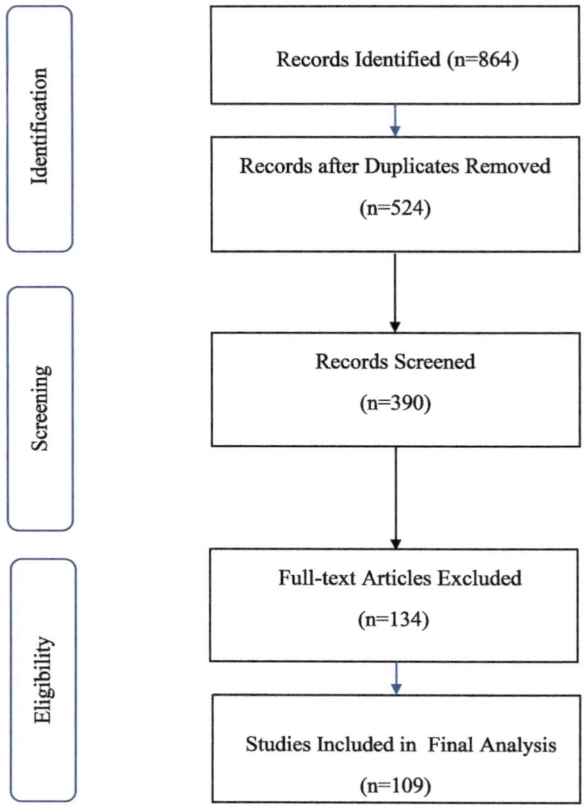

As shown in Table 1, the clusters revealed the following research themes. These thematic areas reflect the interdisciplinary breadth of AI integration in green finance. Specifically, they encompass domains such as AI-driven innovation in sustainable and climate finance; the impact of green finance on both economic and environmental performance; and the application of machine learning in financial modeling and risk evaluation. Other clusters focus on ESG frameworks, sustainability governance, institutional change, and the role of advanced technologies and AI in supporting energy transition and sustainable development goals (SDGs) alignment. Finally, the research highlights the growing interest in digital transformation and the need for robust, AI-related policy infrastructure to ensure responsible deployment.

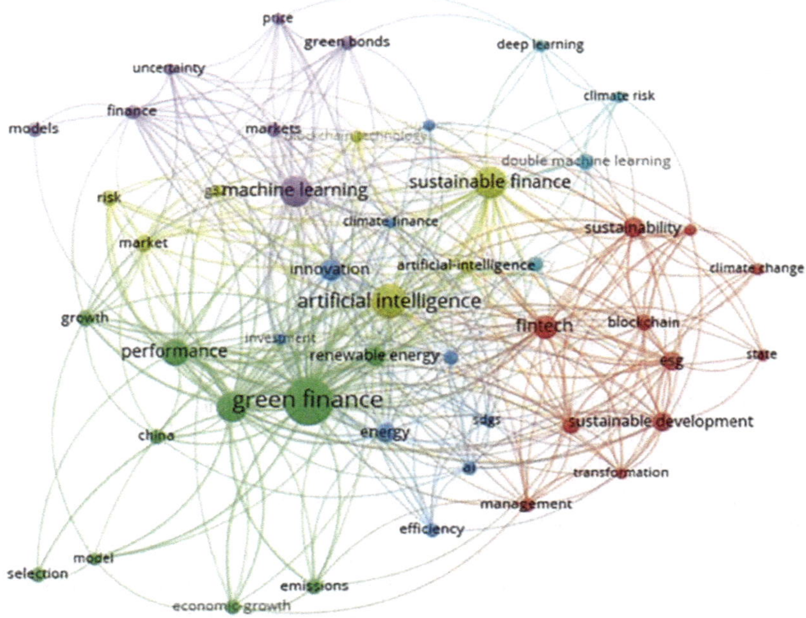

Fig. 2 Keyword co-occurrence network from VOSviewer analysis

Table 1 Thematic clusters identified from keyword co-occurrence analysis

Cluster color	Key terms (prominent)	Probable topic
Yellow	AI, Sustainable Finance, Innovation, Investment	AI-driven innovation in sustainable and climate finance
Green	Green Finance, Performance, Economic Growth, Emissions	Impact of green finance on economic and environmental performance
Purple	Machine learning, Models, Finance, Risk, Uncertainty, Markets, Green Bonds, Price	Machine learning in financial modeling and risk evaluation
Red	Sustainability, ESG, Sustainable Development, Climate Change, Blockchain, Management	ESG frameworks, sustainability governance, and institutional change
Blue	Energy, Efficiency, SDGs, AI, Renewable Energy, Deep Learning	Advanced technologies and AI in energy transition and SDG alignment
Orange	Transformation, Support, Model, State	Digital transformation and AI-related policy infrastructure

4.2 Trend Analysis of Topics (2021–2025)

To capture the temporal evolution of research priorities, a trend analysis was conducted on the final set of included studies using Python. The analysis tracked the frequency of the top ten recurring keywords across publication years. As illustrated

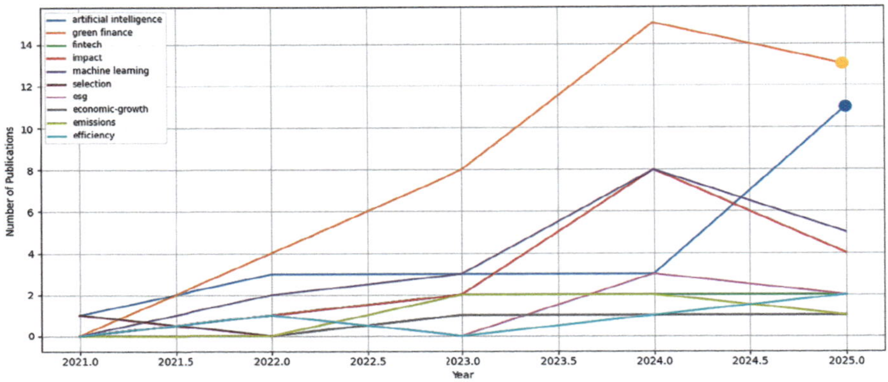

Fig. 3 Trend of research topics over time (top 10 keywords)

in Fig. 3, this temporal mapping visualizes shifts in scholarly attention over time, including the rise of green finance and artificial intelligence and the decline of machine learning and impact investing.

Recent developments in the literature suggest that green finance has grown significantly, establishing itself as a central topic in academic and policy discussions. This growth reflects the financial sector's increasing recognition as a key player in addressing climate and sustainability challenges. Alongside this trend, interest in artificial intelligence has surged, particularly after 2023. This surge is likely driven by advancements in AI capabilities and their potential to improve data analysis, risk assessment, and decision-making in sustainable finance. In contrast, earlier enthusiasm for machine learning, fintech, and impact-oriented studies appears to have peaked, as evidenced by a decline in recent publications in these areas, possibly due to saturation or shifting research priorities. Emerging themes, such as selection methods (e.g., in sustainable asset identification) and efficiency metrics (e.g., in resource allocation or portfolio optimization), are gaining prominence. This suggests a refinement in analytical focus. Despite their importance, topics such as economic growth and emissions continue to receive only modest attention and are often treated peripherally rather than as core research concerns. Overall, these patterns indicate a gradual yet clear shift toward more technical, data-intensive approaches. This shift reflects a maturing field that increasingly relies on computational tools and quantitative methodologies to address the complexities of green finance.

4.3 Research Gaps and Challenges

To complement the thematic and trend analyses, text mining was applied to the final corpus. As shown in Fig. 4, the generated word cloud highlights several dominant terms such as performance and innovation, except for green finance, machine

Fig. 4 Word cloud of keywords

learning, and artificial intelligence, which are the main contexts of this research. These insights guided the identification of major research hotspots in the field.

As shown in Fig. 4, several recurring challenges continue to limit the effectiveness and credibility of AI and ML applications in green finance, as illustrated by the low-frequency keywords. One such issue is the underutilization of XAI, despite its potential to improve transparency and trust in ESG evaluations. Most studies focus on predictive performance, paying little attention to model interpretability—an essential requirement in high-stakes financial decision-making. Additionally, there is a notable disconnect between AI-driven tools and established sustainability frameworks, such as the EU Taxonomy and the UN SDGs. This weak policy alignment undermines the regulatory relevance of many proposed solutions and restricts their practical application in compliance-driven financial environments. Another significant gap lies in the detection of greenwashing. Although natural language processing (NLP) and AI are well-suited for analyzing unstructured ESG disclosures, they are rarely used to systematically identify discrepancies between corporate communications and actual practices.

Data-related challenges further exacerbate these issues. ESG datasets are fragmented and non-standardized across regions, which makes it difficult to compare results or develop models that can be applied universally. The inconsistent quality and availability of data particularly affect the reliability of cross-country assessments and limit generalizability. Additionally, although AI is frequently touted as a means of promoting sustainability, its substantial computational requirements raise concerns about energy consumption, which could undermine environmental goals. The literature insufficiently addresses this trade-off between technological advancement and energy efficiency. Emerging markets are also underrepresented. Few models are designed to function effectively in low-data environments, which leave significant gaps in geographic and socioeconomic inclusivity. Finally, the integration of AI and ML with established financial theories is limited. Most studies prioritize either technical innovation or economic modeling but rarely both. This results in a lack of hybrid models that could more effectively capture the complexity of sustainable finance systems. Addressing these gaps is essential for developing robust, policy-relevant, and ethically aligned AI applications in green finance.

5 Discussion

This systematic review reveals a dynamic yet fragmented research landscape at the intersection of AI, ML, and green finance. The significant increase in attention toward green finance and AI, especially after 2023, indicates the field's growing maturity and societal relevance. However, the relative decline in machine learning and impact investing signals a shift toward more technical, policy-aligned, and explainability-driven methods. Concurrently, the emergence of themes such as efficiency, selection, and energy use is indicating a growing concern for computational sustainability and optimization in decision-making processes. Despite this progress, limited XAI integration continues to hinder stakeholder trust in ESG scoring and algorithmic decision support. Although XAI has been widely discussed in the broader AI literature [17], its application to sustainable finance remains limited, as our findings indicate. This gap is especially critical given the increasing regulatory pressure for transparency under frameworks such as the EU SFDR. Without interpretable and policy-compliant AI tools, financial institutions may struggle to meet the dual mandate of profitability and sustainability [17]. Moreover, fragmented and non-standard ESG datasets, identified across several studies, pose a serious obstacle to replicability and benchmarking. This finding aligns with prior concerns raised by Rahman et al. [16], who emphasized the lack of harmonized metrics in ESG evaluations. These data inconsistencies impair the effectiveness of AI-driven modeling and exacerbate the risk of greenwashing. This is evidenced by the low use of NLP for ESG claim verification.

The analysis also highlights a significant discrepancy between high-performance AI models and climate goals. Many current tools are computationally intensive and energy-hungry, which conflicts with the sustainability principles they are meant to support. Therefore, there is an urgent need to design leaner, context-sensitive AI models, especially for data-scarce emerging markets where financial resources and regulatory capacity are often limited. Finally, the review highlights the absence of hybrid frameworks that integrate financial theory with AI/ML techniques. Most current approaches are either algorithmically sophisticated but economically naïve or financially grounded but technologically shallow. Bridging this divide will require collaboration among AI scientists, financial economists, and sustainability experts. Moving forward, anticipatory research that proactively maps regulatory evolution and integrates foresight methodologies may help align AI innovation with long-term sustainability agendas. All in all, while AI and ML are undoubtedly reshaping green finance, this transformation remains incomplete. Addressing the gaps in explainability, data quality, and policy integration is vital to ensuring these technologies enable—rather than hinder—trust, transparency, and sustainable development.

6 Conclusion

This study confirms that AI and ML are increasingly transforming green finance by enabling more precise ESG scoring, carbon pricing, and climate risk modeling. These technologies promote transparency and facilitate more informed, sustainable investment decisions. However, critical barriers remain, ranging from inconsistent data and algorithmic bias to the high energy demands of complex AI models. The lack of XAI and weak alignment with global policy frameworks further limits trust and practical adoption. To realize AI's full potential in sustainable finance, stronger interdisciplinary collaboration is needed to bridge technological innovation with financial theory and regulatory priorities.

This study has several limitations. First, even though PRISMA guidelines were followed, the selection of databases and keywords may have excluded relevant interdisciplinary studies from nonmainstream journals. Second, the temporal scope (2019–2025) may not fully capture long-term historical developments or very recent unpublished advancements. Third, while bibliometric tools like VOSviewer and keyword-based clustering are useful for pattern detection, they may oversimplify nuanced theoretical contributions. Lastly, the interpretation of research gaps is based on author-coded themes, which may be subjective. Future research should expand the scope of data sources to include not only other databases, such as Scopus and EBSCO, but also gray literature, policy reports, and interdisciplinary publications, which may offer insights that complement those from mainstream academic outlets. Additionally, broadening the temporal range and incorporating continuous or real-time data updates could enhance the identification of emerging trends and recent innovations, especially in rapidly evolving fields such as AI and green finance. Methodologically, combining bibliometric analysis with qualitative content analysis or expert interviews could help uncover deeper theoretical insights and reduce the risk of oversimplification inherent in keyword clustering. Furthermore, developing standardized coding frameworks or conducting collaborative coding with multiple reviewers could improve the reliability and objectivity of thematic interpretations.

References

1. Chen, Y., Wang, X., Li, Z.: Climate change attention and systemic financial risk: a TENET approach. J. Financ. Stab. **60**, 100123 (2024)
2. OECD: OECD Review on Aligning Finance with Climate Goals: Assessing Progress to Net Zero and Preventing Greenwashing. OECD Publishing (2024)

3. Climate Policy Initiative: Global Landscape of Climate Finance 2024: Insights for COP29. Available at: https://www.climatepolicyinitiative.org (2024)
4. Ahmad, F., Boumaiza, A., Sanfilippo, A., Al-Fagih, L.: A detailed comprehensive role of digital technologies in green finance initiative for net-zero energy transition. Adv. Energy Sustainability Res. **2500066** (2025)
5. Friede, G., Busch, T., Bassen, A.: ESG and financial performance: aggregated evidence from more than 2000 empirical studies. J. Sustain. Financ. Invest. **5**(4), 210–233 (2015)
6. Hassanein, A., Tharwat, H.: Artificial intelligence (AI) and green finance. In: The Palgrave Handbook of Green Finance for Sustainable Development, pp. 859–889. Springer, Cham (2024)
7. Lim, T.: Environmental, social, and governance (ESG) and artificial intelligence in finance: state-of-the-art and research takeaways. Artif. Intell. Rev. **57**(4), 76 (2024)
8. Cremasco, C., Boni, L.: Is the European Union (EU) sustainable finance disclosure regulation (SFDR) effective in shaping sustainability objectives? An analysis of investment funds' behaviour. J. Sustain. Finance Invest. **14**(4), 1018–1036 (2024)
9. Benghiat, S., Lahmiri, S.: Evaluating predictive models for three green finance markets: insights from statistical vs. machine learning approaches. Computation. **13**(3), 76 (2025)
10. Chen, H., Zhao, X.: Green financial risk management based on intelligence service. J. Clean. Prod. **364**, 132617 (2022)
11. Taghizadeh-Hesary, F., Yoshino, N.: Sustainable solutions for green financing and investment in renewable energy projects. Energies. **13**(4), 788 (2020)
12. Roy, P., Ghose, B., Singh, P.K., Tyagi, P.K., Vasudevan, A.: Artificial intelligence and finance: a bibliometric review on the trends, influences, and research directions. F1000Res. **14**, 122 (2025)
13. Li, J., Wu, T., Hu, B., Pan, D., Zhou, Y.: Artificial intelligence and corporate ESG performance. Int. Rev. Financ. Anal. **102**, 104036 (2025)
14. Rolnick, D., et al.: Tackling climate change with machine learning. ACM Comput. Surv. **55**(2), 1–96 (2022)
15. Li, D., Zhang, Z., Gao, X.: Does artificial intelligence deter greenwashing? Finance Res. Lett. **67**, 105954 (2024)
16. Rahman, M.S., et al.: FinTech in sustainable banking: an integrated systematic liter-ature review and future research agenda with a TCCM framework. Green Financ. **6**(1), 92–116 (2024)
17. Arrieta, A.B., et al.: Explainable artificial intelligence (XAI): concepts, taxonomies, opportunities and challenges toward responsible AI. Inf. Fusion. **58**, 82–115 (2020)
18. Benaissa, W.O., Mahjoubi, S., Kabbaj, S.: Sustainability meets intelligence: a PRISMA-guided systematic review of AI'S role in ESG financial decision-making. Int. J. Account. Finance Audit. Manag. Econ. **6**(5), 790–806 (2025)
19. Verdecchia, R., Sallou, J., Cruz, L.: A systematic review of green AI. Wiley Interdiscip. Rev. Data Min. Knowl. Discov. **13**(4), e1507 (2023)
20. Page, M.J., McKenzie, J.E., Bossuyt, P.M., Boutron, I., Hoffmann, T.C., Mulrow, C.D., Moher, D.: The PRISMA 2020 statement: an updated guideline for reporting systematic reviews. BMJ. **372**, n71 (2021)

Enhancing Real-Time Contingency Scenario Planning with Retrieval-Augmented Generation Models

Christophe Bisson and Thierry Warin

Abstract Contingency scenario planning (CSP) has become vital for confronting uncertainties and bolstering organizational resilience. However, traditional CSP methods are limited in their ability to adapt quickly to fast-changing environments. While the use of AI in CSP has grown recently, little is known about how generative AI—specifically Retrieval-Augmented Generation (RAG) models—can be leveraged to enhance real-time CSP in unpredictable settings. This study addresses this gap by exploring, for the first time, the integration of RAG models into real-time CSP processes for climate-change scenario creation based on Intergovernmental Panel on Climate Change (IPCC) reports. Our qualitative analysis (including expert insights and empirical data) provides theoretical and practical perspectives on how AI can transform CSP, offering a more robust tool for knowledge workers involved in strategic planning under volatility. In particular, applying RAG to IPCC-based climate scenarios could enable faster and more effective scenario development, leading to greater risk awareness. This research not only illuminates the transformative potential of AI in strategic decision-making but also contributes to the broader discourse on AI-driven innovation in business management. Ultimately, our findings show how RAG models can enhance organizational responsiveness and strategic adaptability in an era defined by uncertainty, filling an important research gap in applying RAG to scenario planning for climate evolution and its consequences.

Keywords Contingency Scenario Planning · Retrieval-Augmented Generation · Generative Artificial Intelligence · Sustainable Development · IPCC

C. Bisson (✉)
SKEMA, Université Cote d'Azur, Paris, France
e-mail: christophe.bisson@skema.edu

T. Warin
HEC Montreal, Montreal, QC, Canada
e-mail: thierry.warin@hec.ca

N. Omrani et al. (eds.), *Human-Machine Synergy and the Digital Future - Exploring Collaboration and Competition Volume 1*, Springer Proceedings in Business and Economics, https://doi.org/10.1007/978-3-032-21347-1_20

1 Introduction

In today's volatile and increasingly unpredictable landscape, organizations face heightened risks and uncertainties. Geopolitical tensions, climate emergencies, and the fast pace of technological change have a profound impact on business environments. In such a context, linear decision-making systems become obsolete, and organizations need a paradigm shift toward decision-making based on possible futures rather than relying solely on past events. As a result, effective contingency scenario planning (CSP) has become essential for navigating disruptions and ensuring organizational resilience (see [1]). However, traditional CSP methods often fall short in adapting to fast-changing environments. Indeed, these approaches are typically conducted via expert brainstorming when qualitative or rely on static models and historical data when quantitative, making them time-consuming and labor-intensive to update [2]. Examples of such traditional methods include:

- Morphological Analysis—a structured brainstorming of all possible combinations of factors to build scenarios [3].
- Delphi Method—an iterative survey of expert opinions to reach consensus on likely scenarios [4].
- Cross-Impact Analysis—exploring how the occurrence of one event could affect the probability of other events [5].

In contrast, the advent of generative artificial intelligence (AI), particularly large language models (LLMs), has introduced transformative capabilities that can greatly enhance the speed, adaptability, and contextual relevance of scenario planning. Generative AI has already revolutionized various domains by automating processes and enhancing knowledge-worker productivity and output quality, while also offering real-time data processing. Its potential to augment CSP lies in the ability to generate diverse scenario narratives and provide dynamic, data-driven updates as new information becomes available. This convergence of AI and strategic planning increases the efficiency of scenario generation and enables more informed decision-making, especially in highly dynamic environments where real-time adaptation is critical.

While existing literature has begun exploring AI applications in scenario planning and improvements in knowledge work productivity [6, 7], a significant research gap remains. Specifically, little is known about how generative AI—and RAG models in particular—can be leveraged to enhance real-time CSP in unpredictable settings. The combination of AI-driven scenario generation with external knowledge retrieval in RAG holds promise for improving both the efficiency and adaptability of CSP, yet empirical research on this specific application is limited.

This study aims to address that gap by examining the integration of RAG models into real-time CSP for climate-change scenarios based on IPCC reports. Using qualitative methods (expert elicitation and empirical analysis), we seek to provide both theoretical and practical insights into how AI can transform CSP application on climate-change scenarios is especially pertinent. Leveraging RAG could enable faster and more effective development of climate scenarios, leading to higher risk awareness and better preparedness for climate-related disruptions.

This research offers a comprehensive view of AI's transformative potential in strategic decision-making and contributes to the broader discourse on AI-driven innovation in management. Ultimately, our findings illustrate how RAG models can become critical tools for enhancing organizational responsiveness and strategic adaptability amid uncertainty (see [8]). We thus fill an important research gap by applying RAG for the first time to scenario planning using IPCC reports—a step that could help anticipate climate evolution and related consequences more effectively.

The remainder of the paper is organized as follows: first, we review recent literature on generative AI for scenario planning and articulate our research question and hypotheses. We then outline our methods, followed by concluding remarks and limitations.

2 Literature Review

Traditional scenario planning involves developing multiple plausible futures (typically 3 to 5) and preparing strategies for each [9]. Many organizations use qualitative approaches (like expert workshops) and/or quantitative techniques (like trend extrapolation) for this. Combining qualitative and quantitative methods is a known frontier in scenario research [2]. The conventional process, however, is time-consuming and resource intensive. The rise of AI has led to growing interest in automating scenario creation [1]. Since 2022, generative AI—particularly LLMs such as OpenAI's GPT-4—has shown significant potential to enhance scenario planning. For example, a recent study found that GPT-3 and GPT-4 can generate future scenarios that are difficult to distinguish from human-crafted ones, underscoring AI's capability to produce high-quality scenario narratives. Foresight expert Sohail Inayatullah has suggested that tools like ChatGPT can handle the "grunt" of data gathering and research, allowing futurists to focus on deeper design work and human insights [10]. In his view, while analytic skills remain important, they may "pale in front of the ability to discriminate and assist in inner transformation," meaning the value of human foresight work will increasingly lie in interpretation and guidance rather than basic analysis.

Generative AI thus offers a transformative approach by automating and expediting scenario generation, improving both efficiency and adaptability. Key themes emerging in recent research include:

- Efficiency in Scenario Generation: Generative AI can rapidly produce diverse scenarios by analyzing vast amounts of data and recognizing patterns not immediately apparent to human planners. This addresses a key limitation of traditional methods often criticized as slow and labor-intensive. For instance, Finkenstadt et al. [11] demonstrate that AI-driven tools can compress scenario planning

cycles from months to days in some cases. Generative models can identify baseline scenario elements by mining historical data and trends, providing a solid foundation on which planners can build.
- Adaptability and Real-Time Updates: The dynamic nature of generative AI allows for real-time adjustments to scenarios as new data emerge. This is crucial in CSP, where rapid response to changing conditions is essential. An AI system can continuously ingest up-to-date information (e.g. news, sensor data) and adjust scenario assumptions or probabilities accordingly. Finkenstadt et al. [11] note that traditional scenario planning's time-consuming processes are especially problematic for CSP and argue that generative AI tools can significantly improve CSP effectiveness by enabling on-the-fly scenario revision.

By providing detailed and varied scenario narratives, generative AI enables decision-makers to consider a broader range of possibilities and to make more informed decisions, especially in uncertain and volatile environments. Kozachek [12] found that AI-generated scenarios can be as rich and plausible as human-generated ones, which means decision-makers using AI have access to scenario sets that are both diverse and credible. This breadth of scenarios helps avoid cognitive biases and "tunnel vision," prompting leaders to prepare for surprises rather than only expected trends.

Methodologically, studies in this area often use case studies, simulations, and field experiments to evaluate generative AI's effectiveness in scenario planning. For example, Finkenstadt et al. [11] illustrate a hypothetical automotive industry scenario planning exercise where an LLM-driven system helped manage supply chain disruption scenarios more effectively than traditional means. Early evidence suggests generative AI can indeed overcome some shortcomings of conventional scenario planning (such as the failure to quickly incorporate new information) and produce actionable insights faster.

Despite these promising developments, there is limited research on the long-term impacts of using generative AI for scenario planning. Most studies to date focus on short-term benefits or isolated cases, leaving open questions about broader implications and potential risks (e.g. over-reliance on AI or scenario quality issues).

The integration of AI into knowledge-intensive tasks has been a major focus of recent research. AI tools, particularly LLM-based assistants, have been shown to enhance productivity by automating routine tasks, providing decision support, and even fostering creativity [6]. In multiple randomized trials, knowledge workers augmented with AI completed tasks faster and with higher quality than those without AI. Key findings and themes include:

- Productivity Enhancement: AI can significantly increase knowledge-worker productivity by automating repetitive or low-value-add tasks, thereby freeing human workers to concentrate on complex and creative activities [6]. For example, in consulting tasks, those given access to GPT-4 completed ~12% more tasks and 25% faster than a control group, on average, while maintaining or improving quality.

- Quality of Work: Studies have also found that AI assistance can improve the quality of output. Mollick et al. [13] report that AI-assisted workers produced work that was evaluated as more than 40% higher in quality (e.g., more insightful and error-free) compared to work produced without AI support. The ability of AI to quickly provide relevant information and even draft content is likely to contribute to these quality gains.

Researchers describe emergent collaboration patterns such as "Centaurs" and "Cyborgs." Centaurs refer to humans who delegate distinct subtasks to AI (as one might to a junior assistant), whereas Cyborgs denote a more integrated workflow where humans and AI continuously interact throughout the task. Both approaches have shown success; for instance, consultants in one study adopted either a centaur strategy (selectively using AI for certain subtasks) or a cyborg strategy (deeply integrating AI into their process), and both groups saw performance improvements. Effective use of AI thus involves balancing delegation and integration to maximize productivity and quality [14, 15].

While the productivity gains are compelling, there is a need for more research on the ethical, social, and psychological impacts of AI in the workplace. Questions remain about long-term effects on job satisfaction, skill development, and organizational dynamics. Additionally, some worry that AI tools could exacerbate inequalities (e.g., between those who have access to them or know how to use them effectively and those who do not). These considerations underscore that adopting AI for knowledge work should be accompanied by training, governance, and an emphasis on human–AI complementarity.

The convergence of generative AI in scenario planning and its impact on knowledge work productivity sets the stage for a unique intersection of research. Both streams highlight AI's transformative potential but also the need for a nuanced understanding of long-term implications. Notably, few studies have explored how generative AI can be specifically leveraged to enhance real-time, dynamic contingency scenario planning for knowledge workers. This gap is especially salient in volatile environments where rapid adaptation and decision-making are critical (e.g. climate crises, geopolitical conflicts, pandemic response). Moreover, to the best of our knowledge, RAG architecture has not yet been applied to scenario creation and planning. Ramirez et al. [16] describe scenarios as "pictures of the future" used to stimulate interesting research and strategic insight; however, no prior work has examined using a retrieval-augmented generator to automatically create and iterate such scenario pictures. Our study addresses this by investigating RAG in the context of climate-change scenario planning, a domain that demands integration of vast, evolving data (scientific, economic, and social) and the generation of coherent futures narratives.

The literature suggests that generative AI could significantly improve CSP by speeding up scenario generation and updating, and by augmenting human planners' productivity. Our work builds on these insights to examine how a RAG-based approach might concretely enhance CSP processes, and what benefits and challenges arise in doing so.

Application Context—RAG for IPCC Climate Scenarios: We focus on the IPCC reports (from 1990 through 2023) as a rich knowledge base for scenario planning in sustainable development. The IPCC [17] assessments are fundamentally about forecasting the future of human development, sustainability, and the complex interactions between the economy, environment, and society. They present numerous modeled scenarios (e.g., emissions pathways, temperature trajectories, socioeconomic futures) which serve as inputs for policy and strategy worldwide. By evaluating how well past IPCC scenario projections have fared and what they included or overlooked, we can derive valuable lessons for future scenario planning.

RAG systems offer a powerful tool for this kind of evaluation and scenario generation. By augmenting human analysis with advanced retrieval capabilities, a RAG model can dynamically pull information from extensive sources (like the corpus of IPCC reports and related data) and use it to generate scenario narratives or to assess existing ones in real time. For instance, RAG has already seen use in specialized domains: researchers have applied RAG in medicine to incorporate up-to-date medical literature into answers, in traffic simulations to generate diverse driving scenarios, and even in cybersecurity to help identify vulnerabilities [18]. These examples suggest that RAG's ability to integrate domain-specific knowledge into generative reasoning can be generalized to new areas like climate scenario planning.

The IPCC scenarios, while comprehensive, inevitably rely on assumptions that may omit certain variables (e.g., disruptive technological breakthroughs or unforeseen policy shifts). Using RAG to retrospectively evaluate IPCC scenario predictions—by automatically cross-referencing what happened with what was predicted—can highlight the impact of those overlooked variables. Such a system can place historical predictions into a modern context, revealing where modeling techniques were sufficient and where they were blindsided by external factors. Ultimately, RAG's capacity to integrate diverse datasets on the fly means scenario generation can become both dynamic and comprehensive, providing a more robust framework for grappling with complex global challenges.

Based on these insights, our primary research question is: How can the evaluation capabilities of RAG systems inform and improve the scenario models proposed in IPCC reports? Put differently, we investigate how a RAG-driven approach to scenario generation and assessment might refine the process and outcomes of climate scenario planning compared to the current state.

To guide our investigation, we propose two hypotheses:

- H1: Integrating RAG systems into scenario planning will enhance the precision and flexibility of IPCC-style scenarios by continuously incorporating updated data and trends, compared to static scenario models. (In other words, a RAG-based process will produce scenarios that more closely mirror evolving reality and can be adjusted on the fly.)
- H2: Evaluating existing IPCC reports with a RAG system will reveal key variables (e.g., the digital economy, global governance changes) that were previously underestimated or omitted. Incorporating these variables via RAG will measurably improve the scenario framework. (Thus, RAG can help expand the

scope of scenario planning to include factors that human forecasters might have underemphasized.)

3 Methods

To explore our hypotheses, we implemented a Retrieval-Augmented Generation (RAG) model tailored to climate scenario planning. RAG is a state-of-the-art approach that combines a generative LLM with a retrieval mechanism, enabling the model to augment its text generation with relevant information fetched from an external knowledge repository. In our implementation, the RAG model uses an input sequence (e.g., a prompt describing a scenario context or question) to retrieve a set of relevant documents, and it incorporates those documents as additional context when generating the output sequence (the scenario narrative or analysis). This allows the model to produce more accurate and contextually enriched outputs by grounding its generation in external knowledge.

The RAG model consists of two key components:

1. Retriever—Denoted $p_\eta(z \mid x)$, with parameters η, which given a query x returns a distribution over text passages z. In practice, the retriever finds the top-K relevant documents for the input x from a large document index.
2. Generator—Denoted $p_\theta(y_i \mid x, z, y_{1:i-1})$, with parameters θ, which generates each token y_i of the output sequence based on the input x, a retrieved document z, and the previously generated tokens $y_{1:i-1}$. Essentially, it's a seq2seq language model that conditions not only on the prompt but also on the content of retrieved documents.

During generation, the model treats the retrieved documents as latent variables that influence the output. We fine-tune both the retriever and generator jointly by marginalizing over these latent documents (i.e., considering the contributions of different retrieved texts to the output probability). We explored two specific RAG variants introduced by Lewis et al. [19]:

- RAG-Sequence Model: In this approach, the same single retrieved document is used to generate the entire output sequence. The retrieved document is treated as one latent variable. The model retrieves top-K documents, then for each document the generator produces a candidate output and its probability. The final output distribution is the marginalization (mixture) over these K possibilities. Formally, if z represents a retrieved document, RAG-Sequence approximates $p(y|x)$ as:

$$p_{\text{RAG-Sequence}}\left(y|x\right) \approx \sum_{z \in \text{top-K}\left(p_\eta\left(\cdot|x\right)\right)} p_\eta\left(z|x\right); p_\theta\left(y|,x|,z\right), \tag{1}$$

- meaning we weigh the generator's output probability by the retriever's score for each document. Intuitively, the model considers "if document 1 were the grounding source, the probability of this output would be X; if document 2 were the source, the probability would be Y," and so on, then averages these, weighted by document relevance.
- RAG-Token Model: In this approach, the model can retrieve a potentially different document for each token generated. Here, the latent document can change at each generation step, allowing the generator to draw information from multiple sources within a single answer. The probability of an output sequence is computed by marginalizing over documents at every time step. Formally:

$$p_{\text{RAG-Token}}\left(y|x\right) \approx \prod_{i=1}^{N} \sum_{z \in \text{top-K}\left(p_{\eta}\left(\cdot|x\right)\right)} p_{\eta}\left(z|x\right); p_{\theta}\left(y_i|,x|,z|,y_{1i-1}\right), \tag{2}$$

- where the inner sum marginalizes different retrieved docs for token i. This model offers more flexibility, as it can draw facts from multiple documents to compose a single answer. In scenarios requiring integration of various data points, RAG-Token can be advantageous, though it is more computationally complex.

Retriever Implementation—Dense Passage Retrieval (DPR) Our retriever $p_{\eta}(z \mid x)$ is based on the Dense Passage Retrieval method. DPR uses a bi-encoder architecture with dual BERT-based encoders: one for queries and one for documents. It encodes each document $d(z)$ and query $q(x)$ into fixed-length dense vectors in the same vector space. Relevance is then computed by the dot product or cosine similarity between these vectors. Specifically, we maximize $q(x) \cdot d(z)$ for relevant (x, z) pairs. We built an index of documents (the "non-parametric memory") consisting of all text from the six IPCC assessment reports (First through Sixth Assessment Reports, including summaries) and related publications. Each document (e.g. a paragraph or section) is represented as a vector. Given an input query (for example, "What are the predicted economic impacts of a 2 °C warming scenario by 2050?"), the DPR retriever quickly finds the top-K most similar passages from the IPCC corpus that may contain pertinent information. We used a pre-trained DPR model for initialization (specifically, a model pre-trained on general QA tasks) and then further fine-tuned it on our domain-specific Q&A pairs to better suit climate content. Under the hood, retrieving top-K documents efficiently are achieved via Maximum Inner Product Search (MIPS) algorithms on the vector index. This allowed real-time retrieval even from tens of thousands of IPCC passages.

Generator Implementation—BART For the generator p_{θ}, we employed BART-large (400 million parameters), a transformer-based encoder-decoder model known for its strong performance on generation tasks. BART was pre-trained on a denoising objective, making it adept at generating coherent text from partially corrupted inputs. In our RAG setup, we concatenate the input query with the content of a retrieved document, separated by a special token, and feed this into BART. For example, if the query is "IPCC projections for sea-level rise," and the retriever provides a relevant paragraph from an IPCC report, we input: "Query: IPCC projections for sea-level rise [Paragraph text]" to the BART model. BART then generates a response that integrates the query context with facts from the paragraph. Because BART's parameters serve as the "parametric memory" and the retrieved text as "non-parametric memory," this approach leverages both the knowledge encoded during pre-training and the specific up-to-date information from retrieval.

Training Procedure We fine-tuned the RAG model (both retriever and generator) on a custom training set of input-output pairs. These pairs were constructed from scenario-related Q&A and summarization tasks based on the IPCC reports. For instance, one training example might use an input: "According to IPCC 2007, what were the expected impacts on biodiversity?" with an output being a summary of those impacts from the report. During training, we optimize the negative marginal log-likelihood of the correct output sequence, marginalizing over the latent documents. In practice, for each training query x with ground-truth answer y, we retrieved K documents and then used the generator to produce a probability distribution over outputs. The loss encourages the model to assign high probability to the correct y across all retrieved evidence. We employed stochastic gradient descent (Adam optimizer) and kept the document encoder (BERT) fixed initially to speed up training, later unfreezing it for a few epochs for fine-tuning. This approach (keeping the retrieval index fixed most of the time) avoids the need to constantly re-embed the entire document corpus, greatly reducing computational cost.

We experimented with both RAG-Sequence and RAG-Token modes during training. RAG-Sequence is simpler and was used for initial training epochs to stabilize learning. We then introduced RAG-Token in later epochs to allow the model to retrieve different mid-generation documents for answers that required multi-source synthesis.

Decoding Strategy At test time, the decoding strategies differ slightly between RAG-Sequence and RAG-Token. For RAG-Sequence, we perform beam search for each of the top retrieved documents and then marginalize the results. Essentially, the model generates one answer assuming document 1 is the source, another assuming document 2, etc., then picks the best overall answer among these (or a weighted combination if needed). For RAG-Token, decoding proceeds token-by-token: at each generation step, the model considers multiple documents for the next token prediction, marginalizes over them, chooses the token, and repeats. We used a beam width of 5 for generation. To maintain tractability with RAG-Token, we limited K to 5 and the number of tokens to 128, which in practice was sufficient for generating a few paragraphs of scenario analysis.

Data and Knowledge Sources Our document corpus consisted of the six main IPCC Assessment Reports (published in 1990, 1995, 2001, 2007, 2014, and 2023, respectively), including their Synthesis Reports and Summaries for Policymakers. In total, these are thousands of pages of climate science and scenario information.

We also included supplementary sources cited by IPCC (for instance, key scenario studies and socioeconomic data) to enrich the knowledge base. In the references, this corpus is summarized as "IPCC (2025) Synthesis Report"—essentially referring to the entirety of knowledge up to the Sixth Assessment Report. By training the RAG model on this domain-specific corpus, we enable it to "learn" how to use external climate data to build scenarios. The retriever becomes specialized in pulling out relevant content (e.g. emissions figures, quotes from scientists, scenario assumptions) that the generator can then weave into its output.

To evaluate H1, we designed experiments where the RAG-augmented model generates scenarios under various conditions, and we compare them to scenarios produced by a static model (one that doesn't have retrieval) and to actual IPCC scenario outcomes. For H2, we analyze which new variables or information the RAG model brings into scenarios that were absent in the original IPCC narratives.

4 Conclusion and Limitations

The integration of RAG models into contingency scenario planning represents a significant advancement in strategic decision-making, particularly for environments characterized by high volatility and uncertainty. Our investigation shows that RAG models—with their ability to dynamically retrieve external data and generate real-time, context-enriched scenarios—offer organizations a powerful tool to enhance both the efficiency and adaptability of planning processes. In the context of climate-change scenarios, for example, a RAG-based approach can rapidly incorporate the latest scientific findings or real-world events into scenario outlooks, potentially leading to better risk awareness and proactive strategy adjustments.

Several specific contributions of RAG to CSP emerged from our study:

- Speed and responsiveness: RAG automates the retrieval of up-to-date information and the generation of scenario narratives, dramatically compressing the timeline for scenario planning. What once might have taken expert teams weeks of research and writing can be accomplished in a fraction of the time. This responsiveness is crucial when organizations face sudden disruptions—RAG can help decision-makers "game out" scenarios on the fly using the most current data available.
- Expanded scenario scope: By drawing from a vast corpus of documents, RAG models can expand the range of factors considered in scenarios. Our climate case study illustrated that the RAG model surfaced several variables (like emerging carbon capture technologies and geopolitical shifts in energy policy) that were underemphasized in some earlier IPCC scenario sets. Incorporating these elements led to more robust scenarios that consider a broader set of plausible futures (supporting H2).
- Improved precision of information: In generating scenario outputs, the RAG model often provided specific quantitative references (pulled from reports)—for

instance, citing exact projections or dates—which increases the credibility and detail of scenarios. This on-demand precision is harder to achieve with purely human-driven processes or with static models that might rely on dated data.

- Decision support and insights: The dynamic generation of scenarios also enables a form of "on-demand foresight." Decision-makers can query the RAG system with hypothetical or specific questions (e.g. "What if global CO_2 emissions peak by 2030?") and receive scenario analyses that draw on established knowledge. This offers a new way to stress-test strategies against an array of scenarios quickly, enhancing strategic adaptability.

Despite these advantages, adopting RAG models for CSP is not without challenges. Key limitations and considerations include:

- Data quality and bias: The output of a RAG model is only as good as the data it retrieves and the training it has undergone. If the document corpus has gaps, outdated information, or inherent biases, the model's scenarios will reflect those. For instance, we noted that if certain socioeconomic variables are not well-covered in past reports, the RAG model might underplay them unless additional data is fed in. Ensuring a high-quality, comprehensive knowledge base (and updating it continuously) is crucial.
- Over-reliance on AI: There is a risk that organizations might become over-reliant on AI-generated scenarios and neglect the critical human judgment aspect. Scenario planning benefits from creativity, interpretative storytelling, and ethical considerations that humans contribute. AI might not fully capture qualitative nuances (like social sentiments or ethical dimensions of futures). Hence, RAG should be seen as an augmentation tool for human planners, not a replacement. A balanced human-in-the-loop approach, where experts review and contextualize AI outputs, is recommended.
- Ethical and transparency issues: The "black box" nature of complex AI models means they might generate content in scenarios that is hard to trace back to sources (though RAG is better in this respect since it can point to retrieved documents). Users must be cautious about inadvertently introducing confidential or sensitive information if the retrieval corpus isn't carefully managed. Moreover, scenario planning often involves value-laden assumptions—if these are hidden in an AI's training data, they should be transparently communicated.
- Resource intensiveness: RAG models, especially at large scale, can be computationally intensive. Retrieving and processing thousands of documents on the fly requires robust infrastructure. Organizations must weigh these costs and ensure they have the technical capacity for deployment. Fortunately, techniques like index pre-loading and efficient neural search (which we utilized) can mitigate this to some extent.

So, RAG models hold transformative potential across multiple strategic domains—from competitive strategy and risk management to corporate finance and operations—wherever scenario planning and rapid information synthesis are key. By enhancing organizations' ability to quickly respond to emerging risks and opportunities with informed scenario analyses, RAG can serve as a vital component of building resilience and maintaining a competitive edge in the fast-changing business landscape.

We advocate for further empirical studies on RAG-augmented scenario planning in different contexts. For example, applying RAG to real-time financial stress testing, or to public health emergency planning, would extend our findings and possibly reveal domain-specific challenges. Longitudinal studies could assess how decision-makers use and trust AI-generated scenarios over time. Additionally, improving the interpretability of RAG outputs (so that users can see why a model says what it says) will be important for adoption. Overall, our work is an early step toward AI-enhanced strategic foresight—an area ripe for innovation as organizations seek to navigate an era of unprecedented uncertainty and complexity.

References

1. Pratt, L., Bisson, C., Warin, T.: Bringing advanced technology to strategic decision-making: the decision intelligence/data science (DI/DS) integration framework. Futures. **152**, 10321 (2023)
2. Bisson, C., Diner, Ö.Y.: Strategic early warning system for the French milk market: a graph theoretical approach to foresee volatility. Futures. **87**, 10–23 (2017)
3. Ritchey, T.: General morphological analysis as a basic scientific modelling method. Technol. Forecast. Soc. Chang. **126**, 81–91 (2018)
4. Linstone, H.A., Turoff, M.: Delphi: a brief look backward and forward. Technol. Forecast. Soc. Chang. **78**(9), 1712–1719 (2011)
5. Gordon, T.J.: Cross-impact analysis. In: Futures Research Methodology (Version 3.0). The Millennium Project (2012)
6. Rajendran, S., Krayer, L., Candelon, F., Lakhani, K.R., Dell'Acqua, F., McFowland III, E., Mollick, E., Lifshitz-Assaf, H., Kellogg, K.C.: Navigating the Jagged Technological Frontier: Field Experimental Evidence of the Effects of AI on Knowledge Worker Productivity and Quality. Harvard Business School Working Paper No. 24–013 (2023)
7. Spaniol, M.J., Rowland, N.J.: Defining scenario. Fut. Foresight Sci. **1**(1), e3 (2019)
8. Bisson, C., Calof, J., Boukef, N.: Exploring the relationship between organizational agility, competitive intelligence and foresight as parts of an anticipatory system. Technol. Forecast. Soc. Chang. **215**, 124112 (2025)
9. Welferinger, S., Bisson, C.: Vaincre la Surprise Stratégique pour l'Économie de la Défense via le Système Stratégique de Signaux Précoces. Vie & sciences de l'entreprise. **214-215**(2), 288–306 (2022)
10. Inayatullah, S.: Reconstructing ChatGPT—part 2. J. Futures Stud. (2023)
11. Finkenstadt, D.J., Sotiriadis, J., Guinto, P., Eapen, T.T.: Contingency scenario planning using generative AI. Calif. Manag. Rev. Insights. (2024)
12. Kozachek, D.: Investigating the perception of the future in GPT-3, −3.5 and GPT-4. In: 15th Conference Proceedings on Creativity and Cognition, pp. 282–287. Association for Computing Machinery, New York (2023)
13. Mollick, E., Lifshitz-Assaf, H., Kellogg, K.C.: Navigating the Jagged Technological Frontier: Field Experimental Evidence of the Effects of AI on Knowledge Worker Productivity and Quality. SSRN Working Paper 4573321 (2023)
14. Dell'Acqua, F., Ayoubi, C., Lifshitz-Assaf, H., Sadun, R., Mollick, E.R., Mollick, L., Han, Y., Goldman, J., Nair, H., Taub, S., Lakhani, K.R.: The Cybernetic Teammate: A Field Experiment

on Generative AI Reshaping Teamwork and Expertise. Harvard Business School Strategy Unit Working Paper No. 25–043 (2025)
15. Kellogg, K.C., Lifshitz-Assaf, H., Randazzo, S., Mollick, E., Dell'Acqua, F., McFowland III, E., Candelon, F., Lakhani, K.R.: Novice risk work: how juniors coaching seniors on emerging technologies such as generative AI can lead to learning failures. Inf. Organ. **100559** (2024)
16. Ramirez, R., Mukherjee, M., Vezzoli, S., Kramer, A.M.: Scenarios as a scholarly methodology to produce "interesting research". Futures. **71**, 70–87 (2015)
17. IPCC: IPCC Sixth Assessment Report Synthesis (Climate Change 2023). Summary for Policymakers (2023)
18. Cheng, P., Wu, Z., Du, W., Zhao, H., Lu, W., Liu, G.: Backdoor attacks and countermeasures in natural language processing models: a comprehensive security review. ArXiv. preprint arXiv:2309.06055. (2023)
19. Lewis, M., Liu, Y.H., Goyal, N., Ghazvininejad, M., Mohamed, A., Levy, O., Stoyanov, V., Zettlemoyer, L.: BART: Denoising sequence-to-sequence pre-training for natural language generation, translation, and comprehension. In: 58th Annu. Meeting Proceedings of the Association for Computational Linguistics, pp. 7871–7880, online (2020)

Mapping AI-Driven Sustainability Research: A Meta-Review Using Topic Modeling

Iandolo Francesca, La Sala Antonio, Maielli Giuliano, and Vito Pietro

Abstract This study conducts a structured analysis of scientific contributions dealing with artificial intelligence (AI) and sustainability. By applying the JS-LDA (JavaScript Latent Dirichlet Allocation) thematic modeling to a dataset of 1295 research articles obtained from Web of Science using the narrowly focused query "artificial intelligence AND sustainab*" in the titles or author keywords of the contributions, this work provides a structured landscape of research on the reciprocal interdependencies between the development of artificial intelligence and the objectives of sustainability and sustainable development, quantifying thematic trends and minimizing subjectivity in thematic classification. The scientific landscape, which has been forced into 15 topics that cover the different aspects of the relationship between sustainability and AI, reveals a fragmentation of research interests, ranging from general topics such as environmental integration and efficiency and economic and application-driven approaches (the topics which scholars pay the most attention) to focused research areas such as corporate adoption of green innovation, education and AI in learning, and others. To help clarify this fragmentation, the correlations between the different topics are analyzed, thus indicating areas of scientific interest shared between disciplinary backgrounds and therefore of potential collaboration and cross-fertilization. From a methodological perspective, the use of unsupervised machine learning techniques in literature review ensures reproducibility and establishes a computational framework that can efficiently process and analyze large and growing datasets without losing accuracy or efficiency. Results of this standardized research framework supports policy formation, academic research and industry decision-making, indicating the ways in which AI applications can align with global sustainability goals, including the United Nations Sustainable Development Goals (SDGs).

I. Francesca · L. S. Antonio · V. Pietro (✉)
Sapienza University of Rome, Rome, Italy
e-mail: francesca.iandolo@uniroma1.it; antonio.lasala@uniroma1.it; pietro.vito@uniroma1.it

M. Giuliano
Queen Mary University of London, London, UK
e-mail: g.maielli@qmul.ac.uk

N. Omrani et al. (eds.), *Human-Machine Synergy and the Digital Future - Exploring Collaboration and Competition Volume 1*, Springer Proceedings in Business and Economics, https://doi.org/10.1007/978-3-032-21347-1_21

Keywords Artificial Intelligence · Sustainability · Meta-review · Topic modeling · Machine Learning

1 Introduction

Artificial intelligence represents a transformative power that enhances global sustainability efforts according to Goralski and Tan [1]. The application of AI-driven technologies received widespread recognition when industries and research teams and governments used these platforms to optimize resources and enhance decision-making while minimizing sustainability risks [2]. AI transforms sustainability management through improved energy efficiency as well as circular economy models [3] and climate change adaptation strategies [4]. AI applications in sustainability grow at an exponential rate while smart cities use predictive city planning [5, 6] and advanced machine learning algorithms improve climate model prediction and biodiversity preservation. Different intellectual fields including environmental science and social sciences along with economics and business and engineering constitute the multifaceted relationship between AI and sustainability. The integration of machine learning and natural language processing and deep learning technologies within supply chain management systems shows a growing trend according to Kamble et al. [7] and these technologies also play an important role in sustainable agriculture [8], renewable energy optimization as well as providing support for climate risk assessment [9]. The extensive research papers currently exist in fragmented parts due to the substantial number of studies which obstacle researchers from extracting general patterns or recognizing essential research areas according to Denicolai et al. [10]. The analysis of how AI promotes sustainability requires a comprehensive method to identify existing research domains along with their scope and necessary investigation areas. Scientists use a systematic methodology to study and classify sustainable contributions made by Artificial Intelligence in this extensive investigation. We have chosen a meta-review method instead of traditional literature review practice because it enables us to evaluate selected literature reviews directly. Through this method we align our research work with other academic investigations in order to showcase its distinctive value. The established framework aims to enhance present sustainability studies regarding AI by identifying main research themes and showing uncaptured scholarly topics in need of additional exploration. Topic modeling serves as our analytic tool because it represents an unsupervised machine learning approach that extracts hidden themes from big textual datasets. The unaided machine learning method of topic modeling helps researchers in systematic classification of research fields and groups similar publications together by recognizing conceptual interconnections between AI and sustainability. The research analysis employs JS-LDA from Cornell University as its probabilistic topic modeling tool for categorizing AI and sustainability studies. LDA allocates numerical probabilities to words and topics, which helps identify linked groups of related concepts that naturally appear together within documents. This method was developed to boost literature synthesis objectivity because human thematic categorization bias would get eliminated. Through computational analysis, we achieve the discovery of unavailable structures which manual literature review techniques may not reveal immediately. The present investigation aims to resolve essential research topics such as which main themes remain prominent within AI-sustainability research. The current literature has several missing components, which AI systems can use to enhance sustainable challenges moving forward. Our research answers fundamental queries that effectively depict AI-driven sustainability concepts while providing essential information to academic researchers and both policy decision-makers and industrial leadership groups. Knowledge of these major themes enables researchers to plan future directions, support policy decision-making, as well as ensure proper AI technology utilization toward sustainable objectives [11]. To address the fragmentation of existing studies and guide future scholarly efforts, this research seeks to answer the following question: What are the main thematic areas explored in the scientific literature on AI and sustainability, and which underexplored topics warrant further investigation? This study embraced structured research to establish key areas of sustainability impact by AI along with evaluating different AI-based technological applications used in environmental conservation and economic development and social benefit efforts. AI-powered innovations drive industrial change mainly through human–robot collaboration systems in sustainable production [12], along with AI and blockchain unified technology for smart city growth [6]. AI will continue developing its sustainable role so future trends should receive ongoing analysis and monitoring [13]. The study builds future infrastructure to connect AI creation with sustainable goals including the United Nations Sustainable Development Goals (SDGs). In addition to its methodological novelty, this study makes an original contribution to the field by unveiling—through computational analysis—the thematic fragmentation and disciplinary clustering that characterize current AI-sustainability literature. By mapping 1295 scientific contributions into 15 data-driven topics and analyzing their interrelations, our results highlight not only the prevailing areas of scholarly interest (such as environmental integration, economic applications, and predictive modeling) but also neglected domains like AI's role in governance, social equity, and ethical deployment. These findings—difficult to derive through manual review—offer a structured foundation for advancing interdisciplinary collaboration and targeted policy development. As such, this research serves both as a diagnostic of the field's current configuration and as a strategic guide for future inquiry aligned with global sustainability objectives.

2 Literature Review

Since our research is a literature review, we studied recent academic publications to show what our work uniquely achieved. Instead of writing a regular literature review we selected and studied several research review pieces to show how our study differs from others in its field. Through this method we base our study on earlier findings while defining areas in research that our work will fill and new angles to explore (Table 1).

While existing literature reviews have extensively examined how AI contributes to various sustainability domains—ranging from agriculture and healthcare to construction and energy—most remain focused on sectoral applications or specific technologies. These reviews often rely on manual qualitative categorization, which, although valuable, introduces subjectivity and limits comparability across studies. Furthermore, only a few studies attempt to provide an integrated perspective on how these various applications relate to broader sustainability goals or how thematic clusters evolve over time. Our study addresses these limitations in two ways. First, by conducting a meta-review focused specifically on the structure and content of existing literature reviews, we identify cross-cutting patterns and recurrent research gaps that might otherwise go unnoticed. Second, the use of unsupervised topic modeling (JS-LDA) allows us to reveal latent thematic structures and inter-topic relationships across a large corpus of scientific reviews, reducing human bias and enhancing reproducibility. In doing so, we contribute both a methodological innovation and a conceptual map that helps organize the fragmented research landscape on AI and sustainability.

The approach we take in this literature review separates from existing research through distinctive characteristics. This research follows a meta-review method by assessing the multiple literature reviews about AI and sustainability instead of compiling individual research studies. This research methodology positions our study against the academic literature base along with revealing main research patterns and missing investigation topics. Our study goes beyond qualitative review by using topic modeling as a computational method that conducts objective research theme classification. The implementation of JS-LDA (JavaScript Latent Dirichlet Allocation) lets our research extract hidden topics from numerous publications to reduce human influence when categorizing topics. This analytical method differs from previous work that depended only on personal evaluation of research reports. The review extends AI-sustainability perspectives through its analysis of various academic fields such as environmental science and engineering together with business along with social sciences. Current literature reviews about AI and sustainability fail to establish systematic affiliation assessments between main themes and research voids. Through this study we group existing research findings and specify dormant fields including AI's environmental impact assessment and governance management as well as interdisciplinary teamwork requirements. The methodology section of our study ensures research reproducibility through a detailed design including defined search procedure and computational framework with distinguished exclusion parameters which maintain documentation and enable research duplicability. The data-driven structured method in our study stands apart from current studies on AI and sustainability because of its research approach.

Table 1 Overview of selected literature reviews on AI and sustainability

Author, year	Type of review	Sample	Main insights about AI and sustainability
Agrawal et al., 2022 [14]	Systematic Bibliometric Review & Network Analysis	165 articles	AI tools integrated with Industry 4.0 enhance Circular Economy practices, reducing waste and improving resource efficiency
Andronie et al., 2021 [15]	Systematic	174 articles	Cyber-physical production networks use AI for automated, sustainable decision-making in manufacturing
Bao & Xie, 2022 [16]	Systematic	131 research publications	AI improves animal farming through behavior detection, disease monitoring, and environment tracking, but challenges remain in accuracy and cost
Cavazza et al., 2023 [17]	Structured	37 contributions	AI enables new business models in agriculture, but barriers include lack of understanding and investment needs
Di Vaio et al., 2020 [18]	Systematic & Bibliometric Analysis	73 publications	AI supports sustainable business models and SDGs but requires ethical and legal considerations
Kar et al., 2022 [19]	Systematic	287 papers out of 8341 search results	AI applications in various industries (construction, healthcare, agriculture) contribute to sustainability through resource efficiency and decision-making
Manzoor et al., 2021 [20]	Systematic	105 research publications	AI enhances civil engineering sustainability, with interconnectivity and data analytics playing key roles
Nikseresht et al., 2022 [21]	Systematic & Bibliometric Analysis	534 research articles	AI assists sustainable decision-making under VUCA conditions, particularly in waste management and circular economy
Rafiq et al., 2022 [22]	Systematic	32 papers from 103 relevant sources	AI is used to enhance privacy in Big Data applications, improving cybersecurity in sustainability reporting
Rahman et al., 2022 [23]	Systematic	42 scientific papers	AI in Life Cycle Engineering (LCE) supports sustainability in production and supply chain, but logistics applications remain underexplored
Smith & Wong, 2022 [24]	Systematic	77 papers	AI-based decision support systems improve sustainability in construction, with hybrid AI models gaining traction
Vasileiou et al., 2024 [25]	Systematic	68 research articles	AI in agriculture, particularly deep learning, enhances eco-friendly weed management and reduces herbicide use

(continued)

Table 1 (continued)

Author, year	Type of review	Sample	Main insights about AI and sustainability
Vishwakarma et al., 2025 [26]	Systematic	89 articles	AI strengthens healthcare resilience and sustainability, particularly in medical research and pandemic response
Waqar et al., 2023 [27]	Systematic	115 research articles	AI optimizes sustainability in oil and gas construction projects, improving efficiency and reducing risks
This study	Meta Review using Topic Modeling	1295 research articles	Identifies thematic patterns, fragmentation, and underexplored areas across AI-sustainability research

3 Methods

3.1 Data Acquisition

The query in Web of Science has been designed to retrieve relevant research articles that focus on artificial intelligence (AI) and sustainability while excluding certain document types that are less relevant for our analysis. The search terms "artificial intelligence" AND sustainab* ensure that the retrieved articles explicitly discuss AI and various forms of sustainability, such as sustainable development or sustainability practices. Searching within the title and author keywords ensures that these topics are central to the studies rather than being mentioned incidentally. The language filter limits results to English to maintain linguistic uniformity, a necessary condition for the correct execution of topic modeling algorithms. The exclusion of document types such as retractions, news items, corrections, meeting abstracts, letters, book reviews, book chapters, retracted publications, editorial materials, and review articles is a deliberate methodological choice aimed at ensuring the reliability, originality, and consistency of the dataset. Retractions and corrections are, by definition, associated with content that has been revised or invalidated, and therefore could introduce distortions or inaccuracies into the analysis. Similarly, meeting abstracts, letters, and editorials often lack the methodological depth and peer-review rigor required for inclusion in a structured literature study. Book reviews and book chapters, while potentially insightful, vary greatly in format, structure, and scientific robustness, and often do not follow standardized empirical or theoretical protocols. Their inclusion would risk compromising the coherence and comparability of the corpus. Furthermore, review articles, although valuable in synthesizing existing knowledge, are excluded in this phase to avoid circularity, given that the present study conducts a meta-review of reviews and focuses on analyzing the broader research ecosystem rather than reinterpreting other summaries. By narrowing the dataset to original research articles published in peer-reviewed journals, the study ensures that the topic modeling analysis reflects primary contributions to the field. This enhances both the validity of the thematic structures identified and the reliability of the conclusions drawn from them. The resulting corpus is therefore composed of autonomous and methodologically sound research outputs, making it suitable for computational analysis and for deriving insights on the conceptual evolution of AI and sustainability scholarship.

For the sake of reproducibility of this study, the query is reported below:

"artificial intelligence" AND sustainab* (Title) or "artificial intelligence" AND sustainab* (Author Keywords) and English (Languages) and Retraction or News Item or Correction or Meeting Abstract or Letter or Book Review or Book Chapters or Retracted Publication or Editorial Material or Review Article (Exclude – Document Types)

The query produced 1381 results. To create a uniform database that would facilitate the subsequent classification of contributions into individual topics, 1295 articles were extracted from these results. These articles included complete abstracts -which were subjected to topic modeling algorithm—along with author keywords and DOIs.

3.2 *Methodology and Tools*

A large collection of text documents receives a pattern discovery and topic detection through unsupervised machine learning using topic modeling [28, 29]. The process analyzes how words co-occur alongside each other to group frequently co-appearing words for detecting the implicit topical structure in a set of documents. The basic concept of topic modeling depends on how similar contextual use of words demonstrates shared semantic meanings which allows the algorithm to cluster words into separate topics. Topic modeling serves exploration-based text data analysis through its uncategorized nature because it avoids needing predefined labels which makes it a strong method for text-based research. The procedure of discovering word relationships and distributing probabilistic interpretations to topics allows researchers to detect latent themes embedded in textual information. The technique proves essential for processing extensive unstructured information which could not be efficiently organized through manual labor. The created topics present an understandable summary of the corpus data which enables understanding field-level conversations and detect both intellectual advances and literature research deficiencies. The technique proves exceptionally helpful during literature review studies where analysts can determine trends and organize research subjects while studying topical transformations through time [30]. The conventional process of reviewing literature uses manual and subjective approach to categorization yet introduces uncertainties and subjectivity into study analysis. Topic modeling represents an automated method for literature analysis through data-driven procedures that enhance the objective and scalable evaluation of academic content. The system helps users visualize intellectual trends to determine idea evolution while tracking the dominant topics that various academic fields and author sources promote. Manual literature synthesis becomes excessively difficult and time-consuming because of the increasing number of available research materials. Our work detects important themes within the research collection as well as showcases the prevalent scientific areas and emerging developments that unite AI with sustainability. The method provides an organized system for examining how AI systems solve sustainability problems across various areas such as energy conservation as well as environmental tracking and circular economic systems and ethical AI management practices. The use of topic modeling in this investigation allows for better understanding of how AI affects sustainability together with creating a predictable analytical method which can scale up. Mechanized learning provides an impartial method to combine diverse knowledge sources which delivers important findings that researchers and policymakers require in this actively transforming field.

The implementation of topic modeling has been conducted through JS-LDA (JavaScript Latent Dirichlet Allocation), developed by Cornell University. Probability distributions drive LDA to assign words such that it extracts thorough thematic structures in a given corpus. JS-LDA stands out as an excellent solution because it combines ease of use with a compact system design and direct web-based processing features for text document sets. JS-LDA enables scalable topic modeling through its system that does not need large computational abilities therefore it works well for studying academic literature databases. The use of JS-LDA topic modeling in this research leads to systematic category organization and synthesis of findings which improved the navigation and reproducibility of findings from AI and sustainability studies.

4 Findings

This section presents the main results of the topic modeling analysis applied to the corpus of research articles. It includes the identification of key thematic areas through keyword association, the distribution of topics across the dataset, the structure of the document classification, and the interconnections between different research themes. Together, these findings offer a comprehensive overview of the thematic landscape at the intersection of AI and sustainability.

4.1 Words per Topic

Table 2 presents the main keywords associated with each identified topic, highlighting the dominant concepts and areas of focus emerging from the dataset.

Table 2 Thematic keyword allocation resulting from topic modeling

1. Systems challenges ethical human change issues food potential technologies social
2. Development environmental process method different used economic also application products
3. Potential insights integration environmental practices framework challenges across within efficiency
4. Learning data machine design system methods building deep detection techniques
5. Smart data urban technologies cities iot technology city systems internet
6. Covid management risk using natural pandemic work health forest method
7. Supply industry chain tourism manufacturing literature production review management construction
8. Concrete water strength agricultural models production materials agriculture properties compressive
9. Performance green innovation data technology relationship impact factors corporate adoption
10. Model models data using performance network neural accuracy used prediction
11. Education students learning educational higher using teaching use teachers tools
12. Development digital technologies goals sdgs economic economy technology industry role
13. Energy power consumption systems system renewable demand optimization production solar
14. Environmental carbon emissions impact climate consumption energy reduction pollution conditions
15. Healthcare health development social sdg science global data public literature

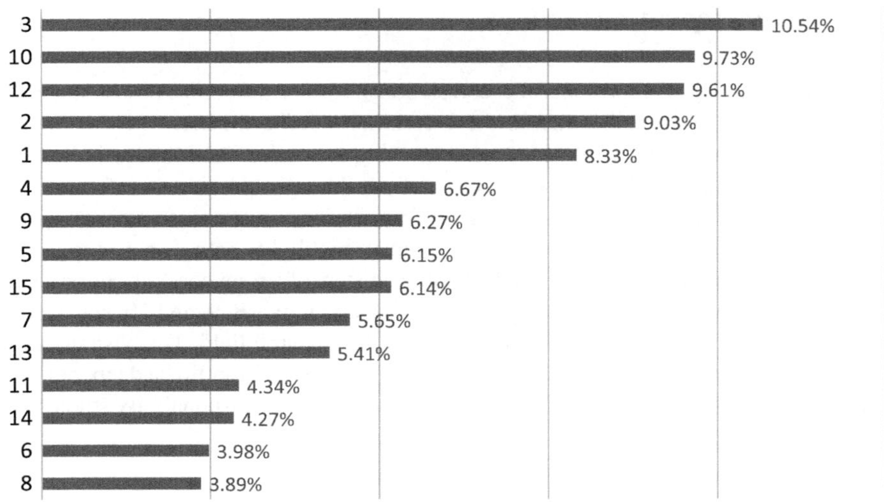

Fig. 1 Distribution of research topics in AI and sustainability (%)

4.2 *Topic Distribution*

The bar chart in Fig. 1 presents the distribution of research topics related to AI and sustainability, illustrating the percentage of articles associated with each topic. The *y*-axis represents different research topics, while the x-axis displays their relative importance in terms of the proportion of studies dedicated to them.

4.3 Documents per Topic

The algorithm generates 15 matrices which have dimensions of 1295 × 10. The research articles exist as rows in each matrix which includes attributes of these articles as columns. The topics column in the matrix indicates article relevance for a particular topic where higher values describe greater relevance. PT represents a classification code. AU maintains a list of all authors in each article while TI presents the document title. The SO entry indicates the publication journal or source which contains the article. DE includes all significant keywords contributed by article authors that characterize the main content of their work. A summary of research appears inside the Abstract section which belongs to AB. Citations of an article are tracked through the TC keyword. Readers can find the publication year through the PY field while they can access the full article by following the DOI link in DI. The complete dataset is not presented within this work but additional material containing the dataset accompanies the original research.

4.4 Topic-Topic Connections

The matrix in Fig. 2 represents the correlation between different AI-sustainability research topics. Each cell indicates the correlation coefficient between two topics, with lighter shades representing positive correlations and darker shades indicating negative correlations. The grayscale color bar on the right provides a reference for interpreting the correlation values, ranging from strongly negative to strongly positive. The distribution of shades across the matrix highlights areas where topics are closely related or inversely associated. Notable clusters of strong correlations or negative relationships can be observed, particularly around topics 8, 9, and 10, suggesting distinct patterns of thematic connections within the research field. This visualization provides insight into how different research areas intersect, supporting a deeper understanding of the structure and interdependencies in AI-driven sustainability studies.

5 Discussion and Implication

5.1 Characterizing Topics

The authors assigned independent descriptive titles to interpret topics by using their knowledge of keywords as well as their contextual connections. Each author examined the connected words inside a topic area to determine its fundamental theme through an evaluation of word frequency and their semantic meaning linkage.

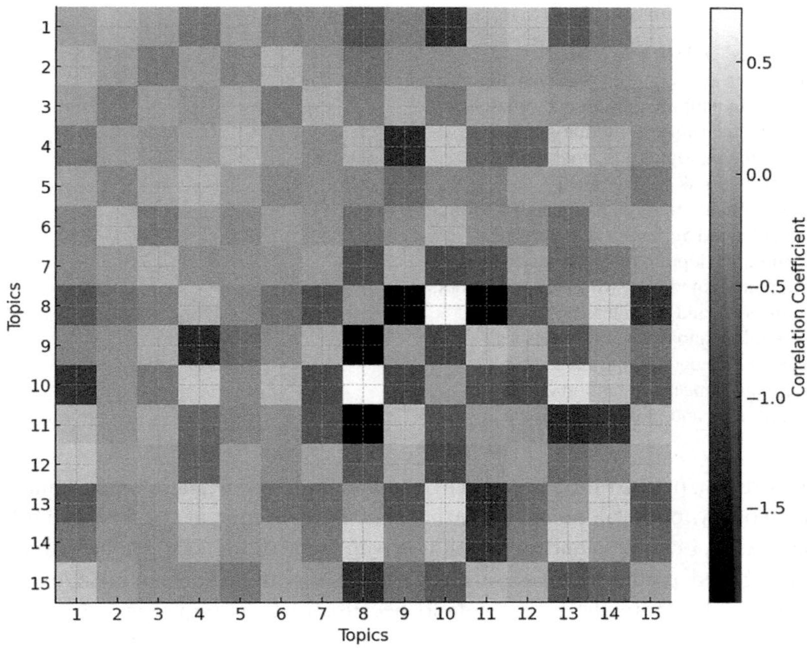

Fig. 2 Correlation matrix of AI-sustainability research topics

Different authors interpreted the topic in different ways because they focused either on technical aspects or economic factors or societal and ethical aspects. Following the distribution of specific research topics to each member the authors evaluated their respective interpretations before they found similarities or differences between them. The Authors addressed their conflicting interpretations by participating in a group discussion that examined both the essential vocabulary items and their environmental meanings to find appropriate heading titles. The authors supported their decision-making process by demonstrating applicability as well as clarity alongside consistency for each title while addressing ambiguities to capture the fundamental meaning of each subject. The researchers worked toward consensus by merging different interpretive elements but maintained a balance of specific and general terms to achieve broad and direct representation of the data structure. The following reports the outcome of this operationalization method (Table 3).

5.2 *Topic Distribution*

The examination topics in the dataset show the varying amounts of interest and research intensity dedicated to sustainability and artificial intelligence disciplines. Due to growing industry and policy-making use of sustainable innovation coupled

Table 3 Thematic titles assigned to topics emerging from the analysis

1. AI, ethics, and societal change
2. Economic and application-driven approaches
3. Environmental integration and efficiency
4. Machine learning methodologies
5. Urban technologies and smart cities
6. COVID-19 risk management
7. Supply chain, tourism, and manufacturing
8. Concrete and agricultural materials
9. Corporate adoption of green innovation
10. Predictive modeling with neural networks
11. Education and AI in learning
12. Digital technology for development
13. Renewable energy optimization
14. Climate impact and carbon emissions
15. Healthcare and global health data

with AI-driven optimization both environmental integration and efficiency and digital technology for development topics become more prominent (10.54% and 9.61%, respectively). Economic and application-driven methodologies together with neural network-based predictive modeling each receive similar substantial attention at 9.03% and 9.73% in the research field because of their importance for sectoral decision-making and efficiency improvement. The combination between AI and ethical and social challenges forms a major research focus area within the dataset. The combination of topics about urban technologies and smart cities with topics on corporate adoption of green innovation demonstrates moderate representation at 6.15% and 6.27%, respectively, thus indicating that AI-driven urban sustainability expands yet remains more specific than typical AI implementations. The use of healthcare and global health data (6.14%) and machine learning methodologies (6.67%) appear in moderate quantities because AI advances these sectors while remaining an emerging technology. Concrete and agricultural materials as well as COVID-19 risk management appear less frequently (3.89% and 3.98%, respectively) than broader economic environmental and technological challenges. AI plays a vital strategic role in industrial sustainability through its applications in supply chain operations and tourism and manufacturing functions (5.65%) as well as renewable energy optimization systems (5.41%) but not as much as it does in economic or predictive analytical areas. The distribution of education and AI in learning (4.34%) and climate impact and carbon emissions (4.27%) remains lower than other areas possibly because AI research in these domains is developing progressively behind economic and industrial and predictive analytics fields. The distribution demonstrates that AI mainly serves sustainability through optimization functions and integration and predictive applications without a substantial presence in specialized areas.

5.3 Topic-Topic Connections

The analysis of topics in correlation shows significant associations between different sections of AI and sustainability because some disciplines impact each other. Neural network predictive modeling shows a strong negative relation (Topic 10) to concrete and agricultural materials (Topic 8) indicating that few applications of AI-driven predictive analytics exist within traditional material sciences and industrial applications for construction and agriculture. Smart cities express moderate negative relationships with corporate green innovation adoption (Topic 9) and climate impact and carbon emissions (Topic 14) at the same time indicating limited direct effects on large-scale sustainability strategies. The integration of ethical considerations with technological progress (Topic 1) shows limited positive relationship with digital technology advancement (Topic 12) throughout discussions about AI governance techniques and fair implementation of technology. The alignment between renewable energy optimization (Topic 13) and machine learning methodologies (Topic 4) is low because AI contributes to energy efficiency while machine learning researchers concentrate on different areas rather than renewable energy applications directly. The adoption of green innovation by companies shows a moderate link between environmental influence and carbon emissions despite rising corporate environmental focus in strategic decision-making (Topic 9, Topic 14). The specific nature of pandemic-related AI applications explains why COVID-19 risk management shows minimal connections to other major topics as it appears in isolation from sustainability discussions (Topic 6). Lower but noticeable relationships exist between education paired with AI learning methods and digital technology strategies for development (Topic 11) since education serves as a key mechanism for AI adoption toward economic growth alongside social advancement (Topic 12). Different dimensions of AI and sustainability show specific mutual synergies based on their relationships that display both clear integrated areas as well as distinct and underdeveloped interdisciplinary connections.

The identified findings present valuable implications which benefit academic researchers alongside decision-making authorities. The research indicates that environmental integration with efficiency and economic applications and predictive modeling represent vital aspects because literature prioritizes optimization achievements and industrial technical efficiency. The rising importance of AI as a solution for measurable sustainability issues is confirmed by this study though it shows that sustainability research does not sufficiently address critical social and ethical components alongside governance issues. Important regions such as AI education at Topic 11 along with climate impact at Topic 14 and social equity aspects in global health at Topic 15 receive insufficient attention compared to other fields although they are essential for reaching sustainable long-term transitions. The research imbalance seems to derive from three main factors including the difficulty of using artificial intelligence to measure social effects and the absence of interdisciplinary collaboration and favoritism toward technological solutions over structural or behavioral modifications. A low association exists between AI ethics work (Topic 1) and activities involving corporate green innovation (Topic 9) and smart cities (Topic 5) demonstrating distant relations between innovation execution and ethical considerations. Full ethical AI development requires strict connection between theoretical norms and actual implementations dedicated to assuring fairness and transparency and accountability. Analysis of the matrix demonstrates multiple chances where different parts of the field could combine their efforts. The low connection between renewable energy optimization (Topic 13) and machine learning methodologies (Topic 4) shows AI technology fails to optimize environmental domains with its current development level. A gap in innovation exists in traditional and resource-intensive industries since predictive modeling (Topic 10) demonstrates no substantial connection to agriculture or materials science (Topic 8). Strategic decision-makers should develop comprehensive research models that fuse computer science approaches with environmental science knowledge as well as public policy procedures and ethically responsible science practices and social science methods. Policy decision-makers and funding institutions need to understand these thematic silos because they should promote integrative research projects that meet sustainability goals particularly focusing on SDGs 4, 5, 10, and 16. The methodological framework presented as unsupervised machine learning with meta-review of reviews reveals ability to identify neglected areas while serving as basis to establish agendas backed by evidence. Research expansion can employ two strategies to understand AI-sustainability theme developments. The first involves monitoring theme progression through time and the second examines institutional and author relationships to reveal active hubs in integrative research.

5.4 *Opportunities for Further Study*

The results of this meta-review highlight not only the richness but also the fragmentation of existing scholarships on the intersection of artificial intelligence and sustainability. The 15 detected topics through topic modeling indicate which sustainability and artificial intelligence topics need additional investigation to achieve stronger integrated research progress. Ethical and societal reflections about AI lack sufficient connection points that guide practical deployments across smart cities and manufacturing as well as corporate innovation sectors. Research must concentrate on ethical principle implementation and practical implementation methods which will achieve transparency alongside inclusiveness and accountability in AI-based sustainability solutions. The research merits intensive work to combine various academic disciplines into unified research projects. The structure of the research shows that most current studies remain within separate academic areas due to limited interaction between technological and environmental as well as economic and social scholarly perspectives. Strengthening programs that connect dissimilar research fields stands vital for tackling complex sustainability problems through integrated solutions. Sustainable projects currently focus greater emphasis on environmental and economic metrics rather than the social aspects. The present research domain dedicates minimal attention to subjects that involve education and social justice and healthcare. The time has arrived to apply AI capabilities toward system optimization as well as inclusive development which involves inequality reduction and well-being improvement for society. A crucial deficiency exists when it comes to sustainability governance of AI systems. Only a small number of research studies concentrate on institutional along with policy frameworks that determine both potential barriers and feasible routes for sustainable AI implementation. Research in the future should investigate approaches to create regulatory systems and decision-making processes and public policies that sponsor responsible innovation which advances global targets. The present studies present fixed observations about the research field. The rapid pace of AI technology development together with sustainability matters necessitates research methods that monitor how new research priorities form during subsequent time periods. Most scientific investigations remain focused on only a few Sustainable Development Goals which include those related to energy along with climate and industrial applications. SDGs that present minimal investigation like peace and justice along with life below water and partnerships require enhanced focus particularly in developing areas and areas with limited resources. The solution of these identified gaps will help future studies combine disciplines while linking AI innovation with sustainability development in a more productive manner.

6 Conclusion and Limitation

The research establishes central sustainability and AI interaction domains which show the primary study directions present in published academic works. Nonetheless, the use of AI in various aspects of sustainability still has more research questions to answer and needs additional work in terms of improvement. One of the significant weaknesses is that much of the work done remains within disciplinary compartments. It implies that for AI to work at its full potential, interdisciplinary collaborations between computer scientists, environmentalists, economists, policy makers, and the practitioners in different industries are required. AI should therefore be integrated with policy-making and regulatory instruments for the realization of sustainable economic development in a globe that requires the achievement of social, economic, and environmental goals.

Research on AI technology and sustainability faces specific limits on what findings can be used. Working with topic modeling produces both intelligent findings and specific analysis barriers during thematic research process. Through JS-LDA LDA discovers hidden topics based on probabilistic models yet users must set parameters for the algorithm to generate effective results based on dataset conditions.

References

1. Goralski, M.A., Tan, T.K.: Artificial intelligence and sustainable development. Int. J. Manag. Educ. **18**(1), 9 (2020). https://doi.org/10.1016/j.ijme.2019.100330
2. Nishant, R., Kennedy, M., Corbett, J.: Artificial intelligence for sustainability: challenges, opportunities, and a research agenda. Int. J. Inf. Manag. **53**, 13 (2020). https://doi.org/10.1016/j.ijinfomgt.2020.102104
3. Bag, S., Pretorius, J.H.C., Gupta, S., Dwivedi, Y.K.: Role of institutional pressures and resources in the adoption of big data analytics powered artificial intelligence, sustainable manufacturing practices and circular economy capabilities. Technol. Forecast. Soc. Change. **163**, 14 (2021). https://doi.org/10.1016/j.techfore.2020.120420
4. Galaz, V., Centeno, M.A., Callahan, P.W., Causevic, A., Patterson, T., Brass, I., Levy, K.: Artificial intelligence, systemic risks, and sustainability. Technol. Soc. **67**, 10 (2021). https://doi.org/10.1016/j.techsoc.2021.101741
5. Allam, Z., Dhunny, Z.A.: On big data, artificial intelligence and smart cities. Cities. **89**, 80–91 (2019). https://doi.org/10.1016/j.cities.2019.01.032
6. Singh, S., Sharma, P.K., Yoon, B., Shojafar, M., Cho, G.H., Ra, I.H.: Convergence of blockchain and artificial intelligence in IoT network for the sustainable smart city. Sustain. Cities Soc. **63**, 16 (2020). https://doi.org/10.1016/j.scs.2020.102364
7. Kamble, S.S., Gunasekaran, A., Parekh, H., Mani, V., Belhadi, A., Sharma, R.: Digital twin for sustainable manufacturing supply chains: current trends, future perspectives, and an implementation framework. Technol. Forecast. Soc. Change. **176**, 13 (2022). https://doi.org/10.1016/j.techfore.2021.121448
8. Rose, D.C., Chilvers, J.: Agriculture 4.0: broadening responsible innovation in an era of smart farming. Front. Sustain. Food Syst. **2**, 87 (2018). https://doi.org/10.3389/fsufs.2018.00087
9. Hannan, M.A., Al-Shetwi, A.Q., Ker, P.J., Begum, R.A., Mansor, M., Rahman, S.A., Muttaqi, K.M.: Impact of renewable energy utilization and artificial intelligence in achieving sustainable development goals. Energy Rep. **7**, 5359–5373 (2021). https://doi.org/10.1016/j.egyr.2021.08.172
10. Denicolai, S., Zucchella, A., Magnani, G.: Internationalization, digitalization, and sustainability: are SMEs ready? Technol. Forecast. Soc. Change. **166**, 120650 (2021). https://doi.org/10.1016/j.techfore.2021.120650
11. Braganza, A., Chen, W., Canhoto, A., Sap, S.: Productive employment and decent work: the impact of AI adoption on psychological contracts, job engagement and employee trust. J. Bus. Res. **131**, 485–494 (2021). https://doi.org/10.1016/j.jbusres.2020.08.018
12. Liu, Q., Liu, Z., Xu, W., Tang, Q., Zhou, Z., Pham, D.T.: Human-robot collaboration in disassembly for sustainable manufacturing. Int. J. Prod. Res. **57**(12), 4027–4044 (2019). https://doi.org/10.1080/00207543.2019.1578906
13. Bhat, J.R., Alqahtani, S.A.: 6G ecosystem: current status and future perspective. IEEE Access. **9**, 43134–43167 (2021). https://doi.org/10.1109/ACCESS.2021.3054833
14. Agrawal, R., Wankhede, V.A., Kumar, A., Luthra, S., Huisingh, D.: Progress and trends in integrating industry 4.0 within circular economy: a comprehensive literature review and future research propositions. Bus. Strat. Environ. **31**(1), 559–579 (2022). https://doi.org/10.1002/bse.2910
15. Andronie, M., Lazaroiu, G., Stefanescu, R., Uta, C., Dijmarescu, I.: Sustainable, smart, and sensing technologies for cyber-physical manufacturing systems: a systematic literature review. Sustainability. **13**(10), 5495 (2021). https://doi.org/10.3390/su13105495
16. Bao, J., Xie, Q.J.: Artificial intelligence in animal farming: a systematic literature review. J. Clean. Prod. **331**, 129956 (2022). https://doi.org/10.1016/j.jclepro.2021.129956
17. Cavazza, A., Dal Mas, F., Paoloni, P., Manzo, M.: Artificial intelligence and new business models in agriculture: a structured literature review and future research agenda. Br. Food J. **125**(13), 436–461 (2023). https://doi.org/10.1108/bfj-02-2023-0132

18. Di Vaio, A., Palladino, R., Hassan, R., Escobar, O.: Artificial intelligence and business models in the sustainable development goals perspective: a systematic literature review. J. Bus. Res. **121**, 283–314 (2020). https://doi.org/10.1016/j.jbusres.2020.08.019
19. Kar, A.K., Choudhary, S.K., Singh, V.K.: How can artificial intelligence impact sustainability: a systematic literature review. J. Clean. Prod. **376**, 134120 (2022). https://doi.org/10.1016/j.jclepro.2022.134120
20. Manzoor, B., Othman, I., Durdyev, S., Ismail, S., Wahab, M.H.: Influence of artificial intelligence in civil engineering toward sustainable development–a systematic literature review. Appl. Syst. Innov. **4**(3), 52 (2021). https://doi.org/10.3390/asi4030052
21. Nikseresht, A., Hajipour, B., Pishva, N., Mohammadi, H.A.: Using artificial intelligence to make sustainable development decisions considering VUCA: a systematic literature review and bibliometric analysis. Environ. Sci. Pollut. Res. **29**(28), 42509–42538 (2022). https://doi.org/10.1007/s11356-022-19863-y
22. Rafiq, F., Awan, M.J., Yasin, A., Nobanee, H., Zain, A.M., Bahaj, S.A.: Privacy prevention of big data applications: a systematic literature review. SAGE Open. **12**(2), 21582440221096445 (2022). https://doi.org/10.1177/21582440221096445
23. Rahman, H., D'Cruze, R.S., Ahmed, M.U., Sohlberg, R., Sakao, T., Funk, P.: Artificial intelligence-based life cycle engineering in industrial production: a systematic literature review. IEEE Access. **10**, 133001–133015 (2022). https://doi.org/10.1109/access.2022.3230637
24. Smith, C.J., Wong, A.T.C.: Advancements in artificial intelligence-based decision support systems for improving construction project sustainability: a systematic literature review. Informatics. **9**(2), 43 (2022). https://doi.org/10.3390/informatics9020043
25. Vasileiou, M., Kyrgiakos, L.S., Kleisiari, C., Kleftodimos, G., Vlontzos, G., Belhouchette, H., Pardalos, P.M.: Transforming weed management in sustainable agriculture with artificial intelligence: a systematic literature review towards weed identification and deep learning. Crop Prot. **176**, 106522 (2024). https://doi.org/10.1016/j.cropro.2023.106522
26. Vishwakarma, L.P., Singh, R.K., Mishra, R., Kumari, A.: Application of artificial intelligence for resilient and sustainable healthcare system: systematic literature review and future research directions. Int. J. Prod. Res. **63**(2), 822–844 (2025). https://doi.org/10.1080/00207543.2023.2188101
27. Waqar, A., Othman, I., Shafiq, N., Mansoor, M.S.: Applications of AI in oil and gas projects towards sustainable development: a systematic literature review. Artif. Intell. Rev. **56**(11), 12771–12798 (2023). https://doi.org/10.1007/s10462-023-10467-7
28. Blei, D.M.: Probabilistic topic models. Commun. ACM. **55**(4), 77–84 (2012). https://doi.org/10.1145/2133806.2133826
29. Blei, D.M., Ng, A.Y., Jordan, M.I.: Latent dirichlet allocation. J. Mach. Learn. Res. **3**, 993–1022 (2003) https://jmlr.csail.mit.edu/papers/v3/blei03a.html
30. Hannigan, T.R., Haans, R.F., Vakili, K., Tchalian, H., Glaser, V.L., Wang, M.S., Jennings, P.D.: Topic modeling in management research: rendering new theory from textual data. Acad. Manag. Ann. **13**(2), 586–632 (2019). https://doi.org/10.5465/annals.2017.0099

Digital Innovation for Sustainable Public Procurement: Overcoming Barriers and Unlocking Opportunities with AI

Alessia Sciarrone, Mario Calabrese, and Kamel Ben Youssef

Abstract Public procurement is increasingly recognized as a strategic tool for advancing sustainability objectives across the European Union (EU). Recent reforms promote the digitalization of procurement processes and encourage the adoption of advanced technologies such as artificial intelligence (AI). While AI holds significant potential to enhance supplier evaluation, ESG performance monitoring, and transparency, its integration in public procurement remains limited and underexplored, especially in relation to sustainability goals.

This short paper sets out to explore the emerging role of AI in sustainable public procurement, with the aim of understanding how AI could support environmental and social objectives and what factors may enable or hinder its adoption in the public sector. The study will be developed through a constructivist Grounded Theory approach, combining literature review, policy analysis, and prospective interviews with procurement officials, policymakers, and technology providers. The intended outcome is the development of a conceptual governance framework that aligns AI integration with sustainability, regulatory compliance, and public value creation. This contribution will lay the groundwork for future empirical investigation and offer early insights for scholars and policymakers navigating the intersection of technology, procurement, and sustainability.

Keywords Sustainable public procurement · Artificial intelligence · Public sector · ESG integration · Digital transformation · Governance framework

A. Sciarrone (✉) · M. Calabrese
Department of Management, Sapienza University of Rome, Rome, Italy
e-mail: alessia.sciarrone@uniroma1.it; mario.calabrese@uniroma1.it

K. B. Youssef
Department of Management et Gestion, University of Paris Nanterre, Nanterre, France
e-mail: benyouss@parisnanterre.fr

N. Omrani et al. (eds.), *Human-Machine Synergy and the Digital Future - Exploring Collaboration and Competition Volume 1*, Springer Proceedings in Business and Economics, https://doi.org/10.1007/978-3-032-21347-1_22

1 Introduction

Public procurement is a cornerstone of the European Union (EU) economy, representing approximately 14% of the EU's gross domestic product (GDP) and involving annual expenditures of €1.9 trillion across more than 250,000 public authorities [1]. As a key mechanism for acquiring goods, services, and infrastructure, public procurement is regulated to ensure equal treatment, non-discrimination, and transparency.[1] However, despite clear legislation, many contracting authorities still prioritize cost over social, environmental, and innovation factors, limiting public procurement's transformative potential [2]. In response, the EU has progressively acknowledged the necessity of strategically reorienting procurement frameworks toward sustainability. Recent policy discussions at the European level emphasize the need to move beyond mere regulatory compliance, advocating for procurement to be leveraged as a mechanism for generating social value, promoting sustainability, and fostering inclusiveness.[2] To drive this transformation, the EU has established a foundational framework for the digitalization of public procurement, advocating for the integration of advanced technologies, including artificial intelligence (AI), to enhance efficiency, regulatory oversight, and decision-making processes. The foundation for this shift was set by Directive 2014/24/EU, which promoted the adoption of electronic procurement processes to improve competition, reduce administrative burdens, and mitigate corruption risks. Building on this framework, several EU Member States have introduced national reforms aligned with these principles. In Italy, for example, Legislative Decree No. 36/2023 mandates the use of certified digital platforms throughout the procurement lifecycle, enabling streamlined access to tender documentation, bid submissions, and contract monitoring. This move reflects a broader ambition to institutionalize digital procurement practices across the EU.

By centralizing and standardizing procurement data, digital procurement platforms not only streamline processes but facilitate AI-driven procurement innovation through data-driven decision-making and predictive analytics. AI is increasingly recognized for its capacity to analyze vast datasets, optimize decision-making [3–5], and enhance strategic resource allocation. Leveraging machine learning algorithms and predictive analytics, AI enables contracting authorities to extract meaningful insights from procurement data, improving efficiency in evaluating tenders, forecasting market conditions, and optimizing procurement strategies [6, 7]. Additionally, AI-powered compliance mechanisms [8] strengthen regulatory oversight by detecting anomalies, assessing supplier credibility, and minimizing integrity risks in real time. AI also

---

[1] European Parliament and Council of the European Union. (2014). Directive 2014/24/EU of the European Parliament and of the Council of 26 February 2014 on public procurement and repealing Directive 2004/18/EC. Official Journal of the European Union, L 94, 1–135. Available at: https://eur-lex.europa.eu/legal-content/EN/TXT/?uri=CELEX%3A32014L0024

[2] *A New Vision for Public Procurement in the European Union* (2024). Conference held in Rome, Italy, 12–13 September 2024. Available at: https://www.anticorruzione.it/en/-/a-new-vision-for-public-procurement-in-the-european-union

holds significant potential for advancing Green Public Procurement (GPP), particularly in optimizing supplier evaluations and improving sustainability assessments [9]. GPP has emerged as a key policy instrument across EU Member States, aligning procurement practices with the European Commission's sustainability objectives [10]. AI-driven analytics support contracting authorities in assessing procurement's environmental and social impact, ensuring compliance with the EU GPP framework. Machine learning and predictive algorithms refine supplier selection, improve supply chain transparency, and enhance process efficiency, strengthening sustainability, risk management, and resilience [11]. Additionally, AI-powered monitoring systems provide data-driven insights, enabling public institutions to track sustainability performance and measure progress toward European Green Deal targets [12].

Despite these advantages, the application of AI in sustainable public procurement remains an emerging field with limited empirical evidence on its effectiveness in integrating sustainability criteria into procurement decision-making. While research has extensively examined AI in private-sector procurement [13–15], its implementation in public procurement remains underexplored [16–19]. More broadly, existing scholarship reveals significant gaps in understanding the complexities of AI adoption within the public sector [20–23], particularly in procurement. Studies highlight the scarcity of empirical research on AI's practical implementation in government operations [24] and the lack of clarity regarding the mechanisms through which AI fosters public value creation [25]. AI's adoption in procurement is not simply a technological upgrade: it is embedded in a broader ecosystem of institutional actors, regulatory frameworks, and operational mechanisms, where success depends on the alignment of digital tools with sustainability objectives. To capture this complexity, the study adopts a multi-layered, interpretative lens, drawing on recent reflections on public-sector digital transformation [26] and systems-thinking approaches to decision-making [27–29]. Within this perspective, AI is viewed not as a linear tool for efficiency, but as a socio-technical system shaped by institutional dynamics, stakeholder interactions, and evolving governance structures [26, 30]. Its implementation raises not only technical and regulatory challenges, but also ethical and institutional tensions, especially where decisions affect citizen rights, service access, and public trust [22]. In this light, ethicality is seen as relational and context-specific, emerging from concrete experiences [31]. These considerations call for reflexive, learning-oriented governance models [32], capable of navigating complexity while aligning AI use with public values such as transparency, fairness, and human oversight [33].

2 Objective

This study examines the adoption of AI in public procurement, with a particular focus on its role in advancing sustainability and the determinants of its integration within governmental procurement systems. The research is structured around three core objectives:

1. Investigate the impact of AI on sustainable public procurement, with emphasis on supplier evaluation, ESG performance monitoring, and supply chain transparency. The study assesses AI's potential to enhance GPP, mitigate greenwashing risks, and improve compliance with sustainability criteria.
2. Identify barriers and enablers of AI adoption in the public sector, analyzing the regulatory, technological, and institutional dynamics that influence its implementation. Specific attention is given to challenges such as institutional inertia, data governance constraints, and skill gaps, as well as policy mechanisms that promote digital transformation.
3. Develop a framework for the sustainable digitalization of public procurement, aligning AI integration with public value creation, transparency imperatives, and long-term sustainability goals. This objective aims to provide a conceptual scaffold for guiding policymakers and public procurement authorities in navigating digital innovation responsibly.

3 Methods

Given the early stage of research on AI in public procurement, this study adopts an exploratory qualitative approach [34] based on a constructivist Grounded Theory [35–37]. This method enables an iterative yet structured analysis, integrating theoretical insights with empirical findings.

1. Literature review and policy analysis. The literature review focuses on three key areas to establish a conceptual foundation for the study:
   - AI in Sustainable Procurement: Examining AI's role in enhancing supplier evaluation, sustainability monitoring, and supply chain transparency, with a focus on its potential to optimize decision-making and reduce sustainability-related risks.
   - AI in the Public Sector: Analyzing AI adoption in public administration, addressing regulatory challenges, data governance, ethical considerations, and institutional resistance.
   - AI in Sustainable Public Procurement: Investigating how AI is being integrated into public procurement processes to support sustainability objectives, identifying empirical evidence on its effectiveness and implementation barriers.
   - A policy review of key directives such as Directive 2014/24/EU and the AI Act will assess their impact on AI-driven procurement.
2. Empirical investigation. Semi-structured interviews with procurement officials, policymakers, and technology providers will explore barriers, facilitators, and AI's perceived impact. Constructivist Grounded Theory will guide thematic analysis.

3. Framework development. Findings will inform a governance framework aligning AI adoption with sustainability and regulatory compliance. This framework will offer strategic guidance for AI-driven procurement.

4 Findings

Findings will offer a deeper understanding of how AI-driven systems contribute to procurement decision-making, particularly in the assessment of suppliers, the monitoring of environmental and social performance, and the enhancement of transparency in supply chains. The study will identify key barriers to AI adoption in public procurement, including regulatory constraints, technological limitations, and institutional inertia, while also highlighting enabling factors, such as policy incentives, digital capabilities, and evolving governance frameworks. By synthesizing theoretical and empirical perspectives, the research aims to delineate a structured approach to the sustainable digitalization of procurement, proposing an adaptive framework for AI-driven procurement, ensuring integrity, accountability, and compliance with sustainability standards. These insights will contribute to a more comprehensive understanding of AI's transformative potential in procurement ecosystems and inform future scholarly and policy discussions on digital innovation in public administration.

5 Implications

This study advances scholarly and practical understanding of AI's role in procurement governance and the digital transformation of public administration. Theoretically, it refines the conceptualization of AI at the intersection of sustainability, governance, and technology adoption, offering a foundation for future research on its institutional integration. From a policy and managerial perspective, the research provides strategic insights for decision-makers, addressing institutional, technological, and regulatory challenges while informing policies that foster AI-driven innovation. It offers guidance on balancing technological advancement, regulatory compliance, and sustainability objectives, particularly within the frameworks of Directive 2014/24/EU and the AI Act. Finally, the study proposes a novel conceptual architecture that bridges AI, sustainability, and public procurement through an integrated, multi-level perspective. By combining governance, technological, organizational, and impact dimensions, the framework advances current theorizing on digital transformation in the public sector and responds to an emerging need for models that connect AI capabilities with ESG-driven value creation.

References

1. Gourdon, J., Messent, J.: How government procurement measures can affect trade. J. World Trade. **53**(5) (2019)
2. Caimi, V., Sansonetti, S.: The Social Impact of Public Procurement. Can the EU Do More. European Parliament (2023)
3. Borges, A.F., Laurindo, F.J., Spínola, M.M., Gonçalves, R.F., Mattos, C.A.: The strategic use of artificial intelligence in the digital era: systematic literature review and future research directions. Int. J. Inf. Manag. **57**, 102225 (2021)
4. Duan, Y., Edwards, J.S., Dwivedi, Y.K.: Artificial intelligence for decision making in the era of big data–evolution, challenges and research agenda. Int. J. Inf. Manag. **48**, 63–71 (2019)
5. Jarrahi, M.H.: Artificial intelligence and the future of work: human-AI symbiosis in organizational decision making. Bus. Horiz. **61**(4), 577–586 (2018)
6. McBride, K., van Noordt, C., Misuraca, G., Hammerschmid, G.: Towards a Systematic Understanding on the Challenges of Procuring Artificial Intelligence in the Public Sector (2021)
7. van der Peijl, S., O'Neill, G., Doumbouyam, L., Howlett, V., de Almeida, J.: Study on Up-Take of Emerging Technologies in Public Procurement (2020)
8. Kingston, J.: Using artificial intelligence to support compliance with the general data protection regulation. Artif. Intell. Law. **25**(4), 429–443 (2017)
9. Parashar, B., Chaurasia, A.: Role of artificial intelligence in green public procurement: (with special reference to European Economic Deal). In: International Conference on Data Analytics in Public Procurement and Supply Chain, pp. 361–371. Springer Nature Singapore, Singapore (2022)
10. Testa, F., Annunziata, E., Iraldo, F., Frey, M.: Drawbacks and opportunities of green public procurement: an effective tool for sustainable production. J. Clean. Prod. **112**, 1893–1900 (2016)
11. Smyth, C., Dennehy, D., Fosso Wamba, S., Scott, M., Harfouche, A.: Artificial intelligence and prescriptive analytics for supply chain resilience: a systematic literature review and research agenda. Int. J. Prod. Res. **62**, 1–25 (2024)
12. Gailhofer, P., Herold, A., Schemmel, J.P., Scherf, C.S., de Stebelski, C.U., Köhler, A.R., Braungardt, S.: The Role of Artificial Intelligence in the European Green Deal. European Parliament, Luxembourg (2021)
13. Constant, F., Berre, M.: Perceived Benefits of Adopting Artificial Intelligence Technologies in Purchasing Processes (2024)
14. Guida, M., Caniato, F., Moretto, A., Ronchi, S.: The role of artificial intelligence in the procurement process: state of the art and research agenda. J. Purch. Supply Manag. **29**(2), 100823 (2023)
15. Meyer, D., Henke, M.: Developing design principles for the implementation of AI in PSM: an investigation with expert interviews. J. Purch. Supply Manag. **29**(3), 100846 (2023)
16. Andersson, P.E., Arbin, K., Rosenqvist, C.: Assessing the value of artificial intelligence (AI) in governmental public procurement. J. Publ. Procure. (2025)
17. Sanchez-Graells, A.: Digital Technologies and Public Procurement: Gatekeeping and Experimentation in Digital Public Governance. Oxford University Press, Oxford (2024)
18. Siciliani, L., Taccardi, V., Basile, P., Di Ciano, M., Lops, P.: AI-based decision support system for public procurement. Inf. Syst. **119**, 102284 (2023)
19. Von Behr, T., Abrahamsson, P.: AI governance and ethics in public procurement: bridging the gap between theory and practice. In: 2022 IEEE 28th International Conference on Engineering, Technology and Innovation (ICE/ITMC) & 31st International Association for Management of Technology (IAMOT) Joint Conference, pp. 1–7. IEEE, Piscataway, NJ (2022, June)
20. Chandra, Y., Feng, N.: Algorithms for a new season? Mapping a decade of research on the artificial intelligence-driven digital transformation of public administration. Public Manag. Rev. **28**, 1–35 (2025)
21. Van Noordt, C., Misuraca, G.: Artificial intelligence for the public sector: results of landscaping the use of AI in government across the European Union. Gov. Inf. Q. **39**(3), 101714 (2022)

22. Wirtz, B.W., Langer, P.F., Fenner, C.: Artificial intelligence in the public sector-a research agenda. Int. J. Public Adm. **44**(13), 1103–1128 (2021)
23. Madan, R., Ashok, M.: AI adoption and diffusion in public administration: a systematic literature review and future research agenda. Gov. Inf. Q. **40**(1), 101774 (2023)
24. Madan, R., Ashok, M.: A public values perspective on the application of artificial intelligence in government practices: a synthesis of case studies. In: Handbook of Research on Artificial Intelligence in Government Practices and Processes, pp. 162–189. IGI Global, Hershey, PA (2022)
25. Wang, C., Teo, T.S., Janssen, M.: Public and private value creation using artificial intelligence: an empirical study of AI voice robot users in Chinese public sector. Int. J. Inf. Manag. **61**, 102401 (2021)
26. Harfouche, A., Merhi, M.I., Albizri, A., Dennehy, D., Thatcher, J.B.: Sustainable development through technological innovations and data analytics. Inf. Syst. Front., 1–8 (2025)
27. Barile, S.: L'impresa come sistema. Contributi sull'Approccio Sistemico Vitale (ASV). Giappichelli (2008)
28. Barile, S., Lusch, R., Reynoso, J., Saviano, M., Spohrer, J.: Systems, networks, and ecosystems in service research. J. Serv. Manag. **27**(4), 652–674 (2016)
29. Calabrese, M., Bosco, G., Grattacaso, R.: Armonia operativa. Processi, controllo e risk management nell'era dell'esperienza imprenditoriale. G. Giappichelli Editore (2024)
30. Vogl, T.M., Seidelin, C., Ganesh, B., Bright, J.: Smart technology and the emergence of algorithmic bureaucracy: artificial intelligence in UK local authorities. Public Adm. Rev. **80**(6), 946–961 (2020)
31. Kinder, T., Stenvall, J., Koskimies, E., Webb, H., Janenova, S.: Local public services and the ethical deployment of artificial intelligence. Gov. Inf. Q. **40**(4), 101865 (2023)
32. Sun, T.Q., Medaglia, R.: Mapping the challenges of artificial intelligence in the public sector: evidence from public healthcare. Gov. Inf. Q. **36**(2), 368–383 (2019)
33. Laitinen, I., Kinder, T., Stenvall, J.: Co-design and action learning in local public services. J. Adult Contin. Educ. **24**(1), 58–80 (2018)
34. Yin, R.K.: Case Study Research and Applications. Sage, Thousand Oaks, CA (2018)
35. Strauss, A., Corbin, J.: Basics of Qualitative Research Techniques. Sage, Thousand Oaks, CA (1998)
36. Glaser, B., Strauss, A.: The Discovery of Grounded Theory: Strategies for Qualitative Research. Sociology Press, Mill Valley, CA (1967)
37. Mills, J., Bonner, A., Francis, K.: The development of constructivist grounded theory. Int. J. Qual. Methods. **5**(1), 25–35 (2006)

Predicting with AI

Addressing Air Quality Estimation Exploiting AutoML

Alessio Carachino, Davide Storelli, Enza Giangreco, and Marco Pinnella

Abstract This paper presents a comprehensive evaluation of three prominent AutoML frameworks (H2O, AutoGluon, and AutoSklearn) for estimating PM2.5 concentrations in Apulia, Lecce. Accurate air quality estimation, particularly for pollutants such as PM2.5 and PM10, is essential for understanding environmental impacts and improving public health initiatives. Leveraging automated machine learning (AutoML) tools offers an efficient alternative to traditional modeling approaches, minimizing human involvement and accelerating both model training testing paving the way for experiments and deployment. We assess the suitability of these tools with respect to a more traditional approach under the aspects of estimation accuracy and computational efficiency. The results indicate that the mentioned AutoML frameworks can provide robust estimations of PM2.5 and PM10 levels. Our findings contribute insights into the application of AutoML for environmental data analysis and suggest the employment of such automated methods for their simplicity of use in building models and efficacy in handling problems that require time and competencies to be addressed, such as missing data values.

Keywords Automated machine learning · Artificial intelligence · Air quality estimation · Accessible artificial intelligence

A. Carachino (✉) · D. Storelli · E. Giangreco · M. Pinnella
Engineering Ingegneria Informatica S.p.A, Rome, Italy
e-mail: alessio.carachino@eng.it; davide.storelli@eng.it; enza.giangreco@eng.it; marco.pinnella@eng.it

N. Omrani et al. (eds.), *Human-Machine Synergy and the Digital Future - Exploring Collaboration and Competition Volume 1*, Springer Proceedings in Business and Economics, https://doi.org/10.1007/978-3-032-21347-1_23

1 Introduction

1.1 Context

When it comes to air pollution, researchers have discovered a wide range of health impacts related to air pollution, including cardiovascular illnesses, respiratory disorders, such as asthma and altered lung function, unfavorable pregnancy outcomes, and in some cases even mortality. To this matter, the World Health Organization (WHO) concluded in 2013 that outdoor air pollution can even cause cancer in people. For this reason, monitoring the levels of air pollutants and the overall quality of air is a delicate task.

However, establishing extensive sensor networks for air pollutant levels monitoring can be costly and logistically difficult, especially in areas with little money or infrastructure. Since it is not always possible to install sensors or there can be faults, and considering that data are needed to establish the quality of air in order to determine pollution levels and react to any health hazards, employing predictive models has become a viable method for estimating the concentration of air pollutants such as the PM2.5 or PM10 in areas without direct data. These models allow smart city administrators to exploit better the potentialities offered by their geographical context, which are generally underused, as described by Earth Observation EO in [1, 2].

Automated Machine Learning (AutoML) frameworks, such as H_2O [3], AutoGluon [4], and AutoSklearn [5], have demonstrated significant potential for automating and optimizing predictive modeling. These frameworks streamline the model selection and tuning process, **reducing the need for domain-specific expertise and expediting the deployment of accurate models**, as described in the Sect. 1.2.

Specifically, in this work, we evaluate the performance of the three mentioned AutoML frameworks in estimating PM2.5 and PM10 levels in the Apulia region, focusing specifically on the city of Lecce by exploiting data coming from both neighbor stations and Lecce itself. Our evaluation considers both the quality of estimations and computational efficiency, despite time not being considered a constraint for this specific case. Besides the advantages related to the employment of applications based on AutoML, the achieved results and performances, described in *Discussion and Implications* section showed the potentialities of these tools in terms of quality of estimations. In fact, during the analysis, results have been collected with three different metrics, widely used for regression tasks, to make considerations based on as many insights as possible.

1.2 *Literature Review*

1.2.1 Machine Learning Development Flow

Implementing solutions based on Machine Learning (ML) and Artificial Intelligence (AI) is generally a complex task since the final model depends on the outcome of several prior phases. However, the development of this kind of solution typically follows a conventional order defined by experts (e.g. data scientists). Thus, the order defines a pipeline, whose phases are reported in Fig. 1. As can be seen, this pipeline is composed of several different **delicate** phases. Once data are collected, they have to be processed by exploiting a series of techniques for different goals (e.g., it could be needed to handle missing data values, normalize the values or even understand how to deal with outliers) before obtaining a model. In fact, model selection and tuning are other delicate phases that have a notable impact on the final performances in terms of computational efficiency and quality of estimations that cannot be performed by the average citizen due to the high complexity of this task.

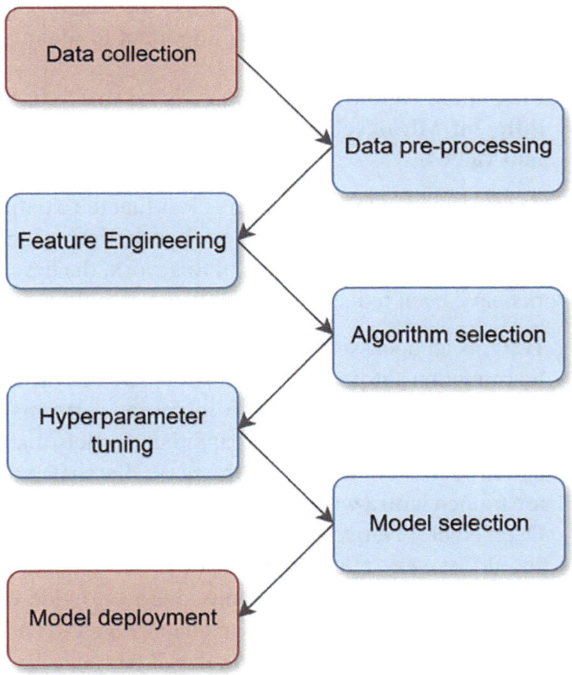

Fig. 1 Machine learning development flow. AutoML automates the phases represented in blue, while red phases are currently not handled by the AutoML frameworks

1.2.2 Automated Machine Learning

Minimizing the effort of people in developing AI models (whose pipeline is reported in Fig. 1), from the data pre-processing phase to the algorithm selection and tuning phases has been under study for several years now. For this reason, in the last years, both in the academic and industrial worlds, applications based on AutoML frameworks started being evaluated and implemented in real scenarios in a wide range of different domains and tasks, such as healthcare [6, 7], finance [8], sentiment analysis [9], fault detection [10], building deep recommender systems [11], and more. Due to the increasing popularity of this topic, several studies [12, 13], have emerged to explore and evaluate the effectiveness of various AutoML frameworks, aiming to identify the most suitable solutions for specific application domains.

The effectiveness of AutoML systems is assessed on the basis of key factors such as:

- Accuracy: AutoML systems should aim as far as possible to achieve high levels of quality of predictions.
- Scalability: AutoML systems should not see performance or efficiency critically compromised as the size of datasets increases.
- Automating capabilities: It is important to identify the phases that can be automated by AutoML systems.
- Flexibility: AutoML systems should be able to handle lots of issues related to the different ML development flow phases output (e.g., handling data containing null values).

As described in [12], it appears clear that the existing AutoML frameworks differ in architecture and other factors such as optimization and search space techniques. In order to match the objectives of this work, the described nine open-source frameworks have been reduced to three, listed as follows:

- **H2O**: is an open-source platform that includes an algorithm based on supervised learning that automates the selection between different models (even ensembles), based on different metrics to represent performance, average prediction time, and so on. In particular, the candidate models that form the ensemble generated by H2O, are very diverse, in the sense that they have a different nature since they are trained with a wide variety of algorithms (such as Gradient Boosting Machine, Deep Neural Networks, Random Forest): this means that the ensemble obtained should be very effective in terms of its generalization capability. Another key quality of H20 is that of being able to provide explanations, thus making the platform compatible with eXplainable AI (XAI) principles and methods, without needing to adapt its results to other XAI tools.
- **AutoGluon**: features a subsystem that handles AutoML for models that make use of tabular data, called AUTOGLUON-TABULAR. Furthermore, unlike other frameworks, AutoGluon does not exploit a pipeline dedicated to tuning hyperparameters but instead exploits combinations of models, put together, both vertically and horizontally, to form a final complex architecture. This architecture is

made of three main layers: the first consists of models trained directly on the data, the second consists of the same types of models as the first but the data it uses are the predictions from the previous layer, while the third (and last) layer combines the predictions coming from the previous layer with an ensemble method that is also used in AutoSklearn. The peculiarity is that it is possible to specify to AutoGluon different configuration presets, implying solutions of different complexity with different training time duration, clearly bearing in mind that too basic configurations may lead to poor performance; alternatively, if the framework algorithm believes that it has already achieved good performance, it may stop the process prematurely and concentrate on training a dedicated module to make the overall model capable of better generalization. This method is particularly important because, from the results proposed by the authors is the one that achieves on average the best results, albeit by a small margin, compared to the nine techniques analyzed in the benchmark [12].

- **AutoSklearn**: was designed to optimize pipelines created on Python using SCIKITLEARN. This framework is strongly based on meta-learning, which consists of a series of techniques used to make models able to adapt faster than normal to new tasks and with less data. Exploiting this concept, the framework tries to find a pipeline that is as suitable as possible for the datasets it knows. An ensemble model is then created. Furthermore, this framework is one of the ones with the most attention; it is no coincidence that AutoSklearn 2 [14] was released in 2022 as a result of an EU-funded project. AutoSklearn 2 consists of a much extended and improved version of AutoSklearn, to such an extent that it is treated as a framework in its own right. The most important changes in AutoSklearn 2 refer to a smaller search space, adaptive performance evaluation strategies and the shift, concerning the initial phase of finding the most suitable pipeline, to a less data-agnostic and more data-specific approach, while maintaining a link to meta-learning.

Unfortunately, none of the described autoML frameworks natively support multitarget regression tasks, implying that it is needed to train a different model for each target/measure to be estimated; thus, for this specific case, it is not possible to train one single model capable of estimating both the PM2.5 and the PM10 values but two different models have to be trained, instead.

1.2.3 Baseline: Multi Layer Perceptron

In the realm of AI and machine learning, air quality estimation can be handled both as a classification task, if the target corresponds to predict qualitative labels such as "poor" or "good" quality, and as a regression task when it comes to estimating the exact levels of air pollutants, with some error, in a context of a dynamic system given a set of observed measurements. Clearly, in this case, the problem has been addressed as a regression task, where the goal is to estimate the PM2.5 values. Since regression tasks can be performed with a Multi-Layer Perceptron (MLP) architecture, which is a Feed-Forward Neural Network (FFNN), many solutions have been proposed, thanks to the holding of the **Universal approximation theorem**, described in [15, 16], according to which it is possible to approximate any arbitrary non-linear function with any arbitrary (small) error with the cost of an increasingly high number of neurons and hidden layers in the architecture (the more complex is the function, the larger will be the architecture), given sufficient data. Unfortunately, in real-world case scenarios, multiple issues usually affect available data (e.g., bias, null values). As reported in the *Dataset* section, the exploited dataset for this work contains null values. Considering the data composing the dataset, an MLP-based solution expects clean, numerical and structured input data, therefore null values cause the mathematical operations in the network (e.g., matrix multiplications) to fail. Thus, specific methods have been applied to replace null values in order to generate an MLP model from the same data and compare the performances with the models obtained using AutoML frameworks instead. Such methods are described in Methods-A.

1.3 Methods

1.3.1 Dataset

In this work, real observed values have been exploited. Specifically, the data have been selected from the collection available on the Open Data Portal related to the Apulia region. The data are related to the air quality monitoring of the year 2023, from January to December and can be downloaded by everyone in different formats. Focusing on the CSV version, which is the one used for this work, each row contains the observed value of an air pollutant in a given day, station and pollutant type. Since this work aims to build estimators for the specific city of Lecce, neighbors' station data have been considered. By analyzing the data, it emerges that each day there are multiple issues related to the stations (e.g., fault, maintenance to sensors) that prevented stations from collecting data for some specific air pollutant for some days; thus, **the generated models for this work are intended to replace the existing station of Lecce when some problems occur in detecting the values of PM2.5 and PM10**. However, the provided data are not ready to be fed to the different frameworks, yet. For this reason, the dataset went through the following phases before being employed:

- First of all, all rows associated with a date for which the PM2.5 values of Lecce's station are missing have to be filtered out.
- Then all rows with the same date were grouped by date in order to obtain single entries characterizing each day. Unnecessary details, such as the station's name and critical limit values are discarded as well.

- In order to obtain structured data (where each column defines a specific measurement), the measurements have to follow a specific order and add null values when any measurement is missing.
- Then, the month of the date has been added as a feature since it can help the models provide better estimations based also on the period of the year, while the full date is exploited as a naive row ID.
- Lastly, the newly obtained data have been shuffled and split into a training set and a test set.

- A general overview of these phases is represented in Fig. 2.

Thanks to these procedures, the final dataset dimensionality **consists of 42** features composed of:

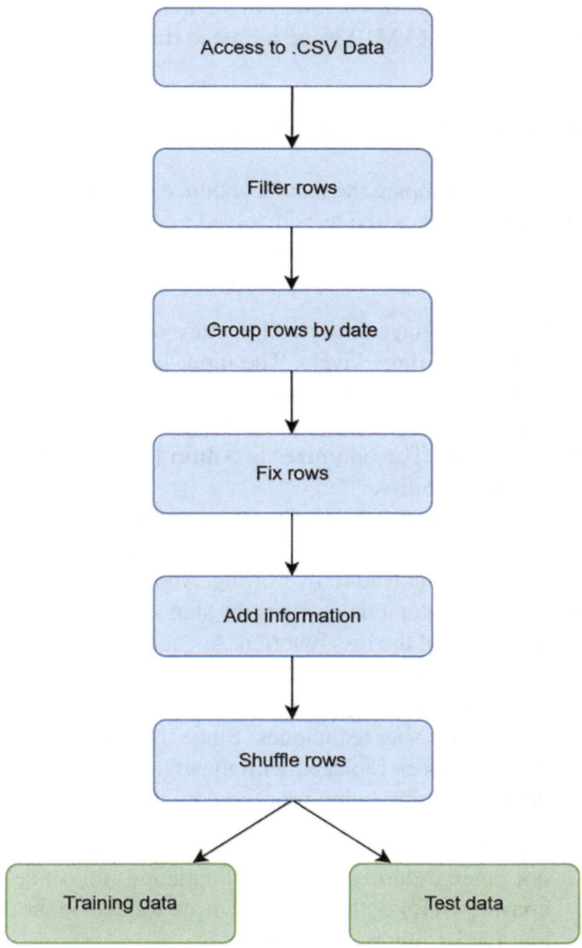

Fig. 2 Data flow from Open Data Portal to the exploited dataset

- Month;
- x10 PM10 observed values of stations within the same region;
- x9 NO2 observed values of stations within the same region;
- x4 O3 observed values of stations within the same region;
- x6 PM2.5 observed values of stations within the same region;
- x5 CO observed values of stations within the same region;
- x3 C6H6 observed values of stations within the same region;
- x3 SO2 observed values of stations within the same region;
- x1 observed PM2.5 value in Lecce (**target feature** of the estimation).

The described features refer to the PM2.5 values estimation case. For the second case, involving the PM10 values estimation, the features are the same, except for:

- x9 PM10 observed values of stations within the same region;
- x7 PM2.5 observed values of stations within the same region;
- x1 observed PM10 value in Lecce (**target feature** of the estimation).

1.3.2 Baseline: Configuration

In order to compare the results obtained with AutoML frameworks with more traditional approaches, the tests involved a Multi-Layer Perceptron, due to its versatility and compatibility with the Universal approximation theorem, built with the following characteristics and hyperparameters:

- Number of layers: the architecture of the employed Artificial Neural Network consists of three layers. The input layer receives 41 inputs (one input per feature), the single hidden layer is made of 128 neurons and lastly, the output layer is based on one single neuron to estimate the target feature.
- Optimizer: The optimizer is **Adam** [17], which is recognized for its efficiency and adaptability.
- Number of epochs: it refers to the number of complete passes through the entire training dataset. More epochs allow the model to learn more from the data, but too many can lead to overfitting. About **85** epochs are considered in this case.
- Learning rate: it determines the step size at each iteration while moving toward a minimum of the loss function. A smaller learning rate makes the training process slower but more precise, while a larger learning rate speeds up training but risks overshooting the optimal point. In this case, the learning rate is set to **0.01**.
- Data processing techniques: Since the MLP cannot handle null values, missing data have been replaced with mean imputation; furthermore, the input was standardized before being processed by the input layer.

- Due to the similarities between the two datasets and since notable differences did not emerge during the experimentation, the same hyper-parameters have been considered for both MLPs which are trained on the datasets containing the PM2.5 and PM10 values, respectively.

- The implementation of a so-defined MLPs has been made possible thanks to the use of the PyTorch framework [18].

1.3.3 AutoML Models: Configuration

The baseline provided a basis for comparing AutoML frameworks such as H2O, AutoGluon, and AutoSklearn, facilitating a thorough assessment of the advantages and disadvantages of each method. On the other hand, AutoML frameworks need a basic yet proper configuration. While for the training and testing the data are the same for the four different approaches, other factors have to be specified framework by framework and are reported as follows:

- **AutoGluon**: The estimators were built using the TabularPredictor class and configured for regression tasks. The model was set to use mean absolute error (MAE) as the evaluation metric, with a focus on prioritizing performance over training time by applying the "good quality" preset. Despite Autogluon supporting Graphical Processing Units (GPUs) to fasten the training, the processing was based on Central Processing Units (CPUs).
- **H2O**: In this case, the models composing the estimators were trained without a limited time budget constraint, while the seed parameter is set to 1 for reproducibility. This ensured a controlled comparison while allowing the system enough flexibility to optimize the models until convergence.
- **AutoSklearn**: The module AutoSklearnRegressors was configured to use MAE as a metric and to fully exploit all available CPU cores.

1.3.4 Findings

It is essential to understand that all the different models performed proficiently this task for both the PM2.5 and PM10 datasets. In this regard, the plots represented in Fig. 3 show the estimated values by each model, including the baseline and the observed values.

As anticipated from the mentioned plots, the four candidates in the comparison performed **similarly**; however, the baseline, obtained with the traditional approach, performed slightly worse in terms of MAE, RMSE, and MAPE for the PM2.5 value estimations case.

In fact, the best results are achieved by the three AutoML frameworks. As for the PM10 case, similar considerations hold, despite the baseline obtaining the best-performing RMSE due to the better understanding of outliers and higher robustness to large deviations. On the other hand, when it comes to computational resources and therefore training and inference times, the considerations are reversed. In fact, while the inference time differences are negligible for small batches, the MLP needed only 15 s to complete the training phase for both datasets, and the **AutoML frameworks needed significantly more time**.

Fig. 3 This plot shows the estimations obtained for the PM2.5 dataset (**a**) and for the PM10 dataset (**b**), including the observed values

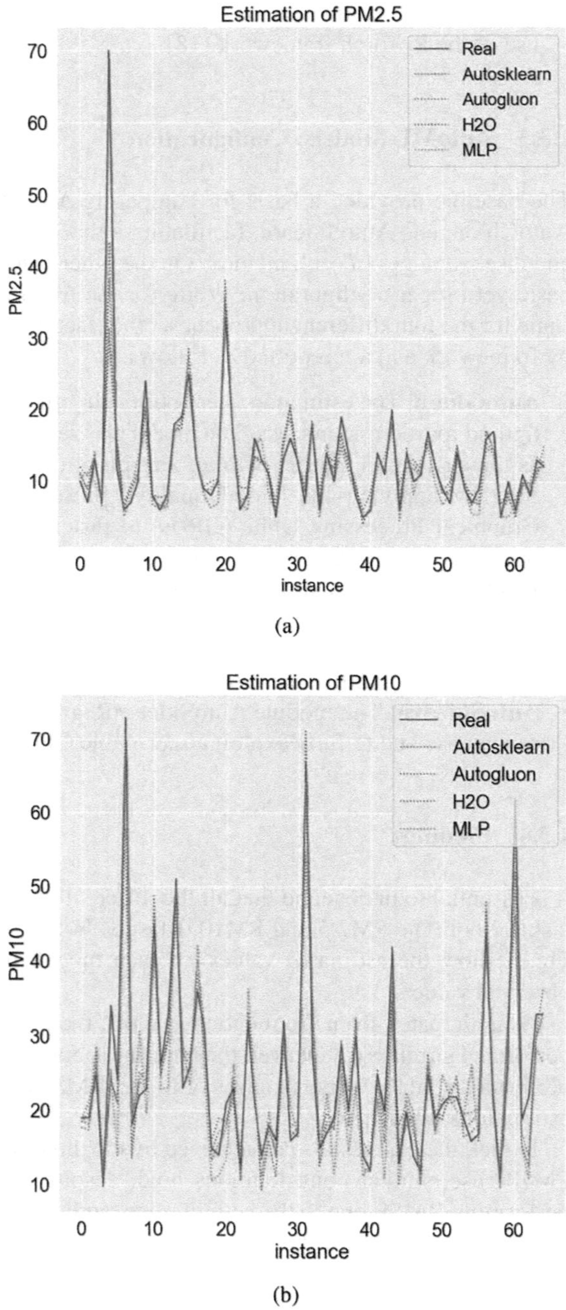

However, in this case, such differences are not critical as time is not considered as a constraint.

2 Discussion and Implications

In this section, the results will be shown and will be explained how the results have been obtained. All codes and algorithms are implemented in Python. The training and the testing were done locally. Furthermore, since the reported training times are clearly hardware-dependent, the specifications are defined as follows:

- Memory: 32 GB 6600 Mhz DDR5;
- Processor: 13th Gen Intel(R) Core(TM) i5–13,500;
- Operative System: Windows 11 23H2;

The results, expressed in terms of quality of estimations, will be provided with three different metrics in order to capture as many insights as possible. The employed metrics are:

- Mean Absolute Error (**MAE**): Measures the average absolute difference between estimations of the models and true values. The advantage of this metric is that it provides a more balanced representation of errors, making it a robust choice when the direction of errors is not critical.
- Root Mean Squared Error (**RMSE**): Penalizes larger errors more heavily due to the square term, often used to understand variance. Thus, the squared term reflects better how the estimator manages the outliers.
- Mean Absolute Percentage Error (**MAPE**): Gives an intuitive percentage measure of error, useful when working with relative values.

The results expressed in terms of the mentioned metrics are reported in Table 1 and in Table 2 for the PM2.5 and PM10 datasets, respectively, while the training times are reported in Table 3.

Table 1 PM2.5—performance of the three frameworks

Model	MAE	RMSE	MAPE
AUTOGLUON	2.136	5.183	0.167
H2O	**1.689**	4.462	**0.116**
AUTOSKLEARN	1.743	4.742	0.117
BASELINE	2.163	**4.178**	0.165

Table 2 PM10—performance of the three frameworks

Model	MAE	RMSE	MAPE
AUTOGLUON	2.879	4.129	0.118
H2O	**2.272**	**3.115**	**0.100**
AUTOSKLEARN	2.438	3.593	**0.095**
BASELINE	4.167	5.195	0.185

Table 3 Wall-clock training time [s], separated by framework and dataset

Model	PM2.5	PM10
AUTOGLUON	312	306
H2O	354	349
AUTOSKLEARN	365	358
BASELINE	15	15

3 Conclusion and Limitations

In conclusion, this study highlights the effectiveness and practicality of leveraging AutoML frameworks (H2O, AutoGluon, and AutoSklearn) for the estimation of air quality based on specific air pollutants (PM2.5 and PM10) levels, in the Apulia region with a specific focus on Lecce. The evaluation underscores how AutoML frameworks can serve as powerful tools, reducing dependency on specialized expertise, and providing robust estimations even when faced with challenges such as missing data. Despite the candidates performing similarly without particular criticality, among the evaluated frameworks and the baseline, H2O demonstrated the best overall estimation capability for both PM2.5 and PM10. However, AutoGluon and Autosklearn offered competitive performances.

Despite these automated tools allowing the building of performance-competitive models, from the results, it appears clear that, in this case, they require significantly more computational resources and training time compared to the more traditional model; in fact, this consideration may not be true for more complex tasks, due to the meta-learning capabilities and exploiting of transfer learning capabilities of AutoML frameworks.

On the other hand, the MLP, while faster to train, delivered slightly inferior quality in terms of estimations, particularly for the PM2.5 case. This trade-off between computational cost and estimating power highlights the importance of context when selecting a modeling approach. For scenarios where real-time predictions or resource constraints are critical, enhancements in AutoML's efficiency or hybrid approaches combining traditional and automated methods may offer a solution.

This study also sheds light on the limitations of current AutoML frameworks in supporting multi-target regression tasks, **as separate models are required for each pollutant**. Addressing this gap represents a promising direction for future research. Furthermore, the integration of AutoML with Explainable AI (XAI) methodologies could improve the interpretability of predictions, fostering trust and usability in environmental applications (e.g., highlighting which input measurements have more impact on the final estimations). Real-time air quality monitoring systems powered by AutoML could also be explored, particularly within smart city initiatives aiming to enhance public health and environmental management.

By demonstrating the potential of AutoML in addressing the described environmental challenges, this work contributes valuable insights into how AutoML tools can be effectively applied to air quality estimation and other domains, considering that sufficient data are available albeit they **showed to be able to handle**

data-related issues, without specialized knowledge required for the user who needs such a system, paving the way for more intelligent, efficient, and accessible solutions.

Acknowledgments This work was partly supported and financed by the NEXUS2030 project (code No. C08SG24).

Declaration of Competing Interests The authors declare that they have no known competing financial interests or personal relationships that could have appeared to influence the work reported in this paper.

References

1. Shelestov, A., Lavreniuk, M., Kussul, N., Novikov, A., Skakun, S.: Exploring google earth engine platform for big data processing: Classification of multi-temporal satellite imagery for crop mapping. Front. Earth Sci. **5**, 232994 (2017)
2. World Health Organization, et al.: Ambient air pollution: a global assessment of exposure and burden of disease. Clean Air J. **26**(2), 6 (2016)
3. LeDell, E., Poirier, S.: H2O AutoML: Scalable automatic machine learning. In: 7th ICML Workshop on Automated Machine Learning (AutoML). https://www.automl.org/wp-content/uploads/2020/07/AutoML2020_paper_61.pdf (2020)
4. Erickson, N., Mueller, J., Shirkov, A., Zhang, H., Larroy, P., Li, M., Smola, A.: Autogluon-tabular: Robust and accurate AutoML for structured data. arXiv preprint https://arxiv.org/abs/2003.06505 (2020)
5. Feurer, M., Klein, A., Egensperger, K., Springenberg, J., Blum, M., Hutter, F.: Efficient and robust automated machine learning. In: Cortes, C., Lawrence, N., Lee, D., Sugiyama, M., Garnett, R. (eds.) Advances in Neural Information Processing Systems, vol. 28. Curran Associates, Red Hook, NY. https://proceedings.neurips.cc/paperfiles/paper/2015/file/11d0e6287202fced83f79975ec59a3a6Paper.pdf (2015)
6. Wan, K., Wong, C., Ip, H., Fan, D., Yuen, P., Fong, H., Ying, M.: Evaluation of the performance of traditional machine learning algorithms, convolutional neural network and automl vision in ultrasound breast lesions classification: a comparative study. Quant. Imaging Med. Surg. **11**, 1381–1393 (2021). https://doi.org/10.21037/qims-20922
7. Zhuhadar, L.P., Lytras, M.D.: The application of automl techniques in diabetes diagnosis: Current approaches, performance, and future directions. Sustainability. **15**(18) (2023). https://doi.org/10.3390/su151813484
8. Agrapetidou, A., Charonyktakis, P., Gogas, P., Papadimitriou, T., Tsamardinos, I.: An automl application to forecasting bank failures. Appl. Econ. Lett. **28**(1), 5–9 (2021). https://doi.org/10.1080/13504851.2020.1725230
9. Mahima, Y., Ginige, T., De Zoysa, K.: Evaluation of sentiment analysis based on automl and traditional approaches. Int. J. Adv. Comput. Sci. Appl. **12**, 612–618 (2021). https://doi.org/10.14569/IJACSA.2021.0120277
10. Santamaria-Bonfil, G., Arroyo-Figueroa, G., Zuniga-Garcia, M.A., Azcarraga Ramos, C.G., Bassam, A.: Power transformer fault detection: a comparison of standard machine learning and automl approaches. Energies. **17**(1) (2024). https://doi.org/10.3390/en17010077
11. Zheng, R., Qu, L., Cui, B., Shi, Y., Yin, H.: Automl for deep recommender systems: a survey. ACM Trans. Inf. Syst. **41**(4) (2023). https://doi.org/10.1145/3579355

12. Gijsbers, P., Bueno, M.L.P., Coors, S., LeDell, E., Poirier, S., Thomas, J., Bischl, B., Vanschoren, J.: Amlb: an AutoML benchmark. J. Mach. Learn. Res. **25**(101), 1–65 (2024) http://jmlr.org/papers/v25/22-0493.html
13. Truong, A., Walters, A., Goodsitt, J., Hines, K., Bruss, C.B., Farivar, R.: Towards automated machine learning: Evaluation and comparison of automl approaches and tools. In: 2019 IEEE 31st International Conference on Tools with Artificial Intelligence (ICTAI), pp. 1471–1479 (2019). https://doi.org/10.1109/ICTAI.2019.00209
14. Feurer, M., Eggensperger, K., Falkner, S., Lindauer, M., Hutter, F.: Autosklearn 2.0: Hands-Free AutoML Via Meta-Learning. https://arxiv.org/abs/2007.04074 (2022)
15. Hornik, K., Stinchcombe, M., White, H.: Multilayer feedforward networks are universal approximators. Neural Netw. **2**(5), 359–366 (1989). https://doi.org/10.1016/0893608 0(89)90020-8
16. Pinkus, A.: Approximation theory of the MLP model in neural networks. Acta Numer. **8**, 143–195 (1999). https://doi.org/10.1017/S0962492900002919
17. Kingma, D.P., Ba, J.: Adam: A Method for Stochastic Optimization. https://arxiv.org/abs/1412.6980 (2017)
18. Paszke, A., Gross, S., Massa, F., Lerer, A., Bradbury, J., Chanan, G., et al.: Pytorch: An Imperative Style, High-Performance Deep Learning Library. https://arxiv.org/abs/1912.01703 (2019)

Managing Risk with Meaning: Explainable AI and Cognitive Turn in SME Governance

Davide Liberato lo Conte, Giuseppe Sancetta, and Nicola Cucari

Abstract Small and Medium Enterprises (SMEs) often confront financial risk under conditions of high cognitive strain, limited resources, and mounting regulatory complexity. This paper explores how Artificial Intelligence (AI), particularly in its generative and explainable forms, can help SMEs move from reactive risk management toward proactive, cognitively sustainable governance. Drawing on a cognitive turn in management theory, we investigate the potential of Explainable AI (XAI) to reduce uncertainty, alleviate decision fatigue, and foster trust-based financial resilience. Using structured financial and organizational data from SMEs, the study applies supervised machine learning models to predict financial distress, while integrating interpretability techniques to ensure managerial usability. Beyond predictive performance, we prioritize explainability through feature importance analysis, local/global model interpretation, and visual narratives aligned with SME financial literacy. Findings show that XAI not only improves risk detection accuracy but also enhances strategic foresight and mitigates the psychological toll of financial decision-making. Importantly, the research reveals that organizational resilience depends as much on cognitive alignment and leadership design as on technical capability. The study concludes by framing XAI as an epistemic infrastructure, enabling SMEs to absorb and act on algorithmic insights in ways that are human-centered, transparent, and strategically coherent. The paper offers actionable implications for management practice, interdisciplinary research, and policy, advocating for inclusive, psychologically informed AI adoption strategies that reflect the lived complexity of SME governance.

Keywords Artificial intelligence · Risk governance · Cognitive decision-making

D. L. l. Conte (✉) · G. Sancetta · N. Cucari
Sapienza University of Rome, Rome, Italy
e-mail: Davideliberato.loconte@uniroma1.it

N. Omrani et al. (eds.), *Human-Machine Synergy and the Digital Future - Exploring Collaboration and Competition Volume 1*, Springer Proceedings in Business and Economics, https://doi.org/10.1007/978-3-032-21347-1_24

1 Introduction

Small and Medium Enterprises (SMEs), though central to economic vitality, often operate under intense cognitive and emotional strain when facing risk-laden decisions [1]. Structural limitations, such as scarce resources, informal governance, and fragmented information flows, amplify uncertainty and contribute to suboptimal risk perception and delayed responses [2, 3]. These behavioral vulnerabilities are further exacerbated by external pressures linked to digitalization and sustainability demands, which increase the complexity of managerial judgment [4]. As such, SMEs require a strategic reorientation that embeds risk literacy, emotional resilience, and anticipatory thinking into the decision-making process [5, 6]. This calls for governance models that recognize and respond to the psychological dimensions of risk, moving beyond compliance toward adaptive, learning-oriented structures [7]. Recent research underscores the transformative potential of Generative Artificial Intelligence (GAI) in enhancing SME risk resilience by supporting every phase of the risk management cycle, from identification to monitoring [6]. Unlike traditional AI systems focused on predictive modeling alone, in fact, GAI enables dynamic access to evolving regulatory and domain-specific knowledge through techniques such as Retrieval Augmented Generation (RAG), thereby supporting more contextual and informed risk assessments [8].

This allows SMEs to foresee financial distress but also to survive in compliance-intensive environments more effectively. Furthermore, integrating GAI assistants within operational workflows enhances managerial understanding, allowing for a more iterative and collaborative governance process [6]. However, the integration of GAI into SME risk practices also introduces new cognitive challenges, such as hallucinations, data bias, and opaque reasoning processes, which may distort judgment and erode managerial trust [9]. Furthermore, these risks directly affect how decision-makers perceive, interpret, and act upon AI-generated outputs. In this context, advancing toward explainable AI (XAI) and transparent governance becomes essential to align algorithmic insights with human cognitive processes. Embedding XAI tools within SME risk infrastructures, in fact, can help mitigate ambiguity, reduce reliance on intuition under stress, and position risk governance as a proactive, cognitively supported capability rather than a reactive or obscure function.

2 Objective

Although AI is increasingly embedded across business domains, its strategic deployment within SME risk governance remains limited [10]. In particular, SMEs often lack the capacity to leverage AI as a tool for enabling transparent, forward-looking decision-making. Structural constraints such as limited resources and evolving regulatory expectations, in fact, intensify organizational vulnerabilities and contribute to heightened levels of financial anxiety among SME decision-makers. This research examines how AI, particularly in its generative and explainable forms, can reduce uncertainty, support resilience, and transform reactive risk management into a proactive, strategic function. We therefore pose the following research question:

RQ: How can AI improve the accuracy of business-oriented financial predictions and support trust-based, anxiety-aware risk governance frameworks for SMEs?

The study then conceptualizes AI as a mechanism for supporting the full risk management cycle, while facilitating greater interpretability and accountability. In this context, XAI is critical not only for regulatory trust and transparency but also for alleviating cognitive burden and perceived financial risk among SME managers. By embedding AI-generated insights into decision-making processes, in fact, SMEs may also reduce the psychological and organizational toll associated with financial volatility. Ultimately, this research reframes AI as an enabling infrastructure for intelligent, adaptive, and resilient governance in SMEs, mitigating both operational risks and the subjective experience of financial distress.

3 Methods

This study integrates machine learning techniques within a governance framework tailored to the specific needs and constraints of SMEs. The empirical analysis is designed to assess how AI systems can improve financial distress prediction while supporting managerial comprehension and strategic usability. The research is then grounded in a real-world dataset composed of structured SME financial and organizational variables, encompassing both quantitative indicators and qualitative attributes. Feature engineering processes are applied to standardize inputs, including normalization, categorical encoding, and imputation for missing values. To ensure robustness, multiple supervised learning algorithms are trained and compared. Each model is optimized through hyperparameter tuning and validated via k-fold cross-validation. Performance is evaluated using established classification metrics, accuracy, precision, recall, F1-score, and AUC, allowing for comprehensive benchmarking across models.

Beyond predictive accuracy, the study prioritizes interpretability through the use of explainable methods, implemented to generate global and local explanations of model outputs, and highlighting feature importance and decision pathways. These insights are presented through interactive visual dashboards and narrative summaries designed to align with the financial literacy levels of SME decision-makers.

4 Findings

The findings underscore that the integration of AI technologies into SME risk governance offers deep organizational and psychological benefits. When supported by explainable and accessible interfaces, in fact, AI systems can significantly enhance strategic risk oversight by reducing the uncertainty and subjectivity that often characterize decision-making in financially fragile environments. In particular, a critical insight concerns the psychological weight of financial risk. Many SME decision-makers operate in conditions of high stress, limited support structures, and persistent financial anxiety; in this context, risk-related decisions are often driven by instinct or short-term urgency rather than structured foresight [5]. AI-supported tools can play a key role in mitigating decision fatigue, offering cognitive relief and more deliberate, future-oriented thinking. The findings also reveal that resilience is deeply tied to organizational design and leadership structure. Firms with more diversified governance layers and adaptive management practices tend to exhibit stronger risk mitigation capabilities.

In fact, early indicators of financial distress are often not purely financial but embedded in shifts in managerial roles, strategic inertia, or reduced agility; factors that AI systems can detect and contextualize if appropriately configured. Importantly, the adoption of AI for risk purposes is most effective when aligned with the risk culture of the organization. Tools that reinforce transparency, support shared interpretation of data, and promote learning over control are more likely to determine long-term engagement. Explainability, in particular, emerges as a cornerstone of adoption, reducing skepticism, building trust, and enabling integration into strategic routines. In sum, the research suggests that AI, when integrated thoughtfully, can serve as a catalyst for evolving SME risk governance: from reactive, compliance-driven models to proactive, reflective, and psychologically attuned systems. Future risk management will then depend not only on algorithmic accuracy, but on the capacity of organizations to absorb, understand, and act upon insights in ways that are cognitively sustainable and strategically coherent.

5 Implications

This study generates a set of implications across managerial, academic, and policy domains, rooted in a cognitive reconceptualization of risk governance for SMEs. Managerially, the integration of XAI emerges as a catalyst for cognitively sustainable decision-making. In high-pressure contexts marked by uncertainty and financial anxiety, XAI tools can, in fact, offload cognitive burden, support more deliberate strategic thinking, and promote a culture of anticipatory governance.

Academically, the findings invite a shift in how financial distress is theorized: no longer solely as an economic condition, but as a cognitive and organizational phenomenon. This perspective opens avenues for interdisciplinary research linking AI, behavioral sciences, and strategic management, with particular focus on how digital tools mediate attention, trust, and learning processes. Future studies may explore the role of emotion-aware AI, hybrid decision architectures, or the long-term cognitive impacts of algorithmic mediation in managerial routines.

At the policy level, the research points to the need for AI adoption frameworks that go beyond technical deployment to embrace a cognitive turn in governance. This entails designing inclusive, psychologically informed ecosystems that enhance interpretability, emotional resilience, and proactive engagement with risk. Public and institutional actors should therefore invest in digital upskilling, but also in cognitive literacy, equipping SME decision-makers to critically absorb, question, and operationalize AI-generated insights in ways that are strategically coherent and human-centered. Ultimately, XAI becomes an epistemic infrastructure for transforming how SMEs perceive, process, and act upon risk, laying the groundwork for more adaptive, trustworthy, and forward-looking governance systems.

References

1. Crovini, C., Santoro, G., Ossola, G.: Rethinking risk management in entrepreneurial SMEs: towards the integration with the decision-making process. Manag. Decis. **59**(5), 1085–1113 (2021)
2. Falkner, E.M., Hiebl, M.R.W.: Risk management in SMEs: a systematic review of available evidence. J. Risk Financ. **16**(2), 122–144 (2015)
3. Renzi, A., Sancetta, G., Orlando, B.: Risk patterns, structural characteristics, and organizational configurations. Strateg. Change. **26**(4), 373–383 (2017)
4. Pereira, L., Tenera, A., Bispo, J., Wemans, J.: A risk diagnosing methodology web-based platform for micro, small and medium businesses: remarks and enhancements. Commun. Comput. Inf. Sci. **454**, 340–356 (2015)
5. El Shoubaki, A., Laguir, I., Den Besten, M.: Human capital and SME growth: the mediating role of reasons to start a business. Small Bus. Econ. **54**, 1107–1121 (2020)
6. Leonard, E., Sheehan, B., Mullins, M., Shannon, D.: Generative AI for enhanced risk management in SMEs. J. Risk Res., 1–34 (2026)
7. Martín-Peña, M.-L., Sánchez-López, J.-M., Kamp, B., Giménez-Fernández, E.M.: The innovation antecedents behind the servitization–performance relationship. R&D Manage. **53**, 459–480 (2023)
8. Soni, V.: Impact of generative AI on small and medium enterprises' revenue growth: The moderating role of human, technological, and market factors. Rev. Contemp. Bus. Anal. **6**(1), 133–153 (2023)
9. Owens, E., Sheehan, B., Mullins, M., Cunneen, M., Ressel, J., Castignani, G.: Explainable artificial intelligence (XAI) in insurance. Risks. **10**(12), 230 (2022)
10. Stein, V., Wiedemann, A., Bouten, C.: Framing risk governance. Manag. Res. Rev. **42**(11), 1224–1242 (2019)

Characterizing the Financial Behavior of Failed Companies During the COVID Crisis

Manuel Ruiz Marín, M. Luz Maté Sánchez-Val, José Noguera Venero, and F. Javier Sánchez-Vidal

Abstract The COVID crisis has prompted insolvency processes in companies which were apparently in a healthy financial condition. This study aims to characterize business failure processes pre- and post-COVID identifying more affected companies in function of different financial distress typologies. To do so, we propose the application of big data algorithms, and in particular, fuzzy qualitative comparative analysis techniques, to identify the combination of financial ratios values, with statistically determined critical thresholds, to differentiate between failed and non-failed companies. Based on this information, we distinguish different business failure processes. We apply this procedure to a sample of 30,101 Spanish companies located in Madrid during pre- and post-COVID periods. We characterize detected financial distress processes as a function of companies' characteristics. We find structural changes in business failure processes as a consequence of the COVID crisis where problems of solvency, because of high debt, and of liquidity play a fundamental role in the quest to survive.

Keywords Business failure · Clustering · Symbolization process · COVID crisis

1 Introduction

The COVID-19 pandemic has caused financial distress in the economies taken as a whole, and with different intensity on their respective sectors. The coronavirus crisis has reduced companies' commercial transactions given the government regulations of social distancing to control the spread of this disease [1]. This situation has caused a significant drop in sales for many companies, as evidenced by, for

M. R. Marín · M. L. M. Sánchez-Val · J. N. Venero · F. J. Sánchez-Vidal (✉)
Universidad Politécnica de Cartagena, Cartagena, MU, Spain
e-mail: Manuel.Ruiz@upct.es; mluz.mate@upct.es; jose.noguera@upct.es; javier.sanchez@upct.es

N. Omrani et al. (eds.), *Human-Machine Synergy and the Digital Future - Exploring Collaboration and Competition Volume 1*, Springer Proceedings in Business and Economics, https://doi.org/10.1007/978-3-032-21347-1_25

example, Fasano et al. [2]. The effect of COVID on companies' performance and survival depends on a set of internal and external factors [3, 4]. Among the internal factors, companies' financial management is a key element to be considered. The well-known discussion about the optimal capital structure becomes a decisive factor, also during the COVID crisis [5]. Literature states that companies posit financial policies to guarantee trusted and cost-efficient access to financing. Solvency depends on management and on the relation between liabilities and equity. The explanatory factors in the tradeoff between equity and debt are exposed in many studies, such as Leland [6], which takes the work of Modigliani and Miller [7] as a base and incorporate real life limitations that affect these authors' hypotheses. More recent theories have highlighted the importance of capital market imperfections in the choice of the enterprises' capital structure, as for example the information asymmetry problem in the pecking order theory, as proposed by Myers and Majluf [8].

Since then, some studies have highlighted the importance of other factors which may affect companies' capital structure and their own survival. A number of these contributions have focused on firms' financial flexibility indicating that some companies are interested in maintaining a financial slack, for the sake of prudence (or because they are forced to, as they cannot lever up because external financing is problematic), or to finance future investment opportunities (Bigelli et al. [9]). But this financial flexibility or financial conservatism is not a generalized practice. Recent research has not found a general trend concluding that deleveraging is the main goal of an average company, which was the expected policy if financial flexibility was a critical driver of capital structure. Zheng [10] explains this evidence by the negative incentives to reduce debt and keep large cash holdings, because, as Acharya et al. [11] point out, cash can be considered as negative debt.

In this context, Fahlenbrach et al. [5] highlight the relevance of firms' financial flexibility stating that companies with large cash holdings and low debt positions are better able to face the unexpected revenue drop caused by the COVID crisis. Our study provides further evidence about the relevant role of firms' capital structure and financial condition, basing it on the well-known Altman's [12] work, which measures each company's financial health by analyzing the values of related, yet distinct, concepts, such as liquidity, solvency, profitability, management, etc. At the end, our study highlights the relevance of financial flexibility in the company's survival. In particular, our research questions are: which are the financial unhealthy conditions that make more probable the death of the company? Have these conditions changed during the COVID crisis? Is there any evidence that Altman values and model should be rethought?

With this purpose, we characterize business failure processes pre- and post-COVID regarding firms' financial characteristics. To do so, we apply big data algorithms implementing recursive procedures based on breaking structural tests and simbolization procedures to define the firms' financial positions during the period 2018–2020. Afterwards, in order to identify business failure processes, we develop specific algorithms based on the Chow test which overcome previous applied qualitative comparative techniques, as the fsQCA developed by Ragin [13]. Our methodological proposal exogenously determines the optimal thresholds in firms' financial ratios to define the different failure processes. After this, we categorize the different pre- and post-COVID business failure processes which are later characterized using multilogistic regressions in function of companies' internal characteristics.

In accordance with previous studies, we identify liquidity and financial flexibility/conservatism practices as a key element to survive during the pandemic [5]. The comparison between failure processes before and after the COVID crisis reveals a clear shift. This study contributes to the existing literature by providing further insight into the firms most affected during the COVID crisis, based on their financial management. In this sense, despite the fact that the COVID shock had a serious impact on companies' wealth [14], the mechanisms that cause business failure are still far from being fully understood. Our paper contributes to several strands of literature. It shows that some combinations of factors that measure a company's financial status have an impact when a company is exposed to an unexpected external shock. Second, our study contributes to the business failure literature by adding new methodology, as COVID shock may have changed the rule of game of companies' survival/death dynamics comparing years before and after this crisis. Our proposal overcomes the limitations of previous literature by identifying the predominant business failure processes during the COVID period and characterizing each based on companies' characteristics.

The study is structured as follows: Sect. 2 presents the main literature focused on bankruptcy prediction and the implications of the COVID shock. Section 3 describes the database and sample used in our study. Section 4 presents the methodology including the specific algorithm we have designed to identify the different business failure processes. Section 5 discusses the results, and we end this study with our conclusions, limitations and future research.

2 Literature About Bankruptcy Prediction

The literature examines explanatory business failure factors from deterministic and voluntaristic perspectives [15]. The former is focused on external companies' factors from which firms have scarce control [16]. These elements depend on general and sectoral environmental characteristics. Initial results in this context used to examine different environmental factors, as for instance crisis or changes in government regulations, as the main determinants in business failure [17]. From a micro-territorial perspective, we find studies which examine firms' surrounding characteristics as potential determinants of business failure [18]. The latter-voluntaristic studies—highlights the existence of firms' characteristics such as financial management, investments, and capabilities, as the main explanatory factors of business failure [19]. Thus, the basic difference between these theoretical backgrounds, deterministic and voluntaristic, is the perspective from which the factors explaining business failure are considered. Most recent studies have indicated the need to integrate a combination of external and internal factors to build a consistent business failure model [20]. Under this global approach, a company's bankruptcy could be explained by a misalignment between its characteristics and its environment [21]. Over time, a series of poor management decisions and adverse external events would lead to a decline in competitiveness, rising debt levels, and ultimately, failure.

2.1 Bankruptcy Prediction Models

As previously mentioned, we are going to use the measures from the Altman Z-score, developed by Altman [12], which is a widely used method for predicting bankruptcy. It uses five financial ratios calculated from the company's balance sheet and profit and loss account, along with some market ratios. Other notorious failure prediction models are:

- The *O*-score, developed by James Ohlson in 1980 [22], which is a multivariate model that uses nine financial ratios, and a constant. The *O*-score was created to address some criticisms of the Z-score and is designed to estimate the likelihood of financial distress for a firm.
- Merton [22] developed a structural model of default risk based on the Black-Scholes option pricing model. This model sees equity as a call option on the company's assets, and bankruptcy happens when the value of the assets falls below the value of the debt.
- The Zmijewski's model [23] is based on three financial ratios and uses a different statistical method (probit analysis) compared to Altman's model (multiple discriminant analysis).
- Other models that have been applied by researchers include the Taffler [24] model, which uses four ratios, including measures of profitability, leverage, liquidity, and performance, and the Fulmer's (Fulmer et al. [25]) Gamma Z model, which uses five ratios to predict bankruptcy in industrial corporations.

2.2 Altmans' Model

Altman's aim was to create a quantitative tool for predicting corporate bankruptcies, stemmed from the increasing number of bankruptcies occurring in the late 1960s, which prompted him to explore whether financial ratios could be used to predict such outcomes. Based on his analysis, Altman identified five financial ratios that were significantly different between the bankrupt and non-bankrupt companies. These ratios represented different aspects of a company's financial position, including liquidity, profitability, leverage, solvency, and efficiency. Altman used discriminant analysis to assign weights to each ratio, based on their relative importance in distinguishing between bankrupt and non-bankrupt companies. These five weighted ratios are combined to create a single score, referred to as the Z-Score. The score is then used to classify a company into one of three categories: safe, grey area, or distress.

The five financial ratios used in the Altman Z-Score model are: working capital to total assets, retained earnings to total assets, earnings before interest and taxes (EBIT) to total assets, market value of equity to book value of total liabilities, and sales to total assets. These ratios were selected based on their ability to predict bankruptcy and their widespread availability in financial statements. The fourth ratio (MVE/TL = market value of equity to book value of total liabilities) cannot be calculated for private or non-listed companies. Various adaptations have been proposed in the years since, such as, for example, the use of the Book Value of Equity instead of the Market Value of Equity. This adaptation is often referred to as the Altman Z-score for private firms [26].

The Altman Z-Score is a simple, yet effective method for determining the financial health of a company, its risk of bankruptcy or the likelihood of defaulting on its debt obligations. One of the benefits of the Altman Z-Score is its simplicity, as it requires only five financial ratios. The Altman Z-Score is widely used by financial analysts, investors, and credit rating agencies, and it continues to be researched and validated. Its accuracy in predicting bankruptcy has been well established, as recently pointed out by Salimi [27] or Altman et al. [28]. Another advantage of the Altman Z-Score is its versatility. The model can be applied to a wide range of companies, regardless of their size or industry, as the financial ratios are relevant to all types of companies and are widely available in financial statements.

In conclusion, the Altman Z-Score is an important tool for predicting the probability of bankruptcy. Recently, several scholars have noted that since the model relies exclusively on financial ratios, it does not take into account other important factors that may impact a company's financial health, such as industry trends or economic conditions.

2.3 Business Failure Prediction: A Review in the COVID Context

In this context, the COVID pandemic is considered as one of the most relevant exogenous shocks changing general market conditions [14]. Because of the pandemic, governments have implemented public health measures including border closures and social distancing protocols. This crisis has triggered a collapse in demand in certain sectors, and a breaking in the supply of many activities. Consequently, unexpected shifts in the economic landscape have disrupted the equilibrium between firms' internal characteristics and their external environments. By creating simultaneous demand and supply shocks, the COVID-19 crisis has generated simultaneous demand and supply shocks, creating situations where companies struggle to generate sufficient cash flows and meet supplier obligations [3].

Pagano et al. [29] find that companies whose activities are less exposed to the social distance showed a less unfavorable evolution in their share prices. De Vito and Gómez [30] examine how much time companies with reduced operating flexibility would be operative before they drain cash reserves. Fahlenbrach et al. [5] conclude that COVID shock has less impact on companies with more cash holdings. In contrast to prior research, we focus on the business failure process examining the typologies and differences in function of firms' characteristics during the COVID crisis.

3 Database and Sample

3.1 Sample

The sample is composed of a set of companies with financial statements from SABI (Iberian Balance Sheet Analysis Systems) database. These companies have available information over the period 2017–2020. We eliminate firms without financial information or with negative total assets [31] from our sample. After this process, we obtained a sample composed of 30,101 observations. We classify a company as failed if it has filed for bankruptcy [32], a definition widely applied in previous studies [33, 34]. In our sample, we consider that a firm has failed in a certain year if it has filed for bankruptcy before the end of 2018, 2019, and 2020, respectively. In our database, there are 1307 failed companies during the 3 years of the sample period.

3.2 Variables

Five financial ratios were computed to measure firms' financial characteristics. We choose these ratios based on the widely applied Altman's *Z*-score model [12]. The Ratio 1 (R_1) is defined as working capital to total assets. Working capital is the difference between a company's current assets and its current liabilities. This ratio is important from a short-term financial point of view and is a measure of the firm's liquidity, as a low value will probably mean that a company will have difficulty meeting its short-term financial obligations because current assets are insufficient. The Ratio 2 (R_2) is computed as retained earnings to total assets. R_2 indicates the amount of profit or loss retained in a company. A low R_2 indicates that a firm relies proportionally less on internally generated funds for financing, thereby serving as a solvency measure. A low value increases the probability that the company will go bankrupt. On the other hand, a high value indicates that the company has proportionally less need to resort to borrowing or to equity issues (external finance). The Ratio 3 (R_3) is computed as earnings before interest and taxes (EBIT) to total assets. This ratio refers to the firm's ability to generate profits from its activity. The Ratio 4

(R_4) is calculated as total assets to total liabilities. A high value implies that the firm does not finance its assets with a high proportion of liabilities. This ratio is another measure of solvency. The Ratio 5 (R_5) is defined as sales to total assets. This ratio defines the efficiency with which management uses assets to generate revenue and is a measure of rotation. A high R_5 means that management needs a small investment to generate sales, which increases the overall profitability of the company.

All financial ratios were incorporated with a one-year lag for each observation period, that is, the ratios that predict the probability of bankruptcy for 2020 are those calculated at the end of 2019. In the logistic analysis, we also consider firms' characteristics such as the size, which is computed as the logarithm of firms' total assets. We consider the Age of the firm considering the years since its constitution. These two variables are usually an inverse proxy of information asymmetry problems, and thus, account for financial constraints problem [9]. We use NACE (Nomenclature of Economic Activities) codes to identify firms' sectors. Table 1 presents descriptive statistics for the study variables during the observation period.

The key findings from the descriptive statistics reveal three main patterns:

Table 1 Descriptive statistics

	2018	2019	2020
Failed companies	445	434	428
R_1 (Working capital ratio)	0.0268 (0.992)	0.0043 (0.989)	−0.0350 (0.948)
R_2 (Retained earnings to total assets)	0.0320 (0.821)	0.0090 (0.931)	−0.1546 (0.648)
R_3 (EBIT to total assets)	0.0495 (0.723)	0.0371 (0.897)	−0.1187 (0.657)
R_4 (Total assets to total liabilities)	2.9187 (1.751)	3.4821 (1.508)	3.2900 (1.260)
R_5 (Sales to total assets)	1.2973 (1.739)	1.4275 (1.952)	1.3365 (1.695)
Size (Logarithm of total assets)	6.658 (2.243)	6.673 (2.242)	6.701 (2.040)
Age (Log of firms' age)	21.41 (13.848)	20.59 (11.673)	20.74 (10.696)
	Number of observations		
Industry and agricultural activities	20	29	19
Building	40	35	51
Trade	104	85	72
Transport	21	13	10
Accommodation	30	33	38
Communications	36	29	33
Financial services	88	83	76
Professional and scientific activities	72	82	72
Others	34	45	57

Mean (sd.)

- The number of corporate failures remained stable compared to previous years;
- Financial ratios R_1, R_2, and R_3 declined in 2020 relative to 2018–2019 levels, while firm size and age showed minimal variation;
- Sectoral analysis indicates generally stable patterns across industries, with modest exceptions: a slight increase in Building and Accommodation sectors contrasted with relative declines in Industrial production, Agricultural activities, and Trade.

4 Methodology

Unlike most of previous studies, we apply qualitative techniques. We propose an algorithm based on the idea of the fuzzy qualitative comparative analysis (fsQCA) proposed by Ragin [13, 35]. This methodology enables us to identify the specific combinations of financial conditions that may precipitate failure. Unlike traditional techniques—such as multiple regression analysis—this approach better captures the nuanced interdependencies driving the failure process. For instance, a critically low level of profitability (R_3) could have a disproportionately negative impact on firms with weak capitalization (R_2) compared to those in higher centiles of R_2. This simultaneous and different impact of one factor on the company's survival depending on the other factors makes a standard OLS analysis (or, for example, a more specific quantile regression approach) unfeasible.

Moreover, multiple regression analysis faces an additional limitation in this context: the potential interconnection among Altman's five financial ratios. The numerator of R_3 is a close proxy of net income, which (after adjusting for dividends) is mechanically linked to the numerator of R_2 via accounting identities [36]. Such collinearity risks distorting regression results, making our combinatorial method a more robust alternative. fsQCA requires different steps: the first is to build a truth table where the selected variables, specifically, our five financial ratios, are coded as binary values (0 or 1) according to pre-established thresholds defined by the researcher. In this sense, the researcher considers whether the specific variable could lead to failure if it takes a value higher than a certain threshold. To address potential subjectivity in this classification stage, we developed an algorithm based on the structural breaking Chow tests along the distribution of each financial ratio.

Based on the previous step, we designed a symbolization procedure to categorize the five financial ratios (R_1, R_2, R_3, R_4, R_5) measured in each firm into a finite set of 32 symbols. Each of these symbols will have a meaning within the financial status of the firm. The symbols distribution will help us to analyze the time evolution of firm failure before and after the beginning of the COVID pandemic. We will then perform a cluster analysis of the failed firms, conducted through the symbols associated with their financial ratios in order to better understand different business failure processes, each one associated with a different combination of the Altman ratios representing the diverse factors previously mentioned. This section concludes with a multinomial logistic regression model analyzing distinct categories of firm failure (each cluster of symbols represent a different type of firm failure) as a function of a set of internal characteristics of the firm in the pre- and post-COVID pandemic era.

4.1 Symbolization of Financial Ratios

Define the set $\Gamma = \{(0,0,0,0,0); (1,0,0,0,0);..;(1,1,1,1,1)\}$ as the set of all vectors of length 5 with entries in the set $\{0,1\}$. Γ has cardinality 32 and its elements are called symbols. For each financial ratio R_i (i = 1,2,...5), we consider the 9 deciles D_k^i (k = 1, 2,...9), that divide the distribution of R_i in 10 equal frequency intervals. With this decile, we divide the sample of failed and non-failed firms in two subsamples, the first one formed by those firms satisfying that R_i " D_k^i and the second subsample formed by the remaining companies (i.e., those with $R_i > D_k^i$). For these two samples, we perform a Chow test with firm failure as the dependent variable (dichotomic) and the five financial ratios (R_1, R_2, R_3, R_4, R_5) as explanatory variables. Then we select the deciles that maximize the value of the Chow-test statistic, namely $\mathfrak{D}^i$. Notice that the subsamples determined by $\mathfrak{D}^i$ (i = 1, 2, 3, 4 and 5) are the variables that maximize the divergence between the linear regression models predicting firm failure, as estimated across the two subsamples. This procedure allows us to identify the threshold from which each of the financial ratios change the way in which they impact on the condition of business failure from an objective perspective. In contrast to fsQCA, we employ the Chow test to objectively establish classification thresholds, thereby exogenously determining the cutoff values for each financial ratio's condition.

Next, we define the symbolization map $S : R^5 \rightarrow \Gamma$ defined by

$$S(x_1,x_2,x_3,x_4,x_5) = \left(\mathfrak{T}^1(x_1),\mathfrak{T}^2(x_2),\mathfrak{T}^3(x_3),\mathfrak{T}^4(x_4),\mathfrak{T}^5(x_5)\right) \tag{1}$$

where:

$$\mathfrak{T}^i(a) = \begin{cases} 1 \text{ if } a > \mathfrak{D}^i \\ 0 \text{ otherwise} \end{cases} \tag{2}$$

serves as an indicator function that equals 1 when the observed value exceeds its corresponding decile threshold $\mathfrak{D}^i$.

Therefore, with the symbolization map S, the vector formed by each company's combination of the five financial ratios is summarized into a symbol that summarizes that particular financial status. Notice that, given the noisy nature of the financial ratios, although we lose the numerical value of the ratios when analyzing the symbols distribution, we gain in robustness when looking for different types of firm failures and their time evolution. Taking values associated with percentiles instead of the actual values has the advantage of controlling for outliers, which are typically numerous and influential in samples containing failed or near bankrupt enterprises [37].

An illustrative example of what one specific configuration from the 32 possible outcome combinations of the whole Γ means, let us take the particular combination: (0, 0, 0, 1, 1). This symbol would characterize those companies with low values for R_1, R_2 and R_3 and values above the threshold for R_4 and R_5, specifically meaning a value lower than that defined by the percentile 10 for the Working capital and the EBIT to total assets ratio, a value for the Retained Earnings ratio lower than that defined by the percentile 20, and values higher than the percentile 50 and 20 for the ratio of Total assets to total liabilities and Sales to total assets, respectively. As a matter of fact, the thresholds for all ratios but R_4 are quite defining, as the companies below them represent reduced subsamples.

4.2 Symbolic Clustering of Firm Failure

Each firm is associated with a symbol through the symbolization map S, applied to its financial ratios. With the symbolic representation of the firms, we perform a cluster analysis applying k-means algorithm with the Hamming distance, which is the most adequate distance in the symbols space. This Hamming distance between two vectors (or strings) of the same length is the number of entries of the vectors that are different from each other. Performing a cluster analysis in this way creates clusters with similar financial characteristics that have been encapsulated in the symbols.

4.3 Multinomial Logistic Regressions

In order to assess how firm' characteristics determine business failure a multinomial logistic regression estimation was carried out. The dependent variable is defined as business failure, which takes the value of zero for no failed companies and values from 1 to 3 in function of the kind of business failure that characterize each of the studied companies. The estimated probability (converted to odds) of each kind of business failure category, predicted by companies' characteristics, is the outcome of maximum likelihood function. Multinomial logistic regression is an adequate method for classification when the dependent variables present more than two choices. In this model, the belonging to a kind of business failure process is a linear function of companies' characteristics. This model can be expressed as follows (3):

$$P_{ij} = \frac{\exp\left(x_i\beta_j\right)}{1+\sum_{l=2}^{J}\exp\left(x_i\beta_j\right)} \tag{3}$$

where P_{ij} evaluates the associated probability with the choice of the jth alternative (one of firms' financial distress categories) by the ith company, x_{ij} represents the explanatory variables and β is the estimated coefficient [38]. This specification is based on the log Weibull distribution which has the advantage that the cumulative density of the difference between any two random variables which have this distribution follows a logistic function [38]. For instance, a company presents a specific financial failure process A if:

$$x_0\beta_B + \varepsilon_B < x_0\beta_A + \varepsilon_A \tag{4}$$

where x_0 is a row vector of firms i's characteristics, then $(x_0\beta_A + \varepsilon_A)$ is the probability of belonging to the kind of financial failure A and $(x_0\beta_B + \varepsilon_B)$ is for the category B. ε_A and ε_B are independently drawn from a log Weibull distribution. Given a company's characteristics, the probability of it belonging to one of three different business failure categories is computed as follows:

$$\frac{\text{prob A}}{\text{prob C}} = e^{x\beta A} \text{ and } \frac{\text{prob B}}{\text{prob C}} = e^{x\beta B}. \tag{5}$$

5 Results

This section shows the results of the business failure processes pre- and post-COVID for our sample of Spanish companies applying the methodology previously defined. Firstly, we apply a recursive algorithm based on the Chow test to the pool of financial ratios from 2018 to 2020 to obtain the firm symbolization as described in Sect. 4.2. Notice that we perform the symbolization procedure in the pool of the 3 years, for the symbols to have the same meaning and therefore, allowing for comparison of their distribution in the pre- and post-COVID pandemic. Secondly, we perform a 3-cluster analysis through the symbolic representation of the firm to identify different processes for business failure. Finally, we characterize these failure processes as a function of business characteristics applying multinomial logistic regressions.

5.1 Pre- and Post-COVID Business Failure Processes

5.1.1 Symbolization and Clustering Process

After applying the proposed recursive algorithm to the pool of financial ratios from 2018 to 2020 for the whole sample, we obtain a different threshold for each of them. Table 2 shows these results:

Table 2 Thresholds based on the Chow test

Threshold	Percentile
$\mathfrak{D}^1$	10
$\mathfrak{D}^2$	20
$\mathfrak{D}^3$	10
$\mathfrak{D}^4$	50
$\mathfrak{D}^5$	20

Table 3 Clustering processes based on the symbols of failed companies

Panel A. Clusters characterization

	Centroid ([a])	Interpretation
Cluster 1	1 0 1 0 1	Cluster 1 is characterized by companies that are not capitalized (low or null proportion of retained earnings) and with low solvency (its assets are proportionally more financed with debt)
Cluster 2	0 1 1 0 1	Companies with low liquidity and solvency (mainly financed with debt)
Cluster 3	0 0 0 0 1	Companies with low liquidity, low solvency (low capitalization from reserves), low current profitability and low solvency (caused by high debt)

Panel B. Percentage of companies in each cluster in the analyzed period

	Cluster 1	Cluster 2	Cluster 3
Pre-COVID	59%	27%	14%
Post-COVID	26%	65%	8%

[a]We find similar centroids for each year of the analyzed period 2018–2020

Based on deciles values and applying the expression (2), we defined for each company a symbol composed of 5 elements representing the five analyzed financial ratios. Each element in the symbol will take the value of 0 or 1 depending on previously determined thresholds.

To characterize the business failure processes among bankrupt firms, starting with the symbolic representation of failed firms, we apply a *k*-means clustering algorithm using Hamming distance. Results of the cluster analysis are given in Table 3. We find three different clusters for the pre- and post-COVID periods.

Panel A of Table 3 includes the interpretation of the characteristics of each cluster. Panel B shows the distribution of clusters before and after the pandemic. Taking an overall look at the clusters, the three have in common that R_5 is not determining.

This is logical, as rotation is quite dependent on the sector (industrial companies, for example, tend to have high proportion of fixed assets, high margins and low rotation, and on the other hand, commercial companies are usually characterized by low margins and high rotation), and what this means is that during the COVID crisis the sector does not matter, as any company can file for bankruptcy. When we compare the changing importance of the different clusters before and after COVID, we conclude that once the COVID crisis comes into play, clusters 1 and 3 are less important, as the weight of the cluster 2 rises in the post-COVID period. Cluster 1 is completely dependent on solvency, as it focuses on R_2 and R_4, which are the only determinant ratios. In cluster 2, the short-term solvency (liquidity) becomes crucial, and this default could also affect companies which have been prudent in the past, as R_2 is 1. Thus, there is a shift in emphasis from long-term solvency toward a greater focus on short-term solvency and long-term prudence is no longer so determinant, as R_2 does no longer defines the inclusion in the cluster. Firms that failed in the COVID period had an evident lack of short-term financial flexibility and liquidity problems, which resulted in the impossibility of not being able to meet the companies' short-term payments, spawning severe problems of liquidity.

5.2 The Multinomial Logistic Regression

In order to characterize each cluster in function of firms' characteristics, we estimate a multilogistic regression for failed companies in each year. The dependent variable FrC takes the value 1 if the company belongs to the clusters 1, 2 if the company belongs to the cluster 2 and 3 in case the company is in cluster 3. The explanatory variables are size, age and the industry the company belongs to. In order to run the analysis, cluster 1 (FrC = 1) is left as the base category. Results of the multinomial logit regression are shown in Table 4.

Our results indicate that during the pre-COVID phase, one-unit risen in the companies' size is related to a decrease in the log odds of being in cluster 2 vs. being in the reference cluster in the amount of 0.0947. The same happens with cluster 3. Thus, as companies' size increases, the probability of being in clusters 2 and 3 is lower in comparison with the cluster 1. This result is also significant in the post-COVID period, but only for cluster 3. Thus, an increase in one unit of companies' size will decrease the probability of being in cluster 3 in comparison with cluster 1. Regarding firms' age, we find that this variable is not significant during the pre-COVID period but becomes significant for the post-COVID period. The probability of a company of being in the cluster 2 rises as the firm gets older, probably old companies which are not as capitalized as their counterparts, and which the pandemic caught wrong-footed, increased their probabilities of failure. Regarding differences between sectors, we find that companies in the Trade and Financial sector present high probability of being in clusters 2 and 3 during the pre-COVID period. During the post-COVID period, we find a lower probability of being in cluster 2 for companies in the sectors of financial activities and other activities during the post-COVID period.

Table 4 Multilogistic regression estimation results, where cluster 1: 1 0 1 0 1 is left as the base category

	Pre-COVID		Post-COVID	
	Cluster2 (0 1 1 0 1)	Cluster 3 (0 0 0 0 1)	Cluster2 (0 1 1 0 1)	Cluster 3 (0 0 0 0 1)
Size	−0.0947** (0.064)	−0.2654*** (0.002)	−0.0015 (0.976)	−0.1988*** (0.047)
Age	0.0315 (0.801)	−0.2134 (0.374)	0.3733** (0.010)	−0.1156 (0.646)
Industry	0.9183 (0.094)	1.4999* (0.086)	0.1323 (0.833)	0.1330 (0.908)
Building	0.4665 (0.243)	0.1956 (0.808)	0.4112 (0.405)	0.3848 (0.687)
Trade	0.7743** (0.026)	1.1176* (0.074)	−0.1779 (0.368)	0.7533* (0.050)
Accomm	0.4487 (0.355)	1.0422 (0.198)	0.0209 (0.963)	0.9557* (0.086)
Transport	0.7325* (0.091)	0.0952 (0.935)	−0.7097 (0.313)	−0.9568*** (0.000)
Communications	0.6868 (0.134)	1.4996** (0.040)	−0.2262 (0.682)	0.5782 (0.557)
Financial activities	1.0058*** (0.005)	1.1668** (0.065)	−0.4646* (0.082)	0.6101 (0.310)
Scientific and profess. Activi.	0.5342 (0.370)	0.8906 (0.173)	0.0780 (0.833)	0.0789 (0.911)
Other activities	0.3802 (0.439)	1.0980* (0.097)	−0.9250** (0.013)	0.2719 (0.746)

*In parentheses the p-value. *** significant at 1%** significant at 5% * significant at 10%. We include those representative sectors with observations for each cluster*

6 Discussion and Conclusions

In this paper, we examine the impact of the COVID crisis on firms' business failure. The most visible change is a break in the business failure processes, as some factors which were determining before the pandemic turn irrelevant, and others become crucial when they were not before. Liquidity and solvency, linked to financial flexibility, seemed critical once the pandemic made a start. This result coincides with previous literature bringing firms' financial flexibility out during periods of crisis [39]. We find that the positive effects of financial flexibility during the post-COVID period is explained by more capacity to get external financial resources [10], of which post-COVID companies seem more dependent. In addition, more mature companies during the post-COVID period have more probability of going bankrupt. Our analysis reveals significant differences between pre-pandemic and post-pandemic bankruptcies when examined by sector of productive activity.

This paper strengths the relevance of financial flexibility which allows companies to be proportionally more financially independent from external resources. This paper provides additional light to the question about the equity-debt tradeoff amid unexpected external shocks, which seemed to intensify the disadvantages of debt during the pandemic. Our results provide further evidence about the relevance of deleveraging and having more financial flexibility during periods of crisis, as the COVID-19 pandemic [40] and the importance of the companies' financial policy. The restarted adequate equilibrium between equity and debt after the pandemic seems to depend on firms' internal characteristics too.

This study opens new possibilities in the analysis of business failure, in which the pandemic has changed the rules of the game. The novelty of this study is both the definition of the deciles that constitute a threshold of the different Altman ratios and the analysis of the diverse combinations of these ratios, through a symbolic analysis. This study opens the way to new approaches for prediction of business failure and new methods of classification. One of the limitations of this study, which in turn entails future research, is the applicability of the results either temporarily: once the pandemic has been overcome, and geographically, as there is a need for more studies exploring these results in other territories, with alternative databases. Further parallel research should try to assess whether the Altman model is still valid and try to identify the new values of the Altman analysis in case they have changed. Finally, this study is mainly based on firms' internal characteristics. The consideration of firms' environmental factors [41] in this context is a research challenge which we will consider in forthcoming studies.

References

1. Baqaee, D., Farhi, E.: Supply and demand in disaggregated Keynesian economies with an application to the COVID-19 crisis. In: NBER Working Paper 27152 (2020)
2. Fasano, F., Sánchez-Vidal, F.J., La Rocca, M.: The role of government policies for Italian firms during the COVID-19 crisis. Financ. Res. Lett. **50**, 103273 (2022)
3. Cook, L., Barrett, C.: How Covid-19 is escalating problem debt. https://www.ft.com/content/4062105a-afaf-4b28-bde6- ba71d5767ec0 (2020)
4. Ramelli, S., Wagner, A.F.: Feverish stock price reactions to COVID-19. Rev. Corp. Financ. Stud. **9**(3), 622–655 (2020)
5. Fahlenbrach, R., Rageth, K., Stulz, R.M.: How valuable is financial flexibility when revenue stops? Evidence from the COVID-19 crisis. Rev. Financ. Stud. **34**(11), 5474–5521 (2021)
6. Leland, H.E.: Agency costs, risk management and capital structure. J. Financ. **53**(4), 1213–1243 (1998)
7. Modigliani, F., Miller, M.H.: Corporate income taxes and the cost of capital: a correction. Am. Econ. Rev. **53**(3), 433–443 (1963)
8. Myers, S.C., Majluf, N.: Corporate financing and investment decisions when firms have information that investors do not have. J. Financ. Econ. **13**, 187–221 (1984)
9. Bigelli, M., Martín-Ugedo, J.F., Sánchez-Vidal, F.J.: Financial conservatism of private firms. J. Bus. Res. **67**(11), 2419–2427 (2014)
10. Zheng, S., Fan, K., Hou, Y., Feng, J., Fu, Y.: Clustering by the probability distributions from extreme value theory. IEEE Trans. Artif. Intell. **4**(2), 292–303 (2022)
11. Acharya, V., Almeida, H., Campello, M.: Is cash negative debt? A hedging perspective on corporate financial policies. J. Financ. Intermediat. **16**, 515–554 (2007)

12. Altman, E.I.: Financial ratios, discriminant analysis and the prediction of corporate bankruptcy. J. Financ. **23**(4), 589–609 (1968)
13. Ragin, C.C.: The Comparative Method: Moving Beyond Qualitative and Quantitative Strategies. University of California Press, Berkeley (1987)
14. Wenzel, M., Stanske, S., Lieberman, M.B.: Strategic responses to crisis. Strateg. Manage. J. **41**(7), 1077–1102 (2020)
15. Heracleous, L., Werres, K.: On the road to disaster: strategic misalignments and corporate failure. Long Range Plann. **49**(4), 491–506 (2016)
16. Amankwah-Amoah, J., Khan, Z., Wood, G.: COVID-19 and business failures: the paradoxes of experience, scale and scope for theory and practice. Eur. Manage. J. **39**(2), 179–184 (2021)
17. Silverman, B.S., Nickerson, J.A., Freeman, J.: Profitability, transactional alignment and organizational mortality in the US trucking industry. Strateg. Manage. J. **18**(S1), 31–52 (1997)
18. Maté-Sánchez-Val, M., López-Hernández, F., Fuentes, C.C.R.: Geographical factors and business failure: An empirical study from the Madrid metropolitan area. Econ. Model. **74**, 275–283 (2018)
19. Kücher, A., Mayr, S., Mitter, C., Duller, C., Feldbauer-Durstmüller, B.: Firm-age dynamics and causes of corporate bankruptcy: age-dependent explanations for business failure. Rev. Manag. Sci. **14**(3), 633–661 (2020)
20. Sabherwal, R., Chan, Y.E.: Alignment between business and IS strategies: a study of prospectors, analyzers and defenders. Inf. Syst. Res. **12**(1), 11–33 (2001)
21. Ohlson, J.A.: Financial ratios and the probabilistic prediction of bankruptcy. J. Account. Res. **18**(1), 109–131 (1980)
22. Merton, R.C.: On the pricing of corporate debt: the risk structure of interest rates. J. Financ. **29**(2), 449–470 (1974)
23. Zmijewski, M.E.: Methodological issues related to the estimation of financial-distress prediction models. J. Account. Res. **22**, 59–82 (1984)
24. Taffler, R.J.: Forecasting company failure in the UK using discriminant analysis and financial-ratio data. J. R. Stat. Soc. **145**(3), 342–358 (1982)
25. Fulmer, J.G., Moon, J.E., Gavin, T.A., Erwin, M.J.: A bankruptcy classification model for small firms. J. Comm. Bank Lend. **67**(1), 25–37 (1984)
26. Altman, E.I.: Corporate Financial Distress: A Complete Guide to Predicting, Avoiding, and Dealing with Bankruptcy. Wiley, New York (1983)
27. Salimi, A.Y.: Validity of Altman's Z-Score model in predicting bankruptcy in recent years. Acad. Account. Financ. Stud. J. **19**(2), 2 (2015)
28. Altman, E.I., Iwanicz-Drozdowska, M., Laitinen, E.K., Suvas, A.: Financial distress prediction in an international context: a review and empirical analysis of Altman's Z-score model. J. Int. Financ. Manag. Acc. **28**(2), 131–171 (2017)
29. Pagano, M., Wagner, C., Zechner, J.: Disaster resilience and asset prices. arXiv preprint arXiv:2005.08929. https://arxiv.org/pdf/2005.08929.pdf (2020). Accessed 8 May 2025
30. De Vito, A., Gómez, J.P.: Estimating the COVID-19 cash crunch: global evidence and policy. J. Account. Publ. Policy. **39**(2), 106741 (2020)
31. La Rocca, M., Sanchez-Vidal, F.J., Fasano, F., La Rocca, E.T.: The misconduct ripple: how corruption and unethical practices affect performance across firm age and size. Manag. Decis. **63**(13), 686–713 (2025)
32. Zorn, M.L., Norman, P.M., Butler, F.C., Bhussar, M.S.: Cure or curse: does downsizing increase the likelihood of bankruptcy? J. Bus. Res. **76**, 24–33 (2017)
33. Muñoz-Izquierdo, N., Segovia-Vargas, M.J., Pascual-Ezama, D.: Explaining the causes of business failure using audit-report disclosures. J. Bus. Res. **98**, 403–414 (2019)
34. Sánchez-Vidal, F.J., García-Marí, J.H., Madrid-Guijarro, A.: SMEs filing for bankruptcy in Spain: The best of luck! BRQ Bus. Res. Q. **28**(1), 141–163 (2025)
35. Ragin, C.C.: Fuzzy-Set Social Science. University of Chicago Press, Chicago (2000)
36. Sánchez-Vidal, F.J.: A cautionary note on the use of accounting semi-identity-based models. J. Risk Financ. Manage. **16**, 1–14 (2023)

37. Sánchez-Vidal, F.J.: High-debt companies' leverage determinants in Spain: a quantile regression approach. Econ. Model. **36**, 455–465 (2014)
38. Kennedy, P.: A guide to econometrics. Wiley, Hoboken, NJ (2008)
39. Sánchez-Vidal, F.J., Hernández-Robles, M., Mínguez-Vera, A.: Financial conservatism fosters job creation during economic crises. Appl. Econ. **52**(45), 4913–4926 (2020)
40. Fasano, F., La Rocca, M., Sánchez-Vidal, F.J., Boutouar, Y.: Why SMEs go to crowdfunding? The role of financial constraints and agency issues. Small Bus. Econ. **65**(2), 1183–1207 (2025)
41. Sánchez Vidal, J., Macan Bhaird, C., Lucey, B.M., Gurdgiev, C.: What determines the decision to apply for credit? Evidence for Eurozone SMEs. Evidence for Eurozone SMEs (2012). https://papers.ssrn.com/sol3/papers.cfm?abstract_id=2170669

Conclusion

As we close "Human–Machine Synergy and the Digital Future: Exploring Collaboration and Competition," one pattern is unmistakable: digital transformation is neither linear nor uniform. It unfolds unevenly across sectors and geographies, combines breakthrough promise with stubborn frictions, and continually renegotiates the boundary between human judgment and machine computation. Across 11 parts, contributors show how AI and digital technologies are reconfiguring relationships among individuals, organizations, and institutions, and how collaboration and competition are both constitutive of, and in tension within, human–machine interactions.

A central message of the volume is that synergy is not a destination but a design effort. It must be cultivated through choices about architectures, roles, incentives, and norms; critically examined through evidence and comparative cases; and ethically guided to safeguard dignity, fairness, and accountability. Whether in workplaces, healthcare systems, city governance, sustainability transitions, or social entrepreneurship, effective integration of AI depends on thoughtful problem framing, inclusive governance, and ongoing calibration of expectations and responsibilities. Machines can expand perception, prediction, and control, but humans must still set purpose, allocate decision rights, and determine what "good" looks like in context.

Three cross-cutting themes emerge. First, context matters. Outcomes hinge on the interplay of institutional arrangements, cultural norms, regulatory environments, and legacy infrastructures. Approaches that thrive in one setting may falter in another; responsible AI integration therefore requires attention to local constraints and capacities, not one-size-fits-all playbooks. Second, synergy is socio-technical. Technical performance alone is insufficient; trust, acceptance, learning, and role clarity shape whether and how people engage with AI. Interdisciplinary perspectives—from behavioral sciences and ethics to organization theory and public policy—are indispensable. Third, the future is co-created. Researchers, practitioners,

N. Omrani et al. (eds.), *Human-Machine Synergy and the Digital Future - Exploring Collaboration and Competition Volume 1*, Springer Proceedings in Business and Economics, https://doi.org/10.1007/978-3-032-21347-1

policymakers, and citizens share agency in shaping trajectories; broadening participation in design and oversight is essential if innovation is to advance inclusion as well as efficiency.

Looking ahead, we envision this book as a foundation for sustained dialogue, collaborative experimentation, and careful institution-building. The most consequential work now lies in translating insights into durable practices and guardrails. To ensure that AI innovation contributes to greater inclusion, AI governance must rely on regulatory approaches that are proportionate to the level of risk and adapted to specific contexts. Such approaches should be accompanied by practical mechanisms, including transparent model documentation, systematic bias audits, impact assessments, and effective channels for contesting AI-based decisions. Democratic values are best protected when procurement, public oversight, and civil society have real leverage over the standards that shape data use, model deployment, and accountability for harm.

Equally important is the human side of hybrid work. Thriving in human–machine environments will demand literacies that cut across disciplines: computational and statistical reasoning, but also design judgment, ethical awareness, and the capacity to reason about causality, uncertainty, and trade-offs. Organizations will need to invest not only in tools but in role clarity, training, and feedback loops that help people calibrate trust, escalate anomalies, and learn from failure safely. Education systems can accelerate this shift by embedding hands-on projects, reflective practice, and collaborative problem framing alongside technical skills.

For research, the priorities are clear. We need comparative and longitudinal studies that reveal boundary conditions for complementarity versus substitution; mixed-method designs that join interpretive depth with causal identification; and sector-specific evidence about safety, resilience, and distributional effects. Open science will be key: sharable code, curated datasets, and reporting standards that make replication and synthesis routine rather than exceptional. Only then can findings accumulate across contexts and inform policy and practice at scale.

For practice and policy, measured deployment should be the norm. Start from concrete problems and user needs; evaluate outcomes beyond accuracy or cost to include robustness, worker well-being, accessibility, environmental footprint, and equity; and treat adoption as iterative learning under uncertainty. In healthcare, this means human-centered clinical validation and post-deployment monitoring; in cities, participatory design and redress mechanisms; in sustainability, aligning incentives so that digital efficiencies do not externalize social or ecological costs; in social entrepreneurship, ensuring that new platform logics expand, rather than concentrate, opportunity.

We invite the DTS community and readers more broadly to turn these commitments into shared infrastructure. Future editions of the DTS International Conference can host policy labs with regulators and city leaders, cross-sector working groups on workforce skills and inclusion, a replication and transparency prize for empirical chapters, and an open repository of teaching cases, protocols, and datasets. We encourage authors and practitioners to contribute comparative cases, benchmarks, and implementation playbooks and to use the International Conference of Digital

Transformation Society 2025 portal (https://dts2025.sciencesconf.org/) as a convening point for these efforts.

This volume is not intended as the last word. Rather, it is a starting point for a community of inquiry and practice committed to building systems that are effective and fair, imaginative and accountable. We invite scholars, practitioners, students, and policymakers to test, critique, and extend what is offered here; to share what fails as well as what works; and to help co-author the institutions, standards, and learning cultures that will guide human–machine synergy in the years ahead. If we succeed, it will be because we paired technical ingenuity with civic responsibility and treated the digital future not as destiny but as a collective design choice.

GPSR Compliance

The European Union's (EU) General Product Safety Regulation (GPSR) is a set of rules that requires consumer products to be safe and our obligations to ensure this.

If you have any concerns about our products, you can contact us on ProductSafety@springernature.com

In case Publisher is established outside the EU, the EU authorized representative is:

Springer Nature Customer Service Center GmbH
Europaplatz 3
69115 Heidelberg, Germany

Batch number: 10628659

Printed by Printforce, the Netherlands